Recovering Solidarity

Catholic Social Tradition Series
Preface to the Series

In *Tertio millennio adveniente,* Pope John Paul II poses a hard question: "It must be asked how many Christians really know and put into practice the principles of the church's social doctrine." The American Catholic bishops share the pope's concern: "Catholic social teaching is a central and essential element of our faith ... [and yet] our social heritage is unknown by many Catholics. Sadly, our social doctrine is not shared or taught in a consistent and comprehensive way in too many of our schools." This lack is critical because the "sharing of our social tradition is a defining measure of Catholic education and formation." A United States Catholic Conference task force on social teaching and education noted that within Catholic higher education "there appears to be little consistent attention given to incorporating gospel values and Catholic social teaching into general education courses or into departmental majors."

In response to this problem, the volumes in the Catholic Social Tradition series aspire to impart the best of what this tradition has to offer not only to Catholics but to all who face the social issues of our times. The volumes examine a wide variety of issues and problems within the Catholic social tradition and contemporary society, yet they share several characteristics. They are theologically and philosophically grounded, examining the deep structure of thought in modern culture. They are publicly argued, enhancing dialogue with other religious and nonreligious traditions. They are comprehensively engaged by a wide variety of disciplines such as theology, philosophy, political science, economics, history, law, management, and finance. Finally, they examine how the Catholic social tradition can be integrated on a practical level and embodied in institutions in which people live much of their lives. The Catholic Social Tradition series is about faith in action in daily life, providing ways of thinking and acting to those seeking a more humane world.

Michael J. Naughton
University of St. Thomas
Minnesota, USA

Recovering Solidarity

Lessons from Poland's Unfinished Revolution

GERALD J. BEYER

University of Notre Dame Press
Notre Dame, Indiana

Copyright © 2010 by University of Notre Dame
Notre Dame, Indiana 46556
www.undpress.nd.edu
All Rights Reserved

Published in the United States of America

Library of Congress Cataloging-in-Publication Data

Beyer, Gerald J. (Gerald John), 1970
  Recovering solidarity : lessons from Poland's unfinished revolution / Gerald J. Beyer.
    p. cm. — (Catholic social tradition)
  Includes bibliographical references and index.
  ISBN-13: 978-0-268-02216-7 (pbk. : alk. paper)
  ISBN-10: 0-268-02216-X (pbk. : alk. paper)
1. NSZZ "Solidarność" (Labor organization)—History.   2. Labor unions and Christianity—Poland—History.   3. Catholic Church—Poland—History.   I. Title.
  HD8537.N783 49   2010
  331.8809438—dc22
                                                            2009041747

∞ *The paper in this book meets the guidelines for permanence and durability of the Committee on Production Guidelines for Book Longevity of the Council on Library Resources.*

To my wife Ania and daughter Julia
Kocham Was całym sercem!

CONTENTS

Acknowledgments ix

Introduction 1

CHAPTER ONE
The Ethic of Solidarity from 1980 to 1989 11

CHAPTER TWO
The Eclipse of Solidarity after 1989 29

CHAPTER THREE
Poverty in Poland after 1989:
Empirical Signs of the Failure of the Revolution 53

CHAPTER FOUR
Recovering and Applying an Ethic of Solidarity to Polish Poverty 85

CHAPTER FIVE
Freedom and Participation as Social Products 121

CHAPTER SIX
Promoting an Ethic of Solidarity as Evangelization:
The Church's Social Witness in Poland since 1989   157

Conclusion: Is Solidarity Possible in a Neoliberal
Capitalist World?   205

Epilogue   215

Notes   219

Bibliography   294

Index   319

ACKNOWLEDGMENTS

I am grateful to the many people who have contributed to this project in myriad ways. Let me start by thanking the numerous scholars, former teachers, friends, and family in Poland who aided me greatly in trying to understand my "second homeland." In particular, Dr. Jan Lencznarowicz and Dr. Janina Filek provided me with access to research materials, stimulating conversation, and friendship. Rev. Prof. Piotr Mazurkiewicz read my dissertation, from which this book arose, and offered valuable feedback. There are so many other Poles who have generously given of their time that it is impossible to mention them all. However, I owe a special debt of gratitude to Dr. Jarosław Gowin, Wojciech Bonowicz, Professor Aniela Dylus, Professor Adam Węgrzecki, Professor Władysław Miodunka, the late Fr. Józef Tischner, and my language instructors at the Jagiellonian University. I also wish to acknowledge my gratitude to the Kosciuszko Foundation and the Polish-U.S. Fulbright Commission, which funded much of my research in Poland.

My friends and colleagues at Boston College also encouraged and challenged me while I completed the dissertation. First among them is Professor David Hollenbach, S.J., who served as my dissertation director and whose work has inspired me for many years. He assisted me in crafting the argument found in these pages and helped me to avoid "not seeing the forest for the trees." Professor Thomas Massaro, S.J., also served on the committee and has continued to mentor me generously. Professor Lisa Sowle Cahill has been a great role model and advisor for Christian ethicists who seek to have a public voice. Maureen O'Connell and Anna Perkins read and helpfully commented on parts of the project.

My friends Ki Joo Choi and John Sheveland urged me to pursue a healthy lifestyle during this arduous process. I thank all the students, faculty, and staff at Boston College for a first-rate education in theological ethics.

I am also grateful for the support I have received at St. Joseph's University, particularly from my colleagues in the Theology Department. I also wish to thank Dr. Owen Gilman of the English Department for continuing conversations about good writing. The university generously has supported my work with a summer research grant and a Faculty Fellowship in the Institute of Catholic Bioethics.

The University of Notre Dame Press has assisted me in bringing this book to fruition. In particular, Dr. Michael Naughton, editor of the Catholic Social Tradition series, read parts of the manuscript and suggested some useful improvements. The comments of two anonymous reviewers and Rebecca DeBoer, Ann Aydelotte, and Katie Lehman of the editorial department helped me to sculpt the final product.

Finally, I thank my family. My mother and father made tremendous sacrifices for many years so that I could receive the education that they were not afforded. My father-in-law and mother-in-law, Dr. Edward and Dr. Krystyna Feliksik, did everything they could to enable me to devote my time to research and writing, including helping to take care of my daughter, Julia, who was born in Niepołomice, Poland. My wife and best friend Ania Feliksik has been with me since its inception on my quest to understand Poland. I am most grateful to her for her love and patience.

Introduction

With the birth of capitalism and democracy in Poland in 1989, solidarity died. Those even vaguely familiar with the Solidarity movement will recognize the irony in this demise. Freedom and democracy were to ameliorate the sickness of Communism. Yet, freedom and democracy are at least in part responsible for stalling the great moral revolution of *Solidarność*.

On the morning of August 14, 1980, a strike in the Gdańsk shipyard began what eventually toppled Communism in Central and Eastern Europe. The whole world watched as ordinary people such as Lech Wałęsa and Anna Walentynowicz led what historian Timothy Garton Ash has deemed "the most infectiously hopeful movement in the history of contemporary Europe."[1] *Solidarność* achieved what most people never dreamed could happen: it galvanized an entire nation to struggle against the Goliath of totalitarian Communism, and it won, without shedding blood.

Many intellectuals and religious leaders, including Pope John Paul II, hoped that after its victory, Solidarity would instill values and principles into "really existing" capitalism and democracy in Poland and beyond. Unfortunately, their hopes were dashed. Less than a year after Poland's democratic elections in 1989, one of the leading voices of the movement, Adam Michnik, proclaimed the "death" of the "idea of Solidarity."[2] In the ensuing years, Solidarity's project was largely abandoned, and the unity in spite of differences that characterized it disappeared. Wałęsa himself declared a "war at the top," a fitting description of the rancorous battles that took place among former allies. Given that Solidarity had inspired people to sacrifice tremendously for others, sometimes to the point of martyrdom, "the war" was no less shocking than the fratricidal tale of Cain and Abel.

Today, Poles exhibit a great deal of ambivalence towards the legacy of Solidarity. Most recognize that Solidarity was indispensable in the battle against Communism. They are grateful to the movement for the rights to freedom of speech and of worship, and for the right to vote. However, the vast majority of Poles believe that Solidarity no longer serves the good of the country. A quarter of a century later, only 24 percent maintained that their lives changed for the better as a result of Solidarity's historic victory, while 31 percent said that their lives became worse, and 45 percent saw no change whatsoever.[3] What became of the fight for "bread and freedom" and for the equality and dignity of its citizens in Poland's new era? How could a movement once so robust and hopeful vanish so quickly, leaving little but historical memories in its wake? As political scientist and former member of Solidarity Aleksander Smolar put it, "the Poland of Solidarity's program was a completely different one than the one we have created."[4]

This book tells the story of the eclipse of Solidarity. It sheds light on the contemporary history of a country little known beyond the images of Wałęsa, the heroic electrician turned president, and "the Polish pope," John Paul II. However, as a work in normative ethics, it goes beyond narrating the death of the Solidarity movement and its ethos. This book is mainly concerned with the viability of a contemporary ethic of solidarity. In other words, it considers whether or not solidarity can be "resurrected" in contemporary capitalist, democratic Poland. The answer to this question, crucial to the fate of millions in Poland, has important implications for people beyond its borders. The social ills of Poland's turbulent transformation to a capitalist, democratic society, such as increases in poverty and inequality, have been replicated in many parts of the world.[5] The causes of these negative phenomena, rooted on the level of ideas, are roughly the same. Solidarity is dead, or "breathing with one lung" at best; and for its demise, "freedom" is largely to blame.

Lest the reader conclude that this is yet another jeremiad against "individualistic" liberty in the name of some collectivist ideal, a qualification is in order. Freedom per se is not the enemy of solidarity. The Solidarity movement quite aptly inscribed its banners with the words, "There is no freedom without solidarity" and "There is no solidarity without freedom." It is precisely the misunderstanding that freedom and solidarity irreconcilably conflict in the capitalist order that has undercut the idea and practice of solidarity today. A particular conception of freedom, which this book describes as "neoliberal freedom," lies at the heart of this misunderstanding.

In the case of Poland, a number of factors contributed to the erosion of the ethic of solidarity. Surely the "hangover" from the Communist era generated numerous social pathologies. This book will treat some of these phenomena in order to explain the fate of solidarity in Poland after 1989. Nonetheless, the clash between the newly embraced ideals of neoliberalism, particularly its understanding of freedom, and the ethic of solidarity was the locus of a decisive battle for the "soul" of Polish society. This book uses the context of "post-solidarity" Poland to explore the challenges to an ethic of solidarity in societies where neoliberalism reigns as the dominant model of human development.[6] As an economic school of thought, neoliberalism assumes three things. First, economic growth alone, most often measured as gross domestic product (GDP), fosters human and ecological well-being. Second, the state should continually shed its responsibilities in favor of privatization. Third, the unfettered market always leads to the best outcomes.[7] On the philosophical level, neoliberalism views human freedom as freedom from constraints, particularly in the economic sphere. In the practical realm, this rejection of freedom understood as freedom realized in solidarity with others led to a sink-or-swim attitude in socioeconomic policy. The primacy of neoliberal freedom contributed to widespread apathy towards the poor after 1989.

Poland represents an important case study because it was the birthplace of one of the most fully articulated visions of a society of solidarity. It is also worthy of close scrutiny because neoliberalism clearly contributed to the deterioration of that vision after 1989. Against the backdrop of the era of solidarity, the birthpangs of Polish capitalism and democracy brought into sharp relief many issues that contemporary societies face in a less publicly tangible way. The resistance to "taming the horse," to use Wałęsa's metaphor for gaining popular support for neoliberal reforms, sparked vigorous debate underscoring the contrast between the ideals of solidarity and the neoliberal order. The rawness of the pain felt by those whose aspirations were abandoned was palpable in the flood of books, articles, speeches, and homilies decrying the derailment of Solidarity's moral revolution. By contrast, powerful political, economic, and social mechanisms have "anesthetized" this pain to a large degree in many advanced capitalist societies, where the masses have largely acquiesced to the status quo.[8] Succinctly stated, Poland provides an entrée to an understanding of an ethic of solidarity that is central to Catholic social thought. The Polish context also reveals the ways that neoliberalism erodes solidarity in the modern world. Moreover, it provides fertile ground for exploring the possibility of the rehabilitation of solidarity. In other words, Poland constitutes the focus of this book. However, the global ascendancy of neoliberalism and its notion of freedom makes both the theoretical framework developed here and its concrete applications to socioeconomic problems relevant to a revival of a contemporary ethic of solidarity in many parts of the world.

—— This book assumes that ideas matter. Sir Isaiah Berlin astutely observed that "when ideas are neglected by those who ought to attend to them ... they sometimes acquire an unchecked momentum and an irresistible power over multitudes of men that may grow too violent to be affected by rational criticism."[9] Of course, Berlin was not talking about ideas *in abstractio*. Any attempt to understand the role of ideas in human history must understand the social forces that breathe life into them.[10] In other words, we must be attentive to the link between theory and praxis. This analysis of the contemporary Polish situation rests on these methodological assumptions. It attempts to keep the link between concepts and actions and the policies that embody them in constant view. In this vein, this book argues that Polish society has lacked three essential elements of an ethic of solidarity since 1989: solidarity, freedom, and participation. Concrete social ills, such as the rise in poverty and inequality, manifest these deficits and reveal their deleterious consequences. In large part these deficits can be attributed to the prevalence of theoretical misunderstandings concerning the nature of solidarity, freedom, and participation.[11]

To revive an ethic of solidarity today, the battle must be fought on the level of ideas and practice. Toward that end, this book clarifies the meaning of solidarity, freedom, and participation and their interrelationship. In addition, it demonstrates how these concepts can be embodied in social structures and policies. Applying these concepts to concrete realities is necessary in order to attest to the possibility of solidarity in a capitalist, democratic context. This book contends that the triad of solidarity, freedom, and participation has the greatest potential for illuminating what a revitalized ethic of solidarity would look like in the new order. Because these three concepts can demonstrate how economic choices and social policies can embody solidarity, they are the most adequate and necessary norms for redirecting public life in Poland towards the goals of the "unfinished revolution." This book employs understandings of these concepts from Catholic social thought towards that end.

Although solidarity languished in Poland after 1989, a number of voices have tried to resuscitate it. They feared that Poland was becoming a highly individualistic society, indifferent to the plight of the marginalized. For example, John Paul II implored the leadership of the Solidarity union to regain its moral compass: "If Solidarity really wants to serve the nation, it should return to its roots, to the ideals that inspired them.... Power changes hands often, but manual workers, farmers, teachers, doctors and nurses and all other professionals need aid in defending their rights no matter who governs. Solidarity must play this role."[12]

This book joins such voices. It agrees with those Poles who see Solidarity as an "unfinished revolution."[13] It assumes that illustrating the relevance of an ethic of solidarity to concrete, exigent issues will most effectively contribute to retrieving this ethic in contemporary Poland and beyond. Therefore, it applies the three aspects of an ethic of solidarity to poverty in Poland after 1989. The dramatic rise in poverty after 1989, and its social and political causes, glaringly reveals the abandonment of the ideals of the ethic of solidarity after 1989. Heeding the admonitions of the French economist Jacques Drèze, who implored Catholic social thinkers to go beyond the level of "vague and sterile" principles, this book demonstrates how the concepts of solidarity, freedom, and participation can inform social policies that effectively combat poverty.[14] It develops this approach in the latter stages of the work, having laid out the theoretical and contextual foundations for its application to contemporary Poland in the first three chapters.

———— A word is in order about how the argument unfolds. It begins with an overview of the ethic of solidarity as embodied in the Polish non-violent revolution, one of the twentieth century's greatest moral achievements. This first chapter demonstrates that Solidarity strove for solidarity, freedom, and the greater participation of all Poles in society. This sets the stage for the rest of the analysis by revealing what was tragically lost after 1989. In doing so, it demonstrates the close resemblance between the ideals of Catholic social thought and the lived realities of the movement. Chapter 2 explains the demise of solidarity in detail, pointing to its causal factors. It portrays the confusion and disappointment that has reigned in public discourse and popular perceptions concerning solidarity, freedom, and participation since 1989. It demonstrates that although Solidarity claimed victory in 1989 when Tadeusz Mazowiecki became the nation's first "Solidarity" prime minister, the "moral revolution" of the movement was derailed. This chapter's survey of the contemporary Polish social and political landscape reveals that an explicit rehabilitation of solidarity, freedom, and participation must take place if they are to be fruitfully utilized in public discourse and embodied in social structures.

Chapter 3 presents empirical signs of the failures of the Solidarity revolution. The analysis focuses on the rising trends in poverty in Poland from 1990 to 2002. These trends illustrate that for the most part, the values and principles of the Solidarity movement have not shaped the Polish economy after 1989, that is, capitalism in its neoliberal form triumphed. The analysis devotes attention to wages, unemployment, and education and their causal relationship to poverty. This chapter also examines how decisionmakers justified policies that contributed to the changes in poverty, wages, unemployment, and education. In doing so, it establishes that particular value choices that conflicted with the ethic of solidarity informed these policy decisions.

Appealing to the Catholic social tradition, chapter 4 begins the prescriptive task of resurrecting solidarity. It develops normative understandings of solidarity, freedom, and participation necessary for the recovery of an ethic of solidarity. It applies this theoretical framework to the domain of poverty in order to demonstrate how a contemporary revisionist ethic of solidarity can and should be embodied in social policies. Because solidarity is often misunderstood, this chapter moves towards a definition of solidarity through a *via negativa*, showing what solidarity is not. It then describes more precisely the nature of solidarity and freedom in order to show that, contrary to what neoliberalism holds, these two values mutually depend on one another. In doing so, it elaborates an understanding of freedom consisting in internal, personalist, and economic freedoms to make its case against the reductionistic neoliberal concept of freedom.

Chapter 5 further explicates the solidarity, freedom, and participation triad, with particular emphasis on the later two concepts. Following Montesquieu and Berlin, who stated that the disputed nature of freedom has perhaps vexed philosophers more than any other issue, this chapter raises the question, "Whose freedom?" Most contemporary discourse on the nature of freedom overlooks that of the poor. It is precisely the freedom of the poor that has been most clearly violated in post-solidarity Poland. Against the neoliberal claim that viewing poverty as a denial of freedom is a hackneyed "Marxist" notion, this chapter draws on the work of economist Amartya Sen to explain how poverty denies human freedom. Using Sen, it also argues that freedom is at least in part a social product. The chapter augments Sen's discussion of freedom by employing the category of economic rights from the Catholic social tradition.

The bulk of this book addresses the "what" and "how" of the resurrection of solidarity. Chapter 6 focuses on the "who," that is, those who can rehabilitate an ethic of solidarity in Poland. It turns its attention to one of the institutions with the greatest potential to do so, namely, the Roman Catholic Church. The Church has received widespread recognition for its important role in the Solidarity movement in Poland leading up to 1989. However, many commentators have scrutinized its activities in "post-solidarity" Poland much less favorably. In spite of this criticism, this book argues that the Church has a pivotal role to play in ensuring that all policy decisions embody solidarity, participation, and a proper understanding of freedom's relationship to these values. Relying mainly on official Roman Catholic social teaching and John Paul II's statements in Poland since 1989, this chapter advances the argument that the Church must play this role in order to be faithful to its mission of evangelization.

It also argues that although some significant work has been done, the Church—in particular, the Roman Catholic Bishops' Conference—has not yet fully realized its potential to promote an ethic of solidarity in Poland today.

―――― As in the case of Poland, the widespread embodiment of solidarity within various societies and on a global scale faces myriad obstacles. This book does not argue that neoliberalism and its underlying conception of freedom represent the only threats to solidarity, nor does it undertake a full-fledged dismantling of the entire neoliberal program. Rather, the conflict betweeen freedom and solidarity, which neoliberalism forcefully brings to the surface, is its main concern. The eclipse of solidarity in Poland has revealed the dangers of misconstruing what freedom means in the modern world. Therefore, a persuasive recasting of the relationship between solidarity and freedom is needed to respond to the claim that freedom and solidarity conflict in capitalist, democratic societies. If a notion of freedom that conflicts with solidarity persists, then solidarity will likely take a back seat in the hierarchy of values in liberal democratic, capitalist societies.

Some readers might be tempted to dismiss this book's central concern as irrelevant to them. Solidarity may well be dead in Poland, a country very early in its development of capitalism and democracy. In advanced capitalist societies such as the United States, however, freedom and solidarity have been achieved harmoniously, such readers may purport. However, prior to putting this book down, they might consider the following statistics on life in the United States:

- gated communities are the fastest-growing type of housing;
- one out of five children live in poverty, and the number continues to rise;[15]
- the federal minimum wage of $5.85 in 2008 does not come close to meeting basic needs and remains far below its real value in 1960;
- more than 45 million people do not have health insurance, leaving them highly vulnerable to morbidity and early mortality;
- 60 percent of murder victims are black, but in 80 percent of the cases where the death penalty was carried out, the victims were white.

This list of sobering realities, by no means exhaustive, belies the claim that solidarity and freedom are thriving in the Land of Opportunity. For those of us who reside in the United States, such as the present author, these facts should force us to ask tough questions. Can we rethink the meaning of freedom and solidarity in order to make the American dream real for the vast tracts of people on the margins of society? Must the gift of freedom come at the cost of solidarity? And must solidarity negate freedom? In recent times a "socialist reawakening" has taken place in Bolivia and Venezuela as a direct challenge to the neoliberal program and its primary global advocate, the United States.[16] Those of us who believe that capitalism, despite its flaws, promotes freedom and solidarity better than socialism ought to think hard about how an ethic of solidarity can better flourish in the free-market context. As William Greider has argued, if we cannot do better, the "ghost of Marx" may come to haunt ever greater parts of the earth.[17]

Those who believe, against the realists, that the world is not "a war of all against all," hope that solidarity can be resurrected. If one hopes to demonstrate that the original Polish ethic of solidarity has important implications for Poland and societies beyond it in the contemporary world, a recasting of the normative content of the ethic of solidarity to meet the needs of the new era must be undertaken. By highlighting the interrelationship of solidarity, freedom, and participation, this book aims to show how the moral revolution of Solidarity can be reignited in a neoliberal capitalist world. It is the product of five years spent by the author in Poland during the late 1990s and into the following decade. Undoubtedly, numerous personal encounters with Polish intellectuals and ordinary citizens have shaped the analysis of trends and events. The story of Solidarity's fate and the negative repercussions of its demise matter to the author both as a Christian ethicist and as a friend to many Poles who have lived out this story. May this book make a small contribution to the call by the great Solidarity chaplain and philosopher, Fr. Józef Tischner, which he issued in his last essay before dying in 2000, to recover the ethic of solidarity.[18]

CHAPTER ONE

The Ethic of Solidarity from 1980 to 1989

In August 2005, Poles commemorated the twenty-fifth anniversary of the birth of the remarkable nonviolent revolution known as *Solidarność*. This ten-million strong movement, comprised of people from diverse walks of life with disparate worldviews, played a crucial role in toppling Communism in Central and Eastern Europe. Historians, sociologists, and philosophers have disagreed about some aspects of the Solidarity movement. For example, some scholars maintain that Solidarity was mainly a workers' movement, while others see the primary impetus coming from the Polish intellectuals of KOR, or Komitet Obrony Robotników (Workers' Defense Committee). In spite of these disagreements, most descriptions of Solidarity contain certain common strands. This chapter provides a theoretical reconstruction of the values and principles that guided and undergirded the movement in its quest for a free and just Poland. It describes the key ingredients of the ethic of solidarity by analyzing both Polish treatises on the subject and accounts of events on the ground.

In a sense, the ideals of the movement may not have ever been fully achieved. They were the stated aims of the movement, but as Saint Paul reminds us, people often know the good but fail to do it (Rom. 7:7–25).

Nonetheless, Solidarity's ethic animated the hearts and minds of millions of Poles, who lived out these ideals at many points during the 1980s, despite moments of human frailty among Solidarity's members. In speaking of the movement's "imperfect solidarity," Adam Michnik eloquently stated, "there were different people, and certainly none of us had achieved that moral elevation; but not only how we live but also how we would like to live is important, after all."[1] How did Poles such as Michnik strive to live during the height of the Solidarity era?

Unity among Differences

One of the most striking features of the Solidarity era was the ability of Poles to rise above differences in political, economic, and theological views in order to reach their common goals.[2] Many accounts of the events of the 1980s describe the experience of "being together" (*bycie razem*), oneness, community, and name it as one of the very goals of Solidarity. This does not deny, for certain, that some members at times experienced factiousness and even hostility within the movement. Solidarity was not the communion of saints; indeed, some members exhibited anti-Semitism and anti-intellectualism. At times, some expressed animosity towards the Communist Party.[3] However, one should not, as Garton Ash correctly argues, deduce Solidarity's program and ethos from impassioned personal statements or ephemeral tactics.[4] Overwhelmingly, people reported that "the most important thing was an unusually intense experience of community. The most essential meaning of the initial solidarity was the widespread awareness of the deep bond with others."[5] Remarkably, this community included many card-carrying Communists. The majority of the party members also belonged to Solidarity in 1981 and participated in the largest strike in the history of the Soviet bloc in March of that year.[6] At its height, Solidarity had close to ten million members out of approximately 12.5 million employees who were theoretically eligible.[7] In regard to economic reform, a diversity of views existed within Solidarity, ranging from economic liberalism to proponents of "socialism with a human face."[8] Thus, the movement unified a massive amount of people with wideranging political and economic commitments.

The Workers' Defense Committee, or KOR, which was formed by intellectuals of various sorts in 1976, laid the early foundations for the movement. This demonstrates that Solidarity built a bridge between social groups that once were antagonistic or indifferent to one another at best.[9] Clearly there were tensions among these groups, and debate continues among academics as to whether Solidarity was a workers' or an intellectuals' movement. Nonetheless, these groups undeniably pulled together in order to achieve their goals in an extraordinary way.[10] The nature of those goals will become more evident in what follows.

Two noteworthy factors contributed to the ability to preserve unity despite differences, namely, *the ability to compromise* and *the existence of social trust*. Despite many disagreements and near breakdowns of dialogue, Solidarity was able to seek compromise within the movement itself. It also sought compromise with the Communist-led government.[11] As the philosopher and chaplain of Solidarity, Fr. Józef Tischner, wrote in *Etyka solidarności*, solidarity must entail genuine dialogue. True dialogue always acknowledges that the other side's argument has some grain of truth and that one side never solely possesses the truth. Dialogue requires that we genuinely attempt to see things from the other's perspective.[12] This willingness to pursue dialogue with the Communists, even after the introduction of martial law in 1981 and the delegalization of Solidarity, eventually led to the historic Round Table in 1989. The Round Table agreements guaranteed democratic elections but gave a majority of seats in the Sejm (one of the two chambers of the Parliament) to the Communists. This was a necessary compromise in the minds of Solidarity members.[13]

Importantly, however, dialogue does not preclude the expression of opposition, even in the form of a strike, when the normal course of dialogue or arbitration fails. According to Tischner, the strike, as it was used in Poland, was not an act of violence or coercion. Ultimately, the strike forms a "communion of people of goodwill" who have "love in their hearts for those for whom they work."[14] As early as 1969, Cardinal Karol Wojtyła broached this subject in *Osoba i czyn*, a work that would adumbrate much of his papal social teaching and inspired the Roman Catholic Church's role in Solidarity. Opposition and political dissent can be an expression of solidarity, he wrote, when it is a form of participation in the common good. In order to play this role, it must ultimately be "aimed at attaining that which is true and just."[15]

In order for dialogue and compromise to take place among opposing camps, a certain level of trust had to be shared. During Communism, Poles lived under a dualistic system of morality in which they devoted little or no attention to the common good; the good of the family was the widest sphere of one's ethical concern.[16] Beginning in the early 1980s, however, Poles came to one another's aid in solidarity on a large scale. This had something to do with a new sense of trust in the human person, a belief in the potential of every person to do the good, which the movement and its Christian ethos (an element of Solidarity to be discussed below) rejuvenated. "Faith in the other, and mutual trust, is the precondition of the functioning of solidarity."[17] This renewed belief in the goodness of human beings spawned mutual trust among people—a trust that enabled Poles to make great sacrifices for one another during the Solidarity era.

An Ethic of Hope

People will not act in solidarity if they do not trust one another, at least on some basic level. If one is convinced, as Thomas Hobbes was, that "man is a wolf to man" (*homo homini lupus*), then one will desperately protect one's own interests, often at the expense of others. In essence, the ethic of solidarity was an ethic of hope—hope in the human person and in the reality of human freedom. Human freedom in this sense is understood as the freedom to do the good, which entails many possibilities not included in merely pursuing one's own interests. Poles were certainly cognizant of the depths of human evil, most horribly exemplified at Auschwitz and Kolyma.[18] Yet, during the height of the Solidarity era, Poles believed in the human ability to do the good. This anthropology of hope was not naïve; it did not forget the evils of Auschwitz, Kolyma, or the 1956 Poznań and 1970 Gdańsk massacres. However, it left room for the possibility of change (conversion, in religious terms), even among those who perpetrated such great evils. Zbigniew Stawrowksi contends that the Solidarity movement was a time of mass conversion. He does not mean by this an explicit return to faith in God. In his view, many atheists and agnostics underwent conversion in the sense that they decided to live according to their conscience, as opposed to the dictates of Communism.[19] In this vein, Michnik speaks of a "religious renaissance," which was "a collective return to issues of transcendence."[20]

According to Tischner, a person cannot be in solidarity with someone who has a severely blunted conscience. However, hope in the human person allows us to believe that even those who have deformed their conscience can restore it, if they truly desire to do so. A person cannot irrevocably destroy his or her conscience; even the most depraved can still undergo conversion. Thus, people can be in solidarity even with those who once caused them great suffering.[21] In solidarity, people engage in dialogue with those who betrayed them in the hope that the offenders will look in the mirror, see themselves as they are, and undergo transformation.[22] This hopeful anthropology undergirded Solidarity's commitment to social change through nonviolence.[23] Space limitations preclude an extensive analysis here, but it should be noted that ultimately this anthropology of hope was profoundly theological: it is grace that liberates human beings from the slavery of sin. As Jarosław Gowin observes, "Christian anthropology, even if as a forgotten or unrecognized heritage, was the real basis of solidarity and Solidarity."[24] Referring to 2 Peter 1:4, Jacek Salij, O.P., puts the matter in explicitly Christian theological terms. In Salij's view, Christ's salvific act enables fallen human beings to participate in His divinity. Salvation in Christ gradually heals the "ambivalent" nature of human solidarity and makes "solidarity in the good alone" possible.[25] Whether or not one explicitly accepted this Christological account, Polish solidarity and its view of the person was, as Tischner put it, "born of the pages and spirit of the Gospel."[26] For his part, Tischner pointed to the symbol of the Cross as a source of hope.[27]

Hope and trust, the font of solidarity, also extend to those who suffer as a result of human evil, in addition to their oppressors. Those who express solidarity with the oppressed hope that they will choose to "conquer evil with goodness," even though they have been trampled upon by others. This paraphrase of Romans 12:20–21, which leaders such as John Paul II and Fr. Jerzy Popiełuszko often repeated, summarized Solidarity's method of political struggle.[28] The hope is that the oppressed will want true empowerment and liberation, which will lead them to work for the common good and act in solidarity with others.[29] This will be explicated further in the discussion below of solidarity's emphasis on participation and its relationship to an "option for the poor." For now, the point to be stressed is that hope in the human person fosters trust, which in turn enables people to go beyond their own self-interest and become members of a community in solidarity. Moreover, solidarity requires people to nurture hope in one another by being faithful to one another in all of their relations.[30]

Self-sacrifice and Heroism

The experience of unity and solidarity far surpassed vague and abstract feelings. The ability to practice self-sacrifice in order to promote the well-being of others and the common good was central to preserving unity. In this vein, Tischner referred to Galatians 6:2 to describe the solidarity he witnessed in Poland in the early 1980s: "This old but also very new word, solidarity, what does it mean? To what does it call us? What memories does it bring back? To explicate it more precisely, perhaps it is necessary to reach back into the Gospel and seek the origin of the word there. Christ explains its meaning: 'Carry one another's burden and in this way fulfill God's law.'"[31] Many heroic deeds brought this ideal to life. For example, Lech Wałęsa once refused to accept a deal that gave the Lenin Shipyard workers in Gdańsk differential pay raises, even though many of the workers were satisfied with it. In his mind, the principle of solidarity demanded equal raises for everyone. When the contented workers began to leave the shipyard, Alina Pieńkowska, Henryka Krzywonos, and Ewa Ossowska exhorted Wałęsa to stop the flow and to help workers from other industries fight for concessions from the Communist regime. In the end, Wałęsa urged the remaining shipyard employees to engage in a broader "solidarity strike" with members from other sectors of the economy. The shipyard workers could not abandon others, even though they had won a raise. Thus, he and the workers created the Interfactory Strike Committee.[32]

The previously unknown unity between farmers, factory workers, intellectuals, and clergy also attests to the nature of solidarity in those days. Workers sometimes traveled long distances to strike with farmers, and farmers sometimes fed striking workers and interned dissidents. Intellectuals such as Michnik appealed to Polish history and culture to rally together Solidarity members from various social strata.[33] Workers from various parts of Poland, along with Michnik and other intellectuals, participated in a "Rural Solidarity" strike in Rzeszów in 1981. During the gathering, Bishop Ignacy Tokarczuk of Przemyśl delivered a key sermon in which he described the unity among the peasants, workers, and intellectuals as "a school of Christian life" and as "one great family."[34] This was the first time in the history of the Roman Catholic Church in Poland that the laity and clergy had worked together in a significant way.[35]

The sacrifices of Solidarity members sometimes involved great risks to themselves and to their own families. As Andrzej Wajda's portrait of a Solidarity activist reveals in the film *Man of Iron,* heroism was in no short supply during the tribulations of the Solidarity era. For example, when confronted with the option of going into exile or going to jail, Michnik chose the latter in fidelity to the movement.[36] The paragon of this heroism was Popiełuszko, whose repeated calls for "life in truth," an obvious condemnation of the regime's lies, prompted the Communist authorities to have him killed.[37] Succinctly stated, people were willing to go to great lengths to serve others and to foster the common good. For some people, such as Popiełuszko, this willingness demanded the highest form of self-sacrifice, martydom; but, more often, it required the willingness to fight for justice in the workplace, the political arena, and in all sectors of society, even at one's own expense.[38]

Equality and Dignity of All Persons

Poles were willing to make sacrifices in order to help those beyond their own familial and vocational spheres because they believed in the equality and dignity of all persons. These values, which Solidarity gleaned from Poland's Roman Catholic and socialist heritage,[39] constituted the goals of the movement and influenced the way it went about pursuing those goals. According to journalist Ryszard Kapuściński, the dignity of the human person was the primary motivation for the events of 1980–81. Respecting this dignity required "new interpersonal relations everywhere and on every level . . . mutual respect for all without exception, a principle according to which one's subordinate is one's partner."[40] Some observers have even spoken of a "republic of equals" in which equality governed all social and political interaction. Professors and shipyard workers, for example, sat next to one another on the ground in protest and considered one another's point of view.[41] The Solidarity movement may not have put this positive characteristic into practice always and everywhere. For example, some recent voices have argued that Solidarity undervalued the often behind-the-scenes contributions of women.[42] However, even if some individuals acted in a sexist or discriminatory manner at times, the statutes and ethos of Solidarity reveal that its members generally all sought the same thing: respect for the dignity of all men and women.[43] It translated into a strong emphasis on the right to participation in the creation and enjoyment of social structures and social goods. In other words, because of its emphasis on the dignity of all people, Solidarity sought to procure basic human rights for everyone.[44] Which concrete rights they fought for will be discussed in due course. At this point, the focus will be placed on the foundational right to participation.

Participation as the Linchpin of Respect for Human Dignity

Solidarity's First National Congress was highly democratic in procedure, sometimes even hindering the efficiency of the proceedings.[45] Each delegate could speak up at any point in the deliberations.[46] Prior to the introduction of martial law in December 1981, the vast majority of Solidarity's nearly ten million members participated in meetings of their local chapters.[47] A tremendous increase in the level of social and political debate took place during the earliest years of Solidarity. It was, in short, a movement toward democracy and civil society.[48] This high level of participation followed from a general conviction that citizens had the right to shape and influence their lives and the life of society.[49] According to Solidarity, the Communist regime had usurped this right.

The movement's demand for participation pertained to social, political, and economic policy.[50] In concrete terms, Poles demanded the ability to maintain free trade unions and to create a system of worker management (*samorządy pracownicze*) in addition to the right to political participation and freedom of assembly. They believed that unless workers "at the bottom" shared decision-making power in a given industry, effective strategies for growth and a just distribution of profits could not be designed.[51] Determining whether or not Solidarity supported socialism or capitalism exceeds the scope of this analysis. The issue is very complex. Tischner, for example, seems to oscillate between a system based on private property and a socialist economy.[52] Regardless of the preferences for a capitalist or socialist economic system, Tischner and the members of Solidarity wanted work to be a form of "dialogue" in which mutuality exists between employees and employers. This is the sine qua non of work that is not tantamount to exploitation. When work becomes exploitation, it becomes "senseless." In this scenario, the fruits of labor—that is, wages—do not suffice for a "flourishing life" and/or the labor itself does not contribute to the good of society. In order for work to have meaning, it must promote the common good.[53]

Bread, Freedom, and the Common Good

What has been articulated thus far hints at the fact that Solidarity fought for both "bread and freedom."[54] In other words, Solidarity believed that the protection of human dignity requires the procurement of both so-called civil and political rights and economic, social, and cultural rights. The first paragraph of the Solidarity Program adopted at its First National Congress in September 1981 demonstrates this commitment. The movement, while not reducing its aims to "bread, butter, and sausage," was concerned with economic rights such as just wages, adequate health care, and family leave. The economic vision of the official Solidarity Program of 1981 was highly egalitarian, demanding, for example, more compensation for the "less prosperous" and resistance to social inequalities between industries and regions.[55] However, it would be a mistake to see solidarity solely through the lens of economic rights. Tischner, for example, claimed that in addition to such rights, the right to maintain hope in a higher being, that is, in God, must be secured if dignity is to be respected. Solidarity also clearly pursued the rights to political participation and freedom of expression, which do not belong to the traditional catalogue of economic, social, and cultural rights.[56] Thus, its egalitarianism pertained to economic, social, cultural, political, and civil rights. In short, Solidarity believed that "bread and freedom" are the rights of all human beings.[57] Moreover, the movement's members postulated that one set of rights cannot be enjoyed without the procurement of the other. As Karol Modzelewski states, "The motto formulated by Jacek Kuroń and chanted at student rallies, 'there is no bread without freedom,' underscored the inherent relationship between the two."[58]

Solidarity championed the rights of the individual person while simultaneously seeking to foster the common good. It affirmed "both the person and the community."[59] In this sense, Solidarity strove to embody the "personalist communitarianism" expressed in Cardinal Wojtyła's *Osoba i czyn*.[60] In other words, the ethic of solidarity sought to empower the marginalized, both to protect their individual dignity and to enable them to take part in building a just society. Once empowered, they in turn "carry others' burdens."[61] A community of solidarity promotes the participation of ever greater numbers so that everyone may contribute to and benefit from the common good. This resembles the understanding of the relationship between human rights and the common good in Roman Catholic social thought, on which the Solidarity movement drew.

The language of human rights entered Solidarity's vernacular via Roman Catholicism rather than through Enlightenment thought or socialism.[62] Cardinal Stefan Wyszyński and Cardinal Wojtyła spoke boldly of the rights of the individual in many homilies leading up to the Solidarity era.[63] For example, Wyszyński expounded on the myriad universal rights and duties that inhere in human nature in one of his famous 1974 "Sermons of the Holy Cross" (*kazania świętokrzyskie*). In it, he cited both John XXIII's *Pacem in Terris* and the United Nations' Universal Declaration of Human Rights.[64] During the first Solidarity strike in 1981 the Polish bishops' conference issued a statement that enumerated the rights to freedom of worship, to unionize, to a just wage, and to know the truth among a long list of "fundamental rights of the human being."[65] Although some individual bishops demurred at the movement's struggle for human rights,[66] the Church clearly stood as a bulwark against the abuses of human rights, and Solidarity drew inspiration from it.

Polish historic cultural and political traditions counterbalanced Solidarity's emphasis on personal rights, interlocking individual and communal well-being. In this vein, Solidarity members often appealed directly to the language of Polish Romanticism, which reacted against the Enlightenment's elevation of the individual over society.[67] In attempting to edify the suffering Poles, John Paul II masterfully recalled the great nineteenth-century Romantic poet Adam Mickiewicz's vision of Poland's unique salvific role in Europe. The pope explained Poland's duty to defeat Communism in these terms during his pilgrimages to Poland in 1978 and 1979. Adding a personalist dimension to Mickiewicz's messianism, he argued that the dignity of the human person required nonviolent resistance because violence turns men and women into objects.[68] In addition to the Romantic heritage, Solidarity returned to the republican ethos of Polish "noble democracy" (*demokracja szlachecka*), which dates back to the sixteenth century. The republican tradition in Poland held that all citizens are responsible for the state and its communal goals and values.[69]

In fact, Solidarity believed that freedom is primarily realized by participation in fostering the common good. The movement certainly sought to protect individuals from coercion, but it resisted simply equating freedom with realizing one's own interests.[70] In short, Poland's communitarian traditions buttressed the Catholic Church's insistence on both human rights and corresponding duties to one another and to the common good. Thus, the ethic of solidarity advocated the full range of human rights, but it avoided overly individualistic and Marxist-collectivist understandings of human rights.

Solidarity and the Option for the Poor

The Polish ethic of solidarity was universalistic in scope. Yet, Tischner also contended in *Etyka solidarności* that solidarity primarily, though not exclusively, is directed towards those who have been wounded by others and whose suffering is avoidable. Tischner bases his argument on the parable of the Good Samaritan. In that biblical narrative, the pain of the man lying in the road is not the result of an illness, natural disaster, old age, or other unfortunate circumstance. Rather, it is the result of human evil. While we can and should be in solidarity with those who suffer from any cause, solidarity with those who suffer as a result of human evil is particularly "vigorous and spontaneous."[71] This was certainly the case if one considers the Solidarity movement, whose members often swiftly and strikingly came to the aid of people whom the Communist regime persecuted in one way or another. The strike in Gdańsk that demanded the reinstatement of Anna Walentynowicz, a shipyard worker who was fired unjustly, serves as one example among many others.[72] Solidarity was ready to defend every oppressed person, simply because he or she was a human being.[73]

These reflections on solidarity generate a salient question: Did the ethic of solidarity include a "preferential option for the poor"? As is well known, official Catholic social teaching endorsed this phrase after controversial deliberations.[74] Did the Solidarity movement share Latin American liberation theology's special concern for the liberation of the poor from all forms of oppression? If so, how can this be reconciled with the universalistic nature of solidarity? Can solidarity "turn towards all" if it places the needs of the poor and oppressed above the needs of others?

In a fascinating comparison of the ethic of solidarity and liberation theology, Tischner explicitly addressed the relationship between the Solidarity movement and the option for the poor. During a lecture given in Caracas in 1989, he stated that "it must be openly admitted that the term 'poor' did not play a crucial role in the movement." He somewhat enigmatically claimed that while Solidarity was concerned with poor persons, they were not the "essence of the Polish situation."[75] However, he went on to say that the movement primarily criticized the tremendous waste of human labor, natural resources, and time. In other words, it decried senseless work in Communist Poland. While Poles worked hard, they found it increasingly difficult to live a decent life.

In his view, Tischner resisted "absolutizing the poor," an error that liberation theology committed in Latin America. Nonetheless, he allowed for particular solicitude towards certain oppressed groups. He also acknowledged that Poles did suffer from poverty, which was the result of the massive inefficiency of the socialist economy. Tischner might have concluded that Solidarity did not explicitly defend "the poor" because Poles rarely discussed the categories of "poverty" and "the poor" prior to 1989. During the Communist era, poverty was not officially recognized. Moreover, he and many other Poles operated with a narrow conception of the problem, equating it only with extreme material deprivation. As chapter 3 of this book will reveal, extreme poverty was relatively rare in those days. Thus, although Tischner spoke of "the exploited," he did not use the word "poor" often to describe their plight. Nevertheless, Solidarity did embrace an option for the poor even though it did not use the precise phrase.

John Paul II's *Laborem Exercens* further clarifies this issue. The Solidarity Program explicitly cited the encyclical several times, referring to it as a "new stimulus to work."[76] It is unlikely that the movement did not embrace the encyclical's explicit exhortations to solidarity with the poor, such as the following:

> This solidarity must be present whenever it is called for by the social degrading of the subject of work, by exploitation of the workers, and by the growing areas of poverty and even hunger. The Church is firmly committed to this cause, for she considers it her mission, her service, a proof of her fidelity to Christ, so that she can truly be the "Church of the poor." And the "poor" appear under various

forms; they appear in various places and at various times; in many cases they appear as a *result of the violation of the dignity of human work:* either because the opportunities for human work are limited as a result of the scourge of unemployment, or because a low value is put on work and the rights that flow from it, especially the right to a just wage and to the personal security of the worker and his or her family.[77]

John Paul II considers those whom Tischner describes as victims of a "sick" system of labor to be "the poor." Furthermore, he claims that solidarity with the poor is part of the Church's mission and "a proof of her fidelity to Christ." Succinctly stated, solidarity by its very nature includes an option for the poor.[78] In other words, Tischner's reluctance to see "the poor" per se as a prominent element of Solidarity's program should not overshadow all that he and the movement did to promote their rights. In fact, the union's efforts even led to initial attempts at formally defining poverty in Poland according to the category of the "social minimum" (*minimum socjalne*). This poverty threshold requires an income that allows for participation in social life. This entails education, access to culture, sports, and medical care, in addition to basic needs such as food, clothing, and shelter.[79]

While solidarity involves special concern for the liberation and the rights of the poor, they are not its exclusive beneficiaries. Importantly, the universalistic dimension of solidarity is retained by the fact that solidarity expresses itself in different ways towards different people. As was described earlier, solidarity towards oppressors sometimes demands peaceful struggle in the name of justice and of the rights of the oppressed, the poor. This struggle not only seeks to empower the poor but also to convert the oppressors. In this connection, it is worth repeating Tischner's famous phrase: "solidarity, the one that is born of the pages of the Gospel, does not need an enemy or opponent to strengthen itself and grow. It turns towards all and not against anyone."[80] Like Martin Luther King, Jr. and the leaders of the Civil Rights movement, Solidarity's goal was not to eliminate or destroy "the other"—white supremacists in the United States, Communist party leaders in Poland. Rather, Solidarity wanted to reveal to their oppressors the truth about themselves. It "held a mirror up" for them, as Tischner put it. This process may involve dialogue, shaming, or, when these methods fail, strikes. However, solidarity always eschews violence and inciting fear in the oppressor; the goal remains his or her conversion.[81] Thus, solidarity with oppressors always involves forgiveness, but never without an insistence on the truth.[82]

In addition to solidarity with the poor and solidarity with oppressors, solidarity extends towards those who directly work to empower the poor. It beckons others to aid and defend them in their struggle.[83] For the sake of clarity, it may be helpful to capture the universal nature of solidarity and its various forms, as seen in Table 1.1. This brief typology illuminates the different ways of embodying solidarity with the poor and the oppressed, and those who struggle with the oppressed towards their empowerment, and the oppressors.[84] Later parts of this book will further elaborate on the various ways of realizing solidarity. The main point here is that solidarity's option for the poor does not preclude solidarity with others, even their oppressors, because solidarity is expressed in diverse, interconnected ways.

Finally, it will be helpful to note that the option for the poor born out of solidarity differs from compassion and almsgiving. Compassion reaches out to a person who remains a passive recipient.[85] By contrast, solidarity does not negate responsibility for one's self and one's obligations. To do so would be to usurp the right and obligation to participation.[86] There may be instances when the poor need to be on the receiving end of solidarity in order to "heal their immediate wounds." This constitutes, however, only an initial step towards solidarity with the suffering. In Tischner's words, "A community of solidarity differs from other communities because it is first 'for someone' and then comes 'we.' First comes the cry of the wounded. Then conscience hears and understands the one who suffers. Then a community arises."[87] The ultimate goal is not merely to alleviate the suffering of the poor. Rather, it is to enable them to become active members of the community of solidarity, to be able to "bear another's burdens."

Life in Truth

The final major aspect of the ethic of solidarity pervades all of its other dimensions. The call to "life in truth" is intimately connected with the anthropology of hope underpinning the possibility of dialogue and

TABLE 1.1 Varying Ways of Embodying Solidarity with Different Persons

Solidarity with:	The Poor and Oppressed	Defenders of the Oppressed	Oppressors
Realities apprehended:	1. Recognition of human interdependence 2. Hearing "the cry of the wounded"	1. Recognition of human interdependence 2. Acknowledging their role in empowering the poor & oppressed	1. Recognition of human interdependence 2. Seeing the oppressor as a person capable of change
Resulting ethical imperatives:	1. Crisis intervention (direct, immediate aid) 2. Contemplation of causes of the suffering of "the other"(social analysis)/understanding "the cry of the wounded" 3. Promotion of the rights of the poor and oppressed through institutions and social structures 4. Promotion of the participation of the oppressed as agent/s for personal and social change	1. Concretely aiding their efforts, through financial, logistical, spiritual, emotional support	1. Dialogue/Confrontation towards conversion 2. Compromise & power-sharing, when possible

with human freedom. It is also an overarching concept that encompasses everything required for the respect of human dignity. Every major voice within the Solidarity movement spoke of the need for life in truth. This demand appeared in the statements, speeches, placards, and myriad conversations among Solidarity's members.[88]

The thinking person in today's postmodern age will inevitably ask questions such as, "Whose truth?" and "Is there such a thing as truth?" For those members of Solidarity who were forced to suppress for decades what they believed to be the truth, these were not pressing questions. In order to understand why, one needs to recognize what kinds of truths were suppressed or erased by the Communist regime. For example, the

Katyń forest massacre, in which the Soviet Army killed 15,000 Polish troops during World War II, was officially nonexistent according to the propaganda pill that Poles were forced to swallow under Communism.[89] Michnik, who eventually was imprisoned for more than five years for refusing to sign a declaration of loyalty to the regime, had this to say on living a life of lies under Communism: "We participated in the mock elections, wrote fallacious articles, we raised our hands at absurd meetings, and cheered at organized mass demonstrations in support of the totalitarian system. We did this out of fear, we were deceitful out of fear."[90]

In Michnik's view, during the Solidarity movement, Poles began to "spit out the gag." They began to openly criticize the abhorrent lies of the regime: the incarcerations, the deportations, the false promises of economic comfort, the deference to the Soviet Union to the detriment of the Polish nation. "Teachers wanted schools to be real schools, universities to be universities, books to be books," claimed Tischner.[91] In other words, Poles wanted the freedom to seek the truth and express their beliefs, and they regained it during Solidarity. Even though repression continued, Poles recovered the virtue needed to live in truth, namely, courage.[92] This had tremendous social consequences. As was said earlier, being able to trust in the sincerity and reliability of others is a necessary ingredient of solidarity. Living a lie, as Michnik argues, is to "establish all of one's relations with other people as relations based on pretence." In this paradigm, people and the world become "a constant threat."[93] In contrast, the era of Solidarity was a time of hope.

Popiełuszko paid for his commitment to truth with his life. For him, valuing one's own human dignity required standing "by the truth in every situation, even if it costs dearly."[94] He argued that lying causes a person to become a slave, which is an affront to human dignity. Therefore, as John Paul II often repeated, human freedom is attained above all else by living in accordance with the truth.[95] This raises the question: Does this require subscribing to a certain set of metaphysical truths and moral truths based on them? To put it another way, were Popiełuszko and others talking about "Truth with a capital 'T'"? Marek Cichocki, for example, argues that Solidarity never really clarified what comprised the "truth."[96] Nevertheless, the following suggests one possible way of interpreting Solidarity's call to life in truth.

Popiełuszko, like the poetic voice in Zbigniew Herbert's "The Envoy of Mr. Cogito," maintained that on the most basic level, living a life in truth meant living in accordance with one's conscience.[97] Conscience is the basis of solidarity. The deepest kind, the solidarity of consciences, calls everyone to be a person of conscience.[98] However, one may further ask whether or not the appropriate shaping of conscience requires belief in the Christian God. Beyond that, does it mandate assenting to Roman Catholic theological and moral doctrines?[99] The answer varied among Solidarity members, and this divergence became a source of contention concerning the nature of freedom and its relationship to truth in Poland after 1989.[100] During the Solidarity era, however, even though some persons held that solidarity requires belief in God, or even in Jesus Christ as the Divine Savior, a diversity of views was possible. Intellectuals such as Michnik and Kuroń, who were either atheists or agnostics, advocated life in truth, alongside Christians such as Tischner and Popiełuszko. However, all those who called for life in truth did share a certain set of beliefs about the human person, a particular anthropology: the anthropology of hope described above. Life in truth required having an understanding of the human person as one imbued with inviolable dignity, the capacity for freedom, and a call to participation. This shared anthropology allowed for the unity in a common cause, which became known as Solidarity, among Christians, Jews, atheists, and agnostics.[101]

This brief sketch of the ethic of solidarity in Poland prior to 1989 has undoubtedly skimmed the surface of many important issues. Nonetheless, it provides a basic understanding of the principles and values that guided the Polish movement that captured the world's attention and changed the course of history. In addition, it gives the reader a sense of what was lost in Poland after 1989. Given the moral and spiritual potency of this movement, it is all the more striking that after 1989, Solidarity and, more important, the ethic of solidarity, met such a rapid demise. That complicated story deserves to be told in a separate chapter.

CHAPTER TWO

The Eclipse of Solidarity after 1989

The collapse of the Solidarity movement shortly after 1989 surprised many outside observers. After it imploded, the movement splintered into new political parties and unions. Traces of it can be found today in Poland; for example, a political party formed under the banner of Solidarity (Akcja Wyborcza Solidarność), and the union NSZZ Solidarność still functions. However, these organizations have little to do with the original movement.[1] Today the vast majority of Poles believe that Solidarity no longer serves the good of the country as a whole.[2] When the current president, Lech Kaczyński, refers to Poland as a "solidarity state," his words are devoid of any real significance. Few people expect the government to translate them into policies that promote the values of the Solidarity movement. As chapter 6 will demonstrate, the Roman Catholic Church has largely abandoned its commitment to Solidarity's original goals and its ethos.

The past illuminates the present state of affairs. Some scholars point to a gradual decrease in the ethos of Solidarity beginning with the introduction of martial law in Poland on December 13, 1981. Martial law not only terminated the fruitful debate that had existed within Solidarity since its inception in August 1980, but it also sowed the seeds of mistrust between those inside Solidarity who supported the regime and those who opposed it. Because the government heightened repression of the opposition, Solidarity members no longer eagerly viewed members of the party who did not unequivocally disavow the regime as dialogue partners. A division between the "elite Solidarity" and the "Solidarity of the people" also arose during this period.[3] Yet, the movement continued its bout with the regime until 1989. Therefore, it is difficult to point to a definitive moment when Solidarity ended. Perhaps it gradually degenerated. Nonetheless, when most Poles think of the end of the era, they recall an event that occurred after Solidarity's first free elections in 1989. It was appropriately called the "war at the top" (*wójna na górze*).

The "War at the Top" and Its Aftermath

The fiery electrician, Lech Wałęsa, declared the "war at the top" in the spring of 1990 at the Second National Congress of Solidarity. He turned against his former intellectual advisors Adam Michnik, Jacek Kuroń, Bronisław Geremek, and Tadeusz Mazowiecki, who were shaping the new order in Poland after 1989 from Warsaw, the capital, while he remained in his native Gdańsk. Mazowiecki had become prime minister on August 24, 1989. Wałęsa, the leader of the early Solidarity movement, felt marginalized. Therefore, he announced his candidacy for the presidency with this declaration and situated himself against Mazowiecki, his former friend from Solidarity. During the presidential campaign, the chasm between "intellectuals" and workers of the Solidarity movement widened. The "war" culminated at a Solidarity meeting in June 1990, when Wałęsa rudely called Jerzy Turowicz, the respected editor of the Catholic weekly *Tygodnik Powszechny*, to the podium. Wałęsa sardonically cried, "Poland is waiting for your criticisms."[4] For many, this event signified the end of Solidarity as a unified social movement. Michnik, the well-known dissident and author, lamented that with the "war at the top," the ethos of Solidarity died and that Lech Wałęsa was responsible for its death.[5] For his part, Michnik did not spare his opponents any of the vitriol that they had spewed towards him. If he was a "crypto-Communist," as they alleged, then they were simply "swine."[6]

It is unfair to blame Wałęsa solely for the fall. Futhermore, he deserves much credit for his role in the movement in the 1980s. Clearly, however, most Poles perceived these rancorous power struggles to signal the abandonment of Solidarity. The hostility between the two camps—one that supported Mazowiecki for president, the other, Wałęsa—polarized Polish society.[7] While the political ambitions of Wałęsa and Mazowiecki largely caused the "war at the top," much more was at stake. Two different visions of the transformation of the political and economic systems lurked beneath the surface of the more visible personal battle.[8] The main differences lay along two lines: the speed and the nature of the economic and political reforms that were undertaken, and the role of the members of the former Communist party in post-1989 democratic Poland.

Both the Wałęsa and Mazowiecki camps generally supported neoliberal economic reforms after 1989. However, they disagreed on the appropriate pace of the economic "shock therapy." Wałęsa advocated giving the government fast-track powers to legislate economic reforms, because as the economic situation worsened, social trust in the reforms dissipated. He therefore wanted to force through as many of these reforms as quickly as possible. Many in Mazowiecki's government, however, became wary of hastily introducing economic reforms that might have harmful social consequences, such as large-scale layoffs and significant decreases in social spending. They also eschewed political reforms that would in one stroke lead to the "decommunization" of the government, one of the Wałęsa camp's key goals.[9] Instead of barring former Communists from public life, Mazowiecki adopted the "broad-line" policy (*gruba kreska*). In doing so, he allowed former Communists to participate in shaping the new Poland.[10] The political issue of "decommunization" split the Solidarity movement, which eventually broke into several new political parties. On the economic front, both Wałęsa and Mazowiecki ultimately opted for neoliberal economic reform, despite the initial misgivings of Mazowiecki.[11] This triumph of neoliberalism in Poland, in addition to the personal enmity between the two old Solidarity allies, contributed to the disappearance of the ethos of solidarity. The support for these economic reforms led some former movement leaders to part from both Mazowiecki and Wałęsa. Many voters felt deceived and became very cynical towards Solidarity, which no longer seemed to protect their rights and interests.[12]

The Ascendancy of Neoliberalism

Both Mazowiecki and Wałęsa believed that the only way to overcome the Polish economy's woes, caused by massive foreign debt, hyperinflation, and stagnation, was to follow the path of neoliberal capitalism. Neoliberalism had had some earlier adherents in Poland.[13] However, it rapidly gained popularity after 1989, when it could be openly considered as a real option. The rise of internal conflicts within Solidarity also coincided with the neoliberal revival's zenith in the West.[14] The fall of Communism guaranteed the triumph of Margaret Thatcher and Ronald Reagan's free-market ideology. Many Poles, particularly new key decision-makers, welcomed it with open arms.

Polish neoliberals have not codified a clear set of values and rules. However, they all espouse at least the following three tenets. First, neoliberals uphold the unconditional supremacy of the economic system. Second, they support unfettered capitalism without the possibility of a "mixed" economy, where government can intervene to correct social problems associated with market failures. And third, they permit all possible points of view concerning issues beyond economics, such as civil liberties, reproductive freedoms, and capital punishment, as long as they do not interfere with economic freedom.[15]

Neoliberalism was not welcomed unanimously. Some political parties, such as Unia Wolności, spoke of building a "social market economy" (*społeczna gospodarka rynkowa*) akin to the *Sozialmarktwirtschaft* of the Rhine countries. Like the Solidarity program, this model of capitalism promotes social goods such as a relatively large number of job opportunities, job-training programs, freedom of association, effective trade unions, unemployment benefits, and mechanisms to promote democratic participation in public life (see Table 2.1).[16] Thus, it appealed to some members of Solidarity. However, voices that falsely likened it to the failed socialist system prevailed.[17] Although the Constitution of 1997 proclaims that Poland's economy is based on the "social market economy" model, politicians generally failed to create laws embodying the general principles found in the Constitution.[18] Capitalism in its neoliberal, Anglo-Saxon form won a decisive victory.

Many Polish economists and politicians found neoliberalism alluring because they had a limited understanding of liberalism. Many of

TABLE 2.1 Models of Capitalism

Neoliberalism/"Washington consensus"	Rhine model/*Sozialmarktwirtschaft*	East Asian or Japanese model
USA, Latin America, England	Germany and much of W. Europe	Japan, South Korea, Taiwan, Chile
Financial deregulation	Focus on "national economy"	"Financial repression": controls on capital flows
Privatization dominates	Corporate ownership controlled by large national banks	State control of large industries
Liberalization of trade	Emphasis on high-quality exports Agricultural subsidies to protect farmers	Protectionism Agricultural subsidies to protect farmers
Deliberate depression of wages to create "comparative advantage"	Collaborative national wage bargaining Wage controls: higher minimum wages, subsidies	Wage controls: higher minimum wages, subsidies Higher prices tolerable effect of higher wages
Encourages consumption as driving engine	Emphasis on "quality of life" for all	Mandatory savings programs
Market alone distributes fairly	Wealth gap smaller due to egalitarian cultural assumptions	Governmental promotion of equitable sharing of growth and wealth
Flat tax and free-enterprise zones	Heavy taxation through graduated tax scale	Heavy taxation through graduated tax scale
Private individuals and institutions tend to welfare needs. State does little	Social programs such as job training and retraining, generous unemployment benefits	Strong social welfare programs such as housing
Unemployment seen as "natural" to a degree. Low-wage jobs in service sector is solution	High unemployment "tolerable" effect of higher wages	Very low unemployment due to "artificial jobs" in private sector
Top-down style of management	Worker participation in ownership, management, and wage negotiations	Tacit agreement between workers and management (e.g., lifetime employment)
Largely ignores role of culture in the market's ability to function. Individualistic view of human person	Culture/nation embedded in market	Cultural norms embedded in market; communal goals supersede private gain
Economic growth first, then social spending	Public higher education and more generous health care	Education, health care, etc., are means and ends of development

Sources: Based on William Greider, *One World, Ready or Not: The Manic Logic of Global Capitalism* (New York: Simon & Schuster, 1997); Amartya Kumar Sen, *Development as Freedom* (New York: Knopf, 1999).

them had primarily associated liberalism with Friedrich von Hayek and the "gospel of the free market" rather than the protection of the individual against governmental abuses.[19] Neoliberalism's appeal resided in Hayek's synthesis of free-market ideology and staunch criticisms of all forms of socialism as totalitarian.[20] Economic advisors to the Polish government such as Milton Friedman and Jeffrey Sachs and the influx of American "Christian neoliberalism" also contributed to the neoliberal moment.[21] In short, the egalitarian ethic of solidarity was replaced by a new system of values that prioritizes individual success, which is measured by the market. The upshot of this shift has been an increase in resentment, individualism that eschews social responsibility, frustration, and the need to prove one's self over and against others.[22]

Neoliberalism is not the worldview of all Poles, in spite of its dominant role in the socioeconomic transformations after 1989. Polish political philosophers, historians, and sociologists have protested against the highjacking of liberalism by neoliberals.[23] The 1990s witnessed vociferous debates about the true nature of liberalism on the pages of the most widely read Polish newspapers and magazines. John Paul II and the Roman Catholic bishops' conference added their own criticisms of neoliberalism in Poland.[24] Moreover, sociological data reveal that the majority of Poles do not subscribe to the economics of neoliberalism. Strikingly, the number of those in favor of governmental establishment of an upper limit for personal income has increased: 39.3 percent in 1988, 47.2 percent in 1991, and 50.5 percent in 1997. More than 65 percent think that the government should bail out failing industries in order to preserve jobs. While most Poles tend to believe that a free-market economy is better than a centrally planned economy, numerous studies have shown that Poles do not support a neoliberal capitalist system that prioritizes minimum government intervention.[25] Nonetheless, neoliberalism has played a significant role in the transformation of Polish society because many influential politicians of the early 1990s aspired to introduce neoliberal reforms.[26] Many of the heroes of the former egalitarian Solidarity era actually believed that "creating a dominant class, in which they themselves might be key players, was in the long-term interest of workers."[27] For them, neoliberalism was the best means to create a prosperous economy. However, today, most Poles reject or do not understand neoliberalism. They believe that the socioeconomic transformations of the 1990s have taken place over their heads.[28]

The manner in which politicians introduced the neoliberal reforms, without the participatory dialogue of the Solidarity era, embittered Polish citizens as much as did the deleterious consequences. Not only did former Solidarity leaders such as Karol Modzelewski, Tadeusz Kowalik, and Bohdan Cywiński decry the departure from Solidarity's values, but they also resented that policymakers did not seek social consensus or compromise on the economic policies known as the Balcerowicz plan.[29] Moreover, Wałęsa and the other Solidarity politicians used their remaining moral authority to "sell" these reforms to the masses in 1989 and 1990, even though they hurt workers and the weakest members of society.[30] They maintained that after the fall of Communism, radical steps were needed to jumpstart the capitalist system in Poland. Wałęsa, for example, tried to appease workers by promising that the painful consequences of economic shock therapy would be short-lived.[31] The former Solidarity leaders also tried to weaken the unions.[32] Eventually they persuaded the Solidarity union that accelerating the neoliberal economic reforms would bring greater benefits to workers.[33] Thus, Solidarity's elite turned away from its Romantic communitarian ideals and were suddenly converted to "elitist liberalism."[34] They even attempted to quell calls for a return to the ideals of Solidarity, arguing that they had no place in a capitalist system.

The years that followed "brought a whole series of Solidarity alliances and Solidarity fiascoes, which ended each time with the announcing of its ultimate destruction."[35] Other than self-interested ideological appeals to the values of the Solidarity movement, decisionmakers did not seriously consider them in their crafting of the new democratic and capitalist system.[36] A backlash eventually erupted against the technocratic imposition of neoliberal policies. Throughout the 1990s there was an increasing number of strikes and protests throughout Poland, which sometimes turned violent.[37] Indeed, the conflict between politicians such as Leszek Balcerowicz and Wałęsa, who perceived their role as "taming the masses," and "the rest," who feel marginalized, is one of the major causes of the collapse of Solidarity's vision for a new Poland.[38]

Neoliberals have contributed to the decay of public discourse and stimulated populist hatred towards any form of liberalism, in addition to allowing the deleterious economic consequences of shock therapy. Despite the apologetics of more temperate political liberals, neoliberals and self-styled ultraliberals such as Janusz Korwin-Mikke have done a good deal to tarnish the image of liberalism in Poland. The neoliberal "demagogy" that rejected any other version of liberalism made defending against antiliberal democratic attacks extremely difficult.[39] In addition, David Ost has argued that the former Solidarity leaders' inability to deal with the "economic anger" of the disillusioned workers after 1989 opened the door to a turn towards the "illiberal right." By 1991, Solidarity could no longer ignore the discontent with neoliberal economic reform. However, it intentionally channeled anger away from economic and class issues towards "identity cleavages." It displaced workers' frustration onto "political, ethnic or religious others" rather than onto the new capitalist class and neoliberal policymakers. This has hindered the growth of political liberalism and democracy and bred intolerance and xenophobia.[40]

Western creditor nations and financial institutions certainly bear some responsibility for the consequences of neoliberalism in Poland. The government negotiated with the International Monetary Fund (IMF) and World Bank in order to receive debt relief and additional loans.[41] As in many other parts of the world, these institutions urged the Warsaw government to adopt neoliberal reforms. However, strong "home-grown" proponents of neoliberalism steered the Polish economy in the early 1990s and took this course of their own volition.[42] To a large degree they are responsible for the abandonment of Solidarity's priorities of participation, the equality and dignity of all persons, and the common good.

Undoubtedly, neoliberalism has created rifts among Poles, stifled public dialogue, and contributed to the abandonment of Solidarity's goals. However, it would be an oversimplification to blame it alone for the nation's social, political, and economic problems. Communism wreaked havoc on Polish society by attempting to atomize it and eradicate civil society for forty years, and the legacy of Communism continues to plague Polish society. This part of the nation's past needs to be explained because its vestiges have also stifled solidarity's ability to flourish in the new era.

Homo Sovieticus as a Challenge to Solidarity

The concurrent existence of the morality of *homo sovieticus* with the ethic of solidarity prior to 1989 sheds some light on the eclipse of solidarity.[43] *Homo sovieticus*, an anthropological construct used to describe the mentality of those who lived under Communism, starkly contrasts with the ethic of pre-1989 Solidarity. Some observers have even argued that the morality of *homo sovieticus* dominated in Poland in the 1980s, and that the ethic of Solidarity was nothing more than a myth.[44] What, then, does *homo sovieticus* look like? Succinctly stated, the character traits of *homo sovieticus* are: eagerness to blame others and not one's self, extreme suspicion of others and their motives, a fatalistic attitude towards life, a sense of entitlement, helplessness, and irresponsibility.[45]

In order to survive the morose and sometimes brutal realities under Communism, Poles developed a private and a public "self." According to anthropologist Janine Wedel, this dualism was a part of everyday life: "One moral code is reserved for the private world of family and [close] friends, another for the public." Wedel notes that among family and close friends, Poles were kind and generous, while in the public sphere they were rude and selfish. The home served as a place of refuge from the harshness of everday public life. Most Poles trusted only those whom they embraced as *swój człowiek* (one of us), usually solely family members and a small circle of close friends. No one else could be trusted.[46] It is easy to imagine why this was the case. One never knew for certain who was or was not collaborating with the Communist regime. Accounts exist of family members betraying other family members as enemies of the regime. This dualistic system of morality that pitted "us" versus "them" fostered the atomization of society and created a "culture of artificial activity." People pretended to work for the sake of appearances. A sense of responsibility for the items they produced and for public goods deteriorated. Stealing supplies from one's place of work was widely condoned. Poles mainly looked out for themselves.[47]

Józef Tischner contended that the roots of this anthropological error lie in materialism. "Selling freedom for bread" comes naturally to this kind of person.[48] Moreover, *homo sovieticus* cannot distinguish between self-interest and the common good. Indeed, the end, freedom from any personal discomfort, always justifies the means.[49] In a world of "us" versus "them," one needs to take care of one's self and one's kin at all costs. Tischner, among others, even went so far as to say this system of morality eroded Catholicism in Poland. In retrospect, he wrote: "a certain conception of religion crystallized that was based on giving our private lives to God, but public life to the party . . . religion concentrated on raising children, family life, pietistic practices, whereas in the social sphere one was absolved from many [duties]."[50] Thus, at home, Poles largely preserved the values of honesty, fairness, care, and justice. In the public sphere, however, they operated with a different set of rules, one of which implicitly affirmed Hobbes's claim, "*homo homini lupus.*" The view of the human person held by *homo sovieticus* was the antithesis of solidarity's anthropology of hope.

Empirical observations confirm these philosophical and anthropological descriptions of *homo sovieticus*. For example, sociological evidence from 1988 shows that Poles believed that their children should be raised to defend their own interests rather than showing concern for others.[51] At the same time, Poles also exhibited "learned helplessness."[52] In this mindset, industriousness is not part of the equation when it comes to ensuring that one's material needs are met. Work is a necessary evil, to be avoided by feigning activity whenever possible.[53] The government, by its nature, "owes us." "It" is to blame for all deprivations. If it does not provide for us, then citizens can rightfully meet their own needs by suspect or illegal means.[54] Although the work ethic has begun to change for the better, many Poles still affirm the popular adages of the former Communist era: "*czy się stoi czy się leży to wypłata się należy,*" and "*wszystkim po równo.*"[55] These phrases meant that whether or not you work, you will be paid, and that everybody deserves an equal apportionment of all goods.[56]

Tischner argued that the Solidarity movement created a new community, which was the beginning of the end of Communism's *homo sovieticus*.[57] Was his prophecy accurate? This may have been the case during the Solidarity era, especially prior to the introduction of martial law. However, a recently published large-scale study of Polish mentalities conducted between 1988 and 2000 concluded that the characteristics of *homo sovieticus* continue to be one of the most serious obstacles to building civil society.[58] Social mistrust can still be readily seen in various aspects of everyday life. In fact, it rose slightly in the 1990s;[59] more than 90 percent of Poles believe that "one can never be too careful in relations with other people."[60] Suspicion of others, which is rooted in a negative view of the human person, precludes solidarity. Corruption, which ultimately stems from and causes a lack of social trust, continues to grow in public life.[61] The number of Poles that perceive corruption to be a major problem rose from 33 percent in the earlier 1990s to 70 percent by 2003.[62] Crime, particularly violent offenses among youths, has risen dramatically since 1989.[63] These crimes often result from a sense of hopelessness and mistrust towards others.

In 1992, Tischner himself wrote that those who demanded their daily sustenance from the Communists ironically now demand it from "the capitalists."[64] Five years later, he stated that much of the economic "sickness" of socialism had disappeared in Poland. Yet, its vestiges collided with the "sickness" of capitalism and globalization, which reduces human labor in favor of technology.[65] *Homo sovieticus* has met *homo oeconomicus*.[66]

To summarize, solidarity existed alongside of *homo sovieticus* in Poland during the 1980s. Perhaps every individual possessed some degree of solidarity and the traits of *homo sovieticus* during the 1980s. Tischner maintained that all Poles were "infected" with the "disease," including himself, but no one person was a perfect incarnation of *homo sovieticus*.[67] By the same token, he lauded the ethical accomplishments of the Solidarity movement, to which roughly one quarter of Poland's population belonged at its height.[68] In the case of Poland, the Church, in spite of its shortcomings and its infiltration by *homo sovieticus*, provided a bulwark against the anthropological and ideological onslaught of Communism.[69] Thus, the characteristics of *homo sovieticus* are more moderate in Poland than in other former Soviet-bloc countries.[70] Nonetheless, solidarity had and continues to have another contender in *homo sovieticus*.

The neoliberal capitalist model in Poland, which was mentioned above, has compounded these issues. "Wild capitalism" (*dziki kapitalizm*), as it is commonly called, is understood as a zero-sum game. Other members of society are seen more and more as competitors for jobs, money, and prestige.[71] In short, others represent a threat, not partners in solidarity. The uncertainties related to the changes that people experience during any systemic transformation have been most traumatic due to the real or perceived sink-or-swim nature of the new capitalist order. This fact has influenced not only the way that people view one another but also social relationships. The frustration of the "losers" spawns more "learned helplessness," and, as Robert K. Merton theorized years ago, often leads to criminal behavior.[72]

While *homo sovieticus* and neoliberalism have different historical roots, they share a common thread on an existential and psychosocial level. Both the attitudes and behavioral patterns of *homo sovieticus* and *homo oeconomicus* arise out of a particular understanding of human freedom. After years of Communist repression, freedom came to be one of the most prized possessions of Poles after 1989. At the same time, the nature of freedom as well as its limitations in a capitalist, democratic society became one of the most controversial subjects of debate. It is worth exploring these debates, as the putative conflict between freedom and solidarity caused many Poles to forsake solidarity in the name of freedom.

Freedom: Enemy of Solidarity?

Poles struggled for freedom against foreign oppressors throughout much of their history because of historical and geographical circumstances.[73] The denial of freedom caused them to value freedom as one of the highest human goods. As Tischner put it, "If I had to place one of the values cherished in Poland first in lexical order, I would choose freedom."[74] In 1995, 83 percent of adult Poles declared freedom to be important always, while a small minority saw it as important only sometimes or never. Moreover, freedom ranks higher than other values such as social justice, welfare, and equality before the law.[75] Thus, Tischner's ruminations on "the unfortunate gift of freedom" after Solidarity's victory may seem confounding at first glance.[76] However, in addition to solidarity, freedom represents another of the most highly contested and controversial ideas in Poland today. Its myriad and sometimes conflicting interpretations cause a great deal of consternation.

In general, the absolutization of "negative" freedom has banished understandings of freedom realized in solidarity with others, that is, "positive" freedom. Negative freedom requires "removal of the obstacles that rise up on the way to realization of the innate rights of the individual, not to decide what the individual should do to be good, wise and happy."[77] A person is free when no other person or institution coerces her. By contrast, positive freedom, that is, "freedom for," answers "the question *for what* man should be free" and links it "to a certain idea of the good, whose attainment is the calling of the individual and collectivity."[78] Important thinkers such as Isaiah Berlin and Leszek Kołakowski have claimed that efforts to promote "positive freedom" or "true freedom" and its inherent relationship to a conception of the good and "truth" lead to totalitarianism. In their view, talk of positive freedom generates political and legal structures that demolish individual rights, as regimes attempt to coerce people into embracing their version of "true freedom."[79] History lends credence to this claim. However, the dominance of negative freedom has eroded concern for both individual rights and the common good in the case of post-solidarity Poland.

Freedom as National Sovereignty

Poland's difficult history inevitably shapes contemporary understandings of freedom among its people. Tartars, Swedes, Teutonic knights, Germans, and Russians all took turns invading Poland.[80] For more than 120 years, it disappeared from the map of Europe until it regained its independence in 1918. Then, on September 1, 1939, the Nazis invaded Poland, and, on September 19, the Soviet army attacked from the East. More than one million Poles were deported to Siberia, half of whom never returned. In February 1945, Franklin Roosevelt and Winston Churchill "gave" Poland to Joseph Stalin, whose army was already occupying it, at the infamous Yalta Conference. For the next forty-five years, Poles lived under the yoke of Communism.[81] In light of this history, Timothy Garton Ash states, "The Poles are an old European people with an unquenchable thirst for freedom: freedom in Polish means, in the first place, national independence. The Polish national identity is defined in opposition to Russia."[82]

Equating freedom with national sovereignty (*niepodległość*) is certainly understandable, given the nation's troubled past. However, this strong emphasis has implications for civil society and an ethic of solidarity. Catholic social ethicist Aniela Dylus claims that the era of Solidarity focused exclusively on negative freedom, or "freedom from." The primary goal was liberation from oppressive structures. This, she maintains, explains why solidarity in Poland dissipated once the Communist regime fell. Today, many of its citizens continue to fight in their minds for "freedom from," finding new enemies in "Communists," "crypto-Communists," "Neocommunists," liberals, and capitalists. As a result, they fail to rebuild society as an exercise of "freedom for" in solidarity with others.[83] It is an exaggeration, however, to propose that Solidarity was solely concerned with negative freedom. Clearly, Solidarity demanded participation in the construction of just social, political, and economic structures. This is an aspect of positive freedom. Moreover, according to the republican origins of Solidarity's ethos, the use of freedom to take responsibility for the community can only be exercised without the threat of foreign domination.[84] In other words, the positive freedom to construct a just society can only exist after the defeat of foreign oppressors. Thus, at least in theory, Solidarity strove for a kind of freedom that included both negative and positive.

Understanding Solidarity as a republican movement explains its emphasis on the common good during its early years. Yet, liberation from the Communist regime and Soviet influence seems to have dominated the minds of many Poles as they approached the historic turn of 1989.[85] The leaders of the revolution devoted far too little attention to creating the democratic structures necessary for preserving the movement's republican ethos. Succinctly stated, Poland's foreign oppression, a constant throughout much of its history, has deeply influenced the way that its people think about freedom.[86] Freedom understood as national sovereignty does not always conflict with an understanding of positive freedom. The ancient republican tradition harmonized the two kinds of freedom. However, freedom from external domination without the republican emphasis on responsibility for the community, along with other distorted notions of freedom, has led to the denigration of positive freedom in contemporary Polish society.

Liberalism's Many Faces

Sociological data reveal that the majority of Poles primarily understand freedom as "freedom from."[87] The historical domination mentioned above is a causal factor, but liberalism's ascendancy after 1989, particularly neoliberalism, has undoubtedly contributed to this phenomenon. When speaking of liberalism(s), one should keep in mind the myriad and sometimes contradictory understandings of the term. In Poland, two different kinds gained sway after 1989. Politicians adopted neoliberalism, that is, economic liberalism, as the modus operandi in the transition from socialism to capitalism. In addition, a brand of liberalism that might be called moral permissivism has shaped the mindset of many Poles. Moral permissivism construes freedom as license to do whatever one chooses, in spite of the existence of objective moral norms.[88]

One need not accept economic liberalism, with its emphasis on economic freedom, in order to subscribe to moral permissivism, which pertains mainly to the sphere of personal freedom and morality.[89] The converse is true as well. Neoliberals sometimes support "conservative" or "right-wing" agendas such as the death penalty or the limitation of so-called political rights.[90] Although many elites and decisionmakers in Poland espouse this kind of (neo)liberalism, a majority of the population generally disavows its economic doctrines. On the other hand, a significant portion of the population appears to subscribe to moral permissivism. These divisions are not intended to be rigid. Rather, they are designed to help illustrate that: 1) some Poles favor neoliberalism, accepting its attendant notion of economic freedom, while condemning moral permissivism; 2) some prefer moral permissivism, adopting its conception of freedom as license, but they do not necessarily see the free market as a guarantor of their liberty; and 3) some adopt both neoliberalism, that is, economic liberalism, and moral permissivism. Regardless of whether one adopts either neoliberalism or moral permissivism or both, each of these options exclusively emphasizes negative freedom. And each of these three stances eschews an understanding of freedom realized in solidarity.

On his last pilgrimage to his homeland, Pope John Paul II decried the fact that many people in Polish society today make decisions according to a "false ideology of freedom." In his homily on August 18, 2002, he said that "[w]hen the noisy propaganda of liberalism, freedom without truth and responsibility, gains sway in our country as well, the shepherds of the Church cannot refrain from preaching the only and unfailing philosophy of freedom, which is the truth of the cross of Christ. That philosophy of freedom is essentially related to the history of our country."[91] Thus, John Paul, along with many others, located the root of a misguided perspective on freedom in a kind of liberalism extant in Poland today. The pope's statement should not be seen as a wholesale rejection of liberalism. During his pontificate he affirmed many of liberalism's goals, such as the protection of human rights. However, he castigated his compatriots who hold the "primitive conviction that the free market is not only the most effective mechanism of economic management, but it is also the ideology that best serves the world's development."⁹² On numerous occasions, John Paul declared that neoliberalism has vitiated his vision of a synthesis between the free market and the ethics of solidarity.⁹³ More specifically, the neoliberal understanding of freedom dashed his hopes for "capitalism with a human face."

Neoliberalism's Understanding of Freedom

Neoliberalism portrays freedom as "freedom from," with the underlying demand of freedom from government intervention in the economic sphere.⁹⁴ Former Minister of Privatization Janusz Lewandowski exemplifies this position: "I choose freedom from the catalogue of values, not equality.... Freedom understood as freedom from coercion and limitations."⁹⁵ Ireneusz Krzemiński and Pawel Śpiewak characterize neoliberalism in Poland today as "the economy first, then everything else."⁹⁶ For example, Balcerowicz, former minister of finance and president of the Polish National Bank, states that "Western countries became wealthy not because they were democratic, but because they were capitalist." He argues that there is "no correlation between democracy in politics and economic progress, in other words economic development."⁹⁷ Economic liberals in Poland demand unlimited economic activity, at the expense of social justice, equality, and the need for security.⁹⁸ Behind this, or perhaps in front of it as an ideological tool justifying laissez-faire capitalism, lies the understanding of freedom as negative freedom.

Hayek, who inspired the Thatcher and Reagan capitalist "revolutions," captivated the minds of Polish neoliberals with his ruminations on the nature of freedom. He equated freedom with the absence of the imposition of the will of others. Freedom amounts to freedom from coercion in the personal sphere.⁹⁹ Hayek's understanding of freedom differs from what Benjamin Constant called "ancient" freedom, or the freedom to participate in the democratic life of the community.¹⁰⁰ The free market, which spontaneously creates the best possible social order, is the only guarantee of Hayekian negative freedom.¹⁰¹ Hayek contended that the most conducive of all social systems to human freedom is one of "spontaneous order," where a society formed on this basis must be governed by certain minimal rules but be devoid of "direct commands." In this vein, Hayek maintains that "intervention" or "interference" in the market order should be eschewed in order to preserve the "balance" of individual interests and aspirations achieved by the spontaneous order.[102] In such a spontaneous order, a common good does not exist; individuals do not share a vision of their goals and the purpose of society. Thus, the idea that all human beings should realize freedom "for something" in common is rendered incomprehensible.[103] Moreover, Hayek perceives the understanding of freedom as empowerment to be a threat to real freedom, that is, freedom from coercion.[104]

Hayek's notion of freedom starkly contrasts with the ideals of Solidarity. Nonetheless, it influenced key Polish decisionmakers during the transition to capitalism and democracy.[105] For example, Balcerowicz expressly appeals to Hayek in *Wolność i rozwój* (Freedom and Development), where he persuades Poles of the felicitous functioning of the "invisible hand" of the market.[106] Ironically, Polish neoliberals exhibit a contrast between what they have putatively aspired to do and what they have done. They have stated that the ideal "invisible hand" of the market must be pulled along by government intervention in this early stage of Poland's road to capitalism. Yet, they imply that this abnormality should give way in time to "true liberalism," in which the state's role in the economy will wither away.[107] "Economic freedom," that is, minimum government intervention, will be attained only after a protracted period of steering the economy. In addition, Polish neoliberals espouse Hayek's view that the concept of social justice represents a dangerous "mirage." Appealing to it threatens freedom because the redistribution of resources demanded by its proponents requires arbitrary coercion dictated by special-interest groups.[108]

Capitalism, Freedom, and Solidarity: An Irreconcilable Tension

The triumph of neoliberal freedom had dramatic consequences for Polish social solidarity. "Polish society in the post-Communist era is driven by individualism, economic egoism—at last," declared Jan Bielecki in 1994.[109] In its most drastic form, "ultraliberals" such as Korwin-Mikke maintain that if the physically challenged desire lower curbs and sidewalks, then they should pay for them out of their own pockets.[110] When the state seeks resources for such projects from taxpayers, some neoliberals consider it an encroachment against the freedom to dispose of one's economic resources as one chooses.[111] This neoliberal understanding of freedom, the cornerstone of neoliberal capitalism, has caused some analysts to posit an irreconcilable tension between capitalism and solidarity.

Canadian philosopher Charles Taylor has said that the Polish ethic of solidarity cannot be fully realized in modern capitalist societies. He argues that capitalism "demands that we put solidarity aside and agree to bend or break the rules of mutuality for the sake of efficiency, which, as it turns out, we cannot forsake." Taylor envisions a tension between solidarity and other human qualities, such as efficiency, ingenuity, and industriousness.[112] Many contemporary Polish thinkers agree with this deterministic understanding of capitalism. They lament the putatively unavoidable conflict between the values of capitalism and the values of Solidarity. Dariusz Gawin puts it starkly: "The new order brought new values with it. The basis of the free market is the principle of competition. In the process of competition, egoism functions as a basic virtue. Those who can eliminate their competitors can best fulfill their own needs. Concepts such as competition, egoism, interest, which are fundamental to the new order, clearly stand in opposition to the concept of solidarity."[113]

Competing understandings of freedom lie at the heart of this conflict. In the early 1980s the Solidarity movement rejected the dichotomy between freedom and solidarity. It adopted the motto "*nie ma wolności bez Solidarności,*" which means, there is no freedom without Solidarity. Whether or not they believed this could be the case in a capitalist system, though, is a matter of debate. Some voices in the contemporary Polish debate envision the possibility of the harmonious coexistence of freedom and solidarity within the capitalist system. In this vein, John Paul II recalled Solidarity's axiom during his pilgrimages to Poland by repeatedly stating, "no freedom without truth, no freedom without solidarity, no freedom without sacrifice."[114] In his social encyclicals, he affirmed a vision of the human person as "free, creative, and in solidarity with others." Moreover, the pope believed that the capitalist system can engender the flourishing of this type of person.[115] In *Centesimus Annus*, which can be seen as a response to the fall of Communism, the pope argued that "freedom in the economic sector [must be] circumscribed within a strong juridical framework which places it at the service of human freedom in its totality."[116] He also posited the possibility of development "achieved within the framework of *solidarity* and *freedom*, without ever sacrificing either one of them under any pretext" in *Sollicitudo Rei Socialis*.[117] Thus, John Paul II rejected a deterministic view of capitalism, which would a priori oppose freedom and solidarity due to the nature of the economic system. However, he did not affirm the neoliberal model of capitalism, as exemplified in the United States. Rather, he had the social market economy in mind when he approved of capitalism in his social teaching.[118]

Contrary to papal social teachings, however, a pervasive conviction exists that the free market is a sink-or-swim system in neoliberal capitalist Poland. Solidarity has been swept away by the new tides of capitalism in the minds of most contemporary Poles. In theory, the Constitution pays equal tribute to the "right to freedom" and the "duty of solidarity," citing them as "the foundation of the Republic of Poland."[119] However, policies rarely embody these words in post-solidarity Poland, where freedom is largely equated with economic freedom.[120] Moreover, economic freedom is narrowly construed along the lines of Hayek's reductionistic view. Indeed, a nuanced discussion of the multiple aspects of human freedom and the interconnections of kinds of freedom is conspicuously missing from public discourse. Polish neoliberals chastised those who promoted a different understanding of freedom. The Polish bishops, for example, were portrayed as "oppressors" or enemies of freedom,[121] and many Poles did not appreciate the Church's critique of neoliberal economic freedom and of understandings of freedom in other spheres of morality.

Moral Permissivism as Freedom

Moral permissivism is mainly concerned with freedom in "private" moral matters, such as sexual behavior, reproductive rights, and freedom of expression. Marian Filar, a self-described liberal politician, claims that "Poles are generally fans of freedom, but only one half of it, which says 'do whatever you want.'" In his view, they forget about the other dimension of freedom, namely, its relationship to responsibility.[122] While it would be imprudent to stereotype the Polish people as "morally permissive," it appears true that there is a tendency among many of them to understand freedom individualistically and as license. One third of adults and two fifths of young Poles understand freedom as the ability to act as one wishes, regardless of objective norms. One observer states that "the perception of freedom as the license to act without barriers is growing. A radically permissive society fosters indifference to the fate of others."[123] Is Poland radically permissive? One should not jump to rash conclusions based on limited sociological data. Moreover, despite the large numbers that espouse moral permissivism, a majority of Poles do not see freedom as license. However, consumerism and moral permissivism clearly play a negative role in Polish society today. After years of Communist control of goods, which often led to material deprivation and censorship, Poles now experience the "freedom to choose" from among fully stocked store shelves. They also have the freedom to say, write, and express their opinions.

This new situation obviously has positive and negative aspects. For example, great technological advances have made their way to Poland, where its people highly value their right to free speech and freedom of association.[124] Polish society is beginning to address many subjects that were once taboo, such as spousal abuse, infertility, and homosexuality. However, there is a great temptation to equate freedom with the unfettered access by consumers to pornography, drugs, and so forth. "At the moment, not everyone realizes that the challenging freedom in post-Communist Poland should not be equated with postmodern free-rein."[125] The Polish bishops condemned the growing culture of consumerism in several Synod documents, linking it with freedom "experienced as following one's instincts" and then selectively following or abandoning objective moral norms.[126] Likewise, John Paul II bemoaned moral permissivism on many occasions, often directly associating it with the issue of abortion.[127] By contrast, he articulated a positive notion of freedom that is measured by the degree to which one is ready to serve others and give of one's self.[128]

The pope's worries have an empirical basis. Several studies conclude that while Poles do not espouse moral relativism, they seem to adopt a live-and-let-live attitude. As one sociologist puts it, "universal agreement exists concerning a great deal of the scope of 'good and evil,' but the majority of evil acts are acknowledged as justifiable in practice."[129] This attitude has significant ramifications for society's level of trust and solidarity. Corruption, for example, is often justified with "creative" situational ethics.[130]

To summarize, "freedom" has become a thorny issue in Poland. The conceptions of freedom rooted in both neoliberalism and moral permissivism suggest that to be free means to be left alone. Freedom realized in solidarity does not fit within either paradigm. Given the myriad conundrums relating to "freedom," it is no wonder that many people have decided that "freedom" is not what they expected. Indeed, some even long for the past, when "freedom" was not an option.

"Fleeing" from Freedom

Another problem compounds the contemporary Polish malaise concerning freedom. Some Poles have rejected liberalism *tout court* and condemn its view of freedom as a pernicious product of "the West." An intense fear of freedom arose, which "became greater than the fear of violence." Many Poles blame the winds of freedom from "the West" for sins such as abortion, pornography, and a lack of respect for religious piety.[131] Tischner described this phobic mentality: "Debauchery is freedom ... Corruption is freedom ... Disagreements among politicians is freedom ... Freedom is horrible. We remember, as Erich Fromm had written, that people flee from freedom and of their own volition chose [someone such as] Hitler for themselves. When we read that book, we said to ourselves, not us Poles, we died for freedom. This is true, but did we know what that freedom is?"[132] Thus, Tischner describes Poles' "escape from freedom" (*ucieczka od wolności*), alluding to Fromm's famous work. The response to this fear of freedom is the temptation to resort to authoritarian structures, because only a vanguard of "moral elites" can protect society from decay. Liberalism and democracy are thus to be rejected. It is easier to find refuge in authoritarian figures than to undertake the constructive aspect of freedom, which requires independent thought and action.[133] Tischner saw this dynamic at work in Polish society as a whole and in the kind of Catholicism often encountered in Poland.[134] He attributed the misunderstanding of freedom to a lack of serious attention to the writings of John Paul II.

Tischner devoted much of his own writings to overcoming this fear of freedom in Poland after 1989, which garnered him both admirers and staunch critics.[135] He promoted "Christian liberalism," which he contrasted with the liberalism of the Enlightenment. Succinctly stated, Christian liberalism does not acknowledge the absolute freedom of human beings. Rather, it situates men and women in the slavery of sin, heralding the possibility of gradual liberation thanks to the gift of grace.[136] Moreover, freedom, according to Christian liberalism, is freedom "for you, through you, and thanks to you"; it can only be achieved in community.[137] While Tischner's Christian liberalism is indebted to his reading of John Paul II, particularly *Veritatis Splendor* and *Centesimus Annus,* he more willingly acknowledges the importance of political compromise than does the pope. On the one hand, his version of positive liberalism, which prioritizes "freedom for" over "freedom from," posits the obligation of the state to protect the right to life of all citizens. Democracy cannot be ethically neutral after Auschwitz and Kołyma.[138] However, democracy requires seeking compromises that sometimes fall short of personal and communal moral ideals while working towards making democracy ever more ethical.[139]

The conflicts among "liberalisms" and other "isms" led to the conundrum that Tischner described as the "escape from freedom." He lamented that Poles have a distorted view of liberalism and have yet to affirm and understand "Christian liberalism."[140] Moreover, in agreement with Michnik, he blames the Church for abandoning its message of freedom from the Solidarity era and spreading the fear of freedom.[141] While this may be true, the undeniable influence of neoliberalism and moral permissivism must be blamed at least in part for the understandable skepticism of some Poles towards freedom. There are, of course, other reasons. The persistence of *homo sovieticus,* as described above, obviously makes people reluctant to accept the responsibility that comes with a positive understanding of freedom—the responsibility for one's self and the community.

As a result, one of the greatest problems in Poland today is the weakness of civil society and the widespread lack of participation in building a society founded on freedom, justice, and solidarity.[142] Many Poles do not place a high premium on civic participation. Others have no choice, as they have been relegated to the margins of society by the turbulent socioeconomic changes in Poland since 1989.

For certain, the rise of nongovernmental organizations (NGOs) concerned with environmentalism, homelessness, women's rights, and consumer protection, to name only a few issues, is a positive sign. Charitable activities, sometimes on a very large scale, such as the Wielka Orkiestra Świątecznej Pomocy, which raises a substantial amount of money for children's medical centers, contribute to the common good. More than 20,000 NGOs have come onto the scene since 1989. However, this number is still comparatively very low (Spain, 150,000; Sweden, 200,000; Finland 100,000). Moreover, two thirds of Poles do not belong to any association of volunteers, which places Poland last among developed countries.[143] Only 7 percent of young Poles belong to some kind of organization or club.[144] The high level of social mistrust described earlier hinders the willingness to get involved in volunteer organizations and often disables cooperation within organizations.[145] People also continue to look to the government rather than personally to undertake efforts to ameliorate social problems.[146] Another disconcerting signal after 1989 was the relatively low voter turnout. Poles very strongly believe that the ordinary citizen has no influence on political decisions (1990, 70 percent; 1994, 92.7 percent).[147]

In addition, the strong emphasis on the family, in itself a positive tendency, leads to a sort of "cult of the family." People in Poland most often rely on their relatives for diverse forms of support. This kind of "familial solidarity" can often fail to move beyond its own sphere to become more universal.[148] Participation of family members in the larger common good, as expressed in Catholic teaching by the vision of the family as a "school of virtue" and "domestic church,"[149] is therefore overlooked or even frowned upon in some cases.[150] The distinction between "us" and "them," a characteristic of *homo sovieticus,* still polarizes the public and private spheres in Polish society.

Today, in Tischner's words, "it is true that no one resorts to violence, but violence is not the only kind of departure from the ethos of Solidarity. Every 'false witness against one's neighbor' betrays it. And there is a great deal of this.... One has the impression that the model of democracy is everybody arguing with everybody."[151] The reasons for this are manifold. One problem lies in the tendency to demonize "the other." In this Manichean brand of politics, the other represents evil and therefore must be tamed with the "right values."[152] The political abuses of Solidarity also caused people to be skeptical of those who declared solidarity with the poor, the sick, or the elderly: they must have an ulterior motive or hidden agenda.[153] Finally, some observers have drawn attention to a Polish "tower of Babel." For example, political parties that declare themselves to be social democratic sometimes support neoliberal economic policies. Neoliberals, as was mentioned earlier, often looked like supporters of "big government" in the 1990s. The political parties are thus hybrids incomprehensible to the larger public, declaring and instituting a mixed bag of policies.[154] It is no wonder, then, that Poles retreat from the political sphere, which they have a hard time understanding and trusting. Gone are the days of dialogue in solidarity, which acknowledges that all sides in a debate must contribute constructively to reach social agreement. As chapter 6 of this book will discuss, some Church leaders reach across boundaries to find common ground, but the invective of some bishops and the unwillingness to listen to other viewpoints has contributed to this woeful state of affairs.

Solidarity and its moral legacy have all but disappeared from this country, where such great hope in human possibilities for just and free social transformation arose in the 1980s. Most members of the movement have either forgotten the experience altogether or speak of it reluctantly.[155] Shelves in Polish bookstores and library catalogues contain a paucity of works on the subject. Polish students of sociology and political science, not to mention the broader public, rarely consider the importance and meaning of Solidarity.[156] Thus, it is not surprising that one recent attempt to recall this part of the nation's past was entitled, "On Solidarity Forgotten."[157]

Despite the tumultuous times in Poland after 1989 and the eclipse of solidarity, there have been some signs of improvement in the lives of ordinary Poles. They are able to cast their votes in free elections. More than two million small businesses have sprung up since the fall of Communism. Poland became a member of the European Union in 2003. In this regard, the remarkable revolution known as Solidarity won its battle, without shedding blood. However, if one harks back to the movement's norms and objectives, the revolution appears to have failed, or at least stalled. Most of the economic, social, and cultural rights that the movement stressed have not been realized. Its emphasis on the solidarity, freedom, and participation of all people has been abandoned by some and abused by others in ideological and political battles. The dramatic rise in poverty, in various forms, evinces this fact.

CHAPTER THREE

Poverty in Poland after 1989

Empirical Signs of the Failure of the Revolution

Poverty has plagued Poland since 1989.[1] The scope and nature of poverty in the nation today reveals that solidarity between the "haves" and "have-nots" scarcely exists. It is perhaps the most blatant area in which the values of solidarity, freedom, and participation have been egregiously neglected. For certain, some Poles live in solidarity with the poor. However, the scale of social solidarity with the poor in Poland today does not begin to compare with that known and experienced in the Solidarity era of the 1980s. This chapter points to concrete spheres in which Polish society lacks solidarity and reveals that a great number of people do not enjoy important freedoms and are precluded from participation in that society. In other words, it points to empirical signs of the Solidarity revolution's derailment. Later parts of this book will demonstrate what a retrieved ethic of solidarity might look like if applied to the domain of poverty in contemporary Poland. First, however, an empirical analysis of poverty's many faces will provide the "data," or "the signs of times," to use Vatican II's terminology.

Solidarity begins with the attempt to understand "the cry of the wounded."[2] Wojciech Bonowicz correctly argues that "it is not only important to hear that cry, but it is most important to *understand* it. This is the case because it is possible to respond to the suffering of some by increasing the suffering of others." In addition, those who understand the poverty and suffering of others will enter into community with those who are trying to understand and change it. They will not choose the road of a lonely crusader who struggles futilely.[3] This claim has important implications for investigating poverty in Poland. First, its complex nature, its causes, and its potential remedies require careful analysis in order to move towards responses that are effective and do not, knowingly or unwittingly, generate still more poverty. As shall become evident, one of the major problems in socioeconomic life stems from the unwillingness to see how one's own choices and demands affect other people's economic situations. This is often the case on the macro- and microeconomic levels.[4] Moreover, well-intentioned activists, ethicists, theologians, and concerned individuals sometimes propose solutions to poverty that simply cannot resolve or assuage the problem in any realistic way.[5] As a result, economists and policymakers often dismiss what nonspecialists recommend in the arena of ethics and economics. In this vein, Leszek Balcerowicz argues that "ethicists often forget about logic" when they write about economic issues.[6] Succinctly stated, in order to begin to tackle the problem of poverty, analysts and societies as a whole must attempt to understand it as precisely as possible. Solidarity demands this attempt, and it must entail establishing what is fact and what is myth in the case of poverty in Poland today.

Measuring poverty presents myriad difficulties. Proposing solutions creates an array of additional problems. An ethic of solidarity cannot claim absolute certitude regarding many of the complex empirical issues related to poverty. This is particularly true of policy proposals. Thus, this analysis attempts, with care and caution, to provide an understanding of poverty in Poland after 1989 based on empirical evidence. It suggests responses to poverty informed by the values of solidarity, freedom, and participation. Its conclusions should be considered "prudential judgments," a category employed in Catholic social thought, which leaves ethical conclusions open to honest and constructive debate.[7] Nonetheless, the analysis of poverty must move beyond the level of moral generalities for two reasons. First, given solidarity's requirement of understanding and responding to "the cry of the wounded," to do otherwise would be a failure of solidarity.[8] Second, "concern for the poorest needs to be translated into more specific programs and effective policies."[9] Otherwise, Catholic social teaching's option for the poor remains at an unhelpful level of abstraction.

Problems in Measuring Poverty

The disputed nature of poverty poses a significant problem for an ethic of solidarity. In this vein, the 2000 World Development Report, *Attacking Poverty,* begins with the following question: "Poverty is a pronounced deprivation in well-being. But what precisely is deprivation?"[10] Answering this question presents numerous challenges. On the empirical level, those who study poverty disagree on the standards by which to measure it.[11] Stanisława Golinowska, a leading economist of poverty studies in Poland, maintains that this lack of common standards leads to conflicts and disagreements among decisionmakers in addressing poverty and its causes. Moreover, inaccurate assessments in a given region generate ineffective aid strategies. Targeting the wrong persons often creates unnecessary dependence on aid and also overlooks those who will remain trapped in poverty unless they are given needed assistance.[12]

Poverty in Poland presents its own context-specific conundrums. Throughout much of the first decade of the Polish transformations, the government had not even designated an official poverty line. As a result, it made no headway in targeting the long-term poor. Because the long-term poor were not clearly identified, policymakers did not devise successful and cost-efficient ways to aid identifiable, vulnerable groups mired in poverty over time.[13] In 1997 the Warsaw government finally adopted an official poverty line based on an income threshold.[14] Debates about the appropriateness of this standard continue.

This lethargy in creating a clear standard can be partially attributed to a Polish historical peculiarity. As was stated earlier, Poles did not carry out an open, widespread dialogue pertaining to the nature and causes of poverty prior to 1989.[15] This lack of dialogue both in academic spheres and among the broader public contributed to the difficulties in defining and measuring poverty after 1989. Nonetheless, some studies did treat "spheres of insufficiency" (*sfery niedostatku*) prior to 1989. This led to the establishment of the so-called social minimum (*minimum socjalne*). As a result of the Solidarity union's pressure, the Institute of Labor and Social Policy (Instytut Pracy i Spraw Społecznych) began to calculate the social minimum in 1981.[16] (The social minimum is defined as "the indispensable level of consumption determining social participation and integration, which demands satisfying not only basic needs but also certain other needs beyond them.")[17] The claim that lacking "non-basic" goods or benefits equates with poverty gives rise to controversy. Guaranteeing the social minimum requires an income equivalent to the cost of a "basket" of goods that allows for participation in social life. Such goods include education, medical care, and access to culture and sports, in addition to one's basic needs such as food, clothing, and shelter. Moreover, the amount and quality of these goods required to safeguard against social exclusion will vary in given societies at different times in accordance with standards of living, cultural mores, etc.[18] The determination of such factors leads to more discrepancies.

Should a person who is excluded from participation in the life of the community because she does not have access to culture, for example, be considered poor? Disagreement on this type of question has caused a great deal of consternation concerning the prevalence of poverty in Poland after 1989. Whether or not one accepts the social minimum standard greatly alters one's perception of the level of poverty. Some scholars, as well as the NSZZ Solidarność labor union, continue to demand that the social minimum be the primary measurement of poverty in the nation.[19] In an article concerning the elusive nature of measuring poverty, Kazimierz Frieske argues that "money is only a means of exchange ... behind the lack of money lies something much more essential, which is the fundamental source of poverty, namely, the long-term deprivation of basic human needs that precludes access to social participation."[20]

In this regard, Frieske's understanding of poverty resembles that of Nobel laureate in economics Amartya Sen, who describes poverty as "capability deprivation." In Sen's view, "poverty must be seen as the deprivation of capabilities rather than merely lowness of income." He does not discount the low income as "one of the major causes of poverty." However, income is *instrumentally* important. Low income can be a "principal reason for a person's capability deprivation." These deprivations, according to Sen, are "intrinsically important."[21] Among these intrinsically important capabilities are the ability to avoid starvation, undernourishment, escapable morbidity and premature mortality, and to have literacy and numeracy, political participation, and free speech.[22] Like Frieske, Sen sees poverty as "something deeper" than income deprivation. However, income standards such as the "social minimum" can be useful in determining if people's lives are impoverished because they are deprived of important goods or "capabilities."[23]

Some economists and policymakers in Poland maintain that the social minimum (and therefore the "goods" that this income level affords) rests far above the level of "real" poverty. Polish neoliberals generally advocate the use of a sole, absolute poverty line, below which individuals would be considered in "extreme" poverty.[24] They also tend to eschew the high levels reported in post-1989 Poland according to the social minimum standard.[25] Other economic liberals completely ignore the subject or deny its widespread existence in their analysis of Poland's socioeconomic transformations.[26] For her part, Golinowska criticizes the use of the social minimum category as a synonym for poverty in "various populist statements." It is, in her view, "*de facto* not a category of poverty."[27] Rather, it indicates those who may be *threatened* by poverty. Especially in a country such as Poland, which cannot afford generous social policies due to lagging economic development, the subsistence minimum (*minimum egzystencji*) should be used to target those threatened by the greatest deprivation.[28] This standard only includes goods immediately necessary for biological survival, such as food, clothing, minimal housing needs, and basic medical supplies.[29]

Those who disagree and defend the social minimum call attention to the denial of social participation, that is, marginalization, as one of the key elements of human poverty.[30] In addition to economists and sociologists, several contemporary Catholic ethicists and the Roman Catholic bishops' conference in Poland embrace a broad notion of poverty that includes the emphasis on social participation.[31] In short, proponents of the social minimum contend that a crucial dimension of human poverty gets lost when poverty is construed solely as an income threshold below which individuals are threatened with extreme material deprivation (starvation, homelessness, illness, and death).

Tadeusz Kowalik, an economic advisor to the Solidarity movement in the 1980s, defends the social minimum by appealing to a different argument. He and his colleague Mieczysław Kabaj contend that many other established poverty lines are unrealistically low. Analyzing the monetary allowances for basics (food, clothing, housing, medicine, etc.) in the subsistence minimum basket, Kabaj argues that a person could not actually survive on the subsistence minimum, which is 55 percent lower than the social minimum.[32] Kowalik, who has decried the decline in the standard of living of Poles since 1989,[33] objects to the standard used by the World Bank to measure poverty in Poland in the early 1990s. In his view, the World Bank's arbitrary use of the minimum retirement pension as the poverty line completely "ignores socioeconomic realities." He points out that prior to 1989, the minimum pension was more than 75 percent of the social minimum, whereas today it is barely above 50 percent. This is the case in spite of the fact that many goods such as public transportation, food, health care, and medications were either free or heavily subsidized, while today they are no longer.[34] Thus, economists such as Kowalik and Kabaj, social democrats who supported the adoption of a social market economy in Poland, differ from neoliberals in their understanding of the measurement of poverty.

These debates may seem esoteric. However, they have far-reaching practical consequences. Politicians utilize these categories to further political and economic agendas, and they shape public consciousness by opting for a particular definition of poverty in their programs and social policy. Choosing a poverty line is clearly a political decision; various lines determine welfare policies, minimum wages, minimum pensions, and the like.[35] As a result, politically and ideologically motivated groups sometimes lobby for one or another conception of poverty.[36] Moreover, despite claims that economics is a "value-free" science, values and moral principles undergird notions of poverty. Some thinkers adopt a conception of poverty that places a high premium on the principle of participation. Conversely, a conception that limits poverty to consumption levels is implicitly rooted in an anthropology that does not envision participation as a central component of what it means to be human. A look at some poverty statistics in Poland will help to make clearer the concrete relevance of the above debates to human persons. Most of these statistics pertain to the critical first decade of Polish democracy and capitalism (with some reference to more recent phenomena). This time period brought about the eclipse of solidarity in Poland and began many negative trends that continued well into the twenty-first century.

Empirical Evidence concerning Poverty from 1990 to 2001

Observers have offered divergent, sometimes contradictory, appraisals of the socioeconomic transformations since the fall of Communism in Poland.[37] Some have lauded the general shape of the transformations, bestowing accolades on the political and social actors responsible for them, while others have sharply criticized many policy decisions and their proponents.[38] Just as persons of different political persuasions selectively use poverty standards, they can also selectively cite various kinds of evidence indicating that poverty increased or decreased in Poland. Ironically, a broader understanding of poverty than neoliberals tend to admit—one that includes "health achievements,"[39] for example—could bolster the neoliberal claim that Polish society has generally benefited from the transitions of the 1990s.[40] Mortality rates, to cite another example, often trump other factors in assessments of a given society's health status.[41] When using this factor to assess Poland's health in the 1990s, there are encouraging signs. The infant mortality rate dropped from 1,934 in 100,000 births in 1990 to 885 in 1999.[42] A similar trend occurred in regard to children from ages 1 to 4. The mortality rate for women due to complications from pregnancy and birth dropped from 15.2 to 7.3 per 100,000 births. The average life expectancy of males and females has risen since 1992: from 67.4 to 68.8 for males and from 76 to 77.5 for females.[43] The risk of dying early, defined by UNDP Poland as death before age 60, has also dropped from 10.4 percent to 8.9 percent for women and from 27.5 percent to 23.2 percent for men.[44]

With the exception of a rise in early death among males in 1990 and 1991,[45] these indicators show an increase in the health and longevity of Poles since 1990. However, statistics concerning the health of Poles in the 1990s do not paint an unambiguously positive picture.[46] For example, a large jump in the rate of registered psychiatric illnesses took place. In addition, there was a steady increase in the number of malignant neoplasms encountered.[47] Thus, statistics to support or deny the claim that the health of Poles has improved can be found. Some indicators of human poverty in the domain of health reveal that Poles are better off today than they were in 1989, while others contradict such an optimistic conclusion.

Health, of course, should not be the only standard used to measure human poverty. In fact, most scholars in Poland continue to use income thresholds such as the social and subsistence minimums to determine poverty levels. According to Golinowska, "It appears that despite the obvious weaknesses of the disposable income category, it remains the most important indicator of the ability to meet one's need in a free-market economy. The correlation between low income and deprivation is very high."[48] Studying incomes and their distribution remains an excellent place to start. According to Sen, "income—properly defined—has an enormous influence on what we can or cannot do."[49] As Sen also points out, numerous factors such as geography, race, and gender affect the relationship between income and the ability to translate it into "freedoms" to be enjoyed. However, the study of human welfare has begun with income for good reasons.

The evidence pertaining to income poverty in Poland in the 1990s is bleak. According to all measurement indices, many people rapidly fell into poverty. Kabaj delineates three phases in poverty growth: 1) a large increase between 1990 and 1994; 2) a slight decrease from 1994 to 1996; and 3) another wave of poverty after 1996. In 1999, Kabaj wrote:

> The number of people living in absolute poverty (income below subsistence level) is estimated at a level of 5–5.5 million persons, i.e., 12–13% of the population of the country. The main reasons are: unemployment (35%), low income (60%), and low pensions (5%). According to the World Bank methodology the poor constitute 18.5% of the population, that is, 7 million people. Using the Leyden methodology or the subjective poverty line, the poor constitute 30.8% or 12 million. As observed by recent research, poverty is closely connected with the size of household, place of residence (60% of the poor live in rural areas), unemployment, and the level of education.[50]

Some observers question Kabaj's claim that "absolute poverty (income below subsistence level)" is as high as 12–13 percent. The Institute of Labor and Social Policy (IPiSS) reports that in 1999, 6.9 percent of the population lived below the subsistence minimum (*minimum egzystencji*).[51] On the other hand, UNDP Poland states that 14.9 percent of the population lived below the poverty line. (It uses the poverty line established by the state to determine eligibility for social assistance.)[52] Thus, different parameters yield different statistics on poverty. Despite these differences, Golinowska, Elżbieta Tarkowska, and other sources confirm Kabaj's portrait of the general shape of poverty trends since 1989: a very sharp increase in the first four years, followed by a slight decrease, with a rise again after 1996.[53] This is the case according to all statistical categories. Table 3.1 illustrates the trends based on the multiple poverty lines used to measure poverty in Poland.

The table does not show the dramatic jump in poverty during the first few years of Poland's transformation to a market economy. In short, during the years 1990–91, income poverty rates almost doubled from their previous levels.[54] In addition to the undeniable rise in poverty,[55] some other disturbing characteristics of Polish poverty raise concern. Unfortunately, a tendency towards chronic, long-term poverty has developed in the nation. This means that more and more of the poor suffer from social exclusion. Lacking participation, they are forming an "underclass," rather than experiencing poverty for a fleeting period of time. The hardships that they endure as a result of the transformations are long-term.[56] Such persons are sometimes referred to as the "hard-core poor," as opposed to the "temporary poor."[57] Poverty in certain social groups has become intergenerational, resulting in what sociologists call "hereditary" poverty.[58] Certain groups have been hit much harder than others by the socioeconomic transformations in the 1990s.

Who Are "the Least"? Particularly Vulnerable Groups

Solidarity's option for the poor requires asking, "Who are the least?" (Matt. 25:40). What persons and groups have suffered from poverty the most, and why? What groups have been relegated to the margins of Polish society? Empirical evidence reveals that those who bear the brunt of poverty the most are children, families with three or more children, women, and farmers and agricultural laborers.[59]

TABLE 3.1 Poverty Rates (Poverty Headcount According to Different Poverty Lines as a % of Total Population)

Poverty Lines	1992	1993	1994	1995	1996	1997	1998	1999	2000	2001
World Bank $2 day (1996 PPP*)							1.2			
Subsistence minimum	n/a	n/a	6.4	5.4	4.3	5.4	5.6	6.9	8.1	9.5
Relative poverty line**		12.0	13.5	12.8	14.0	15.3	15.8	16.5	17.1	17.0
World Bank $4 day (1996 PPP*)		10.0	10.0	10.0			18.4			
Income threshold for social assistance						13.3	12.1	14.4	13.6	15.0
Subjective poverty line***	32.6 (1990)		33.0	30.8	30.5	30.8	30.8	34.8	34.4	32.4
Social minimum	32.4	46.7	47.9	46.7	46.7	50.4	50.0	52.2	54.0	57.0

*PPP = Purchasing Power Parity
**50% of average expenditure per OECD consumption unit[60]
***% of households at the level or under the level of poverty
Source: Adapted from Stanisława Golinowska, "Poverty in Poland: Causes, Measures, and Studies," in *Poverty Dynamics in Poland* (Warsaw: CASE, 2002), 24, 30–31.

Every second child experienced poverty for at least one year in Poland from 1993 to 1996. Moreover, every second permanently poor person was a child. Children also tend to spend the greatest length of time in poverty.[61] Poles still tend to identify poverty with the elderly because retired persons were among the poorest in Communist societies. However, a much higher proportion of children than senior citizens are poor. Moreover, children also experience poverty for a longer time.[62] For example, children under age 15 represent one third of all those living in extreme poverty. As Tarkowska states, Polish poverty is primarily "the poverty of children."[63]

While children in Poland for the most part do not suffer from hunger, those who live in poverty are chronically undernourished. They also lack adequate winter clothing. These two factors make them prone to frequent illnesses.[64] Furthermore, a sense of shame as well as social exclusion often accompany this material deprivation. Poor children sometimes decide not to take part in after-school activities and trips, even when they are given the money to do so. They become reclusive, embarrassed by their "unfashionable" clothes and by their material status. Even simple things such as books are often beyond their reach.[65] In short, poor children are often excluded from enjoying the full benefits of community that broaden their horizons and enrich their lives.

Tarkowska also mentions the phenomenon of "growing up without a childhood," which affects children in many different ways. They take on responsibilities that other children normally do not have. Poor children often have to work rather than attend school and cope with the pathological problems, such as alcoholism, of their parents. Also, children in agricultural settings work more often than children growing up in other areas. In addition, the oldest girl in a family often must undertake the household duties that her mother would perform if she did not have to go to work.[66] Thus, these children may have their education interrupted at a very early age. Because of the strong correlation between education levels and income, this gap generates a poverty trap: children with little schooling are far more likely to remain poor as adults than those with a standard education.[67] Social policies that favor other groups over the needs of children create this situation.[68]

The likelihood of a child experiencing poverty increases dramatically if she or he grows up in a large family. A very strong correlation between the number of children in a household and the likelihood of the family struggling with poverty exists in contemporary Poland. Even though there has been a reduction in the birth rate since 1989, one third of all children in the nation grow up in large families. Such households have the highest poverty risk according to any of the poverty lines used in Poland, even higher than those of single-parent families.[69] In 1997, 84.5 percent of families with four children or more lived below the social minimum, and in the same year, 20.1 percent of such families lived below the subsistence minimum. Thus, their risk of falling below the social minimum is almost double that of the average household, while the risk of falling below the subsistence minimum is almost four times greater.[70] These numbers are staggering for a country whose culture, or at least a prominent part of it, has traditionally lauded large families as the desired norm. The Roman Catholic Church, along with political parties that claim to be aligned with it, has vociferously advocated "profamily politics" (*polityka prorodzinna*) that would enable large families to thrive.[71] Yet, as these statistics suggest, this campaign has not significantly assuaged the plight of large households affected by poverty.

In Poland, family size often corresponds to education levels and geographic location. The lower the level of education, particularly that of the mother, the greater likelihood of three or more children. In addition, families in villages are more likely than those in cities to have three or more children.[72] Six or more people constitute 32 percent of all families in the regions of the formerly collectivized farms (PGR-y), which are now the poorest regions in Poland. It is not uncommon for these families to have more than ten children.[73] By contrast, only 3 percent of all working families nationally are comprised of six persons or more. Moreover, health problems plague 20 percent of persons in large families.[74] Thus, in the case of large families, several related factors converge to put them at a much higher risk of encountering poverty than smaller families. Women experience much greater hardship within such families, and they are much more likely to raise children on their own than men.

The "feminization of poverty" in Poland, which only recently has become the subject of scholarly research, begins in the earliest stages of a woman's life.[75] When a girl grows up in a large, poor family, the responsibilities of raising her younger siblings often fall on her. This sometimes forces young women to forfeit their own plans for the future.[76] In fact, although more women complete secondary and higher education today than do men, some evidence indicates that women may be increasingly at a disadvantage as education moves towards a fee-based system. This may be the case because 33 percent of Poles believe that university education is more important for boys than for girls. If forced to choose for financial reasons between schooling for a son or a daughter, the son will be given the chance to go further.[77] Urszula Nowakowska of the Warsaw-based Women's Rights Center (Centrum Praw Kobiet) argues that marriage laws also prioritize the educational and vocational aspirations of males. The Polish Family Code recently changed the minimum age for contracting legal marriage to 18 for both sexes (it had been 21 for males). However, Family Court can permit 16-year-old females to marry when it deems it desirable. The legal permission to marry at an earlier age rests on the assumption that if a women gets pregnant, then she should marry the child's father. Her priority becomes raising her child and tending to domestic life, while young men are expected to continue their education and pursue careers.[78]

The pattern of having many children often repeats itself in generation after generation, leaving women with little chance of breaking the cycle of poverty. On the one hand, most women in this situation do not desire to have so many children. On the other hand, they accept their role as mothers of large families in accordance with Poland's dominant cultural mores. Despite the fact that a majority of women prefer a "partnership model" of marriage and parenthood, childrearing is still de facto primarily "woman's work." If parents separate, the mother almost always raises the children alone and then goes to work to support them.[79] Accordingly, the poverty of single mothers and their children in large families is the "deepest" in Polish society. In other words, they experience the most extreme poverty and have the most difficulty in climbing out of it.[80]

In addition to doing the housework and childrearing, women in poor families more often than men attempt to find sources of income to survive. Men in Poland are often ashamed to borrow money, to stand in line at social welfare agencies, or to ask their local parish for help. Therefore, women more frequently take on these tasks, adding to their workload at home.[81] Unfortunately, poor women also often have to deal with the alcohol abuse of their spouses. Interviews with the poor reveal that alcohol abuse is "a permanent element of the biographical stories of the poor."[82] As many as 25–30 percent of the unemployed are alcoholics, and 65–70 percent regularly abuse alcohol.[83] Although poor women themselves sometimes abuse alcohol, it is traditionally an element of male culture in Poland.[84] Domestic violence against women often makes matters worse.[85] It is hard to ascertain the scope of the problem because domestic abuse cases commonly remain unreported or are ignored by the police. However, the Women's Rights Center estimates that one in four Polish women live in an "abusive environment."[86] In short, poor women face much more than just income poverty. Rather, one issue often compounds another. The feminization of poverty in Poland has many ugly faces.

It is difficult to prove that more women experience income poverty than men because surveys almost exclusively cover households. In studies of single-parent homes, single mothers are slightly more likely to be poor than single fathers.[87] However, the household-based approach masks the unequal distribution of resources within a family, which some evidence has shown puts women at a higher risk of deprivation.[88] Furthermore, in the case of Poland, women have a higher risk of falling into poverty than men for several reasons: the greater likelihood of single parenthood, a higher long-term unemployment rate among women, the "feminization" of low-wage job sectors, and lower pay for equal work.[89] Clearly, poor women are among "the least" and among the most in need of solidarity.

One other large group has endured major deprivations throughout the 1990s. Rural Poland is known to many as "the other Poland."[90] The gap between the quality and kind of life in rural Poland and in the cities is vast, and one commentator even calls it "the hopeless social question."[91] According to the UNDP's Human Development Index (HDI), which considers life expectancy, adult literacy rate, enrollment rates, and the GDP per capita, urban Poland qualifies as a highly developed country. Conversely, rural Poland's living conditions mirror those in the underdeveloped world.[92]

Rural areas have a much higher concentration of poverty than cities. For example, from 1996 to 1998 around 3 percent of the population of cities lived below the subsistence minimum. The number escalated from 7 to 9 percent in villages during that period. Among individual farmers, the rate climbed to above 10 percent.[93] In 2000 it reached 12.9 percent.[94] In 1997, 28.3 percent of residents of large cities lived under the social minimum. By comparison, 54.5 percent of those in towns with less than 20,000 inhabitants and 62.5 percent of those who lived in villages had incomes below the social minimum.[95]

Farmers suffered tremendously throughout the 1990s. Not all farmers are poor, however. In fact, the largest 20 percent of farms, mainly in Western Poland, produce more than 80 percent of the nation's agricultural output.[96] These large, prosperous farms have given rise to greater inequalities in income and living standards among farmers.[97] According to one study one of every three farmers lives in poverty,[98] and almost 40 percent of small farmers with less than 10 hectares of land are poor.[99] Most of Poland's farmers in the East have subsistence farms, which do not provide a significant source of income. When thinking about the scale of the problem, it is important to remember that Poland is still an agrarian society to a much greater degree than most European countries. Close to 30 percent of all Polish families earn their living in the agricultural sector and live in rural areas.[100] In addition to income poverty and the barriers to education, rural Poland generally has living conditions inferior to those in the cities.[101] UNDP Poland argues that the poorer material living conditions in villages accounts for the lower lifespan of those who reside in them.[102]

While other areas have large concentrations of poverty,[103] it is most acute in the regions (generally in Northeast and Northwest Poland) where the formerly state-operated collectivized farms (PGR-y) are located. Approximately two million Poles lived and worked on the nearly six thousand communal farms. When the government eliminated these unprofitable farms after 1989, some people found new jobs or obtained retirement or disability benefits. Perhaps as many as one half, however, have become chronically unemployed.[104] In terms of poverty's depth, most farmers and their families do not experience hunger, as they can at least eat what little they produce.[105] In the post-PGR-y regions, however, people do not have the ability to live off the land. After 1989 the Warsaw government decided to lease the lands. For the most part, the new owners did not rehire those who had worked on the farms, thus leaving the majority without a source of income to satisfy their basic needs.[106] Moreover, poverty in these regions exhibits a confluence of the characteristics of Polish poverty overall, that is, high unemployment, limited access to education, large families, alcohol abuse, and hardships for women.[107]

The elimination of the PGR-y has been described as a "catastrophe" and the "end of the world as it was known" to their workers and families.[108] In order to understand why, one must know a little more about the nature of the PGR-y. After World War II the Polish government created these farming communes by attracting poor, uneducated workers from various parts of the country with the promise of a better life.[109] While wages were low, employers guaranteed work, free housing kept in good repair, a small plot of land to cultivate, transportation, day care and preschools for children, and vacation time. The PGR-y provided the security and stability that was otherwise unattainable for many people despite the suboptimal quality of many of these benefits. Moreover, they provided a way of life. The PGR-y created a remote, self-contained world because they were located relatively distant from towns and villages. In the new Poland after 1989, this world was taken away, along with its amenities. Its inhabitants became isolated, both culturally and geographically, from the rest of Polish society, with no access to culture and little, if any, intellectual stimulation;[110] they can only dream of expanding their families' lives with travel. People in these regions are often destined to "inherit" poverty and unemployment from the previous generation. Their lack of skills and qualifications excludes them from the job market or destines them to low-paying, dead-end jobs. This leads to "permanent marginalization" and the rise of an underclass.[111]

Today, the negative social consequences of the near-absolute dependency created by the PGR-y represents an example par excellence of the persistence of *homo sovieticus*.[112] Joanna Jastrzębska-Szklarska and Bohdan Szklarski refer to a move from a culture of "clientelism" in the former economic system to "institutionalized paternalism" in the present era. Under Communism, people in the PGR-y were completely dependent on the system for basic goods, and on their supervisors for rare goods that could only be obtained through backdoor channels (*załatwianie coś po znajomościach*).[113] This situation hindered the growth of self-responsibility and creative initiative. In other words, it fostered "learned helplessness."[114]

In the capitalist system, those who lived in the PGR-y look for new "patrons," who will make decisions for them and provide them with essential goods. These new patrons demonstrate paternalistic behavior towards the poor of these regions. Social workers, local political leaders, and shopkeepers, who sometimes permit people to buy items on good faith credit (*na kreskę*), play this role in the new system. For example, shopkeepers decide what can be bought on credit, such as cheaper cuts of meat as opposed to more expensive ones. Social workers often patronize their clients, pontificating about what is good or bad for them. Jastrzębska-Szklarska and Szklarski also found that the level of such condescending behavior rose in relation to higher levels of deprivation among their clients. Succinctly stated, these new patrons have become the "gatekeepers" of access to goods and services in the post-PGR-y world.[115]

To summarize, poverty has risen dramatically since 1989. It afflicts certain groups in particular ways and to different degrees. This empirical "snapshot" of poverty has begun to disclose the lack of solidarity in contemporary Poland. However, an examination of the causes of the rise in poverty will bring solidarity's demise into sharper relief. In a sense, demonstrating that poverty has risen and that it has deeply affected many members of society does not yet fully attest to a lack of solidarity. Poverty may be the result of natural disasters, "impersonal" economic forces, or political and economic decisions at the global level, operating over the heads of Polish decisionmakers.[116] In fact, all of these factors contributed to Polish poverty in the last decade. For example, massive floods wreaked havoc in 1997 and 2001. Nonetheless, policy choices and societal attitudes also contributed to the rise in poverty. Today, Poles shockingly exhibit widespread indifference towards the poor in the country of the great Solidarity revolution. The vast majority do not strive to be in solidarity with the poor as they go about their daily business.

Causes of Poverty in Poland

A revitalized, contemporary ethic of solidarity in Poland must examine unemployment, wages, and educational levels for two reasons. First, these issues have a causal relationship to poverty; changes in wages, employment levels, and education all have contributed to the negative poverty trends described above. Therefore, many policies designed to fight poverty seek to attenuate problems in these domains, which lie at the root of Polish poverty. Assessing these antipoverty policies from the perspective of solidarity, freedom, and participation requires at least a basic understanding of the nature of these root problems. And second, low wages, unemployment, and denials of access to education represent forms of poverty *in se*.

Unemployment

Without a doubt, unemployment was one of the primary reasons that poverty spiked in Poland after the fall of Communism.[117] Prior to 1989, many of the state-operated companies created "artificial jobs" in which workers were highly unproductive.[118] After 1989, privatization and the restructuring of inefficient industries led to massive reductions and job losses. These reductions were deemed necessary in order to make industries more competitive, which became crucial as Poland opened its borders to international competition.[119] In economists' terms, the restructuring of industries, which led to dramatic rises in unemployment, to a large degree revealed previously "hidden unemployment."[120] In addition to workers in industry, many in the agricultural sector lost their jobs. Market competition, the cutting of government subsidies in agriculture, the closing of large state-run PGR-y, and the increased importation of food created many redundancies.[121] This situation led to the creation of "the other Poland." The highest number of unemployed live in villages (44 percent), with the next highest category living in small towns.[122] In addition to these factors, demographics have compounded unemployment in Poland. A relatively large growth in the number of those in the job market occurred in the 1990s, as the children of "baby boomers" finished their education and began to look for employment.[123]

Unemployment grew to 16 percent from 1990 to 1993 in a country that virtually had not known "official" or registered unemployment due to socialism's full-employment policy. According to the government's statistics, it continued to rise over the next decade: 14.9 percent in 1995, 15.1 percent in 2001, 17.5 percent in 2002, 18.1 percent in 2003. Unemployment peaked at 20.6 percent in 2004.[124] Of course, it should be remembered that behind these statistics are the personal misfortunes of more than 3 million people and their families. For them, the loss of a job most often meant plummeting into poverty.

Kabaj demonstrates the interrelationship between poverty and unemployment by pointing out that in regions with higher unemployment, there is a higher incidence of poverty. Long-term unemployment especially generates poverty. Approximately 42 percent of the unemployed in Poland experienced long-term unemployment, with women more likely to remain unemployed for a year or more.[125] Roughly 90 percent of the long-term unemployed lost the right to unemployment benefits. In fact, the number of unemployed eligible for benefits shrank from 79.2 percent in 1990 to 23.8 percent in 1999. In truth, these statistics do not account for those who undertook work illegally. However, even accounting for those "under the table," massive numbers of unemployed were left without income in the 1990s. Those who were eligible to receive unemployment benefits generally did not receive enough income to lift them out of poverty, particularly in the case of large families.[126]

Moreover, less than 10 percent of the unemployed were eligible to participate in state-sponsored job-training and retraining programs. Furthermore, inequities in the distribution of unemployment benefits and retraining occur. The programs that do exist often practice what is known as "cream-skimming," that is, affording participation in training programs to the unemployed with the greatest amount of human capital, often college graduates. Only 4 percent of those without secondary education are eligible for training programs, while 8 percent of high school–educated workers and 10 percent of college-educated workers are eligible. In other words, those with the worst chances of finding work are the least likely to obtain the necessary skills to get a job.[127] Farmers and their children have suffered most acutely. The Polish government began to fund retraining programs for farmers in 1999, while it had supplied such funding for other groups several years earlier. Prior to this time, the government had tried to appease farmers with meager welfare benefits.[128]

Succinctly stated, unemployment has undeniably had traumatic social consequences including and exceeding income poverty in Poland after 1989. Many of the unemployed feel desperate and may even commit suicide because they see no stable future ahead. Unemployment also leads to a greater likelihood of child and spousal abuse and health problems.[129] From an ethical perspective, to what degree was this sudden surge in unemployment avoidable? Was "shock therapy," which was supported by economic neoliberals and required the quickest possible "rationalization" (reorganization) of industry and agriculture, the best course of action?[130] Even if it were, could other forms of social protection have been put in place to minimize the human suffering caused by forced reductions in many sectors of the economy?

Fortunately, since joining the European Union in 2004, the unemployment rate has rapidly decreased. Some economists have attributed the "historically unprecedented" drop to 11 percent in 2007 to the creation of more than two million new jobs.[131] Others have argued that the exodus of more than 800,000 Poles to wealthier European Union countries for work mostly accounted for the decline. While the exact calculation may be complicated, it is clear that the scourge of unemployment is finally waning. Yet, the damage done to many families, when they were left to fend for themselves in the 1990s, cannot be undone. The overwhelming majority of unemployed still remain ineligible for assistance and/or job training. Poverty still wreaks havoc on multitudes of Poles. In fact, at 26 percent Poland continues to have the largest number of children living in poverty in the European Union. Of those, 22 percent have at least one parent who works. According to the European Commission, almost one in five Poles still lives in poverty, in spite of the decline in unemployment. Poland now ranks among those European countries with the highest number of working poor.[132] It also has the second highest number of temporary jobs in all of Europe.[133] These jobs pay low wages and often offer no health benefits. In short, many of the new jobs since 2004, heavily concentrated in the service sector, do not ensure decent wages.[134] Inadequate wages were and continue to be a major source of poverty in democratic, capitalist Poland.

Wages

In addition to the unemployed, the "losers" in the Polish socioeconomic transformations have been those whose wages and salaries declined or rose only slightly during the 1990s. A dramatic decline in real wages after 1989, which took place during a time of economic growth, affected a large number of Poles.[135] Of course, there were also "winners," who reaped handsome salaries. The unprecedented growth in income inequality in Poland led to debates on the relationship between inequality and growing poverty.[136] Neoliberal economists argued that inequalities were necessary for economic growth, which would "trickle down" to everyone's advantage.[137] On the other hand, economists of the post-Solidarity social democratic persuasion saw the rising income gap as one of the primary sources of increasing poverty.[138] Golinowska, who generally shies away from polemics, maintains that "if inequality grows at times of weak economic growth and there is no significant income redistribution or income redistribution may perversely deepen inequalities, then poverty increases." This relationship between income inequality and poverty has been empirically validated in the transition countries of Central and Eastern Europe.[139]

Many people experienced a loss in real income, even though overall incomes for society as a whole rose by over 19 percent from 1989 to 2000.[140] In some instances, these losses were stark. A 1998 World Bank report indicated that about one half of all working Poles earned less than they did in 1989 (despite a 15 percent overall growth in the GDP).[141] Research indicates that 56 percent of working Poles are not satisfied with their wages and that only one in ten states that "work insures him or her good earnings."[142] Succinctly stated, certain groups prospered while others experienced negative repercussions from the changes in the wage structure. Tables 3.2, 3.3, and 3.4 illustrate this fact according to various social groups.

These tables reveal the "winners" of the Polish "income revolution."[143] Table 3.2 displays the increase or decrease in real incomes since 1989 as a percentage decrease or increase from 1989 levels (it shows each successive year as a percentage of 1989 income levels). Table 3.3 shows the percentage differences in monthly earnings levels among those with greater or lesser educational attainment in comparison to those with basic vocational education. Table 3.4 depicts the percentage differences in disposable monthly incomes among members of various sectors of the economy (in terms of negative deviation from white-collar levels, the highest earning sector after 1990). As Table 3.2 indicates, a radical decline took place in real incomes at the outset of the transformation. Fortunately, a gradual increase in incomes in all categories took place from 1994. However, a closer look reveals that employers and the self-employed benefited the most from these gains. These groups essentially did not experience the "income shock" that took place at the dawn of the "free-market" era. As Table 3.3 shows, it is important to notice the increasingly greater relationship between large incomes and higher educational levels,[144] and a steadily increasing gap between the income levels of those with higher educational levels and those with lower ones. This fact clearly points to the need for equal access to education. Another noteworthy trend existed in the income changes of retired persons and those who received disability payments. Contrary to complaints often heard from these groups, their real income rose by 13.6 percent (see Table 3.2). According to the 1999 UNDP Poland report, "[h]ouseholds of retirees and those receiving disability with at least one elderly person had an average nominal disposable income per capita ... higher than the average household in general."[145] The ratio between the average retirement pension and the average salary grew from 53 percent to 73 percent, making it one of the highest in all of Europe. Economists and social commentators often criticized this exorbitant growth in government expenditures.[146]

The occurrence of low wages (two thirds of the average pay) rose from 14 percent to 17 percent among legal workers, which pushed more people into the category of the "working poor," or 60 percent of Poland's poor.[147] Among the working poor, there are more women then men. Irena Reszke explains this by pointing to wage discrimination by gender: after accounting for differences in age, education, and job position, the average wages of women equaled 66 percent of men's wages. In 1998,

TABLE 3.2 Changes in Real Incomes in Poland, 1990–1998 as Percentages of 1989 Income Levels (1989 = 100%)

Incomes	1990	1991	1992	1993	1994	1995	1996	1997	1998	1990–98
All incomes	85.3	90.3	93.5	92.9	96.2	98.2	102.3	114.4	119.7	+19.7
Avg. monthly salary	76.1	75.9	73.8	71.7	72.0	74.1	78.4	86.6	91.0	-9.0
Avg. monthly old age and disability pension	91.1	104.3	97.5	94.7	97.4	100.6	103.1	109.5	113.6	+13.6
Income from private farms	50.1	40.7	46.4	51.6	49.3	56.3	58.8	67.7	64.8	−35.2
Employers and self-employed	—	100.0	109.1	121.9	119.5	121.1	127.1	140.0	145.1	+45.1
GDP*	88.4	81.7	82.9	86.1	90.3	96.9	102.8	109.8	115.1	+15.1

*Fixed prices
Source: Mieczysław Kabaj, *Programme Outline for Actively Counteracting Poverty and Social Exclusion.* UNDP Poland, http://www.undp.org.pl/pages/pl_pov2.htm.

TABLE 3.3 Earnings* Differentials by Educational Attainment from 1988–1995 as Percentages of Income Levels of Those with Basic Vocational Education (Basic Vocational = 100%)

Educational Attainment	1998	1992	1995 (national economy)	1995 (public sector)	1995 (private sector)
University	118.7	146.1	148.3	137.2	188.4
Postsecondary	—	—	98.0	90.9	122.7
Secondary[a]	95.9	109.9	—	—	—
Vocational	—	—	111.3	108.8	113.9
General	—	—	105.8	104.2	106.7
Basic vocational[b]	100.0	100.0	100.0	100.0	100.0
Primary[c]	87.0	93.6	87.3	85.9	88.7

*Earnings = Average net monthly earnings of full-time workers in primary jobs.
a) including postsecondary; b) vocational training (3 years), which does not lead to a high-school diploma; c) including less than primary education
Source: Adapted from Jan J. Rutkowski, *Welfare and the Labor Market in Poland: Social Policy during Economic Transition* (Washington, D.C.: World Bank, 1998), 36.

TABLE 3.4   Income Differentials of Households in Poland per Capita[a] According to Vocational Group

Year	White-collar	Blue-collar	Blue-collar/ Agricultural	Agricultural	Retirees and Disability Recipients	Self-Employed	Unearned Income	Average Deviation (in %)[b]
1990	100.0	74.0	88.2	85.3	72.9	—	—	19.1
1991	100.0	72.9	79.1	70.0	80.4	—	—	19.6
1992	100.0	72.3	74.1	67.7	73.1	—	—	23.0
1993	100.0	66.4	64.3	69.8	82.2	96.8	42.2	26.6/26.4[c]
1994	100.0	66.8	64.7	68.2	81.7	99.0	42.8	26.6/26.3
1995	100.0	65.7	66.7	72.2	81.1	98.8	39.9	26.3/26.3
1996	100.0	62.9	61.4	65.5	76.8	93.2	38.2	30.5/30.6

a) disposable incomes since 1993; b) average deviation in percent calculated as the average deviation from white-collar workers, assumed as 100; c) average deviation for the first five types of households in the numerator; average deviation for all seven types given in the denominator.
Source: Czesław Bywalec, *Społeczne aspekty transformacji gospodarczej w Europie Środkowowschodniej* (Cracow: Wydaw. Akademii Ekonomicznej, 1998), 23.

women's wages were 24 percent lower than men's. These statistics do not include small companies with less than five employees, where many of Poland's female working poor are employed. Reszke mentions in this connection the "feminization" of low-wage sectors such as education, culture, health services, textiles, and retail sales. These sectors are dominated by female employees, while women are forbidden to work in the higher-paying mining, steel, and construction industries. Until such workplace discrimination and "equal pay for equal work" is adopted in Poland, the feminization of poverty will continue.[148]

Tables 3.2 and 3.4 reveal that among all sectors, farmers and industrial workers were struck the hardest in terms of income loss. As will be discussed in more detail below, persons who live in rural areas are much less likely to obtain an adequate education, which makes them more likely to earn relatively low wages. In the 1990s the wages of farmers and agricultural workers radically declined. This is the most direct reason for the "gradual pauperization of 'the other Poland.'" The income of farmers fell from 110 percent of the average wage in 1989 to about 40 percent in 2000.[149] Other groups also suffered real wage decreases. Despite the fact that white-collar workers in general experienced significant gains, certain professional groups received nominal pay increases or even decreases. Health-care providers (especially nurses, who continue to strike frequently), teachers, and professors comprise this group. In other words, while a higher premium has been given to education, as evidenced by the general increase in salaries among white-collar workers, not all those with higher education prospered. The income differentials according to deciles also reveal who suffered and who reaped handsome rewards. Economist Jan Rutkowski encapsulates these trends in the following statement: "The income of the richest decile is now 7.8 times as high as the poorest decile, while before the transition this 'wealth gap' amounted to 5 ... the first 8 deciles have lost their income shares. The losses have been larger in the lower deciles and smaller in the upper deciles. The 9th decile has slightly improved its relative position, but only the top decile has gained substantially. Overall, 5 percent of the total income has been transferred from the bottom 80 percent of the population to the top 20 percent. That is, losers outnumber winners by four to one."[150] In short, 17 percent of all workers earn less than two thirds of the average monthly salary, while one-fifth of those working earn 150 percent of that amount. The vast majority of Poles earn close to the average monthly wage.[151] Thus, as Rutkowski puts it, "poor families have become somewhat poorer, but rich families have become much richer."[152]

The realities described above are to a large degree the result of conscious political decisions. Two political instruments functioned in this regard in the early years of Poland's transition to capitalism. First, Minister of Finance Leszek Balcerowicz instituted a tax (*popiwek*) in 1989 that was to prevent the "inordinate growth of wages" in the public sector.[153] Disobedient companies that allowed such increases were penalized and had to pay an additional, large tax as a result. The majority of companies at that time were state owned; therefore, most companies had to abide by this tax law. Moreover, most private companies adopted Balcerowicz's "appropriate levels" of wage growth of their own accord.[154] The fact that during those years real wages grew ten times slower than the GDP indicates that Balcerowicz achieved his goal.[155] However, some Polish economists criticized him.[156] Balcerowicz's tax was abolished in 1994 and a new Trilateral Commission for Social and Economic Affairs was established. Composed of representatives from the business community, workers of various sectors, and government agents, it began to regulate wages from that point forward.[157]

The second instrument utilized in shaping the wage structure was legislation concerning the official minimum wage. Article 77 of the Labor Code enjoins the minister of labor to establish the minimum wage after negotiations with the Trilateral Commission. The minimum wage in Poland rose pronouncedly in 1991 as a percentage of the average wage and gradually increased through 1993. In 1994 a reversal in the earlier trend occurred. At that point, private employers entered the bargaining process and argued that raising the minimum wage would lead to greater unemployment.[158] Some voices have argued that "the biggest enemies of the unemployed are union leaders" and that raising the minimum wage is the primary cause of unemployment.[159] In April 2000 the Federation of Private Employers (Federacja Pracodawców Prywatnych) issued its "Capitalist Manifesto," in which they demanded "lower labor costs ... flexible labor relations ... and the adjustment of social guarantees to the demands of the market."[160] They made these demands even though the minimum wage in Poland did not even equal the "social minimum" for one person.[161] Thus, those who work for minimum wages cannot afford, as Golinowska puts it, "the indispensable level of consumption determining social participation and integration."

By contrast, two groups deserve individual attention because of their remarkable, controversial gains in income. Politicians and managerial-level civil servants in Poland now earn inordinate amounts in comparison to their counterparts in other countries. For example, civil servants in managerial posts earn 8.1 times more than the average monthly wage in Poland. The corresponding ratio in most European countries is dramatically less: United Kingdom (5.4), Germany (4.9), France (4.6), Belgium (4.4), Switzerland (3.9), Denmark (3.2), Sweden (2.2), and Norway (1.9). Mayors of small towns, such as Ursynów, earn as much as 10,000 PLN (the Polish złoty) per month (7.3 times greater than the average), while the average wage for a physician working in a hospital is 1,200 PLN.[162] When public outcry led to a bill that would limit civil servants' salaries, many of them deplored it as populist and antimarket.[163] Poland has clearly lost the egalitarian ethos of the Solidarity era since 1989.

Like old-age pensioners, coal miners also succeeded in securing high incomes for themselves. From 1990 to 1997 their wages grew faster than any other sector in the Polish economy. According to UNDP Poland, "the unjustifiable chasm between growth in wages and productivity is waning, but in some sectors the opposite is occurring. The mining industry is a clear example; its wages rose the most despite its ailing productivity." The average salary in the coal mining industry was 160 percent of the average salary in Poland in 1996.[164] At the end of 1998, the average monthly salary in mining was 1,833 PLN, compared to 986 PLN in farming, 946 PLN in education, and 845 PLN in health-care services and social work.[165] The government simply capitulated to the strong and vociferous mining unions. Moreover, it offered an early retirement package to many with cash benefits of 40,000 PLN, but such an offer was not extended to workers in other sectors.

The wages of public servants and their reactions to limitations for the sake of the common good manifest the new neoliberal understanding of freedom and capitalism. The demands of certain special-interest groups also attest to the prevalence of a purely negative conception of freedom, which disavows the need for sacrifice for the sake of others. These demands are particularly egregious in the face of the dramatic wage decreases of many of Poland's poor. In addition to low wages and unemployment, the poor also often suffer from educational deprivations that deny them the opportunity to learn and to compete in the capitalist economy.

Educational Deprivations

Poland had one of the lowest tertiary scholarization rates in Europe for much of the twentieth century. Since 1989 the number of students attending colleges or universities has risen dramatically.[166] This is admirable. However, not all Poles have benefited from the changes since 1989 in the educational system. In particular, the poor have less opportunity to receive an education that would make them not only competitive in the job market of today's information society but also able to participate in it.[167] Those with little schooling are very likely to experience poverty and to remain mired in it. Their children will suffer a similar fate: material deprivation leads to poor educational prospects, which lead to meager earnings potential and a continued life in poverty. Thus, a "vicious poverty circle" closes.[168]

The evidence is clear: the lower the educational level, the higher the risk of poverty. Of households where the primary earner has completed basic schooling or less, 10.3 percent live below the subsistence minimum, as compared to 5.4 percent of the general population. As much as 63.2 percent of such households live below the social minimum, as compared to 50.4 percent of the general population. By contrast, extreme poverty is practically nonexistent among those with university-level education (0.4 percent).[169] Of all those living below the social minimum, 75 percent have completed only vocational-technical or primary school.[170] To be certain, much progress has been made since 1970, when one half of Poland's population had only completed primary education. Nonetheless, during the 1990s an entire third of the population did not have more than basic schooling,[171] putting them at greater risk of falling into poverty.

This phenomenon can mainly be attributed to the lower job prospects and earning potential of those with little educational background. While the national unemployment average in 2001 was 18.2 percent, the rate among those with only basic education was 22.9 percent.[172] As was stated above, the wages of those at higher education levels relative to those with vocational or basic education continually increased throughout the 1990s. UNDP Poland reported that the wages of those with tertiary education earn about 44 percent more than the national average wage, while those with basic education or less are paid 17 percent less than the national average.[173] In other words, when those with inferior educations are fortunate enough to find employment, they commonly work in low-paying jobs. They become members of the growing working poor.

The disadvantages of insufficient education also relate to other quality-of-life issues. Low levels of education hinder one's capacity to function in society and to participate in politics and the life of the community. The main precondition of social participation is the ability to make informed, rational choices, and such choices require "an understanding of the world, and therefore the acquisition of adequate knowledge, which concretely means access to the educational system."[174] Those men and women with extreme educational deficiencies may even be deprived of the capacity to articulate their needs and desires through civic and political participation. In this instance, decisionmakers no longer need to listen to their demands because they are no longer a "threat."[175]

When poor persons are literate, they are more likely to be heard in the political arena and therefore their needs are more likely to be met.[176] Furthermore, education has a noticeably salubrious effect on people's lives. For example, one study in Poland revealed that those men who completed tertiary education are twice as likely to live until the age of 65. People with college degrees are much less likely to smoke, have better diet and exercise habits, are less prone to illness, and take better advantage of preventative medical treatment.[177] As Golinowska succinctly states, "the lack of education has become the primary determinant of social marginalization."[178]

Some Poles deny that the poor do not have an equitable chance of obtaining a good education.[179] However, the situation in Poland today belies this claim. For example, children of farmers, who have suffered the negative consequences of the economic transformations disproportionately, clearly benefit less from higher education and the educational system in general. In the 1980s, one in every fourteen high-school graduates from farming or farm-labor backgrounds attended institutions of higher learning. Today, that ratio has changed to one in 140. Only 2 percent of young people from towns and villages with populations under 20,000, where poverty is most prevalent, attend institutions of higher learning.[180] Furthermore, discrimination against children from rural areas begins earlier in the schooling process. They have less access to government-funded preschools and kindergartens, and the quality of their teachers fails to compare to those in the cities.[181] Some gymnasiums (three-year schools prior to high school in the new Polish system) recruit elite students from other regions in order to boost their reputation and rankings. The quality of education at various gymnasiums varies greatly, as some have access to much larger funding pools. Some even segregate students into classes according to their backgrounds, with the children of the poor clustered into homogeneous groups.[182] Thus, a recent study concludes that the segregation of those who are "destined to succeed" and "the rest" already starts at the gymnasium level.[183]

Much of the inequality in education stems from budgetary cuts, which have affected smaller towns and villages more drastically. In the years 1990–91, government spending on education dropped by 20 percent. From 1991 to 1996 the government reduced spending on scholarships by almost one half.[184] When decentralization of the school system took place in the mid-1990s, school boards of small towns and villages struggled with the new responsibility of funding primary schools fully and secondary schools partially. In short, there is much less spending on education per capita in these regions.[185]

Public schooling is theoretically free in Poland. However, numerous costs have been transferred from the state to parents and their children. More than 60 percent of university students now pay tuition, which is well beyond the means of the poor. Even at state-run "free" (*bezpłatne*) schools, students must pay hefty entrance examination fees, room and board, and other costs. State universities have also created a two-tiered system, with evening classes (*studia zaoczne*) that are tuition-based. Moreover, admission to the regular program at state universities is extremely competitive.[186] As a result, parents who can afford it often pay for private tutors for their children, as a pervasive belief exists that public high schools do not adequately prepare students for entrance examinations and university-level study.[187] While there are some exemplary public high schools, they have become the exception to the rule and are generally beyond the grasp of poor children. Given all of these factors, UNDP Poland concludes that "poverty has become the most serious barrier for access to education."[188]

The structural causes of poverty have destined many Poles to live in "the other Poland." Unemployment, the increasing incidence of low wages, and educational deprivations have caused them to plummet into poverty. To some degree, one can argue that these phenomena were going to occur inevitably. The rise in unemployment in many industries, for example, merely reflects the inefficiency of the command economy prior to 1989, and the "hidden unemployment" naturally became visible in a market economy, which demands greater efficiency. The globalized labor market, with demand for profit maximizing, often leads to reductions in the workforce or to "outsourcing" jobs to cheaper labor pools abroad. All of this may be true. However, values and principles always influence those who are responsible for socioeconomic processes. In this vein, former World Bank economist Joseph Stiglitz's critique of institutions responsible for fighting poverty and sustaining economic development is relevant: "the greatest challenge is not just in the institutions themselves but in mind-sets."[189] Indeed, sociological evidence reveals that the majority of Poles will need to undergo a conversion of the heart and mind before they embody relationships of solidarity with the poor at the level of structures and institutions.[190]

Apathy towards the Poor

Dorota Lepianka concludes that "indifference" (*obojętność*) best characterizes Polish society's attitudes towards the poor. She bases her claim on public opinion surveys from 1995 to 1999 and her own interviews with social workers who encounter the poor on a daily basis.[191] The causes of this indifference largely coincide with the causes of solidarity's demise, as described earlier in this book. Among the causes of this indifference, she includes: ignorance about the extent of Polish poverty, a new consumerist lifestyle, "new liberal values," the vestiges of socialism, and fear. According to many social workers, the poor often remain unseen because they adopt strategies to conceal their situation, either by pretending to have more than they do or by simply becoming reclusive out of a sense of shame.[192] In addition, in accordance with the ideology of the former Communist system, Poles tend to believe that all people are needy. Therefore, they do not look beyond their own immediate circles to see those most truly in need.[193] These two factors lead to the widespread ignorance of poverty's ugly faces in the opinion of those who work with the poor. Lepianka demonstrates, however, that more broad-based public opinion polls indicate that most Poles are generally aware of poverty's extent.[194] Yet, "a large gap exists between the verbal expression of sympathy (*współczucie*) towards the poor and the amount of indifference shown in everyday life."[195] In other words, sympathy often does not convert into real solidarity. It will be worth examining the link between liberal values and indifference towards the poor.

Lepianka maintains that by "accepting the new liberal values and endeavoring to create a capitalist system (or trying to adapt to it), Poles tend to judge all members of society by the same criteria. They forget that everyone is not equally efficient, intelligent, creative and industrious." Another aspect of this "new liberalism" is the drive to earn more and to obtain more consumer goods together with a related trend towards workaholism. This precludes devoting time and attention to the needs of others, such as the poor.[196] Add to this the perduring social mistrust and "learned helplessness" of *homo sovieticus*, which expects "the state" (*państwo*) alone to deal with the full gamut of social problems, and one begins to comprehend the indifference towards the poor in a country that once heralded to the world an ethic of solidarity.[197]

Interestingly, on one statistical level the perception of "blameless poverty" has dominated among the majority of Poles since 1989. In other words, they perceive that macroeconomic factors such as large-scale unemployment cause poverty. The majority tend not to name intrinsic characteristics, such as a person's laziness or the inability to function in a capitalist society, among the causes of poverty.[198] However, nearly one quarter of Polish society blames poverty on laziness and/or addiction, while one sixth sees a lack of resourcefulness as the cause. Moreover, 46 percent of those polled attribute poverty to unemployment, while blaming the unemployed themselves for their lot rather than the structural causes of unemployment. Thus, a large number of Poles do, in fact, hold the poor accountable for their situation.[199] It seems that the old saying, "you're poor because you're stupid and you're stupid because you're poor" (*biednyś, boś głupi, głupiś boś biedny*) still functions in today's social consciousness.[200]

Those persons who have prospered in the new era most often hold a view of poverty as blameworthy or culpable, whereas those who have struggled with deprivation and marginalization most often find the causes of poverty in external circumstances beyond the control of the poor themselves. This attitude has significant policy ramifications. Many of Poland's political elites, who earn exponentially more than the national average, operate with a pull-yourself-up-by-the-bootstraps mentality, which often translates into policies unfavorable towards the poor. In addition, those who are financially secure are less likely to see poverty as a major social problem.[201] This should not come as a surprise, because more and more gated communities are built in Poland to insulate the wealthy from the poor. The children of the wealthy often have little or no contact with poorer children, as segregation has begun to intensify in the schools. Succinctly stated, widespread indifference towards the poor, rather than solidarity with them, exists in Polish society. While true solidarity among the poor themselves may also be lacking,[202] solidarity between the rich and poor is even rarer.

Thus far, this book has provided a bird's-eye view of the normative commitments of the Solidarity movement and the discursive and empirical situations that reveal that solidarity has disintegrated in many parts of democratic and capitalist Poland. Both the values of neoliberalism and the moral vestiges of Communism have, in large part, led to this situation.

The evidence in this chapter pointed to concrete spheres in which society lacks solidarity, and it revealed that many Poles do not enjoy important freedoms and are precluded from participation in society. The following chapters will apply conceptions of solidarity, freedom, and participation to these spheres to show the relevance of an ethic of solidarity to Polish poverty. In other words, this book will now undertake its prescriptive task in full and, in the language of Catholic social thought, will move from "observing" to "judging" and then to promoting ways of "acting" to remedy the injustices described heretofore.[203]

CHAPTER FOUR

Recovering and Applying an Ethic of Solidarity to Polish Poverty

> *At one point, solidarity united people in resistance against the politics of the incontrovertibly divisive Communist government ("Divide et impera!"). Today levels of income and the related levels of well-being are a divisive factor and may be even more so in the future. This atomization gives rise to a postulate of a new solidarity: the rich with the poor and the poor with the rich, the unemployed with workers and workers with the unemployed. Evidence [concerning poverty and inequality] reveals the necessity of building this kind of order of solidarity. It would be difficult not to see that this would be an order based on Gospel foundations.*[1]
> —Andrzej Potocki

Having provided a glimpse of the "moral elevation" of Solidarity and the descent into turmoil after 1989, this book may now begin the task of reviving an ethic of solidarity. As Józef Tischner claimed at the height of the Polish revolution, solidarity needs to be reinterpreted amid changing circumstances.[2] It should be clear by now that the new order in Poland demands a revitalized, contemporary ethic of solidarity. This ethic must further develop the relationship between solidarity, freedom, and participation to show that they can coexist in a capitalist, democratic order. Thus, the following chapters elaborate normative understandings of each of these elements of the ethic of solidarity *in relationship to the others*. They apply these normative understandings to the empirical realities of the problem of poverty. Any ethical framework that does not confront this reality is not true to the spirit of the Solidarity program.

While the spotlight may be on one or another part of the triad at various points in what follows, the other two elements are necessarily never out of sight completely. The relationship between solidarity, freedom, and participation advanced here can be summarized as follows: solidarity, freedom, and participation are not conflicting values. Rather, there is a kind of mutual entailment, or necessary interdependence, among these values. Freedom is realized by participating in the construction of a just society in order to promote the participation of others in that society. To act in this way is to act in solidarity with others, because solidarity promotes the freedom and participation of others.

Solidarity and the Option for the Poor Today

John Paul II pointed to the relationship between solidarity and an option for the poor early in his papacy. He returned to this issue in 1987 in *Sollicitudo Rei Socialis*, where he explicitly discussed the option for the poor as a "particular guideline" following his elaboration of the meaning of the more general notion of solidarity.[3] After 1989, John Paul repeatedly urged Polish politicians, members of the Church, and all citizens to "heed the cry of the poor" on his pilgrimages to his homeland.[4] He explicitly called for a return to the ethic of solidarity in Polish social, political, and economic life. In 1999, in a particularly poignant homily in Ełk, which is located in an impoverished part of Northeastern Poland, John Paul underscored the urgency of adopting an option for the poor. Reflecting on Luke 19:1–10, he stated that Jesus calls every person today, just as he called Zacchaeus the tax collector: "make haste and come down, for I must stay at your house today" (Luke 19:5).[5] According to the pope, the accent on "today" is extremely pertinent. The textual "today," in his view, implies "urgency." Here, John Paul implicitly addressed an often-heard argument by Polish proponents of "shock therapy," who maintain that the citizens themselves must bear the social costs of their reforms—higher levels of poverty and unemployment—in the hopes of a better future. Appealing to this biblical text, the pope conversely insisted that:

> There are problems in life that are so grave and pressing, that they cannot be postponed and they must not be put off until tomorrow. The Psalmist beckons, "So that you hear His voice today: 'do not harden your hearts'" (Ps. 95:7–8). "The cry of the poor" (Job 34:28) of the whole world rises unceasingly from the earth and reaches the Lord. It is the cry of children, women, the elderly, refugees, the abused, victims of war, the unemployed. The poor are among us as well: the homeless, beggars, the hungry, the reviled, those forgotten by their families and by society. . . . There are manifestations of poverty in the world that must shock the consciences of Christians and remind them of the urgent obligation to counteract it, both on the individual and social levels.[6]

John Paul went on to say that "the shout and cry of the poor demands an answer from all of us." He spoke directly against the neoliberal dictum of "economic growth first, then everything else," so eagerly embraced by Polish neoliberals. Echoing what he had written in *Sollicitudo Rei Socialis* (nos. 27–34), the pope reminded his Polish audience that "growth and progress should not take place at all costs" and that "economic growth must always make the world a more just and peaceful place." He saw these issues as requirements of "human solidarity" and the Church's "option and preferential love for the poor."[7]

An ethic of solidarity in Poland today must take its cues from John Paul's teaching and unequivocally emphasize an option for the poor. This is imperative given the new situation of the poor after 1989. The evidence concerning Polish attitudes towards them clearly reveals that a revitalized ethic of solidarity must stress the option for the poor. To put it another way, the poor most prominently represent "the person lying in the road" in Poland today. In *Etyka solidarności*, Tischner contended that solidarity is always "with someone and for someone."[8] Solidarity must be with the poor and for the poor in Poland today. Women, children, large families and farmers and agricultural workers are among those most often "passed by" (see Luke 10:31–32). For those who believe that solidarity needs a "common enemy" in contemporary Poland today in order to galvanize mass numbers of people, poverty should be seen as that enemy.

The poor, to a large extent, have been left to fend for themselves and have been relegated to the sidelines of the polis. In general terms, solidarity and the option for the poor have not affected social and political life to a large degree. Polish society's ambivalent, if not outright negative, attitude towards those mired in poverty diametrically opposes solidarity with the poor. Is this picture too pessimistic? Statistically speaking, many Poles do feel sympathy. There has been an extraordinary level of participation in charitable fundraisers such as Jerzy Owsiak's Wielka Orkiestra Świątecznej Pomocy or Caritas Polska's many successful efforts, which John Paul II himself has lauded. After being forbidden by the Communist regime for decades, philanthropy has also begun to grow in Poland. Even though it is not nearly so robust as in other societies, Polish philanthropy has made positive contributions to the arts, education, and environmental protection. Undoubtedly, charitable activity and philanthropy have aided many people in myriad, sometimes life-saving ways. However, Catholic social thought and the Polish experience of the 1980s calls for an ethic of solidarity that requires more than sympathy and compassion. It is important to recognize the distinction between solidarity and sympathy and charitable actions that evolve from sympathy. This distinction evinces that Poles are generally not in solidarity with the poor, despite the significant work of organizations such as Caritas Polska and countless others.

Sympathy, Charitable Works, and the Scope of Solidarity

Many treatises have expounded on sympathy, compassion, and mercy and their roles in the moral life.[9] A review of even a portion of these materials exceeds the scope of this book. For the sake of the argument here, sympathy and compassion, which shall be used synonymously, are understood as a response to the suffering of others primarily on the emotive level.[10] When it does extend in action towards the suffering other, its deeds do not involve reciprocity or mutuality. In other words, compassion is one-directional; the recipient remains its passive beneficiary.[11] Solidarity, as the Polish nonviolent revolution demonstrated, goes beyond compassion understood in this way.

This is not to say that solidarity does not operate at all on the emotive and cognitive levels. Solidarity in the Catholic social tradition, as developed by Heinrich Pesch, Oswald Nell-Breuning, and later John Paul II, entails three distinct, interrelated aspects: 1) solidarity as anthropological "datum"; 2) solidarity as an ethical principle or imperative; and 3) solidarity as a principle concretized in legislative policies and institutions.[12] The first aspect of solidarity, which Pesch called "factual solidarity," entails the recognition of the fact that human beings are by nature interdependent. In regard to this aspect, Catholic social ethicist Franciszek Kampka writes: "this mental dimension of solidarity relates to the attitude of mutual empathy among members of a community, becoming aware of their deep similarities and interdependence, and deepening them by experiencing the needs of others just as we experience our own needs."[13] In other words, this first aspect of solidarity resembles the experience of compassion, or *suffering with others*, because we recognize that we share a common humanity and fate with all human persons. As was mentioned earlier, the Polish ethic of solidarity located the *inception* of solidarity in hearing "the cry of the wounded." This aspect can be conceived of as the first "moment" of solidarity if we think of the realization of solidarity taking place in sequential steps.[14] (See Table 4.1 below.)

The second aspect involves drawing ethical imperatives from the fact of interdependence. The reality of interdependence should have ethical implications for all human interactions in the economic, cultural, political, and religious spheres of social life.[15] This second "moment" of solidarity moves from recognition or acknowledgment to an initial response. In some instances, this may require an act of compassion, a crisis intervention of some kind. In a situation that gravely threatens a person's health, bodily integrity, or psychological well-being, for example, direct, immediate aid is necessary. In such a scenario, the mutuality of fully realized solidarity is not achieved and should not be expected. Barring such extreme circumstances, or when these circumstances have been alleviated, solidarity's response moves in another direction: it attempts to understand the cry of the wounded through contemplation.[16]

More precisely, it attempts to understand the *causes* of the suffering of the other. Only after careful consideration and analysis will action be undertaken to eliminate these causes. Intellectual analysis is crucial to understanding the cry of the poor and to formulating a plan of action in order to do good rather than harm. Furthermore, when action in solidarity is undertaken, it will entail the following two things: an emphasis on the participation of the marginalized, and continuity or perseverance.

TABLE 4.1   The Three "Moments" and Three Aspects of Solidarity

1st Moment	*Recognition of "Factual Solidarity"* • recognition of human interdependence as an anthropological fact • hearing "the cry of the wounded"
2nd Moment	*Initial Response to Solidarity's Ethical Imperative* • crisis intervention (direct, immediate aid) and/or • contemplation of causes of the suffering of "the other" (social analysis)/understanding "the cry of the wounded"
3rd Moment	*Embodying Solidarity in Policies and Institutions* • promotion of and the actual institutionalization of solidarity • promotion of the participation of the oppressed as agent/s for personal and social change

Action that flows from the contemplation of the causes of suffering and takes into consideration the participation of the sufferer or oppressed comprises the third aspect. This third "moment," which is a third, necessary step in the sequential development of solidarity, posits solidarity as a principle of institutions and legislative policy.[17] This is the case because eliminating the causes of the suffering of the wounded and oppressed requires advocating social change on the structural level. It requires embodying solidarity in social policies and institutions. This third aspect will be elaborated on in a later section concerning the institutionalization of solidarity. For now, discussing solidarity's emphasis on participation and its requirement of continuity or perseverance will illuminate the differences between expressions of solidarity and charitable activities. The latter, when not accompanied by further action, should be considered expressions of compassion, not solidarity.

Solidarity as the Promotion of Participation

Solidarity strives ultimately to enable the poor and the marginalized to become full members of the community. In other words, it seeks to procure the right to participation for all persons, a right that has been explicitly stressed in Catholic social thought since the 1971 World Synod of Bishops document *Justitia in Mundo*.[18] The bishops' document conceives of the right to participation as the precondition of all other rights; without it, the realization of all other rights remains in jeopardy.[19] Moreover, the bishops posit a connection between economic deprivation and the denial of the right to participation: "Unless combated and overcome by social and political action, the influence of the new industrial and technological order favors the concentration of wealth, power, and decision-making in the hands of a small public or private controlling group. Economic injustice and lack of social participation keep a man from attaining his basic human and civil rights."[20] To make the matter perfectly clear, the bishops later state that "[p]articipation constitutes a right which is applied both in the economic and in the social and political field."[21] Participation in this sense entails both the right and duty of every member of a given society to contribute and benefit from the common good.

Participation in Catholic social thought denotes a *substantive* contribution to society; it is not just a formal, procedural task to be valued in the abstract from the ends served by it. To use a mundane analogy, if I partake in a discussion "just to say something," I do not genuinely contribute to the discussion, that is, I am not really participating in the sense of the word being used here. If I "participate" in something passively, then, this too does not constitute true participation.[22] To bring the issue into clearer relief, take the example of workers constructing biochemical or nuclear weapons of mass destruction. Although they may enjoy a standard of living that affords them their basic rights through their economic opportunity (their jobs as engineers, mechanics, et al.), the end they serve is not in the interest of the human community. If I am forced to "participate" in labor, in a work camp, for example, it is not participation in the sense being used here. In other words, genuine participation contributes to true human flourishing, the fulfillment of the self, as Karol Wojtyła put it,[23] and the flourishing of the community in concrete ways. Moreover, it is freely chosen and consciously recognized as a duty that all persons share.

As members of a community, exercising this right and duty requires a willingness to cooperate with others, to make compromises when necessary, and to take seriously the expertise and wisdom of others.[24] Nonetheless, it is the very nature and dignity of the human person that requires persons to be meaningfully involved in the decisions that affect their lives and the good of the community.²⁵ The Solidarity movement struggled for the right to this kind of broad participation in economic, political, and social life, and Catholic social teaching has continued to affirm this right. The right to participation can be found, for example, in much of John Paul II's writing, with a clear emphasis on participation in all of these spheres of life. The Polish bishops recall the right and obligation to participation in their Synod document on political life.²⁶

Roman Catholic thinkers have drawn an explicit link between the right to participation and solidarity. Cardinal Wojtyła did so many years ago in *Osoba i czyn*, where he stated that "solidarity is ... the basis of community, in which the common good properly determines and enables participation."²⁷ Participation is the key to explaining the social nature of the human being. Each person has a "right and obligation" to act with others in a way that "fulfills" herself.²⁸ The common good is constituted by participation with others in the community in "authentic acts" through which the person "realizes" herself.²⁹ The person can only fulfill herself, that is, become fully human, by participating with others in the good. By contrast, doing evil always constitutes a lack of self-fulfillment. A community that negates this "right and obligation" is by nature a deformation of community and "totalistic." It negates the person herself and her good.³⁰ Thus, for Wojtyła, participation is a matter of social justice, a requirement of solidarity.

All of John Paul II's later "social" encyclicals emphasized the relationship between solidarity and participation.³¹ In *Christifideles Laici*, he stated that "[t]he manner and means for achieving a public life which has true human development as its goal is *solidarity*. This concerns the active and responsible *participation* of all in public life, from individual citizens to various groups, from labor unions to political parties."³² In like fashion, Andrzej Potocki, O.P., a sociologist at Jagiellonian University, describes the essence of solidarity as "fostering participation in the creation of the common good and orders [all] activity towards this end."³³ Anton Rauscher, S.J., also argues for a conception of solidarity as enabling participation (though he uses the term "co-responsibility"), with particular vigor. In his view, solidarity is not embodied by assuaging the plight of poor, nor is it something owed to the poor. In fact, he resists equating solidarity with the option for the poor: "Solidarity rather means that all, the strong and the weak, must join forces, as we are all dependent on one another."³⁴ Rauscher appropriately amplifies the inherent necessity of the participation of all members of society in the common good in order for true solidarity to exist. However, he misses one important caveat: he does not fully recognize that the participation of "the weak" is often denied by those who hold the power to create institutions and policies that foster the conditions for full participation. To put it more concretely, he does not recognize that poverty, which hinders full participation in the life of the community, is sometimes caused by human choices made by those who wield power. When they are not in solidarity with the poor, those who hold power sometimes exclude the poor from working for the common good. In this sense, solidarity can be something "owed" to the poor out of justice.

In order to clarify this issue, one may appeal to another notion of Catholic social thought, namely, the principle of subsidiarity. According to the principle of subsidiarity, insofar as it is possible, the state should not assume roles and responsibilities that individuals and local civic organizations can perform in order to sustain a society.³⁵ An overbearing state that tries to manage every aspect of the economic and political order will stifle the freedom and creativity of its citizens. This was the grand failure in Central and Eastern Europe of Communism, which gave rise to the phenomenon of *homo sovieticus* and "learned helplessness." Yet, society and the state in particular have the responsibility to create the conditions for the full participation of all in the common good. As John XXIII put it, the "intervention of public authorities that encourages, stimulates, regulates, supplements, and complements, is based on *the principle of subsidiarity*."³⁶ In Roman Catholic human rights thought, this plays itself out in terms of duty-bearers. Subsidiarity helps delineate who bears responsibility for the fulfillment of particular rights. For example, John Paul II argues in *Centesimus Annus* that it is up to the state to "oversee and direct the exercise of human rights in the economic sphere." In other words, while private employers may practically enable the fulfillment of the right to work by providing jobs, the state must erect the legal, economic, and social frameworks necessary for the realization of this right. The pope delineates a middle course between the ill-fated socialist alternative of employment provided solely by the state and the laissez-faire insistence on no governmental interference in the labor market. According to him, "the state has a *duty* to sustain business activities by creating conditions that will ensure job opportunities, by stimulating those activities where they are lacking or by supporting them in moments of crisis" (emphasis added).[37] This explicates what the pope meant when he urged the members of Parliament in 1999 not to "spare any energy in building a state" that "respects the right to work."[38]

Succinctly stated, solidarity demands participation, and it expects the state and society to create laws and institutions that will make it possible, in accordance with the principle of subsidiarity. Such institutions and laws will foster the procurement of human rights for every person, which are the "basic requirements of solidarity."[39] Thus, solidarity is two-directional; it requires the participation of the poor, and those who wish to be in solidarity with them in building the common good. Overcoming poverty benefits all members of the community. It allows for the full flourishing of the community, which, as Catholic social thought maintains, inherently tends towards the thriving of all its members.[40] Furthermore, reciprocity is achieved in solidarity because the oppressed have their own perspectives and abilities to share with those who seek to empower them. In the fullness of solidarity, a relationship or exchange of spiritualities takes place. A mutual sharing of gifts and talents occurs.[41]

Solidarity's Requirement of Continuity and Perseverance

Catholic social teaching's understanding of solidarity demands a lasting commitment to struggle with the poor against their oppression. In other words, solidarity requires continuity and perseverance. Members of the Solidarity movement referred to this element as heroism, which describes the self-sacrifice entailed in persevering in solidarity with the oppressed.[42] In John Paul II's often-cited statement from *Sollicitudo Rei Socialis*, he maintains that solidarity is not a "feeling of vague compassion" but rather "*a firm and persevering determination to commit oneself to the common good.*"[43] He repeated this same demand in his homily in Ełk: "The contemporary Church heralds and attempts to realize the option for and preferential love of the poor. This is not a temporary emotion, or an occasional work, but a real and lasting will to work for the good of those in need and often lacking hope for a better future."[44]

In addition to the lack of emphasis on participation of the marginalized in the life of society, this illuminates why many, if not most, charitable works in Poland cannot be considered expressions of solidarity in Catholic social teaching's sense of the term. Most efforts to give aid to the needy are occasional, one-time donations of money or needed goods. Surveys from the 1990s revealed that more than 50 percent of Poles offered money to charitable causes.[45] One may recall in this regard the spectacular efforts to help the victims of the massive floods in the mid-1990s. However, "Poles are unsystematic, inconsistent and likely to choose the easiest form of help."[46] This problem points to the weakness of civil society in the nation. Aside from one-time donations, Poles rarely undertake any actual involvement in the organization and distribution of aid, which requires time and energy, and possibly contact with the poor. According to a 1998 poll, only 2.5 percent took part in the work of charitable organizations, while only 1.5 percent were active in organizations aiding the poor, elderly, sick, and homeless, and 1.2 percent in aiding children.[47] Many Poles appear to hold in contempt those people with large families. Since the parents decided to have so many children, they themselves should take responsibility for them, the argument goes. Only 46 percent would offer help to children of the poorest families.[48]

Kampka has called this tendency among Poles to offer occasional, short-term aid (most often as money) *akcyjność*, as opposed to *aktywność*, which refers to active participation in a sustained effort. Following José Ortega y Gasset's diagnosis of the contemporary time-constrained, results-oriented human person, Kampka argues that "mass action is tempting because it creates the mirage of quick results." However, "that which is really valuable, is achieved with difficulty, and unfortunately, not quickly." Fundraisers, for example, do not, in his view, "change the social landscape in a lasting way."[49] Complex sociopsychological reasons for mass participation in fundraisers are not always rooted in the desire to "carry another's burdens."[50] The point to be stressed here is that charitable works such as fundraisers only apply a bandage to the problem. While it is sometimes necessary in cases of urgency and is often heart lifting, it does not yet constitute solidarity with the poor.[51] Solidarity, which requires *aktywność*, differs from charitable works in that it contemplates the plight of the poor first. Indeed, well-intended but hastily conceived charitable activities in Poland have sometimes ended in fiascoes, with the poor not really benefiting from these efforts.[52] In short, the weakness of civil society in Poland and the lack of true solidarity with the poor have generated more *akcyjność* than *aktywność*. This applies to both secular and Church-related efforts.⁵³ *Akcyjność* has little to do with the heroism exhibited by the members of Solidarity in the 1980s and does not cohere with solidarity's demand for continuity and perseverance.

Solidarity with the poor, as it is understood in Catholic social thought, is not completely absent from Polish society. There are many fewer NGOs proportionately in Poland than in most other Western European countries. However, the majority of the more than 20,000 Polish NGOs work in the areas of social assistance, health, and education. Many of them embody the rich solidarity of the Catholic tradition and assist people neglected by the government. The government's abandonment has left millions of "wounded by the roadside" during Poland's transformations.⁵⁴ Analysis of some examples of such organizations will appear in chapter 6, which treats the Church in post-1989 Poland. Many of these groups focus on acts of charity and compassion, which are sometimes necessary steps in the development of solidarity but do not constitute its full realization.

Solidarity and the Family

Some observers argue that a kind of "familial solidarity" thrives in Poland. On the basis of surveys done in the 1990s, Potocki concludes that "on the micro scale the majority of Poles experience interpersonal solidarity—they have someone close in whom they find psychological support and practical help in problematic everyday situations." Therefore, he maintains that familial solidarity in Poland is particularly strong.⁵⁵ By contrast, two thirds of Poles believe that social and cultural changes in the 1990s led people to become more self-serving and less altruistic. Thus, social solidarity, especially with the poor, has eroded substantially.⁵⁶ Moreover, the claim that familial solidarity thrives in Poland might be erroneous or misleading. Solidarity can surely exist within families. There are, of course, different kinds of solidarity and different degrees of its realization, and this must be acknowledged when seeking to embody solidarity in public policy, as will be discussed below.⁵⁷ Yet, familial support should not always be equated with solidarity if the goal of solidarity is participation in building and benefiting from the common good.

According to the Christian tradition, families should provide a "school of virtue" that educates its members to serve others beyond their immediate sphere. Recalling Vatican II's teaching, John Paul II wrote that "it is from the family that citizens come to birth, and it is within the family that they find the first school of the social virtues that are the animating principle of the existence and development of society itself."[58] Leading Christian ethicists in Poland have advocated this kind of "build-up" ethic, insisting that social solidarity must be first exemplified and inculcated in the home.[59] While this ethic certainly has merit, the emphasis on the family rarely translates into larger social solidarity in the nation today. A dualistic system of morality continues to exist. In the familial sphere, Poles are readily willing to come to each other's aid, but in the public sphere, this is widely not the case because of pervasive social mistrust.[60] In addition, the desire to help family members is not always born of a sense of solidarity that encourages those who are struggling to flourish, achieve, and contribute to the common good. Some scholars have even suggested that the noticeable generosity of parents in Poland, who often support their children much longer than do those in other Western societies,[61] stems from a desire to gain prestige. "Investing in children" by bestowing on them cars and apartments can become a status symbol. This aid is most often one-directional, especially in the case of the poor. There is no mutuality or give-and-take in the parent–adult child relationship. Those parents are fulfilling their own dreams and ambitions by living vicariously through their children.[62]

Care towards one's family members becomes solidarity only when it aims to inculcate certain values, virtues, and principles in the recipient, prominently among them the option for the poor. Parents can accomplish this by demonstrating solidarity.[63] In raising children today, parents must educate them away from the hedonistic materialism of contemporary consumerist culture towards an "outdated" selflessness.[64] Parents who shower their children, particularly their adult children, with goods also contribute to the continuation of the "learned helplessness" of the nation's Communist past. To put it bluntly, in order for "familial solidarity" to be solidarity in the true sense of the term, it must go beyond creating comfort within the four walls of one's home. It must seek those "lying in the road," wherever they may be. As developmental psychologists claim, parents play a crucial role in engendering the virtue of solidarity in their children because they alone can instill trust in other persons and the world. Renowned psychoanalyst Erik H. Erikson explicitly states that children in the infancy stage who learn to trust develop the "vital virtue of hope."[65] Inculcating this sense of trust and the virtue of hope is vital in Poland because social mistrust, a persistent element of *homo sovieticus,* exacerbated by *dziki kapitalizm* ("wild capitalism," the Polish term describing a Spencerian survival of the fittest capitalism), precludes the flourishing of solidarity. In other words, families must promote the anthropology of hope that inspired the Solidarity movement. As Tischner maintained, human hope needs to be "worked on"; it needs to be cultivated in children, students, and, indeed, in persons of all ages.[66]

A pedagogy of solidarity that emphasizes participation and perseverance as constitutive elements of solidarity is needed in Poland today in order to deal with the problem of poverty. This must go beyond temporary, fleeting aid. As John Paul II stresses, families must work towards creating and supporting institutions and structures that embody social solidarity.[67] For certain, individuals and families must make personal lifestyle choices and engage in practices that reflect the virtue of solidarity before promoting structural and institutional changes. As John Paul pointed out, "external structures of communion" must be born of a spirituality of selflessness in order to be real and lasting means of expressing solidarity. For the Christian, the recognition of the divine presence in others should animate the desire to be in solidarity with them. Seeing God in one's neighbor should also be the foundation of a spirituality that eschews egoistic gratification.[68] Nonetheless, the virtue of solidarity moves beyond one's spirituality and personal way of life. It has important political and social dimensions. "When politics is good politics," Tischner maintained, "it is imbued with the spirit of solidarity. Shouldn't politics aim to organize the sphere of human life so that the human person does not do harm to another?"[69] Towards that end, Catholic social thought insists on moving beyond the abstract level of principles. It insists that solidarity must be concretely institutionalized in order to promote the common good and the dignity of all persons. How is it, then, that a principle such as solidarity can be embodied in social, political, and economic structures? How does solidarity translate into concrete social policy? The next section will begin to address this question on the theoretical level, and other sections of this chapter will further develop the issue, as they will deal with concrete policies in the realm of poverty and its causes.

The Institutionalization of Solidarity

Solidarity demands the creation of "legal regulations that afford the institutionalization of solidarity."[70] Pesch, whose writing on "solidarist economics" influenced the modern papal social tradition, emphasized that solidarity is not just a matter of personal conviction but must be embodied in social and legal structures governing interpersonal relationships.[71] Much of the papal social tradition appeals to solidarity as a principle that should animate various aspects of economic, political, and social life. For example, John XXIII posited human solidarity in management-labor relations as the remedy for "unregulated competition which so-called liberals espouse, or class struggle in the Marxist sense."[72] In *Pacem in Terris,* he demands that solidarity govern international relations.[73] Paul VI appealed to solidarity as the key to overcoming such social evils as racism and discrimination.[74] John Paul II not only argued for solidarity's role in public life in Poland, but he also underscored its importance in relations among nations and various actors in the global economy. The pope articulated his view of solidarity's role in the modern global economy in his first encyclical, *Redemptor Hominis*: "The principle of solidarity, broadly understood, must be the inspiration for the effective search for appropriate institutions and mechanisms in the area of trade, where only healthy competition should be allowed to govern, and on the level of a wider and more immediate distribution of resources and control of them, so that economically disadvantaged peoples may not only be able to satisfy their basic needs, but also to gradually and effectively develop."[75] In short, the whole of modern Catholic social teaching maintains that solidarity can and must be institutionalized. It cannot remain a vague feeling or fleeting commitment to others and to the common good. It will be helpful to further clarify how Catholic social thought envisions the institutionalization of solidarity.

According to David Hollenbach, it is unreasonable to expect that the highest possible levels of solidarity will be institutionalized in society.

This is the case because of the reality of human egocentricity or, to put it theologically, human sinfulness.[76] While the fullness of solidarity may have much in common with Christian charity, which demands that one "love God with all of one's heart, soul, and mind," Hollenbach maintains that this demands too much of citizens in order to be useful in formulating a social ethic and public policy. In attempting to move towards a viable public ethic, he argues that justice "spells out the minimal requirements of the solidarity that is a prerequisite for lives lived in dignity." These requirements "establish a floor below which social solidarity cannot fall without doing serious harm to some of society's members."[77]

The Catholic social tradition further specifies the demands of justice via the notion of human rights, which constitute "the minimal conditions for life in the community."[78] As such, they must be protected in order to safeguard participation. Succinctly stated, while solidarity upholds the ideal for social cooperation, which can and should be sought, human beings will not always attain this ideal. As a result, laws and institutions must stipulate the most basic requirements of solidarity, without which society fails to protect the basic dignity of every person. In this sense, the promotion of human rights is understood as "institutionalizing solidarity."[79] In 1991, John Paul II urged Polish politicians to understand and institutionalize solidarity in this way: "Let us trust that [in] introducing the free market, Poles will not cease deepening the disposition [*postawa*] of solidarity in themselves. An important element of this disposition is concern for human rights ... This means not only demanding one's own rights. It also means striving for the respect of the rights of the mistreated and the weakest, especially those who cannot defend themselves."[80]

Basic participation is the precondition for, and most basic human instance of, "institutionalized solidarity." Without basic participation, the realization of all other human rights remains in jeopardy.[81] Amartya Sen provides empirical evidence to support this claim. He underscores the link between effective participation in democracy and the elimination of various forms of deprivation and inequality. For example, he points out that a famine has never taken place in a functioning democracy, even in relatively poor countries. Historical evidence has shown that countries such as India and Botswana have been successful in averting famines through effective policies despite sharp declines in food output. The point is that democratic governments are accountable to their constituencies, whereas foreign imperial rule, one-party, or dictatorial regimes do not have that kind of accountability. Sen has also demonstrated that when women are *literate, politically active,* and *participate in the labor force,* thereby minimizing economic dependence, their voices are heard. Indeed, empirical evidence shows that when this is the case, their needs as well as the needs of their children (such as health care and nutrition) have a much greater chance of being met.[82] Conversely, when women are denied the right to participation, education, and work, they and their children, especially girls, experience excessively high mortality rates due to poor health care and nutrition.[83] Succinctly stated, the first step in institutionalizing solidarity should be to ensure the right to participation in society for every person and basic human rights such as the rights to food, clothing, shelter, medical care, education, and work.[84] This clearly coheres with the ambitions of the Solidarity movement, which, as was discussed in chapter 1, fought for many of these economic, social, and political rights in the 1980s.[85]

The argument here does not equate with a "statist" approach to the institutionalization of solidarity, that is, the realization of human rights. Although the state has an important role to play, human rights, and specifically the right to participation, are to be procured in accordance with the principle of subsidiarity.[86] Different models of an economy envision various degrees of the institutionalization of solidarity. As Aniela Dylus contends, the social market economy minimizes solidarity organized or institutionalized by the state in favor of "freely-chosen solidarity."[87] Although Dylus lauds it within familial, neighborhood, and professional bonds, she does not altogether dismiss solidarity that is institutionalized by the state. She mentions, for example, a proposal that would enable young people to engage in year-long service projects immediately after college, with the state covering the costs. Such projects might include caring for the sick and elderly, tutoring children, and aiding the poor. This, in her view, might inculcate greater sensitivity among young Poles to the needs of others. However, any such efforts must not devolve into paternalistic welfarism that cripples individuals' responsibility for themselves.[88] It might be added here that such projects would fulfill solidarity's requirements if they aim ultimately at securing the participation of those in need in the life of society. It is easy to see how this might be the case. Take, for example, caring for the elderly. Helping an elderly person may lead her to greater independence, mobility, and the likelihood of taking an active part again in the community. Those who are the recipients of help often, in turn, attempt to extend aid to others.[89] Thus, true solidarity arises.

On the other hand, however, the relationship between subsidiarity and solidarity does not affirm a liberal "umpire" state. Catholic social thought maintains that in an increasingly interdependent world, sustained by a complex web of economic, political, and social ties, the realization of human rights often cannot be guaranteed on the local level. Thus, Dylus's claim that "the state ... must intervene only when natural familial solidarity or the activity of voluntary aid organizations have failed" needs to be qualified. Some further clarification of human rights and corresponding duties will explicate the matter.

The question hinges on the very meaning of human rights, which, to reiterate, represent the institutionalization of solidarity. Acknowledging that people are due certain goods by right has important practical ramifications. For example, those who die because they lack food or basic health care do not only suffer an "unfortunate" death; rather, they also die an unjust death. This is the case because "to have a particular right is to have a claim on other people or institutions that they should help or collaborate in ensuring access" to this right.[90] In other words, rights carry with them corresponding duties. Appealing to the Kantian notion of "imperfect duties," Sen argues that correlative duties are assigned to "anyone who can help." This may mean in some cases that rights may remain unfulfilled, at least temporarily.[91]

Henry Shue adds a helpful addition to the imperfect duties paradigm by recognizing that there are different kinds of interrelated duties attached to each right: "1) duties to avoid depriving; 2) duties to protect from deprivation; and 3) duties to aid the deprived." According to this tripartite understanding, everyone bears *at least* the first kind of duty towards the fulfillment of another's rights.[92] The strength of theories rooted in the Catholic tradition, with its emphasis on subsidiarity, resides in its insistence that in the event no single person or group carries the capacity, the state bears the ultimate obligation to make sure its weakest members do not slide into deprivation. Individual members of society may be first and foremost responsible for the exercise of their rights. Yet, society always has a duty to create the conditions within which this exercise is possible. When the state cannot legitimately fulfill these obligations, it should appeal to international agencies and foreign governments for help. Indeed, according to the concept of socialization, originally promulgated by John XXIII, in today's highly interdependent world, wealthy countries bear obligations towards members of less economically advantaged ones.[93] This is why John Paul II increasingly stressed the need for solidarity among nations and transnational actors. He recognized that for solidarity to flourish on the interpersonal level, steps often need to be taken at the national and international levels in today's highly globalized world.

Interestingly, the Constitution of the Republic of Poland, which was passed in 1997, recognizes that solidarity must be concretely embodied at the level of national policies and institutions.[94] On the level of general principles, the Constitution refers to social justice (art. 2) and solidarity (Preamble, art. 20) as norms to be safeguarded and realized by the Republic of Poland. Article 20 reads: "The social market economy, based on freedom of economic enterprise, private property, solidarity, dialogue, and cooperation among social partners, is the foundation of the Republic of Poland's economic system." The Constitution elaborates on this economic model and articulates concrete realizations of solidarity within its framework vis-à-vis economic, social, and cultural rights.[95] Many of these rights resemble those catalogued in the documents of Catholic social thought. Among them are: the right to a minimum wage (art. 65), the right to unemployment benefits (art. 67), health care (arts. 68, 69), and "universal and equal access to education" (art. 70). Article 71 declares that poor families, especially large and single-parent ones, have the right to "special help from the state." Moreover, the Constitution affirms that the inviolable dignity of every person is the foundation of all human freedoms and rights and that public authorities are responsible for the protection of human dignity (art. 30).

Unfortunately, the evidence concerning poverty reveals that many of these rights remain unrealized for large numbers of Poland's population. Therefore, the state has not fulfilled its obligation to protect the dignity of every person in Poland. Grażyna Skąpska correctly argues that while the Constitution is putatively inspired by the principle of solidarity, it fails to delineate the concrete duties of the state towards the institutionalization of solidarity and the realization of human rights. The articles dealing with these issues leave the concrete means open to individual legislative acts, which are more often the product of haggling among special-interest groups rather than embodiments of solidarity.[96]

Poles today generally fail to perceive poverty as a violation of the human rights of the poor. Talk of human rights is problematic, particularly economic rights, and human rights are sometimes mistakenly equated with statist approaches to justice marred by the kind of entitlement mentality of *homo sovieticus*.[97] Therefore, a return to an ethic of solidarity should emphasize the relationship between solidarity and human rights, in accordance with the Catholic social tradition. The promotion of women's rights, among them the right to equal pay for equal work, should comprise an important element of this ethic.[98] Greater dialogue on the meaning of both solidarity and human rights, with emphasis on how economic rights are to be fulfilled, that is, who are the various duty-bearers, is required to achieve this end.

To summarize, the material poverty in Poland, which is particularly debilitating among children, women, large families, and farmers and agricultural workers, can be largely attributed to a lack of solidarity. Solidarity, which has an intrinsic relationship to an option for the poor and requires perseverance in building a society in which all participate meaningfully, has generally not been operative in Poland during its transformation period. Although scattered large- and small-scale charitable efforts have aided the poor, they remain a far cry from true solidarity, which demands "*a firm and persevering determination to commit oneself to the common good*" (*Sollicitudo Rei Socialis*, no. 38). As Skąpska maintains, "Polish society is more and more divided into the winners and losers of the socioeconomic transformations. The losers are those whose voices are not heard. They are ... children, large families, people who live in impoverished areas distant from decision-making centers, and beyond that those who do not have the means to influence politicians, such as strikes, blockades, protests, and dumping grain."[99] This dire situation of the many poor and marginalized is the cost of poorly institutionalized solidarity. The Constitution pays homage to many of the economic, social, and cultural rights espoused by Catholic social thought and found in the UN Universal Declaration of Human Rights and the 1966 International Covenant on Economic, Social, and Cultural Rights, both of which Poland is a signatory. However, these rights remain little more than lofty aspirations. The misconceptions of freedom have contributed to this situation.

Alternative understandings of freedom must be advanced in order to foster a greater sense of solidarity in contemporary Poland and revive its unfinished revolution.

Freedom and Solidarity: Conflicting or Complementary Values?

The neoliberal understanding of freedom often translates in practice into a disdain for redistributive policies that would "coerce" the wealthy into contributing more to the common good, thereby aiding the poor through "forced" solidarity.[100] The notion of freedom as moral permissivism also often translates into indifference towards the fate of others. Given the predominance of these exclusively negative conceptions of freedom among Poles, it is easy to see why many observers conclude that the values of solidarity and freedom conflict with one another. Moreover, given that so many Poles have become preoccupied with economic success, or are merely just learning to cope in a free-market system, it is no wonder that many believe that solidarity's decline is the cost of "freedom." Any revival of an ethic of solidarity today must address these issues in order to be persuasive. As shall be discussed below, freedom and solidarity need not be considered to be conflicting values. Freedom leads to solidarity as its natural outgrowth.

Given its limitations and aims, this book cannot compare the myriad historical understandings of freedom. The reason is simple. Over the centuries, philosophers have opined that freedom is an elusive and controversial concept. For example, Montesquieu claimed that "there is no other word that has been ascribed more different meanings and which has spoken to people in so many ways than the word 'freedom.'"[101] Thus, this book merely aims to reveal that there is an understanding of freedom that does not conflict with solidarity, and that it is the proper construal of freedom according to Catholic social thought. In this view, solidarity is understood as the fulfillment of one's freedom. Such an understanding sees participation as one of its inherent components.

The recognition of freedom's various interpretations should be the point of departure for promoting an understanding of freedom that counterbalances the predominant neoliberal notion of negative freedom. Neoliberalism, and more widely the bulk of modern economic theory, fails to acknowledge those understandings that predate and contradict its own. More precisely, these schools of thought completely ignore understandings of freedom as positive freedom.[102] One noteworthy exception is Amartya Sen, whose relevant work will be explored in the following chapter. Now, however, a presentation of how freedom can be construed positively in relationship to solidarity is in order.

Internal and Personalist Freedom

The understanding of freedom as the positive ability to share in the governing of one's community has existed since ancient times.[103] Aristotle, for example, held a view that resembled positive freedom. The ability to contribute to the common good constituted self-realization for Aristotle. This understanding of freedom has been called political or communal freedom.[104] Christian thought has long held that freedom amounts to gradual liberation from the bondage of sin, which shackles all human beings. However, it has equally emphasized "freedom *for*," or positive freedom. Freedom *from* sin ostensibly means freedom to do good, or freedom to love in the Christian tradition.[105] Proponents of positive understandings of freedom include, among others, the modern popes and Józef Tischner. As was mentioned earlier, Tischner was Poland's most public advocate of freedom "properly understood" and thus should play a role in reconstruing the relationship between freedom and solidarity.[106] These Christian thinkers may not have always framed their discussions of freedom in terms of its relationship to solidarity and participation, but it can be argued that they at least implicitly affirmed the intrinsic relationship of these values.

Tischner, whose philosophy uses a somewhat different language than Catholic social teaching,[107] framed the question in terms of the dialogical, or dialectical, nature of freedom. Inspired by philosophers of dialogue such as Emmanuel Lévinas and Franz Rosenzweig, Tischner argued that freedom can only be achieved interpersonally. Freedom understood as a solipsistic enterprise in which the individual chooses to do this or that, irrespective of how the outcome relates to another person, is illusory, according to Tischner: "Freedom is first and foremost a dramatic category: it appears between persons. It is not in its origins in me or in you, but 'between us'... The problem of freedom is: respond or not to respond to the question asked of me, to undertake or not to undertake the challenge posed to me, to share bread or not to share it, to kill or not to kill."[108] In short, according to Tischner, freedom is realized in community. By its nature, it is "dialogical," as opposed to the false notions of "monological" freedom held by certain strands of liberalism.[109] Moreover, he states that a person can never be free if others around her or him are not free. In his words, "the real limitation of freedom is the enslavement of the other, not, as it is sometimes maintained, his or her freedom."[110] Clearly, Tischner's thought points in the direction of freedom realized in and through solidarity with others. While he does not parse the relationship between these two values in quite these terms, several other aspects of his thought on this topic support this interpretation.

Furthermore, he argues that freedom is a value that must always be considered in relationship to, or, more precisely, in the service of, other values. Like John Paul II, Tischner heavily stresses freedom's relationship to truth: the truth about the human person.[111] Defending John Paul's use of natural law to speak of the truth, he remarks, "is it possible to respect human rights, not knowing the truth about the human person?"[112] Tischner alludes here to the anthropology of hope that undergirded Solidarity.[113] For Solidarity members, "life in truth" required having an understanding of the human person as one imbued with inviolable dignity, the capacity for freedom, and a call to participation. The exercise of one's freedom, then, entails recognizing this truth and acting in accordance with it, that is, acting in accordance with a person's very nature. This means acting in order to respect the rights that others possess by dint of their humanity, because to be human means to possess inviolable dignity. Because the respect of human dignity requires the participation of all members of a community, one must exercise one's freedom to promote this end. Freedom, in other words, is realized by participating in the construction of a just society in order to promote the participation of others in that society. Given what was said earlier about the relationship between solidarity and participation, exercising freedom in this way is to act in solidarity with others. Thus understood, freedom is at the service of the values of truth and solidarity.[114] The relationship between the three values can be described as follows: if freedom is the interior value, then participation is the external realization of freedom. It is the mode through which freedom is realized. *Solidarity is therefore the outcome of both freedom and participation. Solidarity in turn promotes the freedom and participation of others.*

Exclusively emphasizing positive freedom, of course, can lead to the dangerous denial of the importance of what can be called negative freedom, or the freedom to choose without coercion. The kind of positive freedom envisioned here presupposes negative freedom. The freedom to choose is to be valued per se. Freedom from coercion is a basic good. As Tischner contends, the acceptance and embodiment of all other values requires the "basic" or fundamental value of freedom.[115] In other words, solidarity, for example, cannot be truly solidarity unless it is freely embraced. There is a mutual dependence between solidarity and freedom: "*Nie ma wolności bez solidarności*" (no freedom without solidarity) and "*nie ma solidarności bez wolności*" (no solidarity without freedom).[116] But, according to Catholic social thought, negative freedom must serve the deeper positive freedom that is realized in genuine human solidarity in order to be considered freedom "fully realized."[117]

Tischner maintains that Poland is "free" (*niepodległa*) to the degree to which it respects the dignity of the human person.[118] Thus, he challenges the notion that national sovereignty constitutes true freedom. Can a person be free while under the reign of a foreign oppressor? Tischner answers in the affirmative. If one's conscience is free, he argues, then one is free.[119] In this vein, Tischner accentuates what has been called "internal" freedom. While freedom is ultimately realized interpersonally, it begins with an interior decision of the will.[120] To use an example, Tischner would probably argue that Lech Wałęsa exercised his freedom when he defended the rights of workers such as Anna Walentynowicz in the early 1980s. However, depending on one's interpretation of events, one could argue that in democratic Poland he did not necessarily maintain his freedom, because his will was driven primarily by the desire for political gain, rather than acting in solidarity. The point is that national sovereignty does not necessarily constitute freedom. Tischner also argues that Maximilian Kolbe and numerous other concentration camp internees who made sacrifices for other prisoners were truly free, despite their imprisonment.[121] This emphasis on internal freedom, which can never be extirpated by external forces or threats, resembles the well-known reflections of Viktor Frankl, the Viennese psychoanalyst and Holocaust survivor who reflected on the nature of freedom as follows:

> We who lived in concentration camps can remember the men who walked through the huts comforting others, giving away their last

piece of bread. They may have been few in number, but they offer sufficient proof that everything can be taken away from a man but one thing: the last of all human freedoms—to choose one's own attitude in any circumstances, to choose one's own way.... Every day, every hour offered the opportunity to make a decision, a decision which determined whether you would or would not submit to those powers which threatened to rob you of your very self, your inner freedom.[122]

Elsewhere, Tischner contends that the Beatitudes free us from "the things of this world." They allow us to see earthly things in the proper perspective, including our relationships with others.[123] Succinctly stated, the movement from inner freedom to its external expression (that is, participation), which enables freedom's fulfillment, constitutes the essence of solidarity. Hence, Tischner provides an understanding of freedom that contrasts with an exclusively negative conception. He thereby opens the door to a fruitful retrieval of a contemporary ethic of solidarity that accounts for freedom's positive role. Although he enigmatically supported the neoliberal economic reforms taken by Polish politicians in the 1990s, he criticized versions of liberalism (that is, neoliberalism and moral permissivism) that abused the category of freedom to its advantage.[124] An ethic of solidarity today, inspired by Tischner's work, would need to confront neoliberalism and its notion of freedom for its role in the rise of Polish poverty and the widespread indifference towards it. While Tischner never took up this task, his thought provides the basis for such a constructive ethic.[125]

The modern popes have also described freedom as fulfilled in and through interpersonal relationships, using freedom's relationship to the good, truth, love, and solidarity to flesh out their thinking on the matter. In Catholic social thought this concept has been referred to as "personalist freedom."[126] A complete historical review of the modern papal teaching on freedom cannot be undertaken here. Rather, a few of the key concepts will aid in furthering the argument that freedom and solidarity are two sides of the same coin.

John Paul explicitly referred to economic development "within the framework of *solidarity* and *freedom*" in *Sollicitudo Rei Socialis*. In his earlier encyclical *Redemptor Hominis*, he forcefully critiqued the modern economy. He denounced consumerist culture, greed, and misuse of the world's resources in highly developed nations in the face of hunger and death caused by starvation in poorer nations. The pope linked these woeful signs of the times to an "abuse of freedom." In his view, the abuse of freedom by those who are never satisfied with what they have leads to denials of the freedom of those who lack basic necessities and to conditions of ever greater "misery and destitution." Although he faulted the injustice of the global economy for this situation, he held out hope that human beings can change it by transforming "the structures of economic life." In order for this to happen, persons need to be linked together in freedom and solidarity. Freedom cannot be confused with "the instinct for individual or collective interest or with the instinct for combat and domination, whatever be the ideological colors with which they are covered."[127] In other words, the relationship between freedom and solidarity must be reconceived. Like Tischner, John Paul argued that freedom must be understood in relation to the truth about the human person.[128] Therefore, freedom must take into account that human beings are created to be in solidarity with others. Moreover, the pontiff stated his conviction that the evils of real, existing capitalism can only be overcome by adopting the principle of solidarity in his 2000 World Day of Peace Message: "Experience seems to confirm that economic success is increasingly dependent on a more genuine appreciation of individuals and their abilities, on their fuller participation, on their increased and improved knowledge and information, on a stronger solidarity."[129]

John Paul II clearly expressed concern that economic and political practices of global capitalism are presently not serving the development of the person. Yet, he proposed a return to values such as solidarity and social justice in economics and politics to overcome these problems. While calling into question the very foundations of the modern economy, he basically advocated an ethical rehabilitation of capitalism. He, along with the entire modern papal social tradition, believed that economic freedom, a value to be preserved, can coexist with and serve integral or "personalist" freedom. In other words, it can foster the embodiment of freedom in its fullest form.[130] Although it is morally flawed in its present form in many ways, capitalism, which places a premium on economic freedom, can be conducive to social solidarity. With the proper emphasis on values, starting with the dignity of the human person, capitalism is reformable.[131]

Economic Freedom in the Service of Personalist Freedom

The modern popes, especially those since Leo XIII, have discussed economic freedom and its relationship to freedom understood "integrally" or free "in its totality," as John Paul II put it in *Centesimus Annus* (no. 42).[132] This important aspect of Catholic social thought on freedom indicates that economic freedom is not denied or devalued per se. As a result, in order for Catholic social teaching to be cogent, it must demonstrate how economic freedom relates to personalist freedom and "internal" freedom, which human beings can possess regardless of external circumstances, including economic hardships. Indeed, any ethic of solidarity and freedom that presumes a capitalist system, which affirms private ownership and the role of profit, must show how economic freedom can cohere with "personalist" freedom.

Freedom is never realized in a vacuum. Social, cultural, political, and economic structures provide the frameworks within which freedom is realized.[133] Internal freedom is always mediated by social situations, such as the employer-employee relationship or the producer-consumer relationship. Modern Catholic social teaching has argued that private ownership creates a sphere within which one can exercise his or her freedom.[134] According to John XXIII, the exercise of "human liberty" becomes jeopardized when the right to "act freely in economic affairs" is stultified.[135] At first glance, it is difficult to see how this coheres with a notion of internal freedom, which can never be denied by any external threat. However, if external forces can hamper the ability to exercise freedom, then social circumstances can aid or hinder its use, while never completely eviscerating what Frankl called the last of all human freedoms, the ability to choose one's attitude towards others in any given circumstance. Internal freedom can never be eliminated, but its expression may be deterred by social conditions that preclude its full thriving.[136]

In the case of private property, John Paul II contends that when freedom is considered in relation to "the truth about God and man," ownership of property may become "an occasion for growth."[137] The pope's teaching on the nature of work explains how this may be the case: "Work is work with others and for others: it is a matter of doing something for someone else."[138] Those who organize the productive process, that is, owners and managers, contribute to society's development by using their creative ability to recognize the needs of others and to produce most efficiently the goods to meet those needs. In this sense, economic activity provides an arena for the "responsible use of freedom" in solidarity.[139] Moreover, an economy that denies workers the ability to own the means of production (that is, state socialism) and to "earn a living through his own initiative," impedes freely chosen participation in the creation of a common good in which all can share.[140] The same is true, of course, of an economy that denies access to adequate health care and education and does not afford sufficient wages.

John Paul's reflections on private ownership, which fosters the fulfillment of the right to "economic initiative," were shaped by his own experience in Poland. Socialism created a system in which ultimately no one was responsible for anything, because it was not "their own."[141] In other words, the pope based his teaching on the actual, historical failure of socialism to foster widespread participation in the process of just economic development.

This book cannot go into detail about the nature of the Church's teaching on private property.[142] It must suffice to conclude that ownership of property, when oriented towards the construction of a common good in which all persons participate, can mediate the "exercise of economic freedom placed at the service of human freedom in its totality."[143] An employer who chooses to pay a wage that ensures the basic rights of her workers, rather than purely maximizing profit, exemplifies this. Demanding inordinate wages constitutes an example of exercising economic freedom in a way that does not see it in relationship to personalist freedom. Because low wages constitute one of the major causes of poverty in Poland, and excessive wage inequality has caused social discord, it will be worth exploring this example from the perspective of freedom and solidarity.

Just Wages as Expressions of Freedom and Solidarity

What can be said about wages in Poland after 1989 from the perspective of Catholic social thought, specifically in light of its understanding of freedom and solidarity? The Roman Catholic tradition has championed the right to remuneration that is "enough to support the wage earner in reasonable and frugal comfort" at least since the 1891 publication of Leo XIII's encyclical *Rerum Novarum*.[144] John Paul II astutely perceived just remuneration as the "key problem of social ethics" in the context of worker justice, because without just compensation for work, human beings cannot afford the basics needed to flourish, such as food, shelter, health care, education, and access to culture.[145] In other words, remuneration below a "living wage," or wages below the social minimum standard in Poland, will lead to *marginalization*.[146] Therefore, failure to pay a living wage does not respect the right to *participation*.

Moreover, in accordance with the principle of participation and the principle of subsidiarity, individuals should be able to provide these goods for themselves and their families rather than relying on the government or any other intermediary agency. If all workers were to receive a just wage, which would at the very least be a living wage, then they themselves would, to a large extent, be able to acquire those basics.[147] Their dignity as workers and human beings and their right to participation would be more greatly respected than in a system that heavily depends on government subsidies for food, housing, etc., due to the prevalence of insufficient remuneration for work. Succinctly stated, the procurement of the right to participation requires a living wage, which Catholic social thought has traditionally promulgated as a key method of empowering the poor.[148] From the standpoint of an ethic of solidarity, the living wage must be defended because it represents the best way to ensure the basic human rights necessary for participation in the community.

A living wage represents an indispensable feature of the fight against poverty because of the growing reality of the "working poor." However, many Polish employers have questioned, or even deplored, the idea of raising minimum wages given the nation's high unemployment rate and its bout with inflation in the early 1990s. This was the case despite the fact that the minimum wage did not equal the social minimum standard for one person (for example, it was equal to 35 percent in 2002). Families with only one wage earner were in an even direr situation. In addition, it is true that many small businesses struggle to survive, given a lack of capital and high mandatory contributions to health care and social security (*ZUS*, or *Zakład Ubezpieczenia Społecznego*).[149] In accordance with the principle of subsidiarity, perhaps the Warsaw government should subsidize wages in small businesses that cannot afford to pay a living wage. The government could, for example, simply require less in health care and social security payments from struggling or fledgling small businesses. This may be all the more appropriate given that the government does not seem to be able to provide quality health care at a level commensurate with the employers' and employees' contributions.

These difficulties must be considered. However, many of the arguments in the "Capitalist Manifesto" belie the stated intention of providing more jobs by lowering or abolishing minimum wages. Its authors exhibit a lack of solidarity by relying on slogans rather than on sound evidence. Understanding the cry of the wounded, in this case the unemployed and the "underemployed," requires looking at the facts to avoid further suffering. Linking higher minimum wages and unemployment appears untenable on the basis of empirical studies. The establishment of wages must, of course, consider economic factors, such as productivity and the financial state of the business, as Pius XI acknowledged in *Quadragesimo Anno*.[150] At present, there is no concrete evidence of the minimum wage's effect on employment levels in Poland.[151] In fact, economic research elsewhere supports advocating a living wage. For example, in 1995 one hundred American economists published a statement in the *Wall Street Journal* in which they demanded a raise in the minimum wage. They cited the fact that raising it in the 1980s had had a negligible effect on the level of employment in the United States.[152] Moreover, a growing body of recent evidence in many parts of the United States does not reveal that raising the minimum wage or enacting living wage ordinances has a negative effect on businesses, employment levels, and consumers.[153] In addition, Joseph Stiglitz, the 2001 Nobel laureate in economics, argues that "lower wages might lead some firms to hire a few more workers; but the number of newly hired workers may be relatively few, and the misery caused by the lower wages on all the other workers might be very grave."[154]

Businesses that pay higher wages retain employees longer, thus avoiding the high costs of turnover: lost productivity, recruitment, training, etc. As noted economist George Ackerlof states, "a firm that gives workers a 'gift' of higher wages . . . finds that workers reciprocate with a 'gift' of higher effort norms."[155] Numerous examples have shown that in the long run, employees who are satisfied with their wages will lead their companies to higher profit margins.[156] More efficient productivity offsets higher labor costs. In addition, as American merchant tycoon Edward Filene argued in the early twentieth century, higher wages for the lowest wage earners opens new markets by giving more consumers greater purchasing power.[157] Empowering workers through the living wage also leads to lower expenditures on government subsidies for low-income workers. Small businesses, which lack the "corporate welfare" tax breaks bestowed upon large corporations, are often hit the hardest for these subsidies.[158] Therefore, many small business owners in the United States have adopted living wages of their own volition. For these reasons, in addition to the deontological perspective of Roman Catholic social teaching concerning just wages,[159] Catholic leaders in the United States have continually called for raises in the minimum wage.[160] Catholic leaders in Poland, in order to be faithful to the Church's social teaching and to foster solidarity and the right to participation, should do the same. Polish employers who do not consider paying a living wage to be an ethical mandate fail to utilize their newly found economic freedom in a way that contributes to "human freedom in its totality." They are not fostering the participation of their workers in society. With the minimum wage so far below the social minimum, it is unreasonable to expect minimum-wage employees to be more productive and raise their qualifications, a demand of the competitive, globalized job market.[161] Thus, as John Paul II wrote in *Laborem Exercens,* promoting the right to a just wage, which must at least ensure against marginalization, is one of the most important ways of embodying solidarity with workers and exercising the option for the poor.[162] Unfortunately, many Poles see the legal maintenance of minimum wages that reflect a decent standard of living as a limitation on economic freedom.[163]

The perspective of freedom and solidarity also sheds light on the earnings of those at the other end of the spectrum in Poland. Pius XI contended that "lowering or raising wages unduly, with a view to private profit, and with no consideration for the common good, is contrary to social justice." More specifically, he argued that wages should be set in order to provide as many job opportunities as possible and to ensure a "suitable means of livelihood."[164] Coal miners, politicians, and managers of firms who demanded exorbitant wages violated this teaching. John Paul II, who may have written *Laborem Exercens* with Poland in mind, supports the rights of workers to form unions but staunchly opposes union demands that become "a kind of group or class 'egoism.'" His reminder that workers in any given profession must limit their demands based on "the general economic situation of the country" should be heeded by groups such as Polish coal miners.[165] Those unions, such as the miners, are engaging in the kind of class egoism that their fellow countryman deemed immoral. This class egoism represents a clear lack of solidarity, which sometimes means renouncing one's own claims for the benefit of those who are most in need. In addition, those politicians who have capitulated to the unjust claims of powerful interest groups and unions also act against the principle of solidarity. As Karol Wojtyła contended, solidarity sometimes requires bold opposition to those with power for the sake of the common good and the weakest members of society.[166]

Catholic social teaching has consistently claimed that wages must always be determined with an eye towards serving the common good. According to John XXIII, the following objectives obtain when considering the common good and wage justice on a national level: "to provide employment for as many workers as possible; to take care lest privileged groups arise even among workers themselves; to maintain a balance between wages and prices; to make accessible the goods and services for a better life to as many persons as possible; either to eliminate or to keep within bounds the inequalities that exist between different sectors of the economy."[167] It is very difficult to calculate a just wage concretely. However, Catholic social teaching insists that a just wage is established by considering both the individual's contribution to the economic enterprise and his or her level of participation in serving the common good. In this regard, John XXIII claimed that sometimes "very great remuneration is had for the performance of some task of lesser importance."[168] The salaries of managers in Poland today are anywhere from twenty to fifty times greater than the nation's average.[169] Catholic social teaching calls the legitimacy of such wages into doubt. The exact amount of contribution to the common good escapes any facile calculation. However, as Michael Novak has cogently argued in regard to chief executive officer (CEO) salaries, "there is something supremely social in their achievements.... It is wrong to award them as if they were Lone Rangers."[170] In other words, the CEO's and the manager's capacity to succeed rests heavily on the social system from which he or she benefits. She or he has profited from the educational system and relies more generally on the entire costly edifice of the nation's political economy, such as investments in infrastructure and human capital.

It is difficult to imagine that the contribution of a manager to the common good is that much more valuable than that of a physician, teacher, or professor. Yet, the Polish manager's salary is exponentially greater.[171] In the "information societies" that exist in developed nations, investment in "human capital" is said to be the key to development. But who will develop "human capital," inculcating in students the skills necessary to succeed in today's world, if not teachers and professors? The wages of these professionals, especially in the earliest stages of their careers when they often have families to support, are notoriously low. As a result, many teachers and professors leave their jobs for more lucrative positions. If they do remain in their vocations, they are often forced to teach at several schools, leaving little time to interact directly with their students.[172]

Those politicians who expressed outrage at the prospect of wage cuts for themselves merit similar criticism. As a member of the Advisory Council for Monetary Policy at the Polish National Bank stated, "The regulation concerning the earnings of managers and politicians is contrary to the basic principles of the market."[173] Catholic social teaching on wages rejects this "market mentality," which is rooted in a false notion of neoliberal economic freedom and is contrary to the understanding of economic freedom in the service of human freedom. Rather than bemoaning cuts to their decadent salaries, civil servants should see themselves and their wages in a relationship of solidarity to others in Poland. Solidarity should be embodied in Poland in the context of wage negotiations and demands. Does the politician or coal miner who demands immoderate wages consider, for example, the plight of the 17 percent of workers who earn less than two thirds of the average salary, or the more than 20 percent who earn less than the social minimum?[174] In describing active solidarity, John XXIII argued that civil authority exists, above all, to protect the common good "of the entire human family."[175] Therefore, politicians should acknowledge their role as servants. They were elected to serve, not to earn ten times more than the average Pole and enjoy luxurious fringe benefits. As John Paul II articulated, "[t]he exercise of solidarity within each society is valid when its members recognize one another as persons. Those who are more influential, because they have a greater share of goods and common services, should feel responsible for the weaker and be ready to share with them all they possess."[176]

Solidarity requires everyone to consider the fate of others and to promote the rights of others. In wage negotiations, employers and employees alike should attempt to show mutual understanding: What are the needs, difficulties, and fears of my partner in dialogue? And what consequences might my inordinate demands have for others and for society, directly and indirectly? Poles must ask themselves such questions if they are to build a just economic order that strives to bring freedom and solidarity into harmony. The drastic reduction of wages in some sectors, accompanied by the inordinate gains in others, eroded social support for the economic and political reforms of the 1990s. This book argues that the proper understanding of the relationship between freedom and solidarity is crucial to overcoming many problems in Poland in the economic sphere, most important, poverty. Advocating a living wage is one key instrument in this endeavor. Polish society might encourage this by creating a more widespread and visible "ethical consumer" culture. Nongovermental organizations could publicize information about wages and working conditions in order to encourage consumers and contractors to do business only with those companies that respect workers' rights. Of course, this requires educating consumers to think ethically about the choices they make in the marketplace and to accept higher prices as the cost of just wages and fair trade.[177]

This understanding of economic freedom and its relationship to freedom as a whole vastly differs from a neoliberal notion of freedom. Neither neoliberal economic freedom, freedom as moral permissivism, nor freedom as national sovereignty resembles the kind of positive freedom that has been advocated in this chapter. The personalist freedom envisaged by Tischner and Catholic social thought does not conflict with solidarity understood as promoting the rights of others, above all, the right to participation. This kind of ethic is needed today in Poland to overcome poverty and indifference towards the poor. The freedom of the poor, including their economic freedom, is completely overlooked in public discourse. This issue stems in part from a conception of freedom that fails to see poverty as a denial of it. As was mentioned above, John Paul II alluded to this kind of assault against the freedom of the many people who live in misery and destitution. In *Development as Freedom*, Amartya Sen has confronted economic liberals with the problem of poverty on their own terms, namely, the freedom that they so resolutely tout. The next chapter will explore Sen's notion of freedom, because it provides a sophisticated conceptual analysis concerning the relationship between poverty and freedom that helpfully augments Catholic social thought. This will also facilitate a clearer understanding of the relationship between solidarity, freedom, and participation in a way that deepens what is said in Catholic social thought about these three interrelated realities.

CHAPTER FIVE

Freedom and Participation as Social Products

> [T]rue individual freedom cannot exist without economic security and independence. "Necessitous men are not free men." People who are hungry and out of a job are the stuff of which dictatorships are made.[1]
> —Franklin Delano Roosevelt

The tenth anniversary of Poland's democratic elections was an occasion to celebrate. However, economist and member of Parliament Józef Kaleta instead challenged the notion that all citizens in Poland are truly free. He did not dismiss the importance of democratically elected governments, freedom of expression, and other political freedoms. However, Kaleta asked if it is possible to speak of freedom in a country where more than 50 percent of its population lives below the social minimum and where poverty and the inequality of wealth have reached dramatic levels. He furthermore exclaimed: "Can the hungry person, homeless person, thrown out of work, without any future opportunities really exercise freedom? . . . The freedom of the citizen is primarily economic freedom."[2] Kaleta also suggested that freedom in Poland's "radically liberal version" of the economy is understood as the "freedom of the strong to eliminate the weak." Many Poles, however, hastily dismiss Kaleta's view as "socialist." They see this kind of thinking as passé, if not despicable, ideology because it is responsible for Poland's miserable decades under Communism. In this vein, many Poles disdain numerous putatively "socialist" ideas, such as social justice, which is seen as a threat to freedom. Adversaries of social justice oppose it because it demands the redistribution of resources, which requires arbitrary coercion by special-interest groups.[3] In fact, the association with socialism may have something to do with the negative attitude towards important aspects of solidarity and freedom such as worker participation, an issue that will be treated in more detail below.[4]

Wariness of Poland's socialist heritage, such as *homo sovieticus*, is certainly warranted. However, socialism does not have a monopoly on the category of social justice and notions of freedom associated with the economic circumstances of the human person. Catholic social teaching, for example, clearly affirms social justice. Furthermore, the modern papal social tradition accepted economic rights as an important aspect of human freedom long before it accepted so-called political and civil rights.[5] The arguments of Catholic social thought concerning economic rights as elements of human freedom will be examined more closely later in this chapter. Now, however, an examination of Amartya Sen's thought will enhance the previous chapter's characterization of the realities of solidarity, freedom, and participation in several important ways.

Sen reveals that poverty is a denial of human freedom with an empirical and philosophical depth that surpasses Catholic social thought. His distinction between instrumental and substantive freedom also helps to clarify how freedom in the market and in a democracy represent both ends in themselves and means to solidarity. In addition, his paradigm reveals that because freedom is at least in part a social product, solidarity is necessary for the realization of freedom. Sen's thought has important ramifications because tackling poverty in Poland is often seen as problematic. It conjures up the encroachment of the state into private lives, which is tantamount to a violation of "freedom," according to neoliberals. On the contrary, Sen claims that social solidarity embodied in social institutions is necessary for achieving freedom. On the macro level, his thought reveals the deeply flawed nature of the economic "shock therapy." Although this approach to economic development produced some positive results, such as controlling hyperinflation, it also largely eviscerated solidarity from the "heart of Europe."[6] Finally, appealing to Sen also demonstrates that denying that material poverty is an assault against human freedom because of its alleged socialist ties is ahistorical and ideological. It ignores the many nonsocialists who championed this idea. In Sen's case, a Nobel Prize–winning economist who supports capitalism, has made the argument.

Poverty from the Perspective of Freedom

Most of today's Polish advocates of "economic freedom" in the neoliberal sense do not acknowledge that poverty is an assault against human freedom. Leszek Balcerowicz exemplifies this in his musings on freedom, which are admittedly more nuanced than the freedom-is-the-license-to-do-whatever-I-want credo that one often encounters. Nonetheless, the following excerpt from his book *Freedom and Development* exposes Balcerowicz's neoliberal outlook:

> A reasonable concept of freedom does not apply to the relationship between a given person and the world of material things. For example, the lack of a bicycle does not attest to the lack of freedom, rather [it points] to relative poverty. This understanding of freedom has very important consequences. It forbids the distortion of it [freedom] under leftist influence, especially Marxist ideologies. They generally defined freedom vis-à-vis the situation of persons to material things and—bringing the problem of poverty into relief—tried to give the impression that in actuality freedom does not exist.[7]

For Balcerowicz, any call for government intervention dangerously resembles the Marxist systems that led to the demise of freedom. Interventionists, like Marxists, base their claims "on the false conflict between economic freedom and economic development." (One wonders if Balcerowicz would consider Franklin Delano Roosevelt a Marxist.) Balcerowicz does foresee the necessity of some kinds of government intervention, for example, in order to dissuade industries from destroying the environment. However, economic freedom for Balcerowicz is ultimately freedom from government intervention in the economic sphere.[8] It is a kind of negative freedom, which should be maximized as far as possible. Poverty may be a negative social phenomenon, but it is not a loss of freedom. Balcerowicz has tried to convince Eastern Europeans and Western scholars with "socialist leanings" to banish this thought and the "statism" that he believes accompanies it. One such attempt came in a distinguished lecture at the World Bank in 2003, which he tellingly titled, "Toward a Limited State."[9] However, Balcerowicz fails to acknowledge that in addition to Catholic social thought, widely acclaimed economists such as Sen link poverty with the deprivation of freedom.

Poverty as a Denial of Substantive and Instrumental Freedoms

Sen is no socialist: he clearly sees the free market as the best possible vehicle for the realization of human freedoms.[10] His work places him squarely within the classic liberal tradition, despite claims that his ideas are "leftist."[11] Ultimately, he advocates an understanding of justice based on "the kinds of lives we have reason to value," not on a preconceived notion of human nature or the good. Just social arrangements can only be derived from broad political dialogue and consensus.[12] Thus, Sen most highly values freedom as the ability to choose and to exercise one's agency, which he defines as the ability to "act and bring about change . . . as a participant in economic, social, and political actions."[13] However, his work illustrates that not all liberals espouse the view that freedom amounts to the right to dispose of one's income without coercive interference from the government. Sen would also not agree with Kaleta's claim that economic freedom alone constitutes the freedom of the citizen. Sen also argues that poor persons in places such as India, Bangladesh, Thailand, and Burma value the freedom to participate in the political process just as much as they value freedom from hunger.[14] In short, he demonstrates that economic freedoms, such as freedom from starvation, and political freedoms, such as the right to vote, are inherently interrelated. This is why his work is important for Poland.[15] Yet, while several scholars have noticed his work, Polish neoliberal economists and policymakers have largely ignored it.

At the risk of oversimplification, it will suffice here to elaborate on three of Sen's basic points in *Development as Freedom*: 1) the expansion of freedom is both the primary end and the principal means of development; 2) freedom must be seen "in a sufficiently broad way," which acknowledges the "empirical linkages" between the various kinds of freedoms that persons enjoy or are denied; and 3) there is a reciprocal relationship between individual freedom and social commitments that make individual freedom possible. In making his argument, Sen refers to "substantive" and "instrumental" freedoms. Substantive freedoms, the "ends" of development, are freedoms that people have reason to value in se. With the proviso that his is not a comprehensive list, Sen enumerates the following substantive freedoms: the capability of avoiding deprivations such as starvation, undernourishment, morbidity and premature mortality, freedoms associated with being literate and numerate, political participation, and uncensored speech.[16] Like John Paul II's homily in Ełk, Sen maintains that notions of development that postpone substantive freedoms until economic growth reaches a certain level, measured most often in terms of the GNP, are ill conceived. This view contrasts with neoliberals, who spoke of the social costs of the Polish transformations as the price to be paid for economic growth. In Sen's development paradigm, freedoms such as the capability of political participation and the opportunity to pursue education or health care are among the constituent components of development.[17]

Such freedoms should not be considered only instrumentally, that is, in relation to whether or not they contribute to "economic growth." Rather, development should be measured by the degree to which such freedoms are expanded. As it turns out, however, freedoms such as literacy and access to health care have historically contributed to economic growth. (Recall in this context John Paul II's claim that economic success is dependent on participation and solidarity.) East Asian economies, beginning with Japan, massively expanded education, then health care and other "social opportunities," early on in their rise to economic success. This approach to development also successfully reduced poverty and spawned economic growth in Kerala, India.[18] Unlike Balcerowicz, who sees no historical link between democracy and economic development, Sen demonstrates that democratic participation is both an end of development and a means to it. In order to elucidate this argument further, the category of instrumental freedoms needs to be explicated.

Instrumental freedoms "tend to contribute to the general capability of a person to live more freely" and "serve to complement one another." These freedoms, the "means" to development, include political freedoms (the ability to determine who should govern and according to what principles, uncensored press), economic facilities (access to credit), social opportunities (arrangements for education and health care), transparency guarantees (dealings with one another under the "guarantee of disclosure and lucidity"), and protective security (institutionalized protection against abject poverty, hunger, and death, that is, a social safety net).[19] As Sen contends, these freedoms enhance the substantive freedoms of people, "but they also supplement one another and can furthermore reinforce one another."[20] For example, chapter 3 mentioned the link between education and the ability to participate in civic life and have one's voice taken into account. According to Sen, the "unfreedom" of illiteracy raises barriers to the full exercise of political freedoms: "political participation may be hindered by the inability to read newspapers or communicate effectively with others involved in political activities." He argues that illiteracy may also hinder the ability to participate in the economic sphere; this is the case because people need skills to be competitive in the global economy, which often requires "production according to specification" and "strict quality control."[21] Sen's perspective on the interconnections of freedoms ultimately leads him to conclude that neoliberal development schemes that put the "economy first, then everything else" are inherently flawed.

This understanding of freedom has important implications for poverty analysis and for public policy. Sen's view of poverty as "capability deprivations" implies that there is something deeper than inadequate income that lies at poverty's root, namely, the inability to enjoy substantive freedoms. According to Sen, this notion reflects the ancient words of Aristotle, who claimed, "wealth is evidently not the good we are seeking, for it is merely useful and for the sake of something else."[22] According to this perspective, income is valuable insofar as it is a means to capabilities.[23] Capability, in Sen's vocabulary, is a kind of freedom: "the substantive freedom to achieve alternative functioning combinations," or, in simple terms, "the freedom to achieve various lifestyles." Functionings are those things that persons may value. Capabilities refer to functionings that persons may choose and are really attainable in practice. To put it another way, substantive freedoms are the "capabilities to choose a life one has reason to value."[24] For example, a person may value the functioning of reading and writing but may lack the capability of reading and writing. Thus, she does not have the substantive freedom of attaining literacy; it is not a real opportunity for her.

A comparative scenario may further illuminate the relationship between functionings, capabilities, and freedom. For instance, a woman in Afghanistan under the Taliban does not have the functioning of political participation within her capability set. While she may wish to be active politically, which means that she values the functioning of political participation, it is not a real possibility for her. She is not "substantively free" to do so, as Sen would put it. In a reasonably democratically governed nation, a person may choose not to participate politically, due to his or her disillusionment with the nation's leaders. While both persons may have the same "functioning achievement," that is, they both do not vote or enter into political discourse, the person in a democracy has a different capability set. She or he *chooses* not to participate politically. Nonetheless, the person in the second scenario has the substantive freedom to do so. Succinctly stated, a person's capability set represents the freedom to achieve various functionings, such as literacy, being adequately nourished, and taking part in the civic life of the community. It does not yet, however, tell us whether or not a person "actualizes" the freedoms within his or her capability set.

The interconnections of freedoms may complicate the above comparison. The comparison of the situations of the two persons who do not participate in the political life of the community holds only if the person who chooses not to, of her own volition, is not impeded by the lack of other important freedoms. The mere fact that the second person formally has the right to vote and politically participate (in debate, campaigning, lobbying, etc.) does not guarantee that she truly is substantively free to do so. At the very least, she may not possess the freedom to do so to the same degree as others who are also formally entitled to take part politically. In this vein, John Rawls notes in his *A Theory of Justice* that all persons in a democracy that allows for vast inequalities of wealth and property do not have the same "fair value of political liberty": "Political power rapidly accumulates and becomes unequal; and making use of the coercive apparatus of the state and its law, those who gain the advantage can often assure themselves of a favored position. Thus inequities in the economic and social system may soon undermine whatever political equality might have existed under fortunate historical circumstances."[25]

Rawls argues that for a democracy to truly allow for the fair value of political liberties, private ownership and the means of production, property, and wealth must be "widely distributed." This is necessary because the wealthy have a greater likelihood of influencing politicians and political parties, whose campaigns are privately financed. They also have more opportunity to advance their interests by controlling the media and influencing those who may pass laws that further their interests.[26] Sen's thinking resembles Rawls's claim because he maintains that freedoms often mutually influence one another, positively or negatively. Thus, in the example above, a poor person who formally possesses the ability to participate politically may not in essence possess this substantive freedom in certain circumstances. In order to reinforce his point about the interconnections of freedoms, Sen describes his own childhood encounter with an impoverished Muslim named Kader Mia, who searched for daily work in Sen's own Hindu neighborhood in Dhaka (presently in Bangladesh). Sen recalls the horrifying scene in which he watched the man, who had been stabbed in the back, die as he gave him water. The man told Sen that his wife had warned him not to venture into this unsafe area, but economic need forced him to do so. In retrospect, Sen opines that "economic unfreedom, in the form of extreme poverty, can make a person a helpless prey in the violation of other kinds of freedom. Kader Mia need not have come to a hostile area in search of a little income in those terrible times had his family been able to survive without it. Economic unfreedom can breed social unfreedom, just as social or political unfreedom can also foster economic unfreedom."[27]

These illustrations underscore another of Sen's basic contentions about freedom, namely, that the freedom of the individual is "*quintessentially a social product*" (emphasis added). Both Sen and Rawls maintain that social institutions must be in place in order to procure individual freedoms. In other words, social solidarity must exist in order to achieve freedom as an end. Individual freedom, in turn, must be used to make these social arrangements more effective in protecting freedom.[28] It must promote social arrangements that embody the principle of solidarity. Like the perspective on the fulfillment of economic rights according to subsidiarity in Catholic social thought, this line of thinking cuts through the debate about the loss of individual responsibility when social institutions "overstep their bounds" and provide myriad economic, social, and cultural goods, thereby creating a "culture of dependency." Critics of the welfare state and/or economic rights, Polish neoliberals included, have often rendered such a critique.[29]

To counter this argument, Sen correctly maintains that "responsibility requires freedom." A host of social, political, and economic arrangements must be in place in order for persons to possess the substantive freedoms necessary to contribute responsibly to the construction of a just social order, that is, one that fosters the substantive freedoms of every person. Therefore, the state and society cannot escape responsibility for shaping such arrangements.[30] Sen points out, for example, that a person who lacks the means to escape preventable illness and disease "may also be denied the freedom to do various things—for herself and others—that she may wish to do as a responsible human being."[31] This is obviously where Sen's notion of freedom intersects with the understanding of its relationship to solidarity in Catholic social thought. He demonstrates how poverty can hinder the realization of freedom in solidarity.

In this schema, persons who are "poor" according to income standards may lack multiple important freedoms. In other words, their capability set, or the functionings they may achieve, may be limited due to their lack of income. Seen in this perspective, poverty becomes more than just a lack of income. It is an assault against human freedom, as John Paul states in *Redemptor Hominis*. In this paradigm, freedom does not mean being left alone.[32] If freedom is construed in this negative fashion, poor persons could be considered free as long as they were left to fend for themselves, even if they encounter starvation, illness, and death as a result. In the language of human rights, poverty assaults the freedom of the poor by precluding them from living lives of dignity. It denies them the right to participation and the other rights necessary for its fulfillment. In this sense, poverty arises out of a lack of solidarity, which promotes the participation of all. This will become clearer by looking at how Sen's understanding of freedom applies to some particular groups of poor people in contemporary Poland.

Freedom of Poor Women in Post-PGR-y Poland

Clearly, poor women suffer greater hardships than poor men. Women are at greater risk of falling into poverty.[33] The case of poor women in post-PGR-y Poland (the lands of formerly collectivized farms) lucidly portrays the "coupling of disadvantages and inequality of freedoms" expounded by Sen.[34] As chapter 3 stated, women there are more likely than men to experience long-term unemployment, and those with little schooling often get stuck in low-wage, dead-end jobs. Furthermore, when couples have children, women bear the majority of burdens associated with childrearing. In situations where women have many children, they are often forced to choose between their own health and that of their children. Women in the post-PGR-y regions are faced with many of these deprivations and more. Moreover, due to the geographic isolation of many of these regions, little if any contact is possible with the cultural and political life of the country. Political participation is rare, because people in these regions believe that their government does not represent their interests.

In Sen's paradigm, these circumstances equate with the loss of interrelated freedoms, which contributes to an overall lack of freedom.[35] For example, Sen describes the effects of unemployment in terms of the loss of self-confidence and job skills, an increase in illnesses, morbidity, and mortality, and social exclusion.[36] In other words, it is not only the case that unemployed poor women lack income; they also lack all of these substantive freedoms, which should be the ends of any development scheme. They also do not have the instrumental freedom of economic facilities (work that affords a decent salary, credit, savings, etc.) that would enable them to attain these substantive freedoms. Moreover, many of the women in post-PGR-y Poland cannot escape from illness and premature mortality because most of Poland's unemployed receive little, if any, social assistance. Their material living conditions, far worse than those of the average city-dweller, also contribute to their inability to stave off illness and premature death. As a result, their health needs go unmet. Thus, they lack the substantive freedom of avoiding morbidity and the instrumental freedom of "protective security."

In addition, these women often find themselves in this situation because their education was limited as girls and young adults. Most females and males in Poland achieve so-called basic literacy (more than 70 percent of Poles, according to the OECD Adult Literacy Survey). Yet, the vast majority of those living in the post-PGR-y regions do not have "functional literacy."[37] In other words, they do not have the necessary skills to function as members of the work force and of political, social, and cultural communities in today's "knowledge society."[38] They do not, therefore, truly possess the freedom of literacy, which is both substantive and instrumental. This is the case because it is an end in itself, and a clear relationship exists in Poland between one's educational attainments and the ability to possess economic facilities.

A certain level of education is the sine qua non of social and political participation. Poor women with little schooling in the post-PGR-y world undeniably lack the genuine freedom of political participation. The likelihood of a poor woman from this region holding an elected office is minimal, and the same applies to her ability to influence the political process. Again, this is a result of several "unfreedoms": her lack of freedom associated with limited literacy, her marginalization due to her social standing, her inability to finance a campaign (which requires a good deal of personal resources),[39] and the social unfreedom of gender discrimination. The fact that women are gravely underrepresented in the Polish political forum attests to this last unfreedom. Poland ranks thirty-fifth in Europe in terms of gender parity among members of Parliament: only 20 percent of *Sejm* representatives and 23 percent of senators are women; and among local government representatives (*radni*), only 15 percent are women. They have a much harder time earning slots on party tickets. Party leaders decide whose names will appear on election ballots, thus opening the door to corrupt, often gender-biased political jockeying. When the issue of gender parity in politics is raised in Poland, it is summarily dismissed by remarking on the few women who have made it to the top; or that in "free" elections, quotas should not be used; or by recalling that a woman's place is in the home, not in the "dirty" world of politics.[40] In this connection, it is worth reiterating Sen's claim that when women are represented in government, both their needs and those of their children are much more likely to be met. Poor women in post-PGR-y Poland, and in general, are not likely to compete with powerful special-interest groups such as coal miners, who either lobby or use strident protests to promote their agendas.[41] The government's limited resources must be allotted to an array of competing groups. Poor women in Poland have little chance of having their voices heard.

The elimination of the national alimony fund (*fundusz alimentacyjny*) in 2003 typifies the bias against women. In the past, the fund had provided alimony to those raising children whose fathers avoided paying even though they were legally obligated. The state paid up to 631 złoty per month to those whose income did not exceed 612 złoty per person. The new law eliminates this fund, replacing it with a "family benefit" of

170 złoty per child for those whose income is less than 504 złoty per person.[42] Moreover, under the new system no agency will try to enforce the fathers' responsibility for paying alimony, as the fund once did, even if largely unsuccessfully. Thus, men will be permitted to shirk their responsibilities as fathers, while women will continue to struggle to support themselves and their children. This law took effect on May 1, 2004, despite outcries from the women whom it harmed. Groups of women (*Stowarzyszenia na rzecz Praw Odpowiedzialnych Rodziców*) have officially proposed changing the new law. Their "citizens' proposal" seeks to create alimony funds controlled by local governments (*gminy*) and enforce payments by fathers more strictly. However, only one politician sent a staff member to a meeting in Cracow to listen to the testimonies of mothers who have been forced into desperate situations.[43] While there may be some debate about whether or not the new system's targeted aid better serves the most needy women and children, public discussion did not take place due to a lack of willingness on the part of the politicians. To make matters worse, more than four million single mothers did not receive their new entitlement during the first two months of its existence, as the local governments botched the transfer of payments.[44] This situation discloses that women who face the unfreedom of poverty also do not have the freedom of political participation. It also attests to the lack of solidarity in Poland today.

Mothers of large families, which are prevalent in the post-PGR-y regions, have further limitations placed on their substantive freedoms because their lives often consist solely of meeting their children's needs and serving their husbands. In this regard, Sen has touted the connection between female literacy levels and the reduction of fertility rates as a means to promote the well-being of women and children. Sen rightly maintains that high birth rates disproportionately deny the "substantive freedoms" of women, particularly in African and Asian countries.[45] This same situation applies to the post-PGR-y regions, where women often have many children for reasons beyond their own control.[46]

Responsible parenthood must entail the consideration of how many children can be adequately cared for and loved, as Pope Paul VI acknowledged in *Humanae Vitae*. "Serious reasons" may legitimate limiting the number of children "with due respect to moral precepts."[47] Parenthood should not lead women in Poland to suffer from material deprivation and a loss of other freedoms such as literacy, economic facilities, and political participation. Sen argues that optional family-planning campaigns should be put in place to assuage the plight of poor women.[48] This may be the case. However, fertility-rate reduction should not be seen as a panacea, especially given Poland's overall low birth rate. Other measures should also be considered so that childrearing can be a means to freedom rather than an unfreedom, as Sen sees it. For example, John Paul II urged the passage of laws that would facilitate the harmonious combination of women's roles, thus enabling them to take part in public life and still be responsible mothers.[49] He also proposed grants to mothers who "devote themselves exclusively to the family."[50] In other words, he advocates a woman's right to choose not to work outside the home in order to raise her children. Of course, this should be considered work, as quality childrearing is an invaluable service to society as a whole. The negative social costs of parents' failure to raise their children in a loving, responsible way are well documented and need not be repeated here.

John Paul II's suggestions have merit. However, they fail to re-envision the role of fathers. To some degree, Poland has already embodied policies similar to the pope's proposals, albeit in the form of meager two- to three-year parental-leave benefits (*zasiłek wychowawczy*).[51] However, a true "paradigm shift" is necessary for poor women fully to regain the freedoms stifled by the overburdening of childrearing. Men can and should share more domestic work to eliminate women's "double shift," and society, including employers, should expect them to do so. In countries such as Italy and Spain, women do seven times more domestic work than men.[52] In order to encourage men to share the duties of childrearing and domestic work, some countries have enacted legislative measures. Indeed, many countries, mainly in Scandinavia, have adopted relatively generous paternal leave policies. Germany has introduced "parents' pay," which can be taken by mothers or fathers, and guaranteed daycare after a child's first birthday.[53] Great Britain announced a plan that will allow both parents of children under age 6 to request flexible hours.[54]

Unfortunately, however, the experience of Scandinavia has shown that relatively few men actually avail themselves of paternal benefits.[55] This is also the case in Poland, a country where, notoriously, only women are asked about their family plans during job interviews. Societal attitudes must change, along with the law, in order for men to take on greater responsibilities as fathers. The roles of fathers and mothers need to be reconceived in order to create more just family and work structures that, at the same time, do not come at the expense of children. Perhaps only this kind of paradigm shift will eliminate women's disadvantage in the labor market, as they tend to be seen as potential mothers who will quit or devote less attention to their jobs, while men are perceived as workers who can devote themselves fully to their employer. This should lead to less long-term unemployment among women and to equal wages for women, whose productivity, real or perceived, would not be any more threatened by motherhood than men's productivity would be by fatherhood.[56]

Shedding "the shackles of childrearing," to use Sen's words, should not mean that all people should divest themselves of responsible parenthood—only "the shackles." Having and raising children should be a source of joy for those who choose to do so. It should also be seen as an important way of exercising "contributive justice," which emphasizes the right and duty of participation in society.[57] Parents have a duty to society to be good parents, and societies have an obligation to enable them to do so. This includes fathers. Indeed, fatherhood in freedom and solidarity does not entail "occasionally helping out," as one often hears in homilies, pre-Cana encounters, physicians' offices, and popular parenting guides in Poland.[58] Freedom realized in fatherhood, which is vital to recapturing the freedoms of mothers oppressed by poverty, requires acting in a way that promotes the freedom of the other, in this case, a mother and her children. This translates into equal partnership in parenthood. This idea coheres with the earlier-described realization of human rights in accordance with the principle of subsidiarity. In other words, the realization of human rights and freedoms begins in the home, with the state and society providing structures, such as flex-time work schedules, that support it. This approach will require an entirely different way of viewing the process of development in Poland.

Development as Freedom contra "Shock Therapy"

Sen's conception of development as freedom has profound implications for the overall approach taken to Poland's socioeconomic transformations after 1989. It also overlaps with Catholic social teaching in important ways. For example, both see freedom as at least in part a social product: both view solidarity as a means and an end. On the most basic level, Sen and Catholic social teaching urge us to look first at the lives of real human beings rather than numbers such as the GNP to determine whether or not a nation's economy promotes development. However, Sen brings an empirical as well as a philosophical sophistication to the discussion, which can enhance what Catholic social teaching maintains on human freedom and economic development. Moreover, his notion of development as freedom directly contrasts with the neoliberal understanding of economic development heralded at the outset of Poland's socioeconomic transformations.

Sen does not deny the potentially positive relationship between economic growth and poverty reduction. However, he and several esteemed economists persuasively argue that economic growth does not always translate into poverty reduction, or "the real expansion of freedoms for human persons," nor did the anti-inflation wars of standard economic policy in the 1990s promote human welfare.[59] Sen points out that people in places such as Gabon, Namibia, South Africa, and Brazil are "richer" in terms of the GNP per capita but have much shorter lives than people in China or Kerala, India, where the GNP per capita is much lower.[60] Adjudicating the debates among economists concerning anti-inflation policies exceeds the scope and competence of this book. Nonetheless, at the very least, Sen's claim that a case cannot be made "for eliminating inflation altogether—irrespective of what has to be sacrificed for that end," raises doubts about some of the measures used to control hyperinflation in Poland in the early 1990s.

Hyperinflation, of course, can seriously harm the lives of people, as Sen and all economists would admit. But the price paid in Poland for Balcerowicz's shock therapy was a massive increase in unemployment and a large decline in real wages, as was discussed in detail earlier. The *popiwek* tax may have been designed to help fight hyperinflation. However, employees did not always demand inordinate wage raises in the 1990s.[61] Therefore, imposing such a draconian wage-limiting scheme (recall that wages grew ten times slower than the GNP) on workers without their taking part in deliberations is unjustifiable from the perspective of solidarity, freedom, and participation. The crux of the matter here is that the public participation in the "valuational debates," as Sen calls them, on such matters was missing. Politicians intentionally squelched public debate. The people themselves should have taken part in the "valuational debates" over the major budgetary sacrifices in the areas of education and health care. Indeed, such debates are a crucial part of democracy and development, as Sen contends.[62] Moreover, Sen proffers wisdom that Polish officials who clamored about "fiscal responsibility" would do well to heed: "Financial conservatism should be the nightmare of the militarist, not of the school teacher or the hospital nurse. It is an indication of our topsy-turvy world in which we live that the school teacher or the nurse feels more threatened by financial conservatism than does the army general. The rectification of this anomaly calls not for the chastising of financial conservatism, but for more pragmatic and open-minded scrutiny of rival claims to social funds."[63]

Poland's military spending has increased substantially, sometimes in ways that are clearly questionable.[64] Perhaps most Poles quite understandably see NATO membership as a priority, given the fragility of Poland's national security in the past. However, the required costly modernization of the nation's military must be weighed against the deep cuts in other public expenditures, such as primary and secondary education, scholarship aid, and health care.[65] The drastic cuts in health care, for example, negatively affect people on a daily basis. Their inability to receive treatment due to inadequate state funding, which leads to physicians' and nurses' strikes and the refusal to perform various operations in state-run hospitals, has become a common affair.[66]

Most Poles, including the Church's hierarchy, do not see military expenditures with this kind of critically comparative eye. Given Catholic social teaching's historical critique of an unjustifiably costly arms buildup in the face of grinding poverty, one would expect that the Polish bishops would have raised their voices in protest.[67] Some Poles, however, have drawn attention to this inauspicious situation. Jan Nowak-Jezioranski, for example, maintained that the future of Poland depends on professors and teachers, one of the most poorly paid social groups, not on generals and soldiers, who earn much more.[68] Many of these same military personnel kept the oppressive Communist regime in place. Interestingly, on the issue of military salaries, even some staunch neoliberals such as Professor Wacław Wilczyński agree. He laments that professors earn one half the pay of army colonels.[69] One wonders if he would equally bewail nurses' paltry salaries, which force them to work two or three jobs to survive. That is precisely what solidarity requires: fighting for the rights of others, not just one's own.

Finally, Sen's notion of development as freedom brings to light one other important issue for Poland's consideration of its problem of poverty. Sometimes Poles, particularly neoliberals, aver that they do not encounter "real" poverty in contemporary Poland. Poverty, the argument goes, is what one sees in "Third World" countries such as Ethiopia or Afghanistan or, closer to home, Romania. They maintained that those who claim that Polish poverty has risen since 1989 exaggerate the gravity of the situation. Furthermore, the rapid economic success of some Poles creates a situation in which the "losers" of the transition see themselves as downtrodden by comparison. Meanwhile, they have television sets, washing machines, and perhaps even a dilapidated car. Yet, they perceive themselves to be poor because they are relatively worse off than those who have larger houses and newer cars and who take expensive vacations.

As was mentioned earlier, some scholars and NGOs, such as the Solidarity labor union, continue to advocate the social minimum standard as the official poverty line. It is obvious that this kind of poverty is different from that experienced by an Ethiopian in her famine-stricken nation. This should not be surprising, nor should it enable Polish economists and politicians smugly to dismiss poverty's existence in their own country. Experts on the problem have long acknowledged that poverty "is a historically and spatially conditioned phenomenon."[70] Some even question whether poverty can be defined in an objective fashion, despite the fact that modern medicine and nutritional studies may bring us closer than ever to precise measurements of human physiological needs.[71] From the perspective of poverty as capability deprivation, what a person needs in order to possess certain freedoms will differ from one society to another. As Sen puts it, a person's "situatedness" relative to other persons in society matters: "being relatively poor in a rich community can prevent a person from achieving some elementary 'functionings' (such as taking part in the life of the community) even though her income, in absolute terms, may be much higher than the level of income at which members of poorer communities can function with greater ease and success."[72] Sen further notes that Adam Smith pointed out this obvious fact in *The*

Wealth of Nations. Thus, those who argue that Polish poverty is "shallow" or that it is not nearly as dramatic as, say, Ethiopian or Afghan poverty, miss the point.

The loss of freedoms can take many forms, as Sen argues. For example, although Poland has not nearly achieved the level of financial wealth of the G-8 nations, the introduction of market reforms has begun its move towards a knowledge-based society. As has been demonstrated, the market economy in Poland generally rewards those with higher education levels and punishes those without them. Success in the job market will depend more and more on educational achievements, specifically, computer software literacy, as technological advances digitalize most services.[73] Moreover, despite the fact that starvation is not as rampant in Poland as in poorer countries, the chronic malnutrition of many of its children threatens avoidable morbidity and premature death.[74] In short, while many of Poland's poor may not suffer the unfreedom of the inability to avoid starvation, they do not have many of the substantive freedoms that Sen cites as necessary for overall freedom. For this reason, using the social minimum category as a means to measure human poverty remains important.

One may reasonably ask why Sen's understanding of freedom should trump any other, such as the neoliberal understanding. In other words, why should his ideas play a major role in evaluating the freedom of Poles today? Sen's notion of freedom complements Catholic social teaching's understanding of freedom and of economic rights. It adds the perspective of freedom to the sometimes more legalistically construed language of rights. To put it another way, Sen exposes the paucity of notions of freedom understood negatively by revealing that they omit vast dimensions of human freedom. As such, he makes an important addition to Catholic social teaching. For its part, Catholic social teaching more lucidly stresses that the freedoms described by Sen are owed to persons by right.

Economic Rights as Necessary for Human Freedom

The Roman Catholic tradition has deemed economic rights rooted in and required by the dignity of the human person. Explicating why will add another dimension to Sen's discussion of freedom and will have ramifications for the problem of poverty in Poland today. Catholic social thought views economic rights as necessary for human freedom. Denying poor persons these rights impinges on their ability to exercise their freedom by participating in the building of and benefiting from the common good.[75] The denial of economic rights is not just an unfortunate situation. Such denials of human rights, whether economic, social, civil, or political, are violations of justice that give rise to a claim against society and to an ethical mandate to correct the wrong done.[76]

Catholic social teaching determined that economic rights are owed to persons by reflecting on human experience. David Hollenbach has written that the process of the "specification of the concrete conditions for the realization of dignity in action has been the continuing endeavor of the tradition since Leo XIII. It is this very process that has produced the Catholic human rights tradition."[77] The historical, social, economic, and political conditions reveal what is necessary for the protection of human dignity. For example, Pope Leo's cognizance of the "misery and wretchedness" of the poor and the "callousness of employers and the greed of unrestrained competition" prompted him to promote the right "to procure what is required to live."[78] For the poor, this can only be achieved through work and just wages.[79] Leo argued that the right to a wage that is enough to "support the wage earner in reasonable and frugal comfort" is grounded in a "dictate of human nature." According to natural law, human beings must preserve their lives, and this can only be done through work and wages.

In more recent Catholic thought, the emphasis on economic rights has shifted from the natural law demand of self-preservation to the right to participation in the life of the community. This obviously does not imply that self-preservation has become irrelevant. Rather, economic conditions must grant human beings more than the ability to survive. They must enable them to flourish, to become who they are destined to be in accordance with human nature. According to Catholic social thought's anthropological vision, the "ends" towards which human nature tends and how inherent human capacities must be protected and fostered determine the scope of and content of human rights (and thus the demands of human dignity). One of those ends is freedom fulfilled through participation.

Human beings are created to be free and to participate in the common good.[80] Therefore, persons and societies must do what is necessary to afford the realization of freedom and participation. Catholic social thought argues that while material conditions do not constitute the totality of human dignity, they are necessary for human dignity and human freedom. In Christian theological terms, decent living conditions are necessary components of "integral development." In other words, the temporal and transcendent dimensions of a person's development are related.[81] They are relevant to salvation history because "the construction of a just society 'in a sense' does anticipate the inauguration of God's kingdom."[82] Economic rights are instrumental; they are necessary for the full ability to contribute to the common good. They are also important as intrinsic components of human dignity because economic deprivations do "violence to the dignity" of persons.[83] As Hollenbach maintains, "minimum economic resources are due people by right, and not simply as a desirable part of the full common good. This is the case because persons can be just as effectively excluded or left out of the life of the community by long-term unemployment or homelessness as by the denial of the vote or freedom of speech."[84]

In other words, economic deprivations lead to marginalization, which means that a person's ability to participate in society in accordance with her nature as a free, creative, rational, emotional, and spiritual person has been obstructed. Therefore, Catholic social thought, like the United Nations Universal Declaration on Human Rights, upholds a host of human economic rights, such as the right to life, food, clothing, shelter, rest, medical care, basic education, higher education, employment, work without coercion, a just wage, and social security in cases of sickness, permanent disability, or unemployment as well as the right to development, economic initiative, and private property.

Catholic social thought does not articulate the interconnections among these rights with the same nuance and empirical verification that Sen provides concerning the interconnections among freedoms. But it does argue that rights are intrinsically related. *Justitia in Mundo* made this point explicitly by calling the right to development a "dynamic interpenetration of all those fundamental human rights upon which the aspirations of individuals and nations are based."[85] The realization of the right to economic initiative, for example, depends on a number of more basic human rights, such as universal access to education, the right to choose one's vocation, and the right to private property.[86] Thus, Catholic social thought affirms Sen's position that human freedoms are interrelated and that the realization of one depends on the realization of others.

This has another important ramification for understanding the realization of human rights as an important means of institutionalizing solidarity. While some have criticized Roman Catholic rights theory for embracing an overly expansive list of human rights, which makes their realization financially implausible, modern Catholic teaching has moved towards a strategy of "progressive realization." This strategy, which the 1966 International Covenant on Economic, Social, and Cultural Rights recommends, acknowledges that the implementation of economic rights is "subject to the availability of resources ... and the obligation is one of progressive realization."[87] Therefore, priority must be given to those rights whose fulfillment absolutely cannot be postponed. This spawns the idea of "basic rights," which, as Henry Shue states, "are everyone's reasonable minimum demands upon the rest of humanity. They are the rational basis for justified demands the denial of which no self-respecting person can reasonably expect to accept ... rights are basic in the sense used here only if the enjoyment of them is essential to the enjoyment of all other rights ... if a right is basic, other, non-basic rights may be sacrificed, if necessary, in order to secure the basic right. But the protection of a basic right may not be sacrificed in order to secure the enjoyment of the non-basic right."[88] John Paul II and the United States Catholic Conference of Bishops affirmed the full panoply of rights in the Catholic social tradition, but they concluded that the most "elementary" or "basic" are the rights to life, food, education, health care, and shelter.[89] Of course, as the Solidarity movement believed, there are civil and political rights that are equally basic, such as the right to religious freedom and bodily integrity. For the moment, however, this discussion will focus on the necessity of "bread," while acknowledging that the human person does not "live by bread alone."

For example, a person cannot benefit from preventative medicine if she lacks adequate nutrition; insufficient caloric intake leads to diminished cognitive functioning and eventually to death. Nutrition, in turn, is of little value to someone who must endure the threat of avoidable illness. Generally speaking, a person should have a right to that which enables her to live an average lifespan without the need for tragic interventions. Over time, deprivation of any of these basic rights causes serious deficiencies, such as malnutrition or fever due to exposure, that eventually lead to brain damage, other incapacities, or death.[90]

Catholic social thought recognizes that rights claims often conflict, given limited budgetary resources, and that these conflicting claims must somehow be adjudicated. The basic rights theory maintains that, in cases of conflict, those rights that are absolutely required for a dignified human existence cannot be forgone. As John Paul II stated in regard to any right defined as basic, "vis-à-vis these rights, all other rights are secondary and derivative."[91] He placed the onus for the denial of poor persons' basic rights on "a wealthy minority" in "societies where greed and the search for material goods" exist.[92] Thus, he repeated his teaching on the abuse of freedom as a cause of poverty, an assault against freedom of the poor, in the more binding terms of human rights.

There are several implications of advocating basic rights for combating poverty in Poland today. As was stated earlier, the economic, social, and cultural rights set forth in the Constitution have not been fulfilled for many Poles. This is certainly due in part to politicians promoting their own and special interests rather than the common good. This issue can and should also be examined from the perspective of basic rights. For example, the decline of the health-care system, which has especially generated "unfreedoms" for the poor in Poland "B," cannot be justified by a purported lack of funds. When spending has increased in areas such as defense, higher education (which is a right, but it cannot be considered basic in the sense used here), and retirement and disability pensions, the denial of reasonable health care must be seen as unjust. Meanwhile, those with financial capital in cities can afford to take advantage of a growing private, often superior, health-care market. From the perspective of basic rights, Stanisława Golinowska and others are correct to say that the "subsistence minimum should function as the basis for immediate and indispensable aid" from the state.[93] The social minimum can and should be used as an important measure of poverty and the various forms of marginalization that accompany it, such as cultural marginalization. Ideally, this kind of poverty must be eliminated in order for all persons in Polish society to live in dignity. Yet, when choices need to be made due to real budgetary constraints, aid must be given first to those who fall below the subsistence minimum. From the perspective of basic rights, the right to have access to culture or to higher education, for example, is of lesser immediate priority than the right to nutrition, health care, and shelter.

The basic rights of children, moreover, are most egregiously violated in Poland today. This can in part be attributed to a lack of solidarity among generations. Pensioners, who are relatively financially secure because their income per capita is higher than that of the average household, tend not to see the exorbitant rise in costs of their pensions in the 1990s as a strain on the state's ability to fund children's rights to nutrition, housing, and basic medical care. While some retired persons struggle to survive financially, far greater numbers of children live in poverty in Poland. Furthermore, those who did well under the Communist system, such as military generals, now reap very handsome pensions. According to the principle of solidarity, basic rights must trump all other rights claims. Thus, the demands of retired persons for increases in their pensions, especially those who already had fairly generous ones, cannot be condoned from the perspective of solidarity. As was mentioned earlier in the case of wages, the disappearance of this willingness to make sacrifices for the good of others, the "heroism" so prevalent in the days of Solidarity, has caused many of Poland's social problems today.[94]

The progressive realization strategy does mandate, however, moving towards the fulfillment of those rights necessary for the standard of living afforded by the social minimum. This is especially important because, as has been demonstrated, those with greater access to higher education and culture have a much greater chance of fulfilling their basic rights. Moreover, such rights cannot be denied on the basis of what may be called illusory rights conflicts.[95]

This affirmation of the priority of basic rights in Catholic social thought is an expression of solidarity and the option for the poor. These rights represent the absolute minimum requirements for participation in the life of the community. While much has been said heretofore on the right to participation, which is both the precondition of all other human rights and dependent on them, the following section will explicitly demonstrate that fulfilling this right is the key to overcoming poverty in Poland. It will describe several concrete forms of participation that would be fruitful for the attempt to embody solidarity in the struggle against "the enemy" of poverty.

Overcoming Poverty through Participation

An examination of a few concrete forms of participation in Polish society today demonstrates how their absence has contributed to poverty. This section will highlight worker participation and farming as two such forms. It will also discuss some policies that are needed to foster these forms, such as micro lending, job retraining, and access to quality education. These particular forms of participation and policies enabling them must be instituted in order to combat the problem of poverty. In other words, they are indispensable, concrete forms of solidarity with the poor. While other forms of participation in society such as fair and equal political participation exist, those discussed here have special relevance to some of the groups most threatened by the problem of poverty.

Aniela Dylus sees participation as the key to understanding poverty as something greater than material deprivation. She correctly argues that participation is the best approach to attack poverty.[96] Solidarity does not require handouts for the poor. In fact, much evidence demonstrates that long-term financial assistance that does not enable persons to work, develop their skills, and be responsible citizens erodes their desire to participate.[97] Rather, solidarity requires respecting and enabling their duty and right to participation. As John Paul II stated, "[t]he technical details of certain economic problems give rise to the tendency to restrict the discussions about them to limited circles, with the consequent danger that political and financial power is concentrated in a small number of governments and special-interest groups. The pursuit of the national and international common good requires the effective exercise, even in the economic sphere, of the right of all people to share in the decisions which affect them."[98]

According to Catholic social thought, the free market is not the enemy of the poor. Rather, bringing the poor "into the very center of the market" is the best chance of overcoming poverty and marginalization. Unleashing the untapped potential of the poor can be achieved by making them "producers and co-owners," thus they are "invited to full participation, to the co-creation of the common good."[99] Although Dylus points to the social market economy as conducive to this kind of economic participation, she does not elaborate the steps necessary for achieving this in practice. The following examples aim to move in that direction.

Worker Participation: The Unfinished Agenda of Solidarity

The workers' movement of the 1980s in Poland believed in the power of the workers themselves to create strategies for growth and a fair distribution of the fruits of industries' labor. An ethic of solidarity, freedom, and participation mandates that this agenda, which was largely abandoned after 1989 by those with economic and political power, must be revitalized. Unfortunately, vigorous resistance to the idea of worker participation is found among private employers today in the country where Solidarity fought for worker management schemes (*samorządy pracownicze*). William Greider, who sees worker participation as a key ingredient of truly democratic capitalism, mentions that the Warsaw government accepted the opinions of Western experts that worker ownership would derail what they saw as the necessary downsizing of Polish industries.[100] Despite the fact that Poland is bound by international and European legal agreements to foster worker participation, large private employers pressed not to have any mention of it in the nation's labor law.[101]

Like paying just wages, fostering worker participation should be seen as the exercise of freedom in the service of integral, personalist freedom. For example, an employer may encourage employee participation in decisions that affect the production process, profit-sharing schemes, and the overall vision of her company. By doing so, she exercises her economic freedom, embodied in the right to private enterprise, in a way that promotes the participation of the workers in the life of the community. Thus, she exercises her freedom in solidarity. In this sense, worker participation alleviates the form of poverty that can be called "helplessness" or marginalization. Moreover, as former director of General Motors Elmer Johnson contends, "a highly centralized autocratic management style undermines quality and productivity because the masses of employees rightly sense that their feelings, insights, and suggestions are not considered, even in respect to decisions of utmost relevance to their work lives . . . ; managers tap only a fraction of employees' potential for quality workmanship, innovation, and productivity."[102] Admittedly, the goal of fostering participation may sound idealized, as the short-term profit of owners and executives often becomes the sole motivation for defending and exercising a misconceived "economic freedom." However, Johnson's claim, along with other economists' evidence, indicates that worker participation increases productivity and profits. Polish employers generally claim the opposite to be true.[103]

Nonetheless, the possibility of economic freedom fostering personalist freedom, participation, and solidarity through worker participation exists. While employers and corporations that view and exercise economic freedom in this way may be few and far between, some do put solidarity into practice in the realm of free enterprise. Although worker ownership has not been achieved on a widespread scale due to the weaknesses of the Universal Privatization Program, about 200 profitable worker cooperatives arose in the early 1990s.[104] Modern Catholic social teaching has long advocated such worker cooperatives as sources of respect for the dignity of workers as persons and as a means of assuring that their rights are respected in the production process and in the distribution of profits.[105] John Paul II advocated worker ownership in *Laborem Exercens*, criticizing both state socialism and forms of capitalism that generate large concentrations of wealth and property: "we can only speak of socializing only when the subject character of society is ensured ... when on the basis of his work each person is fully entitled to consider himself a part-owner of the great workbench at which he is working with everyone else. A way toward that goal could be found by associating labor with the ownership of capital."[106]

Unfortunately, Poland's road to capitalism has turned from a system in which the Communist party controlled the means of production to one that largely resembles crony capitalism. Privatization led to excessive concentrations of capital and enabled former Communist officials to reap large profits, illegally. This latter violation of justice has been called *prywatyzacja nomenklaturowa*.[107] Succinctly stated, "social justice ... requires creating access to participation for all citizens in the resources generated by the entire society's efforts."[108] Worker-owner companies provide opportunities in Poland for ordinary citizens to undertake responsibility for the necessary, albeit difficult, privatization process. Workers are more likely to act responsibly and to promote the good of the company, which corresponds with their own interest, when they are in control of their own destiny.[109] While some workers in contemporary Poland have demanded inordinate wages, in the few companies that became cooperatives workers did not make excessive demands in terms of wages. Rather, they decided themselves that downsizing was painfully necessary, against the predictions of Polish and Western government officials and employers.[110]

In this regard, Balcerowicz's "wage tax" was unjustifiable from the perspective of participation on several counts. To reiterate, the anthropological assumptions undergirding the policy were false; not all workers in Poland are incapable of weighing the common good above their own gains in wages. Self-interest does not always win the day in a cooperative rather than confrontative environment. (The Polish government, unfortunately, fostered the latter.) When workers understand the ramifications of their own demands and feel responsible for the fate of their companies, they then can come to equitable wage and benefit agreements with their employers. In order for this to happen, though, a spirit of dialogue must exist. Post-1989 Poland has suffered from the lack of this spirit, which was characteristic of the early days of Solidarity.

Catholic social teaching sheds light on the ethical status of political processes that shape wages. It questions the equity of wage policies such as the Balcerowicz tax, which hurt the poorest workers to the largest extent. On the contrary, Catholic principles commended the establishment of the Trilateral Commission for Social and Economic Affairs in 1994. Composed of representatives from the business community, workers from various sectors, and government agents, it began to regulate wages from that point forward. The right to participation in all levels of society, including wage negotiations, flows from the principle of social justice.[111] Economic processes, including wage and price determinations, must not take place over the heads of workers, especially the poor, whose livelihood depends on them. Such formal institutions may only be successful in embodying the principle of solidarity if their participants exhibit the ability to compromise and trust in each others' intentions, which, to recall, were important elements of the pre-1989 ethic of Solidarity. Grażyna Skąpska contends that after a short period of functioning in the spirit of solidarity, the Trilateral Commission became a battleground for employers and unions each trying to get the upper hand.[112] Whether or not this is the case, a multilateral process of wage negotiation should continue to be the goal from the perspective of participation, rather than a centrally determined policy such as Balcerowicz's wage tax in the early 1990s. Moreover, moving towards greater worker ownership may further aid in overcoming the dichotomy between labor and capital, as Catholic social teaching has maintained.

Creating worker management and ownership schemes on a massive scale in Poland will face obstacles. Dylus rightfully maintains that the lack of capital, both financial and human, precludes worker co-ops from competing with bigger, international corporations that have superior technological, financial, and managerial resources. However, abandoning the goal of widespread ownership will lead to a more entrenched form of oligarchical capitalism and greater social unrest as inequalities deepen. More credit should be made available for worker buyouts. In addition, the need for more human capital among workers bolsters the arguments pertaining to the universal right to education and job training.

Unemployment and a Lack of Job Training among Farmers and Agricultural Workers

The discussion of worker participation presumed that workers are involved in an enterprise that feasibly can supply needed goods and services to local and international markets while paying fair wages, maintaining ecological standards, and turning profits that allow for future investments. In Poland's new market economy, these types of opportunities have been hard to come by. Chapter 3 revealed the dismal plight of many farmers and agricultural workers today, many of whom are either unemployed or are victims of "hidden unemployment." Solving the problems of Polish agriculture will be a very complex endeavor and certainly exceeds the limits of this book. The point here, rather, is merely to show those ways in which, from the perspective of justice, solidarity, and participation, farmers and agricultural workers found themselves in this situation not by happenstance but by morally irresponsible choices of those in power. In some instances, members of this group may also be culpable, as lethargy and apathy sometimes hinder their growth towards participation. However, policy choices played an unmistakable role in creating "the other Poland." The policy recommendations here should be taken as possible solutions to very complicated and vexing problems. They are "prudential judgments," to use the language of Catholic social thought. Nonetheless, solidarity requires making an effort to comprehend the nature of these problems and to initiate further debate in the spirit of dialogue.

The government's role in hampering agricultural development prior to 1989 contributed to the unjust situation today. As Catholic social ethicist Józef Majka explained, "the Department of Agriculture [prior to

1989] not only did nothing to strengthen individual farms, but in many instances, and even in the entire politics of collectivized farming, it created particularly difficult conditions for agriculture."[113] As a result, farming in Poland has not kept up with the innovations in agriculture made in Western Europe and the United States.[114] Moreover, farmers "lost faith in themselves and the possibility of recovery and development."[115]

This fact is extremely relevant to assessing the current plight of farmers and agricultural workers. It reveals that the Polish government should take primary responsibility for the debacle it helped to create in the farming industry. For most of the 1990s, farmers have been left alone to struggle to survive. In the last few years, programs sponsored by the European Union and by the government have injected capital into agriculture. For example, the World Bank in 2000 began the Program for Revitalizing Rural Areas in cooperation with the government. Some of these programs move in the direction of instituting solidarity by promoting participation. Of particular value are those that teach new skills to farmers, such as accounting and marketing. However, it is doubtful that the scale of these programs even begins to redress the years of neglect and their consequences.[116]

Micro lending to farmers has been instituted in Poland, for which Balcerowicz deserves some credit.[117] This could be one of the best ways to bring poor farmers "into the very center of the market" by enabling them to modernize and meet the demands of competition from Western Europe. Regrettably, it has only been provided to farmers who already have a substantial amount of capital.[118] However, as chapter 3 related, the earnings of most farmers radically declined in the 1990s. Whether or not subsidizing farmers is justifiable from the perspective of solidarity and social justice is, of course, debatable. Catholic social thought has approved this way of protecting the income levels of farmers in the past.[119] However, the effects of agricultural subsidies, particularly those of the European Union (of which Poland is now a member) and the United States, have greatly disadvantaged underdeveloped nations in gaining access to the markets of wealthy nations.[120] As John Paul II has repeatedly emphasized, solidarity must have a global reach, and the option for the poor must extend to struggling nations.[121] This should give observers reason to pause over the validity of price supports and high import taxes to raise farmers' income. On the other hand, the government owes a debt in justice to its farmers, as was pointed out above, and Polish farmers must compete with Western European farmers whose output is unjustly more heavily subsidized than their own. Resolving this thorny issue will be difficult. One thing is certain: Poor farmers continue to stagnate and live in poverty. They cannot obtain credit and other means of advancement, while those with more capital gain further advantages. This situation violates their right to participation and the principle of solidarity.

The ability of poor farmers to modernize and meet the demands of the Polish and European markets would, of course, be an important form of participation. In addition to providing healthier and safer food products, they would generally strengthen the Polish economy, which currently runs a large deficit with the European Union in the agricultural sector. Some Polish crops and livestock find their way to these markets, but they are not produced by the small farmers who cannot afford the expensive credit needed to modernize and institute European safety controls. From the perspective of solidarity, the fact that credit is available only to those who have capital and are generally better educated—not to the poorest farmers—is unacceptable.[122] This should be seen as another form of "cream-skimming," which, like the "cream-skimming" practiced in job-training programs for the unemployed,[123] clearly stands opposed to solidarity with "the least."

As many farmers and agricultural workers as possible should be empowered to remain in the industry by enhancing their "human capital." However, not all of them will be able to survive in agriculture. The European Union believes that one half of all farmers in Poland will need to retrain in order to work in other occupations. About 30 percent of Poles work in agriculture, as opposed to some 2 percent in the United States and 5 percent in Austria.[124] This means that in the next twenty years, 1.5 million new jobs must be created in Poland "B."[125] Unfortunately, the government did not fund retraining programs for farmers until 2000, although it had supplied such funding for other groups, such as miners and steelworkers, for a number of years earlier. Prior to this, the government had tried to appease farmers with paltry welfare benefits.[126]

Catholic social teaching commends several policy decisions in regard to this situation. First, according to the principle of social justice, "persons have an obligation to be active participants in the life of society," and "society has a duty to enable them to participate in this way."[127]

Catholic social teaching does not insist that the government props up unproductive sectors of the economy ad infinitum. Indeed, some farmers will have to equip themselves with new job skills. However, Catholic social teaching does demand that workers are not left unprotected from the devices of the market. If Polish farmers need to be retrained in order to contribute to the common good, then the government bears an obligation to enable this shift.[128] The numbers of those who are eligible for free job retraining is still very limited, even after the antidiscriminatory legislation was removed.[129] Job training for farmers is a demand of participation in the sense that they should be able to benefit from the common good, but participation also requires serving the common good. By gaining new skills, they are equipping themselves to help build a stronger economy and serve society in areas that are needed. This is much better than handouts, such as disability benefits for those who cannot continue in farming but could fruitfully work in other sectors of the economy.[130]

Some of the few individuals who are eligible for training courses choose not to take advantage of them. Lethargy, disillusion with the job market, or perhaps fear dissuade farmers and agricultural workers from embarking on a new career path. The right and duty to participation requires that the opportunities for new career paths exist. Those persons who cannot contribute to society in the agricultural sector should accept new roles, provided that these new roles allow for growth and procure the right to a living wage. Unfortunately, the jobs offered to the unemployed pay poorly and sometimes offend the dignity of those trying to re-enter the job market.[131] Of course, this discussion of the necessity to equip villagers with more "human capital" so they can successfully re-enter the job market assumes that there are employment opportunities. Currently, such openings are scarce in "the other Poland." When businesses resist investing in rural Poland, one of the main reasons they cite, in addition to poor infrastructure (especially roads), is the low educational status of villagers.[132] As will be argued in more detail below, education is perhaps the sine qua non of fulfilling the right to participation in Poland

Finally, unemployment benefits for those farmers and agricultural workers who find themselves and their families in desperate need are also an important way of maintaining "economic freedoms," such as the ability to escape illness and avoid malnutrition.[133] Throwing money at the poor does not solve the long-term issues leading to their marginalization. A combination of monetary benefits in order to lift persons out of dire need and retraining courses and investment opportunities produces much better results. Such an approach was instituted in the former PGR-y regions from 1995 to 1997, only to be tabled thereafter.[134] Moreover, as chapter 3 stated, unemployment benefits were drastically cut in 1998.[135] In addition to policies that further marginalize unemployed farmers, the current social safety net (*KRUS*) requires poor farmers to pay in the same amount as those who are well educated and run highly profitable farms. Because this form of social assistance is subsidized by the government, it subsidizes poor farmers and wealthy landowners alike. Once again, solidarity and its relationship to the option for the poor have been overlooked. As economist Irena Wóycicka persuasively argues, "it is time to think about not only the state budget but also farmers through their social insurance contributions participating in the financing of benefits for those who cannot afford to pay higher contributions. The rich should help the poorest."[136] She might have added Józef Tischner's well-known claim: "solidarity requires carrying one another's burdens."

The grave disadvantage endured by farmers, agricultural workers, and their children in regard to education, for example, is not just unfortunate. It is a violation of their right to education, which has a profound influence on the ability to fulfill other basic rights and the foundational right to participation. In other words, educational obstacles represent perhaps the primary cause of marginalization in Poland. Like many other challenges faced by the poor, this situation is not a matter of happenstance. Some of the reasons for this predicament will be outlined here, with some preliminary suggestions as to how to remedy it. Employing basic rights theory points to a way of fulfilling this right amid competing rights' claims that place fiscal burdens on the state's resources.

Education as the Precondition to Participation

Educational deficits are a common denominator among all groups of the poor in Poland today. The lack of educational skills, such as literacy and numeracy, are both causes and forms of human poverty. The fact that only 5 percent of all lyceums, or high schools, are located in villages and that tens of thousands of rural schools are doomed to become extinct is morally problematic. It should also be obvious that such situations preclude the right to participation. In *Etyka solidarności oraz homo sovieticus,* Tischner argued that "people rightly say that learning is a good that belongs to the whole of humanity. In other words, learning is for everyone."[137] In today's global economy, scholars across many disciplines often speak about the primacy of "human capital" (that is, skills, educational background, and knowledge), and they point to education as the primary vehicle for attaining "human capital."[138] Without an education that allows people to participate freely and equally in the marketplace and, more broadly, in the polis, they often find themselves in the throes of a cycle of poverty.[139] Without proper training, skills, and knowledge, these people tend to be relegated to the sidelines.[140] As Sen puts it, educational deficiencies seriously detract from the ability to convert multiple functionings into freedoms that all persons wish to enjoy.

In *The Future of Capitalism,* M.I.T. Professor of Economics Lester Thurow contends that "the knowledge investments that have to be made to generate man-made brainpower industries have to be made in a social context completely foreign to the individualistic orientation of capitalism."[141] Polish capitalism receives a failing grade from this perspective. The failure of the Polish government to ameliorate the educational disadvantages of children from poorer, especially rural, backgrounds in any significant way represents perhaps the greatest lack of solidarity in post-1989 Poland. This is all the more reprehensible given that the Constitution guarantees "citizens universal and equal access to education." It also purports to fulfill the right to education by "creating and supporting a system of individual financial and organizational assistance for pupils and college students." The problem resides in the fact that "legislation will specify the conditions of granting aid." The meaning of the right to education demands specification. There have been some praiseworthy improvements. The dynamic creation of new private institutions has led to a dramatic increase in the number of students attending college. However, the tuition costs have made access to such institutions virtually unattainable for the poor, even though student loans have been made available in recent years. Balcerowicz rightly maintains that when education is co-financed by the students themselves, they tend to value it more. But with high interest rates and restrictive co-liability conditions, such resources are of little value to the poor.

Polish policymakers can try to justify reductions in basic and secondary educational spending and slashing of scholarship funds as necessary due to budgetary constraints. However, the basic rights approach advocated above does not accept the educational inequities in Poland quite so easily. The right to education competes with those interests described earlier, such as national defense, and disability and pensions. The latter consumed as much as 26 percent of the national budget.[142] Just as solidarity requires prioritizing the basic rights of the poor to housing, nutrition, and health care over some of the unnecessarily high expenditures for disability and retirement payments, solidarity necessitates evaluating the denials of the right to education in Poland from this perspective. In other words, competing rights claims must be resolved in terms of each good's contribution to the participation of all members of society, particularly the weakest. Because education is central to active participation in Polish society, it too can be considered a basic right. The inability to forsake one's own claims is the antithesis of solidarity and is one of the vestiges of *homo sovieticus* in contemporary Poland. It is also an expression of "false freedom." When individuals conceive their freedom to be the ability to pursue their own interests unabashedly, without consideration of others, they have fallen prey to what John Paul II calls a false ideology of freedom. The personalist freedom of Catholic social thought is often fulfilled by renouncing one's own claims, particularly those that are less urgent for the fulfillment of the right to participation.

Given the inseparability of the right to participation and the right to education, several concrete steps should be proposed towards ameliorating the educational apartheid among Polish youth. First, every effort should be made to maintain quality preschools, grammar schools, and high schools in villages. Incentives such as free housing should be used to attract qualified and committed urban teachers to these areas, as teachers from large cities are more likely to pass on to students the skills necessary to thrive in today's globalized, informational age. Second, as Catholic social teaching recommends, "every effort should be made to ensure that persons be enabled, on the basis of merit, to go on to higher studies, so that, as far as possible, they may occupy posts and take on responsibilities in human society in accordance with the natural gifts and skills they have acquired."[143]

The situation among Poland's poor today reveals quite the contrary. From the perspective of fulfilling human rights according to solidarity and subsidiarity, it is not a violation of the right to higher education per se to require tuition payments or fees from families who can afford them. However, the right to higher education *of the poor* is not respected in Poland today. All fees, such as those charged for entrance examinations, room and board, etc., which create insurmountable financial obstacles for the poor, should be waived. Current state-based financial aid does not meet the needs of the average student of poor parents from rural Poland. The heavy reduction of state funds spent on scholarship aid (*stypendia socjalne*) is unjustifiable. Moreover, fulfillment of the right to higher education first and foremost requires quality basic and secondary education in "the other Poland." In short, priority should be given to meeting the right to equal and adequate education at the basic and secondary levels. However, more must be done to afford all persons their right to higher education in accordance with the progressive realization strategy of human rights. Studying at a university or college is a right of the poor, not just a desirable goal, because in countries such as Poland the poor cannot convert their functionings into capabilities without it.[144] To put it another way, higher education for the poor is the only way to prevent the passing on of poverty and marginalization from generation to generation.

Education must equip marginalized persons with the necessary human capital to move "to the very center of the market." In addition, schools must adopt a pedagogy of solidarity like the one described in terms of the family earlier. This will entail illuminating the ways that individual and group decisions affect other groups. One example might be discussing Polish farming within an unjust global system that favors wealthy nations. This type of cosmopolitan education is imperative in Poland's rural areas, where many people do not even understand the European Union's rules, let alone their own role in marginalizing poorer African farmers.[145] Another way of fostering pedagogy would be, as Dylus suggests, a kind of civil service for college students in order to build relationships of solidarity with the poor. Such efforts should also be undertaken in the earliest stages of education. To recall Tischner's claim, hope must be "worked on" at all levels of human development. Education must attempt to instill the anthropology of hope in young Poles so that they do not adopt the pessimistic view, *homo homini lupus*. Social mistrust must be attacked at its roots, namely, a Hobbesian-Spencerian anthropology that leads individuals to seek their own interests at all cost, rather than striving to promote the common good. In this regard, John Paul II observed that solidarity is a virtue as well as a principle to be embodied in social structures. In other words, when human persons encounter the other, each must see in him or her a "partner," as Adam saw in Eve and Eve in Adam in the Creation story found in Genesis.[146] The Roman Catholic tradition has a key role to play in inculcating a pedagogy of solidarity. Thus far, it has had successes and failures in doing so during Poland's "era of freedom."[147] The degree to which the Roman Catholic Church has advanced perspectives on solidarity, freedom, and participation warrants special consideration given its unique place in Polish society.

CHAPTER SIX

Promoting an Ethic of Solidarity as Evangelization

The Church's Social Witness in Poland since 1989

> *The Polish Church has a long tradition of providing aid to the needy, so-called works of mercy: preschools, centers for mentally challenged children, shelters for the homeless, etc. This has always been there and continues to be in the Polish Church.... It crystallized in the unwavering support for the underground Solidarity activists. Therefore, it is a distressing paradox, that basically the Polish Church has not put forth any answers to the specific moral challenges of the new era. Why?*[1]
> —Roman Graczyk

This book has considered the meaning of solidarity, its disintegration in Poland after 1989, and its potential recovery. It has attempted to show that solidarity, freedom, and participation can and should be embodied in policies and institutions that work toward overcoming the evil of poverty. At this point, the focus will turn to one of the institutions in Poland with the greatest potential to promote solidarity, namely, the Roman Catholic Church. In other words, this chapter shifts from the *content* of an ethic of solidarity, freedom, and participation to one of the most important *agents* of the promotion of this ethic in Poland today.

The Roman Catholic Church has received widespread recognition for its important role in the Solidarity movement leading up to 1989. However, many commentators have scrutinized its activities in the "era of freedom" much less favorably. The Church no longer needs to champion the rights of the oppressed in the same way as it did under Communism. With the fall of Communism, most of the so-called civil and political rights, such as the freedom to vote in democratic elections, the freedom of expression, and the freedom to worship, have been enshrined in law. Dissidents are no longer incarcerated for their opinions and religious believers are not persecuted. However, the Church has a pivotal role to play in ensuring that all policy decisions embody solidarity, participation, and a proper understanding of freedom's relationship to these values. Relying mainly on official Roman Catholic social teaching, and John Paul II's homilies and speeches in Poland after 1989, this chapter advances the claim that the Church must play this role in order to be faithful to its mission of evangelization.

Succinctly stated, the institutional Church—more specifically, the Polish bishops' conference—has not yet fully recognized the promotion of concrete structures and policies that would embody an ethic of solidarity, freedom, and participation as "a constitutive dimension of the preaching of the Gospel."[2] It has seldom championed the economic rights of the poor even though the Church's mission of evangelization demands this stance.[3] Because poverty is the arena in which an ethic of solidarity is most needed, the Church must evangelize by more vigorously combating poverty. Thus, this chapter provides a critique of the bishops' response to the signs of the times on two levels: 1) their social policy prescriptions and appropriate social and political engagement; and 2) the theology that stands behind these activities.

Given the constraints of the book, this chapter largely focuses on the official statements and actions of the Polish bishops' conference. Some attention will be given to practical initiatives taken by the larger Church in order to attack poverty. The largest NGO and Catholic organization in Poland, Caritas Polska, will serve as a case study in order to show the kinds of action undertaken and the kinds of action that ought to be undertaken by the Church. A few other key initiatives of Catholic organizations will be mentioned briefly. However, this chapter cannot provide a detailed analysis of the myriad Catholic organizations, both lay and clerical, that have sprung into existence in Poland since 1989.[4]

This gap is admittedly a weakness. A complete analysis of the promotion of an ethic of solidarity by the Church would certainly entail a discussion of the economic, social, and political activities of the many groups that constitute the Church. However, this chapter contends that the bishops' conference is a logical and justifiable place to begin an analysis of the social witness of the Roman Catholic Church in Poland. According to Catholic social teaching, bishops hold a particular responsibility for analyzing the signs of the times in the light of the Gospel. However, this claim in no way implies that Catholic social teaching is not influenced "from below." Grassroots movements and events "on the ground" have often contributed to the shaping of the Church's social teaching.[5] Nevertheless, only the bishops can learn from these movements and promulgate authoritative teaching. With this disclaimer about what this chapter can and cannot accomplish, a word about the unique role of the Roman Catholic Church in Polish society is in order.

From Defender of Freedom and Human Rights to "Besieged Fortress"

The Roman Catholic Church has historically advocated the freedom of the individual in Poland, while also stressing the obligation of each member of society to contribute to the common good. Importantly, though, the Church did not support the Solidarity movement only on the level of ideas. It is true that some leaders of Solidarity felt dissatisfied with the level of support offered by the Church at times. For example, Cardinal Józef Glemp, who became the Primate of Poland after the death of the legendary Cardinal Stefan Wyszyński in 1980, was criticized for being too conciliatory towards the Communist regime and not unequivocal enough in his endorsement of Solidarity, particularly of its method of strikes.[6] Nonetheless, the practical activity of the Church in support of Solidarity was crucial to the movement's success. A historical reconstruction of the role of bishops and clergy in Solidarity exceeds the scope of this analysis. Others have chronicled the heroic deeds of Church members, both clerics and laity.[7] It suffices to say here that in spite of these occasionally justifiable criticisms, the bishops and clergy often acted in the practical realm to abet the movement and its goals in myriad ways.

As a result, virtually all Poles recognize the Church's pivotal role in the defeat of Communism. Leszek Kołakowski, a former member of the Communist party and critic of the Church, echoed in 1987 what most Poles continue to believe: "Today it is clear that Catholicism in Poland should be acknowledged as the main factor during the entire postwar period that led to a society and country that could not be 'Sovietized.' Even if Catholicism can be criticized on a philosophical or intellectual level, it was the most important aspect of resistance to the Sovietization of Poland. It was decisive."[8]

The reputation of the Church as the defender of freedom and human rights in Poland took a different turn after 1989, however. After its victory in its bout with atheistic Communism, the Church encountered harsh criticism. According to Polish polling agencies, from 1989 to 1995 the approval of the Church's role in public life fell from slightly above 90 percent to about 50 percent.[9] Catholic historian Jarosław Gowin enumerates a series of controversial decisions as contributing factors to this decline: the demand to return Roman Catholic religion classes to public schools, the hierarchy's repeated uncompromising stance on abortion (including its prohibition even when the mother's life is in jeopardy), the political campaigning of clergy and bishops for certain candidates during the 1991 elections, the call for "respect of Christian values" in education and mass media, and the attempt to regain Church property expropriated by the Communists, even when this meant the closing of state-administered schools, hospitals, and shelters.[10] In addition to these reasons, Polish citizens feared the Church's desire to create a theocratic state. Moreover, the post-Communists, in order to restore their reputation and thereby position themselves to regain power, criticized the "black dictatorship" of the clergy, which, in their view, replaced the pre-1989 "red dictatorship."[11] Whether or not the fears of theocracy were legitimate is debatable. Nonetheless, many members of Polish society decried the "theocratic tendencies" of the Church. Luminaries such as Nobel laureate Czesław Miłosz and philosopher Leszek Kołakowski were among their ranks.¹² Its real or perceived attempt to "legislate morality" contributed to the rising mistrust towards the Church.

In response to these criticisms, the Church largely took a defensive, sometimes hostile, stance, rather than patiently explaining its decisions and searching for dialogue. Former Solidarity leader Adam Michnik, who had once admired it for its tolerance, respect, and efforts to instill hope in all people, lamented that "for a significant number of people the Church has become like a besieged fortress, whose defenders look everywhere for enemies and cast calumnies upon them."¹³

"Secularizing Solidarity" Not the Answer?

Given the decline of the Church's authority concerning its role in the public sphere, one might conclude that it has exhausted its ability to be a force for solidarity, freedom, and human rights in Poland. Would the promotion of solidarity in democratic Poland be better served if the Church were to extract itself from the public sphere? Might the task be better undertaken by nongovernmental organizations that do not "lay hold of God" by making absolute-truth claims? Some contemporary voices in Poland have joined the ranks of Enlightenment thinkers such as Pierre Bayle, Voltaire, and David Hume in calling for the privatization of religion as the means to serve justice and the common good. Hume argued in his famous treatise *Dialogues Concerning Natural Religion* that dogmatic religions that claim to "lay hold of God" erode the human "attachment to the natural motives of justice and humanity."¹⁴ In a similar vein, contemporary Polish philosopher Jan Woleński writes that the "desacralization of nations, that is, the freeing of them from overarching conceptions of the good, was one of the foundations of modern European civilization, and it is a good idea not to vitiate this [in Poland today]."¹⁵

Myriad religious wars, persecutions, and injustices committed "in the name of God," of course, have tarnished religion's record concerning the promotion of peace and human rights throughout Western history. However, the matter is not as simple as "throwing the baby out with the bathwater." The complete demise of religion's public face is highly unlikely. Samuel Huntingdon's empirical data pertaining to the "unsecularization of the world" represent just one of many studies indicating this.[16] As Peter Berger trenchantly put it, "every human society is an enterprise of world-building. Religion occupies a distinctive place in this enterprise."[17] In Berger's view, religion is that which prevents human beings from plunging into anomie. Emile Durkheim also contended that religion is the "glue" that binds society together. In short, religion will survive the attacks of the "cultured despisers." The question turns on *what kind of religion will survive*. As R. Scott Appleby argues in *The Ambivalence of the Sacred*, most religions are inherently polyvalent; they contain both elements that divide and ostracize "the other" while also possessing resources that promote justice and peace for all people, regardless of their faith commitments. Strong but moderate religions make key contributions to civil society in the areas of trade unions, independent media, civic organizations, and private schools.[18] "Religions will not be easy allies to engage, but the struggle for human rights cannot be won without them."[19] This is particularly trenchant in the case of Poland.

Moreover, Roman Catholicism has been and will continue to be a mainstay in Polish culture and society. In sixteenth-century Poland the phrase "a Pole is a Catholic" (*Polak, to katolik*) became a part of common parlance. To this day, more than 90 percent of all Poles identify themselves as Roman Catholic. This means that in a country of almost 39 million people, approximately 35 million are Roman Catholic.[20] Religiosity in Poland intriguingly illustrates the ambiguity of the so-called "secularization thesis." Unlike most societies in Western Europe, and in defiance of negative predictions made in the early 1990s,[21] more than 90 percent of Poles profess belief in God and 63 percent attend Sunday Mass. One can readily find the influence of religious values in Polish poetry, philosophy, art, and politics. In fact, the Warsaw government, in accordance with the wishes of John Paul II, vociferously pressed (to no avail) for explicitly mentioning "Christian values" in the European Constitution.

For certain, however, the reputation of the Church has been tarnished since 1989. Its "triumphalism" after the victory against Communism generated harsh criticism. Nonetheless, the institutional Church continues to occupy an extremely important place in contemporary Poland. In spite of his criticisms of the Church after 1989, Michnik correctly contended that "Polish democracy needs the church; it needs the voice of conscience. It needs a church that speaks the language of the Gospel."[22] The Roman Catholic Church is the largest organization in Poland, after the government, and continues to exert a great deal of influence.[23] Even those who oppose any public role of religion in Poland begrudgingly concede that the Church is one of the most significant non-governmental actors in the social and political spheres.[24] Thus, as Michnik and others have argued, there is "no alternative" to Catholicism in Poland; it will continue to influence Polish society. The real issue is what kind of Catholicism will perdure in the nation throughout the early part of the twenty-first century. Will the Church advocate normative visions of solidarity, freedom, and participation rooted in Catholic social thought? Conversely, will it be a source of division, appealing to polarizing categories in defense of "true freedom" and attempting to "separate the wheat from the tares"? The Roman Catholic Church is poised to play an important role in revitalizing an ethic of solidarity to meet the demand of contemporary Polish society given its unique place in that society. However, it must choose to play this role.

The record since 1989 is mixed. At times, numerous groups have instrumentalized the Catholic tradition for the sake of goals that dubiously resemble the tenets of Catholic social teaching. One example relates to the "Catholic pro-family politics" promoted by groups such as the Polish Federation of Associations of Catholic Families. While such groups do promote some goals that cohere with Catholic social teaching, such as counting a mother's childrearing years towards her retirement fund, other parts of the agenda do not promote solidarity with the poor.[25] Social critic Ewa Nowakowska has persuasively argued that a proposed tax reduction proportionate to the number of children (thus promoting the Catholic procreation agenda) would, in effect, aid only families with middle- to high-bracket incomes because most low-income families with many children subsist purely on public assistance.[26] The latter, the truly poor, therefore would not benefit from the proposed tax policy.

Admittedly, because of the complicated nature of such policies, their validity can be debated among people of goodwill. Yet, other examples more glaringly illustrate the Church's failure as a witness of solidarity after 1989. For example, those who have demonized others in the name of the Catholic faith because of their points of view have exhibited a clear lack of will towards fostering solidarity. As was noted earlier, Michnik and others have drawn attention to the vitriol with which some, including certain bishops, maligned "crypto-Communists." Among them, Bishop Michalik chastised those who opposed catechesis in public schools, referring to them "as enemies of the Cross and the Gospel" and "echoes of the voice of Satan."[27] In another statement, the same bishop urged Catholics to vote for Catholics, Jews for Jews, Muslims for Muslims, Freemasons for Freemasons, and Communists for Communists.[28] In addition, many Catholics have caricatured "liberals" as licentious, sex-driven heathens.[29] Tischner aptly characterized the problem after 1989: "Who is a 'real Catholic'? Who is a 'real Christian'? Who is a 'real Pole'? . . . These questions serve the wrong goal today: exclusion, derision, accusation."[30] Cardinal Francis Macharski went so far as to say that "social divisions, even religious ones, are a real Polish sickness, an epidemic" in a homily during the celebration of the 750th year of Saint Stanisław's canonization.[31] In short, a lack of will to promote solidarity, which "turns against no one," clearly exists among many Roman Catholics in Poland today.

Some Catholic groups and organizations have admirably sought to foster solidarity, freedom, and participation. Tischner and editors of the Catholic periodical *Znak* attempted to debunk many of the negative stereotypes of "liberals."[32] Catholic media outlets such as *Znak*, *Tygodnik Powszechny*, and *Więź* have tried to address social issues that were considered taboo for Catholics. For example, many bishops and conservative Catholics have no interest in hearing the claims of feminists. Indeed, they see feminism as one of the nefarious "isms," which, along with liberalism, will erode the morals of Polish society. While more could be published to promote greater understanding of feminism, in its myriad forms, these media sources have made initial efforts. *Więź* devoted one of its monthly issues to the topic of "new feminism." For its part, *Tygodnik Powszechny* publishes a column on women of the Bible written by Elżbieta Adamiak, one of the few published feminist theologians in Poland today.[33] All of this may seem insignificant. However, in a country where most Catholics think that feminist theology is not a legitimate enterprise and where women face many discriminatory practices, these are steps in the right direction. They are attempts to foster dialogue and mutual understanding, which are important ingredients of social trust, the foundation of solidarity. In terms of realizing solidarity with the poor, Catholic organizations such as Caritas Polska and Fundacja Nadzieja have made strides in the right direction. However, as will be discussed below, more can and should be done by Catholic organizations to develop real solidarity with the poor.

In short, the Church has exhibited tendencies towards both hindering and promoting an ethic of solidarity in post-1989 Poland, where it has failed to reach its full potential as an agent of solidarity, freedom, and participation. This issue in large part turns on the understanding of the Church's mission of evangelization.

Evangelization and the Pursuit of Social Justice

Prior to Vatican II, the magisterium considered the pursuit of social justice, called the "social apostolate," to be "pre-evangelization."[34] It was not seen as a part of the Church's mission in the same way as, for example, celebrating the sacraments.[35] Vatican II's *Gaudium et Spes* initiated a reconceptualization of the meaning of evangelization and its relationship to social justice.[36] The 1971 World Synod of Bishops went further in *Justitia in Mundo*. They argued that "[a]ction on behalf of justice and participation in the transformation of the world fully appear to us as a constitutive dimension of the preaching of the Gospel."[37] This text, in particular the word "constitutive," generated concerns about excessive "horizontalism." As a result, Paul VI clarified the issue in *Evangelii Nuntiandi* (1975). He proclaimed that evangelization would be incomplete without concern for human rights and social justice. In other words, evangelization must include the pursuit of social justice and the defense of human rights as a necessary component, albeit a secondary one.[38] Announcing that God offers salvation to all in Jesus Christ constitutes the "foundation" and "center" of evangelization.[39] However, Paul VI located the primary means of evangelization in "the witness of an authentically Christian life, given over to God . . . and at the same time given over to one's neighbor with limitless zeal."[40]

Succinctly stated, the Church must take some stance regarding socioeconomic issues, and this constitutes an indispensable dimension of evangelization. However, disagreement arises concerning the level of specificity appropriate to the magisterium's teaching on such matters. On the one hand, in *Octogesima Adveniens* (1971), Paul VI challenged local churches to "discern the options and commitments which are called for in order to bring about the social, political, and economic changes . . .

urgently needed."[41] Yet, *Justitia in Mundo* stated that the Church's mission does not entail offering "concrete solutions in the social, economic, and political spheres for justice in the world."[42] John Paul II portrayed the issue in a similar vein in *Laborem Exercens*.[43] However, he, along with the previous popes, did not hesitate to offer specific policy proposals. For example, John XXIII recommended agricultural subsidies in *Mater et Magistra*.[44] In another case, John Paul II offered concrete proposals concerning wages and joint ownership of the means of production in *Laborem Exercens*.[45]

The U.S. Catholic Conference of Bishops clearly responded to Paul VI's challenge in *Octogesima Adveniens* with their pastoral, *Economic Justice for All*. They claimed that while their "prudential judgments" do not have the same level of authority as their moral principles, they "feel obliged to teach by example how Christians can undertake concrete analysis and make specific judgments on economic issues." They contended that the Church's teaching cannot remain on the level of "appealing generalities."[46] The Catholic Bishops' Conference of England and Wales wrote likewise. In their view, remaining on the level of broad generalities to avoid controversy would be a "failure in moral courage."[47] They recommended such policies as a statutory minimum wage, suggesting that it should equal a living wage.[48]

This book argues that Paul VI correctly challenged local churches to apply the Church's social teaching to their specific contexts in *Octogesima Adveniens* (no. 4) and that these bishops' conferences appropriately heeded him for several reasons. Policy proposals must consider the empirical realities of a given society in order to be effective. Therefore, local bishops' conferences cannot simply reiterate universal social teaching.[49] Of course, the more specific Church teaching becomes, the less certitude it can claim; complex policy issues require technical expertise sometimes beyond the competence of bishops. In addition, outcomes are often hard to predict. Thus, differences of opinion regarding concrete courses of action should be respected.[50] Nonetheless, while recognizing this fact, bishops have an obligation to attempt to propose the concrete means to protect the dignity of the human person. Lay experts can and should lend their knowledge to this task. Practically speaking, the bishops' collective voice carries more weight than those of individual Catholics or Catholic organizations. Theologically speaking, if the bishops possess a special duty to proclaim the Gospel,[51] and this involves the effective pursuit of social justice, then they must be willing to propose policies that embody the Church's social teaching. Hence, in the case of Poland, bishops must be willing to demonstrate how solidarity, freedom, and participation can be embodied in social policies.[52]

The Bishops' Response to the Signs of the Times after 1989

The Polish bishops seldom spoke out on economic issues for most of the first decade after the fall of Communism. When they did, their remarks were general and uncritically supportive (that is, seen as "painful, but necessary") of the government's reforms.[53] While the bishops did mention issues such as poverty at times, they never made a serious attempt to diagnose its causes and propose solutions.[54] This was the case in spite of John Paul II's numerous pleas to read the signs of the times and respond to them. For example, during his 1997 pilgrimage, the pontiff stated: "We stand before the great challenges of the present day. I have drawn attention to this before, in my speech to the Bishops' Conference of Poland during my pilgrimage in 1991. At that time, I said 'the human person is the way of the Church.' . . . The task of the Episcopate and the Church in Poland is to somehow translate that into the language of concrete problems and tasks, utilizing the conciliar vision of the Church as the People of God and the related analogy of the 'signs of the times.'"[55] Exploring how the bishops perceive the relationship between evangelization and social justice and their understanding of the specificity question will illuminate their shortcomings and more recent strides since 1989. While in the 1990s the bishops were largely reluctant to promote solidarity, freedom, and participation in the domain of poverty, they made several concerted efforts to grapple with the problem since the year 2000, as shall be shown below.[56] Yet, more work needs to be done.

Evangelization and Social Justice in the Minds of the Bishops

When asked in 2000 why the Church had not issued a separate document on poverty in Poland, the late Bishop Jan Chrapek of Radom responded: "Up until this point, action has been more important. I fear that we still speak too uninterestingly about the Lord Jesus; social issues cannot dominate the basic mission of the Church, namely, evangelizing."[57] He maintained that solidarity with the poor is a "consequence of faith." It does not belong to the most important task of the Church, which is to "proclaim the risen Christ." Yet, he also argued that the Church is not faithful to its mission if it does not "stand unequivocally on the side of the poor and the marginalized."[58] There is a tension in what the bishop stated. On the one hand, he seems to view action on behalf of social justice as secondary to the Church's mission. However, he sees it as an intrinsic part of it. It is simply not a part of what he calls "evangelization." He appears to be thinking in the pre-Vatican II terminology of "pre-evangelization." This confused notion of evangelization helps to explain the bishops' inertia in the face of the deleterious socioeconomic trends after 1989 in Poland.[59] Several important episcopal documents directly address the relationship between evangelization and social justice. Rather than making rash judgments based on one interview, an examination of these documents must be undertaken here.

In a document published by the 309th Plenary Assembly of the Conference of Bishops, the bishops justified their concerns regarding poverty, unemployment, corruption, and rising crime by appealing to John Paul II's notion of "new evangelization."[60] According to the pope, "[t]he 'new evangelization' which the modern world urgently needs . . . must include among its essential elements a proclamation of the Church's social doctrine."[61] It is noteworthy that the bishops claimed to view concern for social problems under the rubric of "new evangelization." However, can it be concluded on this basis that they fully accept the promotion of social justice as a constitutive element of preaching the Gospel? The following analysis will attempt to answer this question.

The Polish bishops devoted the first document of the II Plenary Synod, which lasted from 1991 to 1999, to the topic of "new evangelization" at the end of the millennium. The accent on the social justice dimension of evangelization is unmistakable here: "The Church's mission of evangelization also concerns temporal realities. Making the world more human belongs to the essence of the economy of salvation, first, because the divine plan of making everything anew in Christ touches all of creation, and next because the inhuman dimensions of earthly realities hinders, and sometimes even precludes, accepting the gift of salvation."[62] The bishops pointed out that evangelization entails witnessing to Christ's

Gospel "by word," in addition to deed (no. 11; compare no. 13). However, they stressed the following among the "priorities of new evangelization" in Poland: propagating the principles of Catholic social teaching (no. 52); the formation of consciences and the building of the moral order, which includes promoting the common good and care for the needy (no. 54); and special concern for the poor, which stems from the Church's preferential option for the poor (no. 55). The individual parish should facilitate attaining these goals. For example, the parish community should teach and act in order to aid families, children, the sick, the unemployed, and various professional groups (no. 48). Hence, the bishops clearly highlighted concern for social justice as an aspect of evangelization in this document. In this connection, they cited the pope's exhortation to analyze the signs of the times (no. 15), in democratic, capitalist Poland.

In the Synodal document on the role of the laity, which has been traditionally neglected in the Church in Poland, the bishops also described "proclaiming the Kingdom of God" through word and deed. In their view, the laity "in their own way" participate in evangelization, which takes place, as *Lumen Gentium* puts it, "in the ordinary surroundings of the world."[63] Pondering this phrase, one wonders if and how the laity and the ordained evangelize differently. This question will return later in this chapter. For the moment, the discussion of evangelization in the document on the missionary activity of the Church is of immediate interest.

In this document, the bishops appear to have qualified some of their ideas from the document on evangelization. They chastised "excessive horizontalism," which they also referred to as the "secularization of salvation."[64] Citing John Paul II's admonitions in *Redemptoris Missio*, the bishops insisted that "Christians first and foremost should 'clearly affirm our faith in Christ, the one Savior of mankind, a faith we have received as a gift from on high, not as a result of any merit of our own.'"[65] Furthermore, "bearing witness to and proclaiming salvation in Jesus Christ and creating local churches" comprise the primary missionary activities of the Church. Helping the poor, contributing to the liberation of the oppressed, aiding development, and defending human rights represent legitimate missionary enterprises, but they must be deemed secondary.[66]

Does a tension or even contradiction exist in the bishops' statements from various documents? Claiming that professing salvation in Jesus Christ *ad gentes* constitutes the primary goal of evangelization does not preclude viewing concern for social justice as part of its essence. This seems to be the position of the Polish bishops, which is entirely consistent with Paul VI's position as it was described earlier. However, Paul VI also maintained that the primary means of evangelization, or proclaiming Christ to be our savior, comes in the form of an authentically Christian life given over to God and one's neighbor.

John Paul II and the Polish bishops have rightfully confronted religious indifferentism.[67] Giving "an account of one's hope" (1 Pet. 3:15) must, of course, remain a perennial task of the Church.[68] However, this goal becomes problematic if it hinders or omits striving for social justice.[69] Paul VI's formulation of "an authentically Christian life" as the primary means of evangelization precludes truncating evangelization in this manner. While the admonitions of John Paul II and the Polish bishops may be judicious, they can lead to an improper relativization or prioritization among the goals of evangelization. A dangerous lapse into seeing social justice as merely an addendum to the Gospel, important but not necessary, lurks around the corner. In this case, the emphasis of *Justitia in Mundo* on "constitutive" is completely eradicated.[70]

This type of prioritization among the goals of evangelization, whether conscious or not, partially explains the Polish bishops' scant attention to socioeconomic issues. Some of their teaching has clearly underscored social justice as a key ingredient of evangelization. Yet, Bishop Chrapek's statement and the qualifications regarding the promotion of social justice as intrinsic to the Church's missionary activity discussed above attest to the ambivalence of the bishops on this issue. In this regard, they have misconstrued the message of John Paul II, who told them that bishops especially must "lead the People of God ... in announcing the Gospel of love, in calling attention to those whom no one mentions." In his words, the "enduring and selfless witness of active love has an inextricable link with evangelization because it witnesses to God's love ... let the voice of the Church be clear and audible everywhere where the fate and the rights of the homeless, deserted, hungry, disabled, and the marginalized need to be recalled."[71] Even if the pope maintained that evangelization first entails the proclamation of Jesus as our Redeemer and then the promotion of social justice and concern for the poor and oppressed in that order, he did not intend to say that the latter can be attended to selectively and sporadically.

Differences exist among individual bishops regarding the weight that they should accord to social issues. For example, in an interview concerning the mission of the Church in Poland, several bishops were asked what they perceive to be the most important tasks of the Church today. Bishop Adam Śmigielski named "announcing the message of salvation to all people without exception" as the "basic task." He placed helping poor families and charitable activities to relieve victims of disasters and addictions as the fifth and sixth items, respectively, on the Church's pastoral agenda.[72] When asked the same question, Bishop Marian Gołębiewski responded quite differently: "Taking into consideration the specific conditions in which the faithful of the Koszalin-Kołobrzeg diocese live, I would say the Church must first and foremost realize the option for the poor." He went on to say: "This means imbuing the structures of state life, institutions of social life, local government and congressional communities, and a wide range of human activity with the spirit of the Gospel and [the norms of] Catholic social teaching."[73]

Divisions clearly exist within the bishops' conference on certain issues.[74] The differences in the documents on "new evangelization" and "mission" are not irreconcilable. However, they may manifest disagreement among the bishops. In truth, a host of other factors inhibited them from speaking out against the negative consequences of the socioeconomic reforms after 1989. Reviewing them will further demonstrate that the bishops did not sufficiently grapple with the "signs of the times" throughout most of Poland's era of freedom.[75] It will explain why the bishops were not more active in promoting solidarity, freedom, and participation.

Aniela Dylus attributes the bishops' reticence during the first several years of the socioeconomic transformations to three things. First, she points to their fear of being perceived and portrayed as biased towards a political party. Approval or criticism of given social policies might be construed as approval or disapproval of the party that crafted those policies. Second, she claims that the bishops wrote relatively little about the highly complex socioeconomic reforms because evaluating socioeconomic issues, such as privatization, requires expertise that the bishops do not have. Such expertise exceeds the general knowledge of Catholic social thought. In her opinion, appealing to abstract principles and values such as the common good, social justice, or the primacy of labor over capital does not suffice. In this sense, she believes that it was appropriate for the bishops to use restraint when considering the socioeconomic realities of the 1990s in Poland. And third, many outcomes of the social and economic policy decisions were still unclear. Thus, it would be inappropriate to make rash judgments about them early in the transformation process.[76]

Gowin blames the lack of serious, sustained reflection in this area on several factors.[77] First, the bishops were not prepared for this "unexpected meeting with capitalism." In other words, they lacked the kind of training needed to undertake serious reflection on economics. Unfortunately, distrust towards laypersons continued to hinder fruitful consultation with lay experts after 1989.[78] Second, Gowin maintains that the antiabortion theme dominated the speeches and statements of the bishops' conference.[79] While this may have changed in the latter part of the decade, abortion certainly absorbed the bishops' attention until 1997. And third, the Church feared that if it criticized the reforms, it would be attacked and deemed "anti-Polish" or "anti-national." In fact, the left and the right did criticize the Church. For example, the head of Prime Minister Hanna Suchocka's cabinet claimed that the Church's hierarchy still acted as though they were in a battle with Communism by not supporting the government's (neoliberal) reforms. On the other hand, Catholic intellectuals such as Church historian Bohdan Cywiński criticized the hierarchy's blind acceptance of neoliberal economic proposals that invariably hurt the weakest members of society the most, thus violating the preferential option for the poor.[80]

This onslaught of criticism, coupled with the general decline of the Church's authority in Poland, led many bishops to believe that it should withdraw from the political sphere.[81] Bishop Tadeusz Pieronek, the secretary general of the Polish episcopate from 1993 to 1998, proposed this course of action on many occasions.[82] However, like John Paul II, he has called for a Church that is politically neutral but socially engaged. Bishop Pieronek offered an apologetic for the Church's insufficeint scrutiny of the socioeconomic trends and policies instituted in Poland in the last decade:

> Has the Church in Poland sufficiently called attention to the fate of the weakest? ... It was difficult to protest against appropriate re-

forms. It was difficult to demand that the bishops proposed to the economists better solutions, especially because the economists assured us that the economic recovery would benefit all. The Church was nonetheless accused of not supporting the reforms strongly enough. However, the Church can never give up calling attention to the most needy.... Enough of that voice did not exist in recent years, or at least it was not heard enough.[83]

Bishop Pieronek directly acknowledged that the Church mistakenly closed its eyes to the uneven sharing of the burdens of the economic transformation, which led to a "serious increase in the number of people below the social minimum."[84] In his pastoral letter of 2001 on unemployment, Archbishop Damian Zimoń of Śląsk went even further, criticizing the Church's acceptance of neoliberal economic reforms that had caused greater unemployment. Therefore, he argued, the Church should now lucidly articulate a position that does not accept the negative effects of the economic transformation.[85]

Succinctly stated, the Church did not live up to the demands of solidarity and the option for the poor. Pieronek and Zimoń are among the few bishops to admit the failures of the Church in the face of poverty in the 1990s. Their frank observations adumbrate the related question pertaining to the specificity of Catholic social teaching. What level of specificity is required of the Church's social teaching in Poland today if it is to be a church of solidarity and the option for the poor?

Specificity and Application of Catholic Social Teaching

Should the bishops say nothing at all if they cannot adeptly handle complex socioeconomic policy questions, as Dylus implies? A substantial number of Roman Catholics in Poland believe that the Church should never pronounce on social issues such as unemployment, regardless of their knowledge of the subject.[86] Franciszek Kampka, a former advisor on social issues to the bishops' conference, contended that when "it seems that the economic system does not respect the dignity of the human person, the Church cannot be silent and must take a strong stance." Yet, he maintained that the Church's teaching on economic life must remain at a certain level of generality. The Church should not analyze the technical, economic changes that economists handle. For example, it might speak in favor of private property, but it should not propose a concrete model of privatization.[87]

As was alluded above, the bishops did write about the socioeconomic transformations of the early 1990s, but only sporadically throughout most of the decade. They did delve into some specific policy areas in a few of the Synodal documents and in the 2001 pastoral, *W trosce o nową kulturę życia i pracy* (In Concern for a New Culture of Life and Work). On these occasions, they have taken positive steps. However, they still have not gone far enough. They have not persistently promoted policies that embody solidarity, freedom, and participation.

Prior to the Synodal documents, the bishops' conference touched upon privatization and reprivatization,[88] poverty, unemployment, and the "wealth gap" in Poland in a few places.[89] Appealing to *Centesimus Annus,* the bishops mentioned that those plagued by unemployment and poverty deserve protection by "political organizations, unions, and greater interest and aid from society."[90] They failed, however, to recommend concrete ways in which these various agents can and should help those who suffer. The documents lack analysis of the causes of poverty and unemployment, and no relationship is shown between low wages and poverty. To their credit, the bishops note that "blameless poverty" (a term that the World Bank has used in contradistinction to "deserved poverty") often precludes educational opportunities for advancement. Yet, there is no mention of policies to remedy this injustice, such as targeted scholarship aid and raises in salaries for teachers in villages. In short, these documents, along with others similar in nature and tone, represent necessary attempts to address social ills in Poland. However, they do not respond to Paul VI's call to "discern the options and commitments" necessary for social, economic, and political change that would embody solidarity, freedom, and participation, thereby making Poland more just.

In the Synodal document entitled "The Church on Socioeconomic Life," the bishops stated that although the Church does not provide specific policy recommendations, it must denounce all forms of social injustice and formulate general principles that should govern socioeconomic life.[91] The bishops reiterated this stance in several other documents.[92] They also pointed out that some politicians mistakenly expected the hierarchy to designate "the Catholic position" in cases where the Church leaves room for debate and disagreement on concrete applications of its teaching.⁹³ Appealing to *Gaudium et Spes,* the bishops argued that the laity themselves should look for their own answers, and that it is wrong to expect concrete solutions to every problem from the bishops.⁹⁴ Unfortunately, they excluded a significant qualification from the same paragraph of *Gaudium et Spes*: bishops must undertake "unremitting study" in order to engage in greater dialogue with the world and to ensure that "all earthly activities ... will be bathed in the light of the Gospel."⁹⁵

Many Poles had great expectations for the documents of the II Polish Plenary Synod of Bishops. Committees headed by esteemed theologians such as Fr. Józef Tischner and Fr. Andrzej Zuberier wrote the preparatory documents. Lay experts also contributed to them. However, many Polish bishops did not want to analyze problems seriously. They treated the Synod as another celebratory, perfunctory event. They eventually limited the role of the laity, with the head of the conference, Archbishop Glemp, spearheading the way.⁹⁶ The preparatory documents, published in a collection, did not stimulate discussion among the hierarchy and eventually were tabled. Bishop Pieronek expressed his disappointment by saying that "we must openly admit that the bishops neglected the pastoral opportunity created by the Synod."⁹⁷

Much of the Synod's output amounted to "nice generalities," as Gowin correctly puts it.⁹⁸ For example, the document on evangelization spoke of all people taking on their responsibilities in the Church and in society (no. 39) and concern for the poor (no. 55). The bishops did not go into details. The document on political life failed to go beyond prioritizing "effective education, a just distribution of goods, and conditions that foster creating jobs" (no. 17). It also tended to be less critical of the obvious failures of the last decade than other documents, thanking "Mary, Mother of God, Queen of Poland" for the "decade of miraculous transformations in solidarity" (no. 54).⁹⁹ The document on education, a worthy topic given Poland's sweeping educational reforms, did not describe discriminatory patterns regarding the right to education, which the Constitution of 1997 enshrines.¹⁰⁰ However, in spite of their claims to provide norms only, the bishops moved to the level of concrete realities and policies in some places. If the first document merely attempts to provide the theological basis for social concern by linking evangelization and social justice, to be expanded on in the other documents, then remaining on the level of generalities seems justified. As such a foundation, it is quite successful. However, the less than apparent links between the documents, along with outright tensions, cause the reader to wonder if the various committees responsible for each document view the specificity question differently.

The document on socioeconomic life is the most promising, along with some noteworthy portions of other documents. This document initially provides a philosophical framework that emphasizes solidarity while critiquing neoliberal economic policies and understandings of freedom that value profits over people (see nos. 8, 12, 26, 31, 45). Here for the first time the bishops explicitly and unequivocally echo John Paul II's criticisms of neoliberalism and its "false notion of freedom" in Poland.[101] Furthermore, they attempt to demonstrate what an ethic of solidarity looks like in socioeconomic life. For example, they urge politicians and corporate board members to remember that "demanding and earning incommensurably high salaries is an expression of a lack of solidarity with millions of poor and it extinguishes the hope for a justly managed country" (no. 32). This is a timely exhortation given that Polish politicians earn disproportionately high salaries in the face of the public's profound distrust.[102] In a manner reminiscent of Tischner's *Etyka solidarności* and John Paul II's *Laborem Exercens,* the bishops called on employers to "humanize" work by respecting the rights of workers and for the latter to do their job diligently and honestly. This will forge healthy relations between labor and capital, which will be built on a "foundation of the virtue of solidarity" (no. 42). The bishops also exhorted all citizens to be in solidarity with the decisionmakers who undertake often painful, but necessary, reforms. This does not preclude real dialogue and the ability to raise doubts about specific policies. However, citizens should not berate public figures; this does not contribute to genuine public debate (no. 31).

The bishops discussed many other policy issues in this document, contrary to their stated intention to limit themselves to norms. For example, they opposed high taxes, which, in their conviction, hinder economic growth (no. 21). They proposed a system that would "equally distribute burdens and foster the creation of new jobs"; it should also be "stable, just and take into consideration the taxpayer's number of dependents" (no. 33). The bishops repeated this last plea, which is part of the call for "pro-family politics" in several of the other documents. The document on family life, placed immediately after the document on evangelization, pointed to specific rights of the family, which include having children, a residence, employment, medical services, and family benefits.[103] They deemed the current tax system "anti-family." It does not secure these rights and denies children of large families the chance for an education and access to other cultural benefits (no. 20). As the document on socioeconomic life mentioned, children from poor families in villages complete higher education less frequently than children of other backgrounds (no. 27). The same document also described some of the various aspects of poverty and proposed concrete ways of combating it. For example, it pointed to the rising mortality rate of young men in Poland. It attributed this rise to their poor health, which is a consequence of environmental degradation, the organization of work, harmful technologies, and the stress caused by deprivation (no. 24). It is unfortunate, however, that the bishops seem to have overlooked the many aspects of the feminization of poverty in Poland. Perhaps this should come as no surprise, given their general attitude towards feminism.

The document also encouraged low-interest, long-term loans in order to ease the housing crisis (no. 36). In addition, the document on charitable work showed sensitivity to the many dimensions of poverty: the material, the social (that is, marginalization), the psychological (helplessness), the intellectual, and the spiritual. The bishops correctly maintained that poverty can be measured objectively, according to empirical criteria, and subjectively, considering the individual's determination of his or her own social status. They rightly note that "the scope of human poverty, seen on various levels, has widened" (no. 21). However, the bishops would have done well to address many of the other contours of Polish poverty, such as the fact that women and children suffer from long-term poverty disproportionately. Instead, they reinforce the false notion that poverty particularly affects retired persons (no. 24). As was stated earlier in this book, many senior citizens certainly endure various forms of impoverishment, but the statistics reveal that children of the poor are at a much graver disadvantage.

For the sake of brevity, this book cannot examine every policy proposal in the Synodal documents. It has merely attempted to demonstrate that the document on socioeconomic life, to a much greater degree than the others, exemplifies the direction in which the bishops should move. This is not to say that this document is without flaws. Some of the concrete analysis lacks sophistication. In addition to the topics already mentioned, the discussion of taxes, which generates considerable debate among ethicists and economists, fails to cite from the ample research on the subject.[104] When do high taxes become inefficient and unacceptable? Are burdens shared equally by a "flat tax," which some economists in Poland have suggested? John Rawls, for example, argues that progressive tax schemes are necessary in order to prevent excessive concentrations of wealth, which obviate fair equality of opportunity.[105] It is interesting to note that the bishops themselves deem "excessive differences in income" unjust in the same document. Should there be a tax on dividends? How will the expensive social programs involved in their "pro-family politics" be funded? The discussion of poverty points to the rise in poverty in Poland without citing any sources. This may seem unnecessary. However, given that some observers dispute the fact that poverty has risen in Poland, the bishops should provide some empirical verification. Agriculture certainly also merits attention. However, simply reiterating John XXIII's support for small family-owned farms oversimplifies the issue, given the contemporary challenges of Polish agriculture described earlier in this book.

Despite any shortcomings, the document on socioeconomic life represents the best effort of the Polish bishops to take *Octogesima Adveniens* (no. 4) and John Paul II's exhortations more seriously. In this vein, the bishops noted that while charitable endeavors remain important, the Church must "first and foremost shape the structures of social life, so that they will more effectively protect the weak and guarantee all people equal access to the common good."[106] The bishops even recommended the creation of a permanent institute dedicated to the study of socioeconomic affairs (no. 49). These are significant steps, given the historical neglect of Catholic social teaching in Poland and previous lethargy in the face of the crippling socioeconomic transformations.[107]

After the Synod, the bishops published a pastoral letter on socioeconomic issues to commemorate the 110th anniversary of *Rerum Novarum*, along with several other shorter statements. Only a few of the strengths and weaknesses of the pastoral letter may be noted here.[108] Importantly, the bishops again stressed the relevance of an ethic of solidarity today. Not unlike Amartya Sen, they underlined an understanding of development that encompasses more than economic growth. They also intensified their critique of a "radical ideology of capitalism":

> After twelve years of systemic changes in Poland, we must contend that many people responsible for the shape of public life uncritically believed that the fall of Marxism would automatically lead to a just society and in free-market mechanisms, which would guarantee the well-being of all in every sphere of life. In the place of collectivist ideology appeared a distorted version of liberalism, which ... conceived the whole of reality solely in economic categories. In this manner the development so desperately needed in our country was identified only with economic growth.[109]

In addition, the letter auspiciously situated concern about unemployment, its focus, within the framework of "new evangelization," which requires the propagation of Catholic social teaching.[110] The treatment of unemployment itself largely recapitulated John Paul II's teaching on the dignity of labor from *Laborem Exercens*. It provided a helpful statistical overview of unemployment according to sectors, regions, and age groups. However, the scant policy proposals were largely taken from *Centesimus Annus*. For example, the bishops mentioned the role of the government in creating jobs. In doing so, they cited the pope's balancing of solidarity and subsidiarity and his recommendation of unemployment benefits and job retraining in order to facilitate workers' transition from faltering industries (compare *CA*, no. 15). They rightfully disapproved of the fact that 80 percent of the jobless in Poland cannot obtain unemployment benefits. The bishops did assert that education must change with the times, in order to prepare young people for the new conditions of the labor market, which require the lifelong acquisition of skills. However, one searches for more specificity concerning unemployment in Poland.

In this pastoral letter, the bishops repeatedly stated, "proposing technical solutions to the problem of unemployment exceeds our competence and our mission." Yet, clearly they have suggested some concrete policies in the past, particularly in their Synodal document on socioeconomic life. In fact, their discussion of unemployment in that document accomplished more than did the pastoral letter.[111] In this connection,

Archbishop Zimoń's pastoral letter *Kościół katolicki na Śląsku wobec bezrobocia* (The Catholic Church in Silesia concerning Unemployment) is worthy of mention. His letter gives a very concrete analysis of unemployment in the Śląsk region of Poland, where the decline of heavy industries led to a 75 percent increase in joblessness from 1998 to 2000.[112] The archbishop does not hesitate to make numerous policy recommendations, many of which resemble those discussed in this book. Among them are: the recognition that women suffer disproportionately from unemployment and that domestic work merits a salary and benefits, workers' participation in management, and the importance of retraining programs for the continual upgrading of skills. He also mentions the possibility of reducing the hours in the work week in order to provide more jobs, a solution that has had some positive results in countries such as France. Significantly, the archbishop places all of this discussion within the framework of solidarity and subsidiarity, arguing that without sensible economic development and solidarity, the plague of unemployment will never cease to exist.[113] Clearly, he has the vestiges of *homo sovieticus* in mind when he calls for "personal responsibility for individual and social growth." At the same time, he contends that the government must foster the conditions in which this can be done. For example, he calls for the expansion of a social safety net to preclude more unemployed persons from falling into poverty, but he also cautions against the abuse of such a safety net. It should be geared towards mobilizing the workforce.[114]

The only shortcoming of the analysis is in regard to education, which, this book has argued, is inextricably related to the problems of poverty and unemployment. While Archbishop Zimoń prevails upon the individual to see how crucial the pursuit of education is today, he fails to address the social conditions that prohibit the kind of "investment in one's self" that he proposes.[115] Despite this oversight, his effort goes beyond generalities and tries to read "the signs of the times" carefully in his archdiocese. He also links this endeavor to the very mission of the Church, because, in his words, "there is no area of human life that can be treated outside the divine plan for salvation."[116] In short, he provides a model for engaging in the kind of concrete analysis needed to foster solidarity, freedom, and participation in Poland today. It is unfortunate that all of the bishops have not followed his lead and that the bishops' conference has not progressed in its own work since the achievements of Synod documents.

Several tensions in the bishops' writing continue to exist today. On the one hand, they often repeated that their teaching must remain on a certain level of generality. On the other hand, they moved at times to the level of policy. Hence, it appears obvious that the bishops continue to struggle with the appropriate level of specificity of Catholic social teaching. As was discussed earlier, they posited a close relationship between evangelization and social justice in some of their writings in recent years. The effort put forth in the Synodal document on socioeconomic life attests to their belief in this link. While it still does not contain the degree of careful analysis found in the U.S. bishops' *Economic Justice for All*, for example, it is a significant step in the right direction. However, the pastoral letter on unemployment, while containing much of value, does not accomplish enough to demonstrate a desire among the bishops to take *Octogesima Adveniens* (no. 4) seriously. It is difficult, perhaps impossible, to discern why the bishops did not put the same amount of energy into this document in order to build on the momentum from the Synodal document on socioeconomic life. Do not the bishops wholeheartedly see promoting solidarity, freedom, and participation as a constitutive element of preaching the Gospel? While this may be true of some bishops, recent statements have posited the relationship between the Church's social mission and evangelization. To repeat what was said earlier, some bishops still view this dimension of new evangelization as necessary, but secondary. This mindset has contributed to the relativization of issues such as poverty. Another contentious issue resides in the bishops' interpretation of *Octogesima Adveniens* (no. 4). This issue undoubtedly further contributes to the bishops' reluctance to engage in the kind of structural analysis necessary for the promotion of solidarity and social justice.

The Polish bishops maintain that Paul VI's challenge imposes the duty of creating specific policy options exclusively on the laity. In their pastoral letter, they cite *Octogesima Adveniens* (no. 4) in its entirety. Immediately following the citation, they appeal to *Octogesima Adveniens* (no. 48), which states that "it belongs to the laity, without waiting passively for orders and directives, to take the initiative freely and to infuse a Christian spirit into the mentality, customs, laws, and structures of the communities in which they live." Key Polish commentators on the Church's role in society echo this sentiment.[117] This book has argued that the American as well as the English and Welsh bishops appropriately taught by example how Catholic social teaching should be applied to the particulars of a given society. A number of other bishops' conferences have produced detailed policy analysis, such as the conferences of Canada, Cameroon, Congo, Germany, Australia, and the Philippines.[118] As Archbishop Weakland said upon the tenth anniversary of *Economic Justice for All*, "the teaching has grown and become more refined precisely because there were attempts to apply it to different problems at different periods of time."[119] Bishops must be a part of the task of translating Catholic social teaching into "the language of concrete problems and tasks," as John Paul II told the Polish bishops.[120] Certainly, the Church teaches that the laity and clergy have different roles in the world; laypersons can and should hold political office, while priests should not. However, Paul VI did say that discerning the options necessary for social change belonged to "Christian communities, with the help of the Holy Spirit, in communion with the bishops who hold responsibility" and in dialogue with other Christians and persons of goodwill (*OA*, no. 4).

Ultimately, only the bishops can put forth an authoritative reading of the signs of the times in local churches. The unified voice of a bishops' conference will be able to project its ideas onto decisionmakers in politics and business more effectively than will lay groups. Thus, the role of laypersons is indispensable because they often possess expertise in fields that the bishops do not. They can and should affect politics "on the inside" by holding office and by lobbying for just causes. If the Polish bishops truly want to shape socioeconomic realities in the way that they have indicated, then employing lay lobbyists, as the U.S. bishops do, seems appropriate. This would fit within the parameters of the "cooperation for the good of the human person and common good" called for by the Constitution and the Concordat between the Holy See and the Republic of Poland.[121] As Archbishop Zimoń contends, the Church can and should influence local politicians to take the problem of unemployment and poverty more seriously.[122] Because such political activity was forbidden under Communism, the Catholic Church in Poland lacks experienced lobbyists.[123] The time is ripe, however, for the formation of such a cadre of dedicated Catholic laypersons in democratic Poland.

To summarize, the Polish bishops have recognized the inherent relationship between evangelization and social justice in some of their more recent writings. However, an expressed concern for "excessive horizontalism," coupled with a lack of thorough, sustained reflection on the problem of poverty and its causes may attest to continued ambivalence, at least among some bishops, to an important aspect of the Church's mission of evangelization. The problem may also reside in a reluctance to delve deeply into policy areas and propose concrete solutions that would embody solidarity with the poor. Yet, there have been encouraging signs for the future, such as the Synodal document on socioeconomic life and Archbishop Zimoń's pastoral letter on unemployment. It will be useful to point to a few more future directions that can and should be pursued by the bishops as part of their contribution to the revitalization of an ethic of solidarity in Poland today. This discussion, which presupposes familiarity with the numerous policy proposals made in earlier chapters of this book, cannot be exhaustive. Rather, it will underscore some of the key issues and hopefully stimulate further reflection.

Future Directions for a Church of Solidarity

The current tensions within the Church and between the Church and the larger society need to be addressed in order to foster greater solidarity. First, all bishops, clergy, and laypersons must learn to respect one another in dialogue, as did those who had differences during the Solidarity era. Although there are examples of Church leaders who listen attentively to laypeople—"feminists" and "crypto-Communists" included—more must embrace the kind of dialogue that thrived during those days in Poland's past. Second, a large number of Catholics do not believe that the Church should concern itself with issues such as poverty and unemployment. Although the latest research shows an increase in recent years in the number of Catholics who think that bishops and clergy should take a public stance regarding unemployment (72.6 percent) and social inequalities (70 percent), the majority still argue that the Church should not become "entangled in politics." Furthermore, a majority of Catholics (57.3 percent) believe that the Church should not comment on government policies.[124] These two opinions indicate that the majority of Catholics in Poland do not understand two important issues: 1) the problem of unemployment cannot be resolved apart from politics and if the Church is going to fight unemployment, it must critique and suggest concrete governmental social policies; and 2) "the Church is called to be the critical conscience of society," as the Synod document *Kościół wobec rzeczywistości politycznej* maintains.[125] Thus, the bishops must ensure that a large-scale educational program concerning Catholic social teaching is undertaken, perhaps most aptly in every parish.

All Catholics do not understand that realizing the option for the poor is an indispensable part of the Church's mission of evangelization, and that solidarity with the poor requires more than occasional charitable works. If they did, then many more would probably live in true solidarity with the poor and support the Church's concern for policies aiding them. As the bishops pointed out, only 4 percent of Roman Catholics participate in civic organizations.[126] This percentage indicates a lack of an understanding that all persons are responsible for promoting the common good. It demonstrates that many Church members do not wish to fully participate in the life of the community. As was discussed in chapter 2, the legacy of *homo sovieticus* can be blamed, and one hopes that with time this mentality will change. There are some signs of growth already. While the number of Catholics involved in organizations is small relative to Western European and North American countries, there has been a gradual increase since 1989.[127] These criticisms apply to clergy as well as to laypersons. Many clergy do not recognize the importance of the Church's social teaching and the need to study various disciplines, such as economics, sociology, and political science, in order to scrutinize the "signs of the times."[128] For example, the Tischner European School of Higher Education in Cracow and the National Bank of Poland co-sponsored seminars in economics and business management for priests. These two organizations assumed that priests in Poland today should have some facility in these fields in order to grapple with important contemporary pastoral and social problems. However, the clergy showed little interest, and many priests think that economic issues are not relevant to their work.[129]

This attitude betrays solidarity's call to "understand the cry of the poor." Succinctly stated, the bishops should do all that they can to insist that the "tragic separation between faith and earthly affairs" decried by *Gaudium et Spes* is bridged. Better theological education, particularly in Catholic social thought and interdisciplinary study, in seminaries, local parishes, and universities is crucial to this goal. Calling special attention to the fate of "the least"—children, women, members of large families, poor agricultural workers and farmers, people in the former PGR-y regions—is essential to realizing the Church's option for the poor. More can and must be done in this regard. For example, the Polish bishops criticized the abolishment of the earlier mentioned national alimony fund. However, their statement did not explicitly mention the detrimental effects that this decision will have on poor women and their children. Rather, they focused on the fact that it will encourage more divorce.

Another area in which the bishops could say more pertains to economic rights. This is appropriate given that they represent the "institutionalization of solidarity" and are essential to the realization of freedom. The bishops' social teaching contains only a few scattered references to economic rights.[130] Given the emphasis on economic rights in Catholic social thought, one wonders why the bishops have not addressed the topic more frequently and systematically. In post-Solidarity Poland, it behooves them to do so. Despite the fact that the Solidarity movement advocated both "bread and freedom," economic and social rights are viewed very cynically in today's Poland. They are often construed as remnants of *homo sovieticus* that should be eradicated at all costs in order to construct a strong free-market economy. For example, neoliberal economist Jan Winiecki stated that the ideals of Solidarity, such as worker ownership, amount to "anti-Communist bolshevism."[131]

Perhaps more disconcerting is the fact that a leading Catholic social ethicist such as Aniela Dylus views the legal guarantee of economic rights as a "violation of equality before the law." The meaning of this statement is not entirely clear. However, she seems to believe that the constitutional protection of economic rights lends itself to too many political squabbles among competing parties who make empty promises. Furthermore, she maintains that the legal guarantee of economic rights can create a sense of entitlement, which leads to the "incapacitation" (*ubezwłasnowolnienie*) of the human person.[132] In response, the bishops should herald Roman Catholic human rights theory, which emphasizes both the duty of society to aid in securing human rights for all people and the duty of individuals to exercise their rights responsibly and to foster those of others.

In addition to the theoretical misunderstandings about economic rights that abound, they are violated on a regular basis in Poland, as has been demonstrated throughout this book. Interestingly, Jarosław Gowin maintains that both workers' rights and employers' rights are also regularly violated. In the case of the latter, government bureaucracy hinders the economic freedom of many businesses, not in order to protect workers' interest but for its own self-gain through graft. In short, there are sufficient reasons for the bishops to promote greater understanding and realization of economic rights. Among economic rights, the bishops should highlight the right to a just wage and worker participation. The Church in Poland has not undertaken a campaign to support the legislation of a living wage, as the U.S. and English and Welsh bishops have done.[133] The Polish bishops have said relatively little about the issue, which is controversial in a country where a "Capitalist Manifesto" decries talk of a living wage as populist. More stress should also be placed on worker ownership, which, as has been discussed earlier, also meets with great resistance, especially among neoliberals. Although Bishop Zimoń clearly endorses worker participation in his pastoral letter on unemployment,[134] one struggles to find references to it in the bishops' conference documents.

In addition, the Church's teaching concerning "true freedom" must be more audible and nuanced enough to avoid merely chastising "liberals." Such talk divides rather than unites. In this vein, Tischner rightly criticized those members of the Church, including the hierarchy, who advocated what he called flight from freedom. This book has attempted to show one way that an understanding of freedom can be in harmony with the demands of solidarity by appealing to Catholic social thought and the work of Amartya Sen. The Christian tradition provides numerous other resources that can aid in explicating that freedom is neither the ability to do whatever one pleases nor the slavish submission of one's self to doctrines or laws. The bishops should mine these resources to teach about the nature of freedom and its relationship to solidarity.

The bishops are certainly aware of this issue. They, like John Paul II, criticized "false notions of freedom" stemming from neoliberalism and moral permissivism. To counter such notions of freedom, the bishops, like the pope, emphasized the relationship between freedom and truth.[135] This last point, however, has led to deep rifts between the Church and some observers such as Michnik, who fear that the Church wants to legislate the whole of its moral teaching. In such a quandary the Church, in particular the bishops, must be patient, yet persistent, in explaining the nature of freedom and its relationship to solidarity. It must also embrace sincere dialogue in the spirit of solidarity on this matter.

The Polish bishops should not jettison the emphasis on the relationship between freedom and truth. Yet, the issue must be approached in a manner sensitive to its explosive nature. The best way, perhaps, to move towards some agreement would be to espouse a notion of "truth" reminiscent of Solidarity's call to life in truth. Solidarity's insistence on "life in truth" did not require the profession of the Christian faith nor did it require adherence to the entire gamut of its moral teachings. Rather, it first and foremost demanded living in accordance with one's conscience. It is worth emphasizing again that this does not equate with choosing whatever one wishes to do. Much ink has been spilled over the question as to whether or not following one's conscience means always obeying the teaching of the Roman Catholic magisterium. Prescinding from this technical question of moral theology, one might reasonably conclude that in a pluralistic society it is not feasible to maintain that true freedom requires assent to all of the truths held by the Roman Catholic magisterium.[136] At the very least, it is not plausible to maintain that the Church seeks to legislate the whole of its moral teaching. The universal magisterium itself has acknowledged this on more than one occasion.[137] In *Dignitatis Humanae*, for example, the Second Vatican Council accepted John Courtney Murray's distinction between the common good and the public order. In the words of the Council, the government must protect the public order, which requires "genuine public peace," "true justice," and the "guardianship of public morality." Only those actions and behaviors that preclude these three things are to be prohibited by law because, as the Council goes on to state, "the freedom of man is to be respected as far as possible and is not to be curtailed except when and insofar as necessary."[138] While he uses a different framework, that is, that of natural law, Saint Thomas Aquinas poses a similar stance on the relationship between law and morality. Aquinas's position has been nicely summarized as follows: "Human law should suppress the more grievous vices from which most people are able to abstain—especially those that are harmful to others—because such prohibitions are necessary for the good of society."[139] In other words, those actions that may be morally reprehensible, but not so egregious as to threaten the good of society, should not be outlawed. In this vein, Aquinas cites Augustine's toleration of legalized prostitution.[140]

While the following may fall short of an ultimately satisfying answer to the question of the relationship between law and morality, this book argues that the Church should promulgate a notion of freedom that stands in relation to the most basic truth about the human person, namely, that she is imbued with inviolable dignity, the capacity for freedom, and a call to participation. Any genuine exercise of freedom will respect this basic truth about the human person, in regard to one's self and those affected by one's actions. Anything that incontrovertibly degrades this truth can and should be considered a violation of the justice required by the public order. As such, laws should be created against such actions.

In the case of Poland, this truth about the human person is most often overlooked in reference to a particular group, namely, the poor. To reiterate what was stated earlier, herein lies the strength of Sen's understanding of freedom: it directly calls attention to the freedom of the poor and fleshes out what is necessary for its realization. The Polish bishops certainly do not have an easy task on their hands, but perhaps emphasizing *these aspects* of freedom in *these particular times* is what is called for at present. They must unequivocally state, with the full force of their authority, that the dignity, freedom, and right to participation of the poor is non-negotiable. This does not imply that they should not also condemn abortion as a violation of truth and a violation of the Catholic notion of public order.[141] The concept of public order, however, may assuage some of the fears that pushing legislation against abortion exemplifies a larger agenda to legislate all of Catholic moral teaching. Succinctly stated, the bishops should emphasize that there are some issues that are nonnegotiable, while there is a range of others open to debate in a democratic, pluralistic society. They could clarify this position by appealing to the notion of public order. This tack may quell the negative, sometimes hostile reaction to any talk of freedom's relationship to the truth. If done with humility and patience, perhaps this understanding of freedom will have greater success in galvanizing, rather than polarizing, the currently highly divided Polish nation.

Finally, in conjunction with a positive understanding of freedom, the Church has a pivotal role to play in rebuilding in the human person hope and social trust, which, to repeat, is the foundation of an ethic of solidarity. The Church possesses another important resource for a pedagogy of hope. The Christian theology of grace acknowledges that human beings often fail to love. It is not naïve considering the extent of human evil, which has led to genocides, wars, and poverty. The Christian concept of grace, however, assumes two things: 1) that human beings are in need of grace; and 2) that human beings are capable of receiving it.[142] It ultimately holds that the human person is capable of breaking free of egocentricity to love and serve others. This theology of grace must be heard in the Church today, when it is tempting to look both at history and at the present and conclude, as Hobbes did, *homo homini lupus*. The Church must teach that in these times dominated by consumerism, greed, and corruption, the grace of Jesus Christ can break through and inspire people to embrace an ethic of solidarity. Tischner's thought, for example, provides the Church in Poland with a rich theology of grace underpinning hope in the human person, human freedom, and solidarity among people.[143] In addition, an understanding of the Eucharist that stresses its liberating power and connection to social justice might aid in this regard. Unfortunately, the celebration of the Eucharist often fails to highlight this dimension of what Johannes Baptist Metz calls the "Bread of Survival."[144]

This chapter has mainly focused on the "educational-cultural" and "legislative-policy" functions of the Polish bishops' conference. In other words, it has dealt with the Church's official role as a teacher, through its social teaching and its role as a political actor, through direct policy advocacy.[145] These are indispensable elements of the Church's mission of evangelization. There are, of course, other ways to "infuse the world with the light of the Gospel," and the bishops certainly are not the only members of the Church entrusted with this task. One of the other ways to evangelize is to aid the needy directly. In the context of this book, the question to be raised is whether or not the Church's direct aid to the poor constitutes solidarity.

As was stated earlier, Polish direct social aid in response to poverty and marginalization has entailed more *akcyjność* than *aktywność*. In other words, true and lasting solidarity with the poor is often overlooked in favor of fleeting charitable efforts. The latter provide a "fish" but not a "fishing rod" and so do not teach the poor how to fish, to cite an old Chinese proverb. This is not to deny that acts of charity, known as the corporal works of mercy in the Catholic tradition, are another way of infusing the world with the light of the Gospel. However, this book has argued that solidarity requires advocating structural change that will enable the participation of the poor in the life of society, that is, eliminate marginalization, and that Poland needs first and foremost a return to solidarity to overcome its social ills. For example, feeding the hungry by opening soup kitchens may indeed be needed in many situations, but it does not eliminate the structural forces at work in society that lead to the problem of hunger. As was mentioned above, the bishops themselves acknowledged the primacy of advocating structural change in order to fulfill the option for the poor.

Catholic Organizations Acting in Solidarity

Any consideration of the work of Catholic organizations combating poverty in Poland after 1989 must consider the following important fact: this type of activity was banned in Poland during the Communist era. Thus, those organizations that function today suffer a grave disadvantage. First, they lack experience with the democratic and capitalist structures within which they must operate. In addition, there is a shortage of personnel trained in the fields most relevant to combating poverty, such as economics, sociology, and psychology. Second, Poles are generally not accustomed to being proactive in promoting their own welfare and the welfare of others through organized activity. Hence, there is still reluctance among the faithful to play an active role in Church-related agencies. And third, the pastoral agenda of the Catholic Church during Communism privileged popular traditional piety over intellectual and socially progressive currents within the Church. The ritual and devotional aspects of traditional piety in Poland played a key role in overturning Communism by unifying Catholics under difficult circumstances. However, it did not encourage the kind of rigorous analysis of social ills such as poverty that is desperately needed today, nor did it encourage the laity to take responsibility for the Church and its mission.[146]

Despite these historical impediments, most Catholics in contemporary Poland realize that Catholic charitable organizations can and should play an important role in creating a more just society. However, parish members very seldom organize in order to serve the Church's social mission.[147] Moreover, the more than two hundred Catholic groups, comprised of about 500,000 Poles (a number quite low in a country with over 35 million Catholics), generally prefer to help the poor directly rather than by seeking to build just economic and political structures. There are a few exceptions, such as the Association of Polish Catholic Lawyers, which lobbied the Warsaw government concerning the necessity of privatization, equitable labor conditions, and agricultural subsidies.[148] Nonetheless, much work needs to be done in order for Catholics as a whole to embrace an ethic of solidarity with the poor.

Caritas Polska as a Case Study

After forty years of Communist-government suppression, Caritas Polska reappeared in Polish society in 1990.[149] Clearly, its resurrection has made a difference in the lives of tens of thousands of underprivileged Poles. Already in 1993, 40,000 volunteers formed about 5,000 groups to serve in soup kitchens, therapy centers for the physically and mentally challenged, shelters for homeless persons and single mothers, orphanages, summer camps for children, etc.[150] It is important to have a sense of the scale of this aid. For example, in 1993 around 45,000 people were given meals from Caritas-sponsored soup kitchens. In the same year, Caritas provided 316,000 children with some form of financial or material assistance. More than 230 medical centers cared for the chronically ill and mentally and physically challenged. Some dioceses, such as the Archdiocese of Lublin, maintained discount pharmacies; for example, Lublin's archdiocesan pharmacy helped more than one million people in 1995. The summer camps for children from underprivileged families, one of the most popular Caritas programs, have been growing in attendance. In 1992, 13,500 children attended; in 1994, 60,000; and in 2003, more than 100,000.[151] Children from Polish families in the Ukraine and Belarus also are invited to attend these summer camps.

Caritas Polska also assists persons beyond Poland's borders. For example, in 1994, Caritas collected around 900,000 PLN (approx. $300,000 U.S.) for the countries ravaged by war in the former Yugoslavia and about 1.4 million PLN (approx. $460,000 U.S.) for the people of Rwanda. These funds were used to purchase and transport clothing, food, medical supplies, and coal to these areas.[152] More recently, Caritas sent 400 gift packages to children in orphanages in Afghanistan and transferred $25,000 U.S. to Caritas International in Kabul. In addition, it undertook numerous and diverse efforts to aid the victims of the earthquake in Indonesia, Sri Lanka, and India in December 2004. For example, Poles will become permanent sponsors of children who have lost their parents by sending monthly stipends through accounts set up and managed by Caritas Polska and its local partners. In addition, Caritas Polska has transferred over 800,000 PLN and $47,000 U.S. in cash, medical, and other supplies to Caritas India to relieve victims in India and Sri Lanka. Adam Dereń, director of Caritas Polska, said that "this assistance is an expression of the solidarity of Polish society with the victims of the Asian cataclysm. The resources transferred will provide the most needed aid to the people suffering as a result of the earthquake."[153]

Caritas Polska clearly helps tens of thousands of people and deserves accolades for its tremendous work. The purpose of this analysis, however, is to discern the degree to which this work embodies the rich solidarity of Catholic social thought. Based on this concept of solidarity, much of Caritas's endeavors involves the first and second "moments" of solidarity (described earlier in Table 4.1), encountering the need of "the other" and acting to alleviate it. However, more steps must be taken for solidarity to become fully realized. What is missing is the contemplation of the plight of the poor, *together with the poor themselves,* in order to devise a plan of action that will alter society in a positive way. Sometimes crisis intervention is necessary, but ultimately people must work with the poor in order to encourage their active participation in overcoming their problems and then contributing to society.[154]

Although Caritas reaches a significant number of poor people, the magnitude of the problem of poverty necessitates pursuing other avenues, particularly structural reform. In Leon Dyczewski's words, "love must complement justice in solidarity, not surpass it."[155] Justice is "the first virtue of social institutions," as Rawls put it. Laws and institutions that are unjust must be "reformed or abolished."[156]

A complete analysis of the myriad forms of assistance provided by Caritas Polska exceeds the scope of this book. However, a closer look at a few of its most typical activities in the light of solidarity will reveal that Caritas must advocate structural reform through legislative policy. While this "justice lens" must be adopted in order for Caritas to embody greater solidarity with the poor, a number of its activities clearly empower impoverished people to participate, while others merely assuage their plight. Thus, although it is necessary to point to the road ahead, Caritas is already doing the work of solidarity in many ways. As has been said earlier, even though solidarity is in short supply in Poland today, it is certainly alive in some places and worthy of recognition and emulation on a broader scale.

Caritas Polska divides its activity into the following categories: aid to the sick, aid to the homeless, aid to the unemployed, aid to single mothers, and aid to the physically challenged. Several different kinds of assistance are offered to these groups at various sites. The largest in scope are soup kitchens, summer camps for children, medical and therapy centers, and shelters for the homeless. In addition, each year Caritas launches special fundraising campaigns such as "*Kromka chleba*" (A Slice of Bread) and "*Wigilijne Dzieło Pomocy Dzieciom*" (The Christmas Eve Children's Aid Event). These fundraisers primarily are designed to pay for various programs that also have an important pedagogical component, which is to be incorporated into catechesis from first grade up through high school. Generally speaking, it aims to increase sensitivity to the needs of the poor.[157] Its strength resides in its insistence that to love God, one must love one's neighbor, and that as Christians, we have obligations to the poor. Unfortunately, there is no mention of the structural causes of poverty and injustice and what citizens can do to dismantle them.

Tens of thousands of poor persons benefit from Caritas's soup kitchens on a daily basis.[158] These soup kitchens serve warm meals throughout the year, but especially in the colder months. During the winter season these meals can become a matter of life and death for the homeless. It is easy, therefore, to see that this aid represents a kind of crisis intervention: the persons fed in these locations are often desperate, and there is no time to deliberate about how to encourage their participation or empowerment in society. The "moment" of solidarity that involves contemplation of the causes of suffering cannot take place. For the most part, beneficiaries of this type of aid remain passive recipients. Thus, soup kitchens alone do not constitute a form of solidarity. Yet, this indispensable aid can be seen as a step along the road to the flourishing of solidarity. It is fairly obvious that someone who suffers from hunger and/or malnutrition cannot participate in the life of a community. A certain minimum of calories and nutritional values is essential for proper physical and mental health, a precondition of participation and the ability to be in solidarity with others.[159] In order to "carry another's burdens," the human person must have certain basic needs met first.

If the meals provided contain these bare minimums of calories and nutrition, then they may be considered a precursor to, or step towards, action in solidarity.

The summer camp program, Wakacyjna Akcja Caritas, has been in existence for fifteen years and serves more than 100,000 children yearly. The program explicitly intends to "prevent the marginalization of poor persons" and to make sure that children do not fall into a poverty trap. Therefore, the program is seen "not only as temporary aid, but as preventative aid understood as an investment in human capital." The summer camps afford children from poor regions a vacation that they would otherwise not enjoy. This may be the only way that these children "can be children," as youngsters from impoverished families often are forced to lead adult lives in some ways. Moreover, the program includes an educational component, which fosters the "love of one's neighbor" through concrete actions, concern for the common good, and care and acceptance of one's self together with some foreign language instruction.[160] Each of these aspects addresses important issues for the young campers and is geared toward facilitating participation in society and inculcating solidarity. As such, this program is an excellent way to promote an ethic of solidarity in Poland.

Two possible drawbacks, however, come to mind. First, two weeks out of the year is far too short a time for an at-risk child. Many parishes under the auspices of Caritas have *świetlicy* for children throughout the year, which are something like afterschool programs.[161] Yet, one wonders if there is enough continuity between the program's efforts in the summer and the activities at these afterschool programs, which are not supervised by Caritas directly. Insofar as they replicate or continue what occurs in the summer camps, they may meet solidarity's requirement of continuity and perseverance. For example, a tutoring component should be intensified in reading, mathematics, science, and foreign languages for those children whose parents cannot afford the private tutoring that has become popular among the affluent. In light of the evidence concerning poverty and educational and testing disparities, this is crucial to breaking the poverty cycle. In short, the ideal would be for each child to be assisted throughout his or her school years in order to ensure that he or she has every chance for success.

Second, inviting children from families who are *dobrze usytuowane* (well off) could promote greater solidarity among those who are fortunate and those who endure hardships. It could help overcome the indifference that so many Poles have felt towards the poor, because an encounter with a real person who struggles can often erode one's prejudices and lead to a change of heart. Perhaps dialogue concerning the problems in Polish society could take place among children who will become the leaders of tomorrow. Because the wealthy of "Polska A" and their children are often isolated from the poor, this could be a way of breaking down social barriers. There are, of course, problems with this idea. This kind of endeavor might be too challenging psychologically for the impoverished children, who desperately need some respite from their difficult lives. Furthermore, how many children whose parents can afford to take them to the Tatra mountains, the Baltic seacoast, or exotic places abroad, will want to attend such a camp? Moreover, who will pay for such a program? Perhaps it may seem too idealistic, but the Church can call upon its more fortunate members to encourage their children to benefit from such an opportunity and to defray the costs themselves. These are merely suggestions for possible improvement to a program that appears to be on the right track already. The program is designed very well, that is, it is the fruit of "contemplation," one of the key "moments" of solidarity. Caritas and those who volunteer to lead this program are acting in solidarity with many of Poland's disadvantaged children, who are among "the least" in the nation today.

The therapy centers (*stacje opieki*) administered by Caritas Polska also exhibit elements of an ethic of solidarity. Morbidity is a form of poverty itself and is also often a cause of poverty. To reiterate what was said earlier regarding participation, one's health is the precondition of participation in the life of the community. Caritas attempts to the best of its ability to work with patients in their homes, which enables those who are immobile to undertake therapy. Insofar as Caritas provides these services for those who could not otherwise afford them, it is contributing to the ability of patients to overcome physical and psychological obstacles to participation. It is unclear, however, if Caritas explicitly and always challenges its clients, in turn, to "carry the burdens of others," which would complete the "circle of solidarity": solidarity with the poor leads to participation by the marginalized, which then leads to solidarity with others who suffer. The summer camp program has recently come upon an idea in this vein. In 2003, Caritas invited sick persons to pray for the young campers, while the children would learn how to aid those who suffer from illnesses. This type of "circle of solidarity" should be incorporated into Caritas's programs whenever possible, including in the therapy centers.

Two other Caritas programs are worthy of specific mention because they assist groups among "the least": shelters for single mothers and victims of domestic violence, and programs for the unemployed. The women's shelters attempt to deal with some of the symptoms of the feminization of poverty. Caritas has nine centers for pregnant women who have been ostracized by their families because they have conceived a child out of wedlock. The Church must stand firmly by women in this situation, especially given its pro-life stance. It has another nine centers for women and children who have been traumatized by domestic violence. These centers house women temporarily, up to a one-year maximum. The degree to which Caritas aids them in finding permanent housing, jobs, health care, and quality, affordable daycare determines whether or not this is a form of solidarity. In order for solidarity's requirement of continuity and perseverance to be met, this kind of "firm and persevering determination," to paraphrase John Paul II's definition of solidarity, must be exhibited towards these women. The description of one of the shelters in Cracow maintains that "women leaving the center can count on emotional and spiritual support and financial assistance depending on the center's present ability." In order to exemplify solidarity, this commitment must be definite and concrete; it must enable women to become fully functioning members of society. In addition, more of these shelters must be built in order to meet the demands of women in need in Poland today. Given the immensity of the needs of poor women, Caritas should urge the state to do more. For example, it could put its weight behind supporting the reinstatement of the alimony fund for poor mothers.

Programs for the unemployed have increasingly become another element of Caritas Polska's mission. The goal of these programs is

> to help marginalized people to find trust in themselves and reclaim all that in an unemployed person has been stifled and silenced by his or her feeling of uselessness. A marginalized person is distant from others, and is not able to participate in the life of society, find meaning and the goal of his or her path.... However, while keeping in mind this particular sensitivity of unemployed persons, we cannot

treat them as if they were crippled. On the contrary, it is important to support and sometimes awaken their feeling of responsibility for themselves and for others.[162]

This is undoubtedly an urgent task in a country where more than three million people and their families suffer the negative consequences of unemployment. Solidarity with the poor demands addressing the causes of their poverty, and in Poland unemployment is certainly one of them. Caritas Polska has been working with Caritas France to develop new approaches to helping the unemployed get back on their feet. This is a Herculean task in a country where structural unemployment, downsizing, and industry collapses continue to increase. It appears that most of the assistance provided constitutes job placement as opposed to job training.[163] There is an opportunity to learn valuable job-search skills, but the acquisition of new vocational or technical skills is essential for many unemployed persons in Poland's changing economy. To provide such courses depends on a good deal of resources, and Caritas may not be in a position to do so at this time. Nonetheless, this is the direction in which solidarity calls its programs for the unemployed to move.

A stable, meaningful job should be the outcome of any program for the unemployed. The best way to enable someone to feel responsible for himself and others is to place him in a job that contributes to the common good. While interviewing skills and resumé writing are necessary tools for the unemployed, job training, retraining, and, first and foremost, jobs must be made available. In other words, Caritas should advocate: 1) changing the laws that severely limit access to job-training programs; and 2) policies that stimulate job growth in the areas hit most hard by unemployment, such as the former PGR-y. Towards this end, Caritas undertook a promising venture in the Koszalin-Kołobrzeg and Warsaw dioceses. It purchased two large farms where it employed many local residents who had lost their jobs in agriculture. The next step could be to provide financing for a group of unemployed agricultural workers and farmers who would modernize an existing farm to make it competitive and become worker-owners. This approach has been used by the U.S. Catholic bishops' successful Campaign for Human Development. In short, the job-search programs in place are necessary for solidarity with those who have lost their jobs, but much more needs to be done to grapple with this complicated socioeconomic problem.

The focus on acts of compassion as a first step towards realized solidarity makes sense given that Caritas had to undertake massive efforts to rebuild its infrastructure, including dilapidated buildings appropriated and neglected by the Communists in the former era. Nonetheless, the motto of Caritas is "*być głosem ubogich*," that is, to be the voice of the poor.[164] In order to cohere with the ethic of solidarity, speaking with and on behalf of the poor in order to fight poverty will require advocating sweeping social reforms in addition to providing direct aid. Catholic Relief Services, which is based in the United States, reached this conclusion recently in its history of serving the marginalized and the oppressed in more than sixty countries worldwide. Recognizing the severity and scope of the problems faced by the populations whom it serves, it began to see the need for widespread reform at the level of governmental and international social policy. It described the change in its mission as a shift from a charity-based approach to trying to tackle social problems through a "justice lens."[165] This also included giving the poor themselves a say in how their problems and needs should be addressed, assuming that they themselves best understand their plight. It appears that Caritas Polska should consider such an adaptation in order to be in solidarity with more of Poland's many poor and marginalized—a change from being the voice of the poor to a stance that allows the poor to have their own voice.

Perhaps some of the blame rests on the poor themselves. The mission statement of Caritas's programs for the unemployed indicates that the poor may not always feel responsible for changing their situation. According to Agnieszka Homan of Caritas Kraków, this impedes her organization's ability to operate according to an ethic of solidarity. People often approach Caritas's various ministries in search of a handout or what is "owed to them." This will continue to hamper true solidarity until broad-based efforts at changing this mentality take root. Caritas should be an important contributor to this change through all of its programs.

While detailed analysis of other Catholic organizations cannot be undertaken here, it is worth briefly mentioning several exemplary programs that have sprung into existence recently. To their credit, the Polish bishops acted in solidarity by creating a foundation in 1999 that awards 1,200 scholarships annually to children of poor families from villages and small towns.[166] These scholarships will follow the students throughout their school years, thus ensuring that they will continue to receive a good education. Importantly, scholarships are awarded based on merit and a clear demonstration of financial need. Preference has been given to children from the former PGR-y regions, which, for reasons discussed in chapter 3, is highly appropriate. Scholarship winners are also invited to two-week vacations and to summer language camps. Moreover, the foundation stresses the formation of civic leadership inspired by Christian ideals. In other words, it hopes to shape tomorrow's leaders, who will govern Poland in the spirit of solidarity.

The Archdiocese of Warsaw has also created a foundation that provides loans to unemployed persons who wish to start their own business. The concept of micro-lending, which has had much success in places such as Sri Lanka, is certainly worthy of emulation in Poland. It is encouraging to see that the Archdiocese of Warsaw undertook such an effort to promote the participation of unemployed persons through economic initiatives.[167] Undoubtedly, there are other Catholic groups and organizations that promote solidarity and participation among and with the poor and marginalized. Nevertheless, much more needs to be done, as the laudable efforts described here only begin to address the massive problems of poverty, unemployment, educational deprivation, and lack of access to decent health care for everyone. One can hope that more Catholics and people of all faiths will seek to spread the kinds of solidarity exemplified by some of the programs described above.

Reflections on the Church and Solidarity

This chapter has argued that in order to be faithful to its mission of evangelization, which must include striving for social justice, the Church must promote solidarity, freedom, and participation. It must do so in the educational-cultural, legislative-policy, and prophetic-witness modes. In other words, the Church must function as a teacher, through its social teaching; a political actor, through direct policy advocacy; and a witness, by creating "within the Church a clear counterpoint to existing societal vision and policies."[168] John Paul II continually stressed the need for the bishops to take on this responsibility. On his last pilgrimage to Poland, he implored them to "create and realize a pastoral program of mercy in the spirit of solidarity with others." This program, according to the pope, should shape the internal life of the Church, and, "when right and necessary," it should give rise to involvement in national, European, and global sociopolitical issues.[169] It is understandable that the bishops were not prepared to deal with complex social questions in a capitalist, democratic society. Yet, one must consider the extent to which they have attempted to equip themselves with the necessary skills and knowledge. As Aquinas maintained, ignorance is culpable if the attempt is not made to gain as much knowledge as possible about a given situation.

Another very important way to be a witness to solidarity is to live with and among the poor. Bishop Pieronek believes that Catholics in Poland have a tendency to distance themselves from "others" and to listen to Christ's call "when it is convenient for them." Popular religiosity in Poland has not facilitated "a conversion of the heart," which leads to looking at "the other" through the eyes of Jesus.[170] Does this pertain to the bishops as well? While they have initiated significant programs such as the scholarship aid mentioned above, some of them do not have routine, direct contact with the women, children, and men who experience suffering, prejudice, and marginalization. Most of them remain silent in the face of intolerance towards those with AIDS, immigrants, and minorities.[171]

There are some bishops who live out the option for the poor in an admirable way. Bishop Gołębiewski, for example, has created a committee for socioeconomic affairs in his diocese, which addresses pressing concrete issues. He views this as an important component of the Church's option for the poor.[172] He also has given his salary to families who were devastated by the massive floods in Poland in the 1990s. Bishop Zimoń from Śląsk, which suffers extraordinarily high unemployment, attempts to engage in dialogue with the blighted working class and to defend their interests.[173] His timely and well-drafted pastoral letter on unemployment stands out as an application of Catholic social teaching to difficult and complex local issues. Yet, one wonders if the option for the poor has been fully embraced by all the bishops and clergy in Poland today. Some bishops do not prioritize such attempts at promoting social justice and do not demonstrate solidarity in such ways. Many lead a relatively secluded and privileged lifestyle and have little contact with laypersons. This is not the way to be a prophetic witness to solidarity, which involves being "a sign of contradiction" to the growing individualistic and materialistic culture in Poland. Very few live like Sr. Małgorzata Chmielewska, who recently received an award from the bishops for creating communities for the homeless. She has made a conscious decision to live among the poor and to share her life with them, not just to sporadically reach out to them.

The late Jesuit Stanisław Musiał recognized the many charitable works undertaken by the Church. However, he deplored the fact that hundreds of people freeze to death in Poland each year while Church doors remain under lock and key every night (unlike in France, where churches are opened when temperatures become extreme). Maybe the bishops and the Primate of Poland should attend their funerals, he claimed, in order to raise awareness. Moreover, he maintained that if bishops such as Saint Basil and Saint John Chrysostom lived in Poland today, more money would be spent on scholarships, housing for the poor and elderly, and free catechesis and Bible study rather than on massive basilicas and statues of John Paul II.[174] Perhaps this type of prioritization would take place if the link between evangelization and social justice was more clearly and universally recognized. With more funds available, the valuable work of solidarity carried out by organizations such as Caritas Polska, Fundacja dzieło tysiąclecia, and Fundacja nadzieja could come closer to meeting the demands of widespread poverty and marginalization.

As Christ taught, we should not judge our neighbors before truly repenting ourselves (Matt. 7:1–5). Very few Christians can claim to be in solidarity with the poor always and in every possible way. One hopes, however, that the bishops, as pastors of the Church, will lead the way in striving to fulfill the option for the poor. To a large extent, the witness of the Church's leaders will determine whether or not Catholicism in Poland will remain strong and truly preach the Gospel. This must entail, as Metz points out, demanding less "doctrinal rigorism" and more "radicalism" in the struggle for justice. He believes that people yearn for such a church. Poland needs a demanding church that eschews what Metz calls "bourgeois religion," which legitimates the prosperity of the "haves" by adopting an eschatology that projects God's reign of justice beyond this world.[175]

The Roman Catholic Church in Poland must proclaim the good news with the poor and marginalized by awakening believers from their moral complacency. As the Church in Poland struggles to find its place in a pluralistic, democratic, and capitalist society, it must accept this role. It must become "a church of more freedom and of more demands."[176] For certain, many will resist this call and find solace elsewhere. The "haves" in Poland can now numb the emptiness of life without God and the absence of community by turning to a life of materialistic pursuit, as many people in Western countries have done for a long time. However, as Stefan Swieżawski argues, it is not the number of church-goers every Sunday that counts. Rather, it is more important to have believers who witness to the Gospel with their whole lives.[177] This will be achieved in large part by those who embody solidarity and struggle for the freedom and participation of all persons. For the Church, this means fulfilling its mission of evangelization. Given the scale of poverty in Poland, and the numerous other problems described in this book, Polish society needs the Church to evangelize in this way. The Roman Catholic Church, more than any other nongovernmental organization, is uniquely poised to play this role.

This book began with a recollection of the ideals that animated the "most infectiously hopeful movement in the history of contemporary Europe," to recall Timothy Garton Ash's description of *Solidarność*. At the heart of the movement was a desire to promote unity among differences and a belief in the human desire to achieve unity. The Church, as Poland's largest and most influential nongovernmental organization, can and must be at the forefront of reviving this goal of the Solidarity movement. Church leaders must pursue open and honest dialogue with all groups in Polish society, even with those whom it perceives to be hostile to its message. In order to participate in this kind of dialogue, the Church must exhibit the willingness to seek compromise, as did the members of Solidarity, and it also requires being willing to listen to critics and respond constructively in the spirit of solidarity. Bishop Pieronek, among others, has stressed that the Church has not always been able to learn from its critics.[178] This, however, is a necessary element of solidarity. As Józef Tischner put it, it involves the willingness to forsake a monopoly on the truth. Of course, this does not mean abandoning all of the Church's doctrines in the name of compromise. On the contrary, the Church must be more prophetic, as were the heroes of Solidarity such as Fr. Jerzy Popiełuszko, in regard to its social teaching, for example. This will not be easy in an era dominated by neoliberalism and other false notions of freedom.

Spreading the fear of freedom, however, is not the answer. Rather, fully embracing freedom as a gift of God the Creator and patiently teaching about its true nature can lead to a revival of solidarity.

Although it may be unpopular among many in these times of *dziki kapitalizm* (wild capitalism) in Poland, the Church must better disseminate its social teaching, particularly by clearly and frequently reiterating the relationship between an ethic of solidarity and the option for the poor. On a theological level, it will be important to convince all of the faithful (who constitute the vast majority of Polish society) that by promoting just social structures, they participate in some way in the building of the Kingdom of God, as *Gaudium et Spes* clearly affirmed more than forty years ago. In terms of specific social policies that contribute to social justice and doing God's work, Solidarity's emphasis on "bread and freedom" as necessary for the safeguarding and respecting of human dignity is among the most timely. Just wages and worker ownership were two of Solidarity's most important proposed means of attaining bread and the freedom to participate in the life of society. This book has argued that these goals remain vital to the common good of Polish society today. The Church should lead the way in advocating these two elements of a just economy and participatory democracy because it has a long history of supporting them in its official social teaching. Moreover, building on the ideals of the Solidarity movement, the Church in these new times must promote an understanding of family that fully respects the equality and dignity of all its members. This includes the right of women to participate in the life of society beyond the confines of the home. In order for this to happen, the Church must renew its emphasis on responsible fatherhood, and it must advocate nothing less than a paradigm shift in the way that society conceives gender roles as well as work and family responsibilities.

Finally, and most fundamentally, in the Church resides an important resource for a pedagogy of hope. The Church must unfailingly promote the anthropology of hope that animated the ethic of solidarity in Poland in its past. Without hope, the world becomes a "war of all against all," to use Thomas Hobbes's famous phrase. Without hope, there can be no trust in others. Without trust in others, there can be no solidarity.

Conclusion

Is Solidarity Possible in a Neoliberal Capitalist World?

The Polish people rose to dizzying moral heights in the 1980s. They showed the world that solidarity on a broad social scale is possible, if only for a fleeting moment in the grand scheme of the human drama. This book has narrated the demise of the ethos of solidarity in Poland and explained some of its causes. It has also attempted to reconstruct a viable ethic of solidarity in the contemporary Polish context. The impetus for this project resides in the hope that the ethic of solidarity witnessed in the "unfinished revolution" is not purely a relic of history. Rather, as the introduction intimated, it can provide a basis for the understanding of solidarity in the contemporary world.

By way of conclusion, it may be worth spelling out some of the implications of the ethic of solidarity elaborated in this book for life in a world dominated by neoliberal capitalism. While this book has demonstrated the relevance of a revitalized ethic of solidarity to Poland, it has remained relatively silent about its application to other parts of the world. Thus, a few explicit words about the lessons from Poland's unfinished revolution for other communities and societies are in order. Recognizing that applying the ethic of solidarity, freedom, and participation to various regions of the world well exceeds the scope of this book, most of these remarks pertain to my own context, that is, the United States, and the Church and the academy within it.

In addition to addressing the matter of applicability to other contexts, some other potent challenges to a contemporary ethic of solidarity shall be raised here, albeit heuristically. Future scholars will need to grapple with these challenges if an ethic of solidarity akin to the Polish experience of the 1980s is to function both in democratic, pluralistic, capitalist societies and globally in order to alleviate social evils such as poverty, marginalization, and discrimination. Given the magnitude and complexity of these challenges to solidarity from outside Poland, they may only be signaled here for further scrutiny.

Is Neoliberal Capitalism Regnant Globally?

Is it an exaggeration to claim that the kind of neoliberal capitalism found in Poland after 1989 reigns throughout the world? If this is not the case, then perhaps the ethic of solidarity developed herein loses much of its relevance to other contexts. Two factors indicate that indeed neoliberalism's ascendancy on much of the globe persists today. First, voices from around the world in the recent past have decried the deleterious consequences of neoliberalism and continue to raise concerns. The Latin American Jesuit provincials, for example, characterized neoliberalism as "a radical conception of capitalism that tends toward an absolutist view of the market, transforming it into the means, the method and the end of all rational and intelligent behavior."[1] William Greider describes how neoliberal economic policies such as the free flow of capital and unrestricted trade policies wreaked havoc in Mexico and elsewhere in the 1990s.[2] He believes that neoliberal capitalism is leading us on a collision course because it has generated masses of poor, marginalized, and discontented people throughout the world. German-born theologian Gregory Baum contends that "the neoliberal world project" is undergirded by "an updated version of nineteenth-century social Darwinism" and a culture that "legitimates the public indifference to solidarity."[3] In her recent book on ethics and globalization, Christian ethicist Rebecca Todd Peters states that neoliberalism is the dominant paradigm within which most people think about globalization today. In addition to these secular and Christian critics, Islamic scholars have also critiqued problematic aspects of neoliberalism.[4]

Second, Social Democratic governments in Europe that have traditionally promoted some form of the social market economy have recently fallen on hard times. In Sweden, for example, the Social Democratic party was voted out of office in 2006 for the first time in more than twelve years, in spite of the fact that some observers have dubbed the Swedish version of the social market economy the most successful that the world has ever known.[5] The individualism of neoliberalism seems to have taken hold not only in Sweden but also in Germany, the birthplace of the *Sozialmarktwirtschaft*. Many young, talented professionals no longer wish to sacrifice some of their earning potential for the sake of the common good.[6] Trade union solidarity has begun to deteriorate; some unions are no longer concerned about wage equity across sectors of the economy.[7] Thus, the ethic of solidarity and its remedies for the "market failures" of the neoliberal economy in Poland clearly have implications beyond its borders.

American Socioeconomic Realities and the Ethic of Solidarity

Those familiar with the American socioeconomic and political context will readily ascertain similar problems. Thus, many of the policy proposals in this book, which grow out of the ethic of solidarity, are relevant to the situation in the United States. Of course, the American context is different from Poland in important ways. However, neoliberalism and the reactions against it share commonalities in both countries. Ironically, the hypocrisy of both Washington and Warsaw strikingly mirror one another. On the one hand, both governments have repeated much of the neoliberal rhetoric pertaining to issues such as free trade. Yet, the American government, like the Polish government, continues to support agricultural subsidies that ultimately hurt farmers in underdeveloped nations. In addition, both governments fail to see that realizing the right to an education is both an end in itself, that is, a substantive human freedom, and a means towards economic development.[8] In this regard, Poland and the United States both adopt the neoliberal party line by prioritizing economic growth understood in terms of the GDP as opposed to Sen's much richer understanding of development as freedom.

A plethora of socioeconomic and political issues in contemporary American society point to the need for recovering an ethic of solidarity. Other examples include excessive concentrations of wealth, the scarcity of worker cooperatives, the waning influence of unions, the replacement of a decent livelihood in farming and the industrial sector with low-wage, service-sector jobs,[9] and debates about just tax structures.[10] These examples attest to the fact that the cases of Poland and the United States bear much resemblance. Moreover, a growing body of literature is illuminating similar problems in numerous countries that have vast numbers of the working poor.[11] Clearly, the argument for just wages as expressions of freedom and solidarity is germane to many parts of the world.

The Problem of Freedom

The underlying issue of freedom at the root of Poland's social problems is also not peculiar to the "heart of Europe." For example, Harvard Professor of Law Mary Ann Glendon has written that the UN Universal Declaration of Human Rights' insistence on the links between freedom and solidarity seems untenable to many. In her words, "principles such as freedom and solidarity *do* sit uneasily with one another."[12] Even the great historian and admirer of Solidarity, Timothy Garton Ash, maintained that solidarity probably does not exist in Poland after Communism, or in any other free society.[13] A conception of freedom construed in a way inimical to human solidarity lurks behind this putative tension between solidarity and freedom. The problem resides in the pervasive acceptance of freedom construed negatively. Most Americans, for example, tend to view freedom exclusively as "negative."[14] Whether or not Americans and other members of the human family would be convinced by the argument of this book that freedom and solidarity mutually entail one another is debatable. However, the need for a persuasive recasting of the relationship between solidarity and freedom in American society and elsewhere is indisputable. Failure to do so will have grave consequences for the poor and marginalized, because if negative freedom monopolizes the thinking and action of citizens and decisionmakers, problems such as poverty and social marginalization will not be attenuated. As David Hollenbach has cogently argued, values such as fairness and tolerance are important to the welfare of individuals and societies, but they are hardly sufficient for generating the kind of proactive civic engagement and pro-poor policymaking needed to deal with such serious flaws in contemporary societies. "Tolerance means acceptance of difference, perhaps even a kind of acquiescence in such differences." Thus, tolerance alone can lead to apathy in the face of class barriers.[15] Overcoming the chasm between the "haves" and the "have-nots" in contemporary societies requires more than acceptance of differences. It requires robust and widespread solidarity.

Individualism and the Capitalist Spirit

As chapter 2 described, Polish society had a strong communitarian ethos with historical, cultural roots prior to the transformation to capitalism. How can solidarity, which requires the willingness to make sacrifices for the sake of the common good, be inculcated in all people in societies where the dominant ethos tends to be highly individualistic? Neoliberalism quickly eviscerated much of the Polish communitarian ethos. In a country such as the United States, which has been dominated by a more individualistic ethos, how can an ethic of solidarity take root?[16] Nothing less than a "Copernican revolution" would need to take place. Much of the American "story" would need to be rewritten. Most notably, the myth of self-reliance, which stresses that American success stories are made by "pulling one's self up by the bootstraps," without social support, needs to be tempered. In addition, *homo consumens,* which Eric Fromm ascribed to modern humans decades ago, is alive and well in the United States.[17] Powerful stories via television, movies, and advertisements tell us that "to have" is "to be" in our society today. The promulgation of the consumerist mentality and the unfettered desire to consume must be overcome if solidarity is to flourish.[18] This certainly provides a daunting, if not Sisyphean, task for those who wish to promote the rich ethic of the Catholic social tradition. Nonetheless, this must be done in order to push aside the excessive individualism of American society and make room for solidarity.

"Hard-Wired" for Solidarity?

Given these seemingly insurmountable obstacles, perhaps the demands of solidarity are simply too great for mere mortals. Is it really possible, for example, for solidarity to govern international relations, as both John Paul II and the United Nations have wished?[19] Movements such as Solidarity in Poland and People's Power in the Philippines have demonstrated that the demands of solidarity can be met on a large scale. However, might such examples be isolated anomalies in the grand scheme of human history? Many philosophers and theologians assume that human solidarity is possible on ever greater scales, without considering two salient issues. First, much of human history tells us otherwise. In the twentieth century alone, more than 167,000,000 people were killed in the name of political ideologies, making it the bloodiest century in human history.[20] Some thinkers have argued that in our fragmented, globalized world, differences divide people so severely that talk of solidarity has become obsolete.[21] The colonialist agenda, for example, to "civilize" indigenous peoples in the name of solidarity has rendered the term suspicious, if not discredited altogether.

Second, in the contemporary milieu, a pervasive belief exists purporting that human nature itself militates against the call for solidarity in all spheres of social life. Some sociobiologists and evolutionary theorists would contend that humans are inherently incapable of sustaining the "thick" solidarity of Catholic social thought. Realists and much of modern economic theory eschew the social anthropology of solidarity in favor of *homo oeconomicus*. This view of the human person holds that self-interest dominates the decisionmaking process of both individuals and nations.[22] Perhaps we are not "hard-wired" to practice solidarity. Is it realistic to call for solidarity among diverse and often fractured communities, to say nothing of nations and international bodies? These are difficult and complicated questions. In order for proponents of solidarity to answer them, they ought to turn to the sciences and evolutionary theory to discern whether the normative demands of solidarity are realistic, given what we know about human nature and identity. The time for such conversation is ripe, as evolutionary biologists, anthropologists, primatologists, and psychologists are devoting serious attention to the nature of human and social morality. While genetics and evolutionary theory may not ultimately be able to prove or disprove the viability of an ethic of solidarity, insights from these fields should certainly be considered. In other words, theologians and philosophers who advocate an ethic of solidarity should not ignore the sciences. Rather, they should engage them in seeking to understand human nature and the degree to which human beings are capable of solidarity.

Implications for the Catholic Social Tradition

In addition to this book's implications for and challenges to a universal ethic of solidarity, several suggestions arise pertaining specifically to Catholic social teaching. These issues are complex and full of potential misunderstandings. Thus, these remarks are provisional. Nonetheless, they should at least be mentioned to stimulate further reflection, especially as this book expounds and attempts to enrich the Catholic social tradition.

Roman Catholics and non-Catholics alike often misuse the category of solidarity. In this vein, Ada Maria Isasi-Diaz lamented in 1990 that the meaning of solidarity was "under serious attack." Solidarity, in her view, had become *en vogue* at the time. Yet most people conceived of it as "unthreatening," reducing it to a feeling of sympathy or agreement with a cause.[23] In the early twenty-first century, misunderstandings of solidarity continue to abound. Many people today champion solidarity with the poor. They embark on service-immersion trips to places such as Appalachia, the Dominican Republic, and elsewhere domestically and globally. Their earnest desire to help the poor is laudable. However, the distinction between charity and solidarity often is lost on them. They fail to recognize that to develop solidarity with the poor entails *both* direct contact and mutuality with them *and* the promotion of just and participatory institutions and structures. For certain, their activities embody aspects of solidarity; they have taken some of the necessary steps towards its realization. However, their solidarity with the poor remains incomplete.

Some of the leading thinkers in areas such as ethics and education also use the category of solidarity in a nebulous manner. In his acclaimed book, *Democracy and Tradition*, Jeffrey Stout describes what he calls the solidarity of Americans immediately following the terrorist attacks of September 11, 2001.[24] Paul Locatelli, S.J., president of Santa Clara University, refers to solidarity in a confusing way in his speech, "The Catholic University of the 21st Century: Educating for Solidarity." On the one hand, he mentions the solidarity that Americans expressed towards the victims of the tsunami in Southeast Asia and of the destroyed World Trade Center in New York. On the other hand, he maintains that solidarity requires "sophisticated ethical analysis and actions."[25] He obfuscates how these two aspects of solidarity or, more appropriately, steps towards solidarity relate to one another. In both of these instances, the speakers conflate sympathy, charitable actions, and embodiments of solidarity.

Some scholars have sought to clarify the meaning and scope of solidarity in contemporary Catholic social thought. Christine Firer Hinze's treatment in a recent article ranks among the most helpful.[26] This book shares her desire to elucidate the meaning of solidarity in a world of suffering. Like Hinze's work, this book hopefully makes a contribution by reiterating and perhaps illuminating in new ways the true nature of solidarity, which John Paul II made a key theme in Catholic social thought. To be certain, more is at stake here than just an academic issue. Religious organizations and Catholic universities have begun a campaign to disseminate the call to solidarity. Such attempts to clarify its nature and encourage its practice in various forms are crucial to mending the broken world in which we live. Those who write about solidarity need to do more to help others envision what solidarity looks like "on the ground."

The methodology of this book, which entails moving to the level of empirical realities and public policies to grapple with the problem of poverty, implies another concern regarding Catholic social thought. Theologians and ethicists who advocate the option for the poor must go beyond the level of principles and abstract calls for solidarity. Proponents of the option for the poor rarely delve into the complex host of issues surrounding the phenomenon of poverty. Philosopher Thomas Pogge exemplifies the kind of careful analysis of poverty in his work that is needed.[27] Theologians and Christian ethicists who challenge us to stand in solidarity with the poor must acknowledge the difficulties in understanding poverty and seek to provide answers to the many complicated questions concerning its causes and its remedies. Some have done pioneering work in this vein already. For example, Thomas Massaro, S.J., has delved into the particulars of American welfare reform and illuminated them in the light of Catholic social teaching.[28] More thinkers need to undertake this kind of analysis so that the norms of Catholic social teaching do not remain "vague and sterile," to repeat Jacques Drèze's critique.

Finally, Pope Benedict's encyclical *Deus Caritas Est* has renewed the question about the nature and scope of the Church's mission to promote justice. In particular, it reopens the question raised by this book pertaining to the appropriate level of specificity of official Catholic social teaching. Should bishops become mired in welfare and taxation policies, for example, if "the Church cannot and must not take upon herself the political battle to bring about the most just society possible"? (no. 28). Benedict's multifaceted argument does not yield a simple answer. Therefore, this issue cannot be adjudicated here. However, the thrust of the Church's social teaching as presented in this book reveals that continued discussion is needed. The mixed reactions to this papal encyclical on this matter beg clarification of the current pope's position.[29] This seems all the more necessary, given that what Benedict has written may lead to the conclusion (perhaps mistakenly) that he is taking the Church in a direction different from that of his predecessor, John Paul II, regarding its social mission. It is certainly needed if some Catholics conclude that the call to solidarity involves charity without justice.

Epilogue

Since the completion of this book, Poland has undergone significant changes—some good, and some bad. The great leaders of Solidarity have begun to leave us. First, Jacek Kuroń died. Then, cancer prematurely took the life of Alina Pieńkowska. This past summer, the great intellectual leader of the movement, Prof. Bronisław Geremek, was tragically killed in a car accident; he was 76 years old. Lech Wałęsa said that without Geremek, he would not have changed the face of Europe and the world. He believed that Geremek's influence on the course of events in the 1980s in Poland was the greatest, after John Paul II, and he secretly hoped that Geremek would someday become the president of Poland. Wałęsa himself has been recently maligned in a book that unjustly accuses him of collaborating with the Communist secret police ("SB"). Public scrutiny of Wałęsa in recent times has opened up a retrospective examination of the Solidarity movement in the Polish press. The conversation is sometimes painful, as various players fling vitriol towards one another. The ruling Law and Justice party (Prawo i Sprawiedliwość), to which current president Lech Kaczyński belongs, seems intent on tarnishing the image of Wałęsa and others by insisting on lustration. They contend that Poland has yet to cleanse itself of its Communist past. The tone of their recriminations, and the responses to them, are a far cry from solidarity.

Without the leadership of Pope John Paul II, Fr. Józef Tischner, and the other towering figures from the Solidarity era, what chance does Poland have for recovering the legacy of those days and bringing their lessons to life again? It is deeply saddening that the world has lost so many of those courageous men and women who showed us that it can be done—that human beings can overcome their fears and selfish drives to become one, to act in solidarity. This book has revealed that since 1989 the vision of these men and women has largely been eclipsed, yet, some Poles, at least, remain optimistic. The material conditions of many Poles have improved greatly in the last few years. The rate of unemployment, though still a problem, continues to decrease steadily. Many social commentators look to the future generations to create a Poland untainted by *homo sovieticus*. These younger Poles, a great source of hope, did not experience the nation's difficult past and are future-oriented. They are generally optimistic and more open to divergent perspectives than many Poles of previous generations. One hopes that they will be eager to leave behind the debilitating baggage of the past while cherishing the valuable lessons from the Solidarity era.

In addition, the Solidarity union has returned to fighting for workers' rights. Its leaders seem to have heeded John Paul II's call to eschew direct involvement in politics. Instead, the union has begun a large-scale campaign called "adequate work, adequate retirement" (*godna praca, godna emerytura*). One of its goals is to raise the minimum wage to one half of the average salary. The campaign also demands a return to "authentic social dialogue." Thus, Solidarity has begun to take steps in the right direction. As David Ost has pointed out, the recent revival of trade unionism shows that new kinds of workers are being included, such as those in the service and retail sectors. Many people have awakened to realize that neoliberal capitalism conflicts with the aspirations of the Solidarity movement. A growing collection of movements has sprung up to resist the dominance of neoliberalism and protest against social stratification.[1]

Despite these positive trends, Poland remains far from being a nation founded on the ideals of Solidarity. For example, it still has the highest rate of child poverty in Europe. A recent article in *Polityka* entitled "*Dzieci i dzieci-śmieci*" (Children and Garbage-Children) describes the persistent discrimination against poor children and the mechanisms that perpetuate class divisions, which begin in the earliest years of a child's life. Many of the social and economic forms of marginalization described in this book remain potent obstacles to solidarity. In a recent interview two young, acclaimed playwrights discuss their attempt to raise consciousness of social problems through theater. They attributed the Polish acceptance of neoliberalism as a "new religion" in part to the Church for not speaking the language of its own social teaching. Rather, the Church has reverted to the language of a retrograde amalgam of Catholicism and nationalism tinged with xenophobia.[2] While it is unfair to ascribe this to the whole Church, it is true that some Catholic groups sow the seeds of hatred towards "others." Unfortunately, the Church's leaders have not always repudiated these voices swiftly and forcefully.

Poland's new political leaders have not done much better at rebuilding the ethos of solidarity. In August 2007, Wiesława Warzywoda-Kruszyńska, a professor and sociologist who specializes in poverty research, was asked if the Law and Justice party fulfilled its campaign promise to create a nation of solidarity. Her response sums up the current situation well. In her view, the answer is no, "if we assume that in 'a nation of solidarity' the government tries to lessen the effects of inordinate differences in the material status of its citizens." The government has done very little in this vein. She argues that in a "nation of solidarity" (*państwo solidarne*), the government would not undercut its ability to pay for important social programs such as universal preschool in order to appease constituents or abide by a wayward ideological principle.[3] For those of us who have lived through eight years of the Bush administration and its acceleration of the neoliberal agenda, her perspective sounds frighteningly familiar.

Yet, perhaps a new era is dawning. Some important voices have declared that the recent monumental financial and economic crisis in the United States and beyond has utterly discredited neoliberalism. E. J. Dionne, one of the most astute social and political commentators on the contemporary American scene, recently proclaimed the death of Reaganomics. He mentioned that influential politicians are finally acknowledging that neoliberal capitalism, while serving the interests of the minority, has wreaked havoc on the most vulnerable.[4] David Brooks, who correctly assigns blame to Democrats as well as to Republicans for unreflectively accepting neoliberal dogmas, described the dominance of neoliberalism in politics, economics, and American journalism since the

1980s, and declared that it has at last died.[5] Renowned British theologian Philip Blond lamented the long-term, pernicious social and economic consequences of neoliberalism in Great Britain and urged the creation of a truly "shared economy."[6] The Vatican newspaper, *L'Osservatore Romano,* joined this chorus by printing an article that deems the fundamental assumptions of the "so-called new economy" fundamentally flawed and misguided.[7]

Some observers of the modern global economy such as William Greider predicted its possible wreckage more than ten years ago. He argued that we are headed on a collision course because of the social dislocations generated by global capitalism. At that time, he stated that we could retrace the path to fascism of the early twentieth century if we do not attend to the inequalities and social displacements created by market fundamentalism.[8] The question remains, Will we undertake to repair capitalism and democracy by constructing policies and institutions grounded in an ethic of solidarity, or will we ignore the messages sent to us by the collapse of the market and the failure of the neoliberal project? The stakes are incredibly high. We cannot afford to ignore what history has told us. We can no longer promote interlocking systems of global economy and international relations that allow the powerful to reap benefits at the expense of the suffering and oppressed. We ought to return to the aspirations of people such as Wałęsa, Pieńkowska, and Adam Michnik. We ought to heed John Paul II's repeated calls to make capitalism serve true human freedom and solidarity. This will require courageous and wise leadership. The Catholic social tradition has offered helpful signposts for such leaders. We can only hope that they will follow them and undertake this necessary and difficult task. The Great Depression ushered in the New Deal, which the Catholic social tradition helped to shape. There is no reason to believe that we cannot, once again, chart a similar course.

NOTES

Introduction

1. Timothy Garton Ash, *The Polish Revolution: Solidarity*, 3d ed. (New Haven, Conn.: Yale University Press, 2002), 351.
2. Adam Michnik, *Letters from Freedom: Post–Cold War Realities and Perspectives*, trans. Irena Grudzińska-Gross (Berkeley: University of California Press, 1998), 165.
3. Andrzej Stankiewicz, "Młodzi doceniają 'Solidarność,'" *Rzeczpospolita*, August 16, 2005.
4. Aleksander Smolar, "Rocznice, pamięć, przyszłość," *Znak* 558, no. 11 (2001): 38.
5. For a geographically far-reaching treatment of the turmoil wreaked by capitalism, see William Greider, *One World, Ready or Not: The Manic Logic of Global Capitalism* (New York: Simon & Schuster, 1997).
6. Numerous works have discussed the dominance of neoliberalism. On Latin America, see ibid., 263–84; and Jesuit Provincials of Latin America, "A Letter on Neoliberalism in Latin America," *Promotio Justitiae* 67 (1997): 48. On Central and Eastern Europe, see Jerzy Szacki, *Liberalism after Communism*, trans. Chester Adam Kisiel (Budapest: Central European University Press, 1995), 119–70; and Michel Albert, *Capitalism vs. Capitalism: How America's Obsession with Individual Achievement and Short-term Profit Has Led It to the Brink of Collapse* (New York: Four Walls Eight Windows, 1993). On Canada, see Gregory Baum, "Are We in a New Historical Situation? Must We Rethink What Justice and Solidarity Mean Today?" in *Stone Soup: Reflections on Economic Injustice* (Montreal: Paulines, 1998). On the global economy in general, see Rebecca Todd Peters, *In Search of the Good Life: The Ethics of Globalization* (New York: Continuum, 2004), 41–69; and Andrew Glyn, *Social Democracy in Neoliberal Times: The Left and Economic Policy since 1980* (Oxford: Oxford University Press, 2001). For Islamic critiques of neoliberalism,

see Tariq Ramadan, *Western Muslims and the Future of Islam* (Oxford: Oxford University Press, 2004), 199; and Charles Tripp, *Islam and the Moral Economy: The Challenge of Capitalism* (Cambridge: Cambridge University Press, 2006).

7. See Szacki, *Liberalism after Communism*, 137–38.

8. See Greider, *One World, Ready or Not*, 40. Eric Fromm described the social and psychological etiology of this phenomenon in Erich Fromm, *Escape from Freedom*, 1st ed. (New York: Henry Holt, 1994).

9. Isaiah Berlin, Henry Hardy, and Ian Harris, *Liberty: Incorporating Four Essays on Liberty* (Oxford: Oxford University Press, 2002), 167.

10. See ibid., 168.

11. In this regard, Aniela Dylus states that "at the basis of every sociopolitical decision lies an axiological option." Aniela Dylus, *Gospodarka, moralność, chrześcijaństwo* (Warsaw: Wydawnictwo Fundacji ATK, 1994), 105. Following Joseph Stiglitz, Polish economist Tadeusz Kowalik argues that long-term economic development depends above all on the "sociological factors" of ideas, interests, and coalitions. Tadeusz Kowalik, "Joseph Stiglitz a polska transformacja," *Myśl socjaldemokratyczna* 1 (2002): 95. See Joseph E. Stiglitz, "The Private Uses of Public Interests: Incentives and Institutions," *Journal of Economic Perspectives* (Spring 1998). Stiglitz also takes this up in the final chapter of Joseph E. Stiglitz, *Globalization and Its Discontents*, 1st ed. (New York: W.W. Norton, 2002).

12. John Paul II, "Niech Solidarność wróci do korzeni," *Gazeta Wyborcza*, November 13, 2003. Other notable proponents of a retrieval of the ethic of solidarity in Poland include thinkers affiliated with the Catholic journals *Znak* and *Więź*, some Roman Catholic bishops, and, prior to his death, Józef Tischner.

13. The influential Catholic monthly *Znak* titled its November 2001 issue, "1989—An Unfinished Revolution?" (*1989—niedokończona rewolucja?*). See also Dariusz Gawin, "'Solidarność'—republikańska rewolucja Polaków," in *Lekcja sierpnia: dziedzictwo 'Solidarności' po dwudziestu latach*, ed. Dariusz Gawin (Warsaw: Wydawnictwo IFiS PAN, 2002), 179. Gawin maintains that Solidarity should be seen as a process that was begun in 1980 and continues to present challenges to Polish democracy. It has and will continue to go through phases of greater or lesser institutionalization of its values.

14. Jacques H. Drèze, "Ethics, Efficiency, and the Social Doctrine of the Church," in *Social and Ethical Aspects of Economics: A Colloquium in the Vatican*, ed. Pontificium Consilium de Iustitia et Pace (Vatican City: Pontifical Council for Justice and Peace, 1992), 45.

15. See National Center for Children in Poverty statistics at http://nccp.org/pub_lico6b.html.

16. See, for example, "A Revolution Faces the Voters," *The Economist*, June 29, 2006.

17. Greider, *One World, Ready or Not*, 39–56.

18. Józef Tischner, "Fragment o solidarności," *Znak* 543, no. 8 (2000): 21. Another important article is Józef Tischner, "Solidarność po latach," in *Spór o*

Polskę: 1989–99, ed. Paweł Śpiewak (Warsaw: PWN, 2000). I have written a sketch of Tischner's life and philosophy in Gerald J. Beyer, "Fr. Józef Tischner (1931–2000): Chaplain of *Solidarność* and Philosopher of Hope," *Religion in Eastern Europe* 21, no. 1 (2001).

CHAPTER ONE   The Ethic of Solidarity from 1980 to 1989

A version of this chapter was published as "A Theoretical Appreciation of the Ethic of Solidarity in Poland Twenty-Five Years After," *Journal of Religious Ethics* 35, no. 2 (June 2007): 207–32.

    1. Adam Michnik, "The Moral and Spiritual Origins of Solidarity," in *Without Force or Lies: Voices from the Revolution of Central Europe in 1989–90: Essays, Speeches, and Eyewitness Accounts*, ed. William M. Brinton and Alan Rinzler (San Francisco: Mercury House, 1990), 243.

    2. Gawin, "'Solidarność'—republikańska rewolucja Polaków," 174–75.

    3. Adam Michnik, Józef Tischner, and Jacek Żakowski, *Między panem a plebanem*, 1st ed. (Cracow: Znak, 1995), 314–15.

    4. Garton Ash, *The Polish Revolution: Solidarity*, 269. Some Poles have drawn the conclusion that Solidarity was really nothing more than a political struggle for power. For an example of a realist interpretation of Solidarity, see Marek Cichocki, "Doświadczenie pierwszej 'Solidarności'—między moralnym absolutyzmem a polityczną samowiedzą Polaków," in *Lekcja sierpnia: dziedzictwo 'Solidarności' po dwudziestu latach*, ed. Dariusz Gawin (Warsaw: Wydawnictwo IFiS PAN, 2002). There is some historical truth to this view, as the movement certainly had internal conflicts. However, this interpretation denies the heroic sacrifices and moral achievements of the movement.

    5. Zbigniew Stawrowski, "Doświadczenie 'Solidarności' jako wspólnoty etycznej," in *Lekcja sierpnia: dziedzictwo 'Solidarności' po dwudziestu latach*, ed. Dariusz Gawin (Warsaw: Wydawnictwo IFiS PAN, 2002), 104.

    6. Garton Ash, *The Polish Revolution: Solidarity*, 165, 289.

    7. Ibid., 163.

    8. See Antoni Dudek, "Rewolucja robotnicza i ruch narodowowyzwoleńczy," in *Lekcja sierpnia: dziedzictwo 'Solidarności' po dwudziestu latach*, ed. Dariusz Gawin (Warsaw: Wydawnictwo IFiS PAN, 2002), 148; and Garton Ash, *The Polish Revolution: Solidarity*, 227.

    9. Garton Ash, *The Polish Revolution: Solidarity*, 20; Michnik, "The Moral and Spiritual Origins of Solidarity," 241; Lech Wałęsa, *A Way of Hope* (New York: Henry Holt, 1987), 95–97.

    10. Both Krzemiński and Garton Ash acknowledge these tensions, and the historical debates surrounding them, but reach this conclusion. In his postscript to the third edition of his book, Garton Ash argues that it is precisely this alliance

between the workers and the intellectuals that made Solidarity possible. See Garton Ash, *The Polish Revolution: Solidarity*, 351–55; and Ireneusz Krzemiński, *Solidarność: projekt polskiej demokracji* (Warsaw: Oficyna Naukowa, 1997), 12–20. For a view that starkly underscores the tensions between workers and the intelligentsia, yet does not deny the latter's role in Solidarity, see Dudek, "Rewolucja robotnicza i ruch narodowowyzwoleńczy," 142–50.

11. Garton Ash, *The Polish Revolution: Solidarity*, 266.

12. Józef Tischner, *Etyka solidarności oraz homo sovieticus*, 1st ed. (Cracow: Znak, 1992), 20, 120. The English translation of this book, which helped shape the Solidarity movement, is Józef Tischner, *The Spirit of Solidarity*, trans. Marek B. Zaleski and Benjamin Fiore (San Francisco: Harper & Row, 1984).

13. Michnik, *Letters from Freedom*, 117–21.

14. Tischner, *Etyka solidarności oraz homo sovieticus*, 92–93. Following Reinhold Niebuhr, one may ask if a strike is actually a form of violence, or at least coercion. See Reinhold Niebuhr, *Moral Man and Immoral Society: A Study in Ethics and Politics* (New York, London: C. Scribner's, 1932), 250–56. For a comparison of Niebuhr and Tischner on this issue, see Beyer, "Fr. Józef Tischner (1931–2000)," 36–38.

15. Karol Wojtyła, *Osoba i czyn oraz inne studia antropologiczne*, 3d. ed. (Lublin: Towarzystwo Naukowe KUL, 2000), 325. For the English translation, see Karol Wojtyła, *The Acting Person*, trans. Andrzej Potocki (Boston: D. Reidel, 1979). On this work's importance to the Solidarity movement, see Wojciech Bonowicz, *Tischner* (Cracow: Znak, 2001), 266–67; and Jarosław Gowin, "Kościół a 'Solidarność,'" in *Lekcja sierpnia: dziedzictwo 'Solidarności' po dwudziestu latach*, ed. Dariusz Gawin (Warsaw: Wydawnictwo IFiS PAN, 2002), 26–27.

16. Krzemiński, *Solidarność: projekt polskiej demokracji*, 230–40; Janine R. Wedel, *The Private Poland* (New York: Facts on File, 1986).

17. Władysław Zuziak, "Znaczenie myśli Józefa Tischnera w rozwoju idei solidarności," in *Idea solidarności dzisiaj*, ed. Władysław Zuziak (Cracow: Wydawnictwo Naukowe PAT, 2001), 33.

18. Kolyma was the largest of the Soviet "work camps" in Siberia, in which tens of millions of people died. Millions of Poles were deported to these camps, never to return to their homeland.

19. Stawrowski, "Doświadczenie 'Solidarności' jako wspólnoty etycznej," 115.

20. Michnik, "The Moral and Spiritual Origins of Solidarity," 246.

21. Tischner, *Etyka solidarności oraz homo sovieticus*, 11, 19. See also Michnik, "The Moral and Spiritual Origins of Solidarity," 246.

22. Tischner, *Etyka solidarności oraz homo sovieticus*, 22, 92.

23. For more on Solidarity's commitment to nonviolence, see Garton Ash, *The Polish Revolution: Solidarity*, 54, 164, 255, 257, 269, 271, 301; Gowin, "Kościół a 'Solidarność,'" 30; Michnik, "The Moral and Spiritual Origins of Solidarity," 243–46; Gawin, "Solidarność—republikańska rewolucja Polaków," 166; and Tischner, *Etyka solidarności oraz homo sovieticus*, 64, 82–84, 91–94, 194.

24. Gowin, "Kościół a 'Solidarność,'" 29.
25. Jacek Salij, "Solidarność trochę teologiczniej," *Znak* 543, no. 8 (2000): 48.
26. Tischner, *Etyka solidarności oraz homo sovieticus*, 11. See also Michnik, "The Moral and Spiritual Origins of Solidarity," 246; and Garton Ash, *The Polish Revolution: Solidarity*, 239–41.
27. Tischner, *Etyka solidarności oraz homo sovieticus*, 47, 60, 69.
28. Józef Tischner, *Nieszczęsny dar wolności* (Cracow: Znak, 1996), 71.
29. Gowin, "Kościół a 'Solidarność,'" 28.
30. Tischner, *Etyka solidarności oraz homo sovieticus*, 95. See also Józef Tischner and Jacek Żakowski, *Tischner czyta katechizm* (Cracow: Znak, 1996), 94.
31. Tischner, *The Spirit of Solidarity*, 2–3.
32. Garton Ash, *The Polish Revolution: Solidarity*, 45–46.
33. Ibid., 117–40, 317.
34. Ibid., 135.
35. Jarosław Gowin, *Kościół po komunizmie* (Cracow: Znak, 1995), 37.
36. Adam Michnik, *Letters from Prison and Other Essays* (Berkeley: University of California Press, 1985), 16–24.
37. Tischner, *Etyka solidarności oraz homo sovieticus*, 69–71; Wałęsa, *A Way of Hope*, 299–307; George Weigel, *The Final Revolution: The Resistance Church and the Collapse of Communism* (New York: Oxford University Press, 1992), 149.
38. Wojciech Bonowicz, "Światła etyki solidarności," *Tygodnik Powszechny*, January 7, 2001; Bonowicz, *Tischner*, 350–52; Józef Tischner, *Myślenie według wartości*, 3d ed. (Cracow: Znak, 2000), 8–9.
39. See Garton Ash, *The Polish Revolution: Solidarity*, 237–39.
40. Cited in Gawin, "'Solidarność'—republikańska rewolucja Polaków," 168.
41. Ibid., 169.
42. Two feminist critiques have raised this issue. See Agnieszka Graff, *Świat bez kobiet: płeć w polskim życiu publicznym*, 1st ed. (Warsaw: Wydawn. W.A.B., 2001), 24–26; and Shana Penn, *Podziemie kobiet* (Warsaw: Wydawnictwo Rosner i Wspólnicy, 2003). For a positive appraisal of the role of women in Solidarity, see, for example, Wałęsa, *A Way of Hope*, 99, 112–13, 116–18.
43. Tischner, *Etyka solidarności oraz homo sovieticus*, 55.
44. Ibid.
45. Garton Ash, *The Polish Revolution: Solidarity*, 229–30.
46. Gawin, "'Solidarność'—republikańska rewolucja Polaków," 173.
47. Ibid., 181.
48. See Krzemiński, *Solidarność: projekt polskiej demokracji*, 246–48. This term is used here to describe the renewed emphasis on civil discourse and civic participation. Some scholars have pointed to the various definitions of "civil society" and the problems in applying them to Poland. For an overview of this issue, see Cichocki, "Doświadczenie pierwszej 'Solidarności.'" For usage of the term to describe Solidarity's aim, see Szacki, *Liberalism after Communism*, 73–117; and Anita Miszalska, "Moralność a demokracja—uwagi o stylu moralnym

współczesnego społeczeństwa polskiego," in *Kondycja moralna społeczeństwa polskiego*, ed. Janusz Mariański (Cracow: Wydawnictwo WAM, 2002), 168–69. Szacki acknowledges the ambiguity of the term, but he contends that it was used widely and appropriately to describe the changes sought by Solidarity in the 1980s. He also stresses that the dominant understanding of civil society in Poland at the time did not posit antagonism between the individual and the collective, as Western thinkers on the subject sometimes do.

49. Krzemiński, *Solidarność: projekt polskiej demokracji*, 105.

50. Garton Ash, *The Polish Revolution: Solidarity*, 304.

51. Dudek, "Rewolucja robotnicza i ruch narodowowyzwoleńczy," 149–50; Garton Ash, *The Polish Revolution: Solidarity*, 196–99, 236–37.

52. In one part of *Etyka solidarności*, Tischner criticizes the "socialization" (*uspołecznienie*) of the means of production. On the other hand, he distinguishes between open socialism, which he finds worthy of some merit, and closed socialism. See Tischner, *Etyka solidarności oraz homo sovieticus*, 22–30, 56–59, 119–20. Gowin contends that Tischner advocated some kind of "third way" between socialism and capitalism. Gowin, "Kościół a 'Solidarność,'" 33–36. On this question, see also Garton Ash, *The Polish Revolution: Solidarity*; and Krzemiński, *Solidarność: projekt polskiej demokracji*, 246–47.

53. Tischner, *Etyka solidarności oraz homo sovieticus*, 23–25, 30, 92–93.

54. In the very first worker protest in Poland, which took place in Poznań in 1956, workers printed posters demanding "bread and freedom." See Garton Ash, *The Polish Revolution: Solidarity*, 11.

55. Dudek, "Rewolucja robotnicza i ruch narodowowyzwoleńczy," 149; Garton Ash, *The Polish Revolution: Solidarity*, 232, 38.

56. See Garton Ash, *The Polish Revolution: Solidarity*, 232; Gawin, "'Solidarność'—republikańska rewolucja Polaków," 168; and Tischner, *Etyka solidarności oraz homo sovieticus*, 232.

57. For more evidence confirming this claim, see Garton Ash, *The Polish Revolution: Solidarity*, 11–12, 15, 26, 36, 48, 65–66, 75, 84, 191, 212, 226, 238, 275, 315, 327, 352; Niezależny Samorządny Związek Zawodowy Solidarność, *21 Postulatów z 17 sierpnia 1980 roku* (1980 [cited February 28, 2004]), available from http://www.solidarnosc.org.pl/archiwum/historia/21_post.htm; and Tischner, *Etyka solidarności oraz homo sovieticus*, 33, 38, 54, 89, 92, 100, 13.

58. Karol Modzelewski, *Dokąd od komunizmu?* (Warsaw: "BGW," 1993), 16.

59. Krzemiński, *Solidarność: projekt polskiej demokracji*, 245.

60. Wojtyła does not use this phrase, but clearly he develops his personalist theory along these lines. He draws heavily on Max Scheler rather than on Maritain. The latter is often associated with the term "personalist communitarianism." See Jacques Maritain and John J. Fitzgerald, *The Person and the Common Good* (New York: C. Scribner's Sons, 1947). Some of Solidarity's intellectuals were familiar with Maritain's writings.

61. Gowin, "Kościół a 'Solidarność,'" 28.

62. Garton Ash, *The Polish Revolution: Solidarity*, 66.
63. Ibid., 66, 122.
64. Adam Michnik, *Kościół, lewica, dialog*, 2nd ed. (Warsaw: Świat Książki, 1998), 105–6.
65. Garton Ash, *The Polish Revolution: Solidarity*, 66.
66. For a balanced, critical appraisal of the church's relationship with Solidarity, see Michnik, *Kościół, lewica, dialog*, 246–58; and Adam Michnik, *The Church and the Left*, trans. David Ost (Chicago: University of Chicago Press, 1993), 233–72.
67. Cezary Michalski, "'Desolidaryzacja,' czyli wspólnota jako przedmiot roszczeń," in *Lekcja sierpnia: dziedzictwo 'Solidarności' po dwudziestu latach*, ed. Dariusz Gawin (Warsaw: Wydawnictwo IFiS PAN, 2002), 191–92. See also Garton Ash, *The Polish Revolution: Solidarity*, 69. Also, Tischner often appealed to Romantic poets such as Adam Mickiewicz and Cyprian Norwid in *Etyka solidarności*.
68. Weigel, *The Final Revolution*, 140.
69. Zdzisław Krasnodębski, *Demokracja peryferii*, 2nd ed. (Gdańsk: Wydawnictwo Słowo/Obraz Terytoria, 2005), 282–83.
70. Ibid., 75–76.
71. Wojciech Bonowicz, "Słowa, których nie wolno zapomnieć," in *Lekcja sierpnia: dziedzictwo 'Solidarności' po dwudziestu latach*, ed. Dariusz Gawin (Warsaw: Wydawnictwo IFiS PAN, 2002), 69–70; Tischner, *Etyka solidarności oraz homo sovieticus*, 16–17.
72. See Garton Ash, *The Polish Revolution: Solidarity*, 42–43; and Wałęsa, *A Way of Hope*, 41, 116–18.
73. Andrzej Szostek, "Sztuka jedności—posługa jednania," in *Ziarno czynu: refleksje po V pielgrzymce Jana Pawła II do ojczyzny*, ed. Franciszek Kampka (Cracow: Wydaw. WAM, 1998), 29.
74. For a succinct discusssion of these issues in Catholic social teaching, see Charles E. Curran, *Catholic Social Teaching, 1891–Present: A Historical, Theological, and Ethical Analysis*, Moral Traditions Series (Washington, D.C.: Georgetown University Press, 2002), 183–88.
75. Józef Tischner, *Etyka solidarności oraz homo sovieticus*, 194.
76. Garton Ash, *The Polish Revolution: Solidarity*, 239. On the importance of *Laborem Exercens* to Solidarity, see also Tischner, *Etyka solidarności oraz homo sovieticus*, 113–20.
77. John Paul II, *Laborem Exercens*, in *Catholic Social Thought: The Documentary Heritage*, ed. David J. O'Brien and Thomas A. Shannon (Maryknoll, N.Y.: Orbis Books, 1992), 361, no. 8.
78. See Szostek, "Sztuka jedności—posługa jednania," 29–30.
79. Stanisława Golinowska, "Ubóstwo w Polsce: synteza wyników badań," in *Polska bieda II: kryteria, ocena, przeciwdziałanie*, ed. Stanisława Golinowska (Warsaw: IPiSS, 1997), 307.
80. Tischner, *The Spirit of Solidarity*, 2–3.
81. Tischner, *Etyka solidarności oraz homo sovieticus*, 80–81.

82. Michnik, "The Moral and Spiritual Origins of Solidarity," 246.
83. Bonowicz, *Tischner*, 352.
84. This typology is indebted to Franciszek Kampka's account of the sequential realization of solidarity in Franciszek Kampka, "Solidarność w nauczaniu Jana Pawła II," in *Idea solidarności dzisiaj*, ed. Władysław Zuziak (Cracow: Wydawnictwo Naukowe PAT, 2001), 8–9.
85. Gowin, "Kościół a 'Solidarność,'" 28.
86. Wojtyła, *Osoba i czyn oraz inne studia antropologiczne*, 324.
87. Tischner, *Etyka solidarności oraz homo sovieticus*, 18.
88. Garton Ash, *The Polish Revolution: Solidarity*, 293.
89. Ibid., 44.
90. Michnik, "The Moral and Spiritual Origins of Solidarity," 240.
91. Tischner, *Etyka solidarności oraz homo sovieticus*, 11.
92. Józef Tischner, *Myśli wyszukane*, ed. Wojciech Bonowicz (Cracow: Znak, 2000), 78.
93. Michnik, "The Moral and Spiritual Origins of Solidarity," 239–40. See also Tischner, *Etyka solidarności oraz homo sovieticus*, 98.
94. Jerzy Popiełuszko, *Myśli wyszukane* (Cracow: Znak, 2002), 72.
95. For an extended discussion of John Paul II on this subject, see Gerald J. Beyer, "Freedom, Truth, and Law in the Mind and Homeland of John Paul II," *Notre Dame Journal of Law, Ethics, and Public Policy* 21, no. 1 (2007).
96. Cichocki, "Doświadczenie pierwszej 'Solidarności'—między moralnym absolutyzmem a polityczną samowiedzą Polaków," 79.
97. Popiełuszko, *Myśli wyszukane*, 77. See also Zbigniew Herbert, "Przesłanie Pana Cogito/The Envoy of Mr. Cogito," in *Poezje Wybrane/Selected Poems* (Cracow: Wydawnictwo Literackie, 2000), 94–96.
98. Tischner, *Etyka solidarności oraz homo sovieticus*, 12–15.
99. Following Karl Jaspers, Jacek Salij, O.P., argues that in order for people not to believe that the world is a miniscule part of a chaotic and hostile universe, they must believe in monotheism. See Salij, "Solidarność trochę teologiczniej," 42. Popiełuszko comes close in some of his statements to saying that one must profess belief in Christ.
100. Jarosław Gowin, *Religia i ludzkie biedy: księdza Tischnera spory o Kościół* (Cracow: Znak, 2003), 184.
101. Gowin, "Kościół a 'Solidarność,'" 28.

CHAPTER TWO   The Eclipse of Solidarity after 1989

1. See Krzemiński, *Solidarność: projekt polskiej demokracji*, 244–49; Stawrowski, "Doświadczenie 'Solidarności' jako wspólnoty etycznej," 118; and Zuziak, "Znaczenie myśli Józefa Tischnera w rozwoju idei solidarności," 39–43.

2. See Andrzej Potocki, "Czy społeczeństwo polskie jest społeczeństwem solidarnym?" in *Idea solidarności dzisiaj*, ed. Władysław Zuziak (Cracow: Wydawnictwo Naukowe PAT, 2001), 69.

3. Gawin, "'Solidarność'—republikańska rewolucja Polaków," 180–81.

4. Garton Ash, *The Polish Revolution: Solidarity*, 374–75.

5. Michnik, *Letters from Freedom*, 165.

6. Wojciech Roszkowski, *Najnowsza historia Polski: 1980–2002*, vol. 3 (Warsaw: Świat Książki, 2003), 138.

7. Ibid., 116.

8. Antoni Dudek, *Pierwsze lata III Rzeczypospolitej: 1989–2001*, 2nd ed., Arkana Historii (Cracow: Arcana, 2002), 115.

9. See ibid., 115–24; and Roszkowski, *Najnowsza historia Polski: 1980–2002*, 123–29.

10. Roszkowski, *Najnowsza historia Polski: 1980–2002*, 128; Jerzy Turowicz, "Dekomunizacja, ale jaka?" in *Spór o Polskę: 1989–1999*, ed. Paweł Śpiewak (Warsaw: PWN, 2000), 183.

11. Tadeusz Kowalik, "Społeczna gospodarka rynkowa—konstytucyjnym wyzwaniem dla Polski," in *Człowiek—rynek—sprawiedliwość*, ed. Krystyna Goldbergowa (Warsaw: Towarzystwo Wydawnicze i Literackie, 2001), 147–49.

12. Jacek Kuroń and Jacek Żakowski, *Siedmiolatka, czyli, kto ukradł Polskę*, 1st ed. (Wrocław: Wydawn. Dolnośląskie, 1997), 85. See also Janina Paradowska, "Król Lew. Bilans Lecha Wałęsy: 1990–95," in *Spór o Polskę: 1989–1999*, ed. Paweł Śpiewak (Warsaw: PWN, 2000).

13. See Andrzej Walicki, *Polskie zmagania z wolnością* (Cracow: Universitas, 2000), 35–67.

14. Gawin, "'Solidarność'—republikańska rewolucja Polaków," 185. See also Marek Ziółkowski, "Społeczno-kulturowy kontekst kondycji moralnej społeczeństwa polskiego," in *Kondycja moralna społeczeństwa polskiego*, ed. Janusz Mariański (Cracow: Wydawnictwo WAM, 2002), 35.

15. Jerzy Szacki, *Liberalizm po komunizmie* (Cracow: Znak, 1994), 169. For a similar description of Polish neoliberalism, see Ireneusz Krzemiński and Paweł Śpiewak, "Awantura w rodzinie: jakiego liberalizmu Polacy potrzebują? Doktryner wolności," *Gazeta Wyborcza*, February 16, 2000.

16. The description here of the social market economy is taken from Aniela Dylus, *Zmienność i ciągłość: polskie transformacje ustrojowe w horyzoncie etycznym* (Warsaw: Centrum im. Adama Smitha: Wydaw. Akademii Teologii Katolickiej, 1997), 105. In addition to Greider and Sen, for a comparison of the Rhine model of capitalism and neoliberalism, see Albert, *Capitalism vs. Capitalism*.

17. Dylus, *Zmienność i ciągłość: polskie transformacje ustrojowe w horyzoncie etycznym*, 20–21, 66. See also Szacki, *Liberalizm po komunizmie*, 11; and Kowalik, "Społeczna gospodarka rynkowa—konstytucyjnym wyzwaniem dla Polski."

18. Grażyna Skąpska, "Czy instytucje publiczne budowane są w oparciu o ideę solidarności?" in *Idea solidarności dzisiaj*, ed. Władysław Zuziak (Cracow: Wydawnictwo Naukowe PAT, 2001), 48–54. See also Kowalik, "Społeczna gospodarka rynkowa—konstytucyjnym wyzwaniem dla Polski."

19. Gawin, "'Solidarność'—republikańska rewolucja Polaków," 185. See also Walicki, *Polskie zmagania z wolnością*, 35–67; and Andrzej Walicki, "Ideolog epoki postchlubnej," *Gazeta Wyborcza*, November 8–9, 2003, 17.

20. Walicki, "Ideolog epoki postchlubnej," 17.

21. This is not to say that Polish Christian liberals do not exist. Szacki maintains that Mirosław Dzielski goes even further than Michael Novak in his attempt to reconcile liberalism and Catholicism. See Szacki, *Liberalizm po komunizmie*, 221. The popularity of Novak's works in Poland stem from his offering of something diametrically opposed to what the Poles already had, namely, Communism. Professor Aniela Dylus, chair of the Department of the Ethics of Economics at Cardinal Stefan Wyszyński University in Warsaw, shared this view with me. On the influence of Sachs and Friedman, see Kowalik, "Społeczna gospodarka rynkowa—konstytucyjnym wyzwaniem dla Polski"; and Jeffrey Sachs, *The End of Poverty: Economic Possibilities for Our Time* (New York: Penguin Press, 2005), 109–30.

22. Miszalska, "Moralność a demokracja—uwagi o stylu moralnym współczesnego społeczeństwa polskiego," 176.

23. Among the most noted are Szacki, Krzemiński, and Walicki. Some Polish economists, such as Tadeusz Kowalik, one of the principal economic advisors to Solidarity, also decried neoliberal economic policies. See, for example, Kowalik, "Joseph Stiglitz a polska transformacja."

24. See John Paul II, "Misterium nieprawości i wyobraźnia miłosierdzia," *Tygodnik Powszechny*, August 25, 2002. For the bishops, who largely remained silent regarding neoliberalism in Poland until 2001, see Konferencja Episkopatu Polski, *Kościół wobec życia społeczno-gospodarczego* (Konferencja Episkopatu Polski, 2001 [cited January 24, 2003]); available from http://www.episkopat.pl/dokumenty/synoddokumenty.pdf.

25. See Witold Morawski, "Realizacja zasad sprawiedliwości społecznej w Polsce jako miara 'powrotu do normalności,'" in *Kondycja moralna społeczeństwa polskiego*, ed. Janusz Mariański (Cracow: Wydawnictwo WAM, 2002), 129–31. See also Jadwiga Koralewicz and Marek Ziółkowski, *Mentalność Polaków: sposoby myślenia o polityce, gospodarce i życiu społecznym 1988–2000* (Warsaw: Wydawnictwo Naukowe SCHOLAR, 2003), 219.

26. Examples include: Leszek Balcerowicz, the former minister of finance; Janusz Lewandowski, the former minister of privatization; and Jan Bielecki, the former prime minister. One French commentator observed that it is impossible to find more strident adherents of Milton Friedman's free-market economics anywhere in Europe than in Poland. Cited in Szacki, *Liberalizm po komunizmie*, 6.

Here, I use the word "aspired" quite deliberately. As Szacki maintains, politicians in post-Communist countries who called themselves neoliberals often indulged in steering the economy in all sorts of ways. See ibid., 187–97. See also Paweł Śpiewak, ed., *Spór o Polskę: 1989–1999* (Warsaw: PWN, 2000).

27. David Ost, *The Defeat of Solidarity: Anger and Politics in Postcommunist Europe* (Ithaca, N.Y.: Cornell University Press, 2005), 58.

28. Szacki, *Liberalizm po komunizmie*, 197. See also Miszalska, "Moralność a demokracja—uwagi o stylu moralnym współczesnego społeczeństwa polskiego," 172.

29. Modzelewski, *Dokąd od komunizmu?* 24, 28. See also Kowalik, "Społeczna gospodarka rynkowa—konstytucyjnym wyzwaniem dla Polski," 145–52; Jerzy Jedlicki, "Czas zwątpienia," *Znak* 558, no. 11 (2001); and Gowin, "Kościół a 'Solidarność,'" 37.

30. Modzelewski, *Dokąd od komunizmu?* 28. See Paradowska, "Król Lew. Bilans Lecha Wałęsy: 1990–95," 693.

31. Ost, *The Defeat of Solidarity*, 42, 61.

32. Ibid., 20, 37, 53.

33. Ibid., 83, 92.

34. Michalski, "'Desolidaryzacja,' czyli wspólnota jako przedmiot roszczeń," 185. See also Modzelewski, *Dokąd od komunizmu?* 17–18. A good example of this fatalistic attitude can be found in the thinking of Jacek Kuroń, who laments the suffering caused by the neoliberal reforms while maintaining that there was no other alternative. See Kuroń and Żakowski, *Siedmiolatka, czyli, kto ukradł Polskę*, 75–85. He seems, however, to regret some of the choices made at that time.

35. Gawin, "'Solidarność'—republikańska rewolucja Polaków," 178.

36. Krzemiński, *Solidarność: projekt polskiej demokracji*, 243, 245–49. See Cichocki, "Doświadczenie pierwszej 'Solidarności'—między moralnym absolutyzmem a polityczną samowiedzą Polaków," 99.

37. For statistics pertaining to the number of strikes in Poland, see United Nations Development Programme Poland, *National Report on Human Development: The Changing Role of the State, Poland '97* (Warsaw: UNDP Poland, 1997), 29–30. The report points out that a large decline in strikes took place in 1989 and 1990, with a dramatic increase from 1991 to 1994 as a result of the high social costs of the economic transformation. In the early twenty-first century tensions arose again in Poland, with the first-ever recorded use of violence by Solidarity taking place on September 11, 2003. During a strike of more than 5,000 coal miners, individuals threw Molotov cocktails at goverment buildings and stormed the Russian embassy. See Mateusz Zieliński, "Atak górników," *Gazeta Wyborcza*, September 12, 2003. NSZZ Solidarity declared November 2003 a month of protest against the "anti-social politics of the government," and numerous protests took place.

38. See Garton Ash, *The Polish Revolution: Solidarity*, 373–75; Dudek, *Pierwsze lata III Rzeczypospolitej: 1989–2001*, 97–98; Dylus, *Zmienność i ciągłość: polskie transformacje ustrojowe w horyzoncie etycznym*, 18–20; Kuroń and Żakowski, *Siedmiolatka, czyli, kto ukradł Polskę*, 76; and Paradowska, "Król Lew. Bilans Lecha Wałęsy: 1990–95."

39. Sergiusz Kowalski, "Jedynie słuszny liberalizm," *Polityka*, February 12, 2000.

40. Ost, *The Defeat of Solidarity*, 34–93.

41. For details, see Roszkowski, *Najnowsza historia Polski: 1980–2002*, 132; and Dudek, *Pierwsze lata III Rzeczypospolitej: 1989–2001*, 90.

42. See Modzelewski, *Dokąd od komunizmu?* 27.

43. Russian philosopher Aleksander Zinowiew created this term, which thinkers such as Józef Tischner later popularized in Poland.

44. See Smolar, "Rocznice, pamięć, przyszłość," 25.

45. Tischner, *Etyka solidarności oraz homo sovieticus*, 165–67.

46. Wedel, *The Private Poland*, 24, 26. See also Miszalska, "Moralność a demokracja—uwagi o stylu moralnym współczesnego społeczeństwa polskiego," 165–68, 171–73; and Krzemiński, *Solidarność: projekt polskiej demokracji*, 230–40.

47. Miszalska, "Moralność a demokracja—uwagi o stylu moralnym współczesnego społeczeństwa polskiego," 166–67.

48. Tischner, *Etyka solidarności oraz homo sovieticus*, 166.

49. Ibid., 128.

50. Michnik, Tischner, and Żakowski, *Między panem a plebanem*, 286. See also Tischner, *Etyka solidarności oraz homo sovieticus*, 163–74. For a summary of Tischner's view on *homo sovieticus* in the Church, see Jarosław Gowin, "Zmącona pieśń Pana," *Znak* 3, no. 550 (2001); and Gowin, *Religia i ludzkie biedy: księdza Tischnera spory o Kościół*, 107–12. Andrzej Szostek, M.I.C., discusses how *homo sovieticus* influenced behavior within the Church. See Szostek, "Sztuka jedności—posługa jednania," 16–21.

51. Koralewicz and Ziółkowski, *Mentalność Polaków: sposoby myślenia o polityce, gospodarce i życiu społecznym 1988–2000*, 180.

52. Miszalska, "Moralność a demokracja—uwagi o stylu moralnym współczesnego społeczeństwa polskiego," 168. See also Edmund Wnuk-Lipiński, "Wyuczona bezradność," in *Spór o Polskę: 1989–1999*, ed. Paweł Śpiewak (Warsaw: PWN, 2000). Krzemiński contends that a version of Catholicism that portrays life as something totally granted by God and to be accepted as such has contributed to this phenomenon. Krzemiński, *Solidarność: projekt polskiej demokracji*, 234.

53. Krzemiński, *Solidarność: projekt polskiej demokracji*, 232. Tischner famously said that "Polish work is sick" at the First National Solidarity Congress. See Garton Ash, *The Polish Revolution: Solidarity*, 230–31.

54. See Koralewicz and Ziółkowski, *Mentalność Polaków: sposoby myślenia o polityce, gospodarce i życiu społecznym 1988–2000*, 206–7; and Miszalska, "Moralność a demokracja—uwagi o stylu moralnym współczesnego społeczeństwa polskiego," 167–68.

55. See Władysław Jacher and Urszula Swadzba, "Etos pracy w Polsce," in *Kondycja moralna społeczeństwa polskiego,* ed. Janusz Mariański (Cracow: Wydawnictwo WAM, 2002), 154–59.

56. The number of Poles subscribing to the view that wages should be equal (*każdemu po równo*) rose from 18.6 percent in 1991 to 22.9 percent in 1997, even though wages have become in some senses more meritocratically distributed in Poland since 1989. See Morawski, "Realizacja zasad sprawiedliwości społecznej w Polsce jako miara 'powrotu do normalności,'" 123; and Koralewicz and Ziółkowski, *Mentalność Polaków: Sposoby myślenia o polityce, gospodarce i życiu społecznym 1988–2000,* 217.

57. Tischner, *Etyka solidarności oraz homo sovieticus,* 173.

58. Koralewicz and Ziółkowski, *Mentalność Polaków: sposoby myślenia o polityce, gospodarce i życiu społecznym 1988–2000,* 206–7. See also Miszalska, "Moralność a demokracja—uwagi o stylu moralnym współczesnego społeczeństwa polskiego," 165–68, 171–74.

59. Koralewicz and Ziółkowski, *Mentalność Polaków: sposoby myślenia o polityce, gospodarce i życiu społecznym 1988–2000,* 229–35. The authors of this study report that 50 percent of Poles declared trust towards others in 1988, while 48 percent did so in 1998.

60. Miszalska, "Moralność a demokracja—uwagi o stylu moralnym współczesnego społeczeństwa polskiego," 173. Miszalska points out that 61.4 percent of Americans agreed with this statement during the same time period. See also Krzemiński, *Solidarność: projekt polskiej demokracji,* 231–33; and Jacek Kurczewski, *The Resurrection of Rights in Poland* (Oxford: Clarendon Press, 1993), 400–401. The most recent "Diagnoza Społeczna 2003" concludes that Poles more and more trust no one but themselves. See Wiesław Władka, "Mocne i słabe strony Polaka: Onizm," *Polityka* 45, no. 2426 (2003): 85.

61. Throughout the 1990s, Poland continued to fall in the Transparency International rankings, which measures corruption on various levels of society. See the website at http://www.transparency.pl. For a detailed analysis of corruption and its various forms and perceptions in Poland, see Andrzej Kojder, "Korupcja i poczucie moralne Polaków," in *Kondycja moralna społeczeństwa polskiego,* ed. Janusz Mariański (Cracow: Wydawnictwo WAM, 2002); and Jacek Kurczewski and Beata Łaciak, *Korupcja w życiu społecznym* (Warsaw: Instytut Spraw Publicznych, 2000).

62. "Corruption in Poland: Enough!" *The Economist,* April 17, 2003, 45.

63. Kojder, "Korupcja i poczucie moralne Polaków," 233. He states that the number of registered crimes rose 2.5 times, while the number of robberies rose three times. Jacek Hugo-Bader points out that these numbers only count registered crimes; many more go unregistered. He states that in 1990 every tenth robbery was committed by a youth, while in 1997 a youth committed every fifth robbery. Again, this only includes registered crimes. See Jacek Hugo-Bader, "Chłopcy z motykami," *Gazeta Wyborcza,* September 29, 2003.

64. Tischner, *Etyka solidarności oraz homo sovieticus*, 167.

65. Józef Tischner, *W krainie schorowanej wyobraźni*, 1st ed. (Cracow: Znak, 1997), 90.

66. For an excellent discussion of the reductionistic anthropology accepted in modern economics, often referred to as *homo oeconomicus*, see Amartya Kumar Sen, *On Ethics and Economics* (Oxford: Blackwell, 1987), 1–23.

67. Tischner, *Etyka solidarności oraz homo sovieticus*, 125.

68. Garton Ash, *The Polish Revolution: Solidarity*, 244.

69. Tischner, *Etyka solidarności oraz homo sovieticus*, 167–74.

70. See Miszalska, "Moralność a demokracja—uwagi o stylu moralnym współczesnego społeczeństwa polskiego," 167. The Church in Poland was able to sustain itself in ways that it could not in countries such as Czechoslovakia and Hungary.

71. Ibid., 173.

72. Ibid., 178.

73. Dylus, *Gospodarka, moralność, chrześcijaństwo*, 95.

74. Michnik, Tischner, and Żakowski, *Między panem a plebanem*, 42.

75. Janusz Mariański, "Kryzys moralny czy transformacja wartości? Na przykładzie wartości 'wolność,'" in *Ziarno czynu: refleksje po V pielgrzymce Jana Pawła II do ojczyzny: praca zbiorowa*, ed. Franciszek Kampka (Cracow: Wydaw. WAM, 1998), 117.

76. Tischner, *Nieszczęsny dar wolności*.

77. Szacki, *Liberalism after Communism*, 196. See also Berlin, Hardy, and Harris, *Liberty: Incorporating Four Essays on Liberty*, 166–217. Gerald MacCallum cogently revealed the inherent flaws of the negative/positive freedom dichotomy in Gerald C. MacCallum, "Negative and Positive Freedom," *Philosophical Review* 76, no. 3 (1967). Although MacCallum is persuasive, this book makes the distinction because it functions in the minds of many people today and is still used in many types of discourse. The terms may point to different aspects of a unitary freedom, but many people sever them, thereby conceiving of two different kinds of freedom.

78. Szacki, *Liberalism after Communism*, 196.

79. Berlin, Hardy, and Harris, *Liberty: Incorporating Four Essays on Liberty*, 179–80. For an overview of Berlin's views, see John Gray, "The Case for Decency," *New York Review of Books* 53, no. 12 (2006). Kołakowski has said that seeing "true" freedom as "positive" freedom led Saint Augustine to justify oppressive regimes if they prohibit sinners from sinning. By limiting one's ability to do illicit acts, the oppressive regime creates the conditions for true freedom, which develops as one continues to avoid sin and to do "the good." In Kołakowski's view, this lies as the basis of totalitarian ideologies, including Soviet Communism. See Leszek Kołakowski, "Laik nad katechizmem się wymądrza," *Puls* 62 (1992). Cited in Tischner, *W krainie schorowanej wyobraźni*, 144–45.

80. This historical sketch follows Garton Ash's introduction, which provides a much more detailed account than is warranted here.

81. The degree to which this should be equated with "Soviet domination" is a much-debated topic today. This debate cannot be rehearsed here. It must suffice to say that Poles did not choose Communism in free and fair elections at the end of the war. For more on the history of this period, see Garton Ash, *The Polish Revolution: Solidarity*, 6–8; and Andrzej Paczkowski, *Pół wieku dziejów Polski: 1939–1989*, 4th ed. (Warsaw: Wydaw. Naukowe PWN, 2000).

82. Garton Ash, *The Polish Revolution: Solidarity*, 5.

83. Dylus, *Gospodarka, moralność, chrześcijaństwo*, 95. Władysław Zuziak shares this view. See Zuziak, ed., *Idea solidarności dzisiaj*, 38.

84. Krasnodębski, *Demokracja peryferii*, 280–84.

85. See Garton Ash, *The Polish Revolution: Solidarity*, 295–96, 305, 393. The issue is quite complicated. As Garton Ash notes, most Poles ultimately dreamt of "Poland being Polish," but lived with the tension between the ideal and the necessary compromises made by Solidarity. The description "self-limiting revolution" bespeaks this tension, which manifested itself in the factions within the Solidarity movement itself. On this question, see also Dudek, "Rewolucja robotnicza i ruch narodowowyzwoleńczy"; and Walicki, *Polskie zmagania z wolnością*, 362–63. Walicki denies that Solidarity sought national liberation.

86. While young Poles exhibit this tendency to a much lesser degree, it continues to shape the mentality of older generations today. See Mariański, "Kryzys moralny czy transformacja wartości? Na przykładzie wartości 'wolność.'"

87. See ibid., 118; Miszalska, "Moralność a demokracja—uwagi o stylu moralnym współczesnego społeczeństwa polskiego," 173; Szacki, *Liberalizm po komunizmie*; and Ziółkowski, "Społeczno-kulturowy kontekst kondycji moralnej społeczeństwa polskiego," 25–26.

88. Most sociological evidence indicates that Poles generally accept the existence of objective moral norms. At the same time, they find it easy to justify behavior that disregards such norms. Hanna Świda-Ziemba, "Permisywizm moralny a postawy polskiej młodzieży," in *Kondycja moralna społeczeństwa polskiego*, ed. Janusz Mariański (Cracow: Wydawnictwo WAM, 2002).

89. These distinctions are problematic because human freedom and morality are inherently social realities. They will be used here, however, for lack of a better way to describe the emphasis sometimes encountered on the morality and freedom of the individual, as if they were completely distinct from the freedom and morality of others.

90. Szacki, *Liberalizm po komunizmie*, 169–70. The terminology here is mine, but I am indebted to Szacki for these basic distinctions. He points out that especially "Christian liberals" are not ready to accept moral license but basically approve of economic liberalism. The so-called Conservative Liberal Union of Real Politics (Konserwatywno-Liberalna Partia Unii Polityki Realnej), a political party

led by Janusz Korwin-Mikke, serves as an example. It supports the death penalty while espousing neoliberal economic doctrines. See its website at http://www.upr.org.pl/upr/dokumenty.shtml. Donald Tusk, formerly of the Liberal Democratic Congress party (Kongres Liberalno-Demokratyczny), serves as another example. In 1993 he stated that labor unions should have their rights restricted in order to quell growing strikes. On this, see Karol Modzelewski, *Życiodajny impuls chuligaństwa* (Cracow: Universitas, 2003), 19.

91. John Paul II, "Misterium nieprawości i wyobraźnia miłosierdzia."

92. Marcin Król, "Liberalizm—co to właściwie znaczy?" *Tygodnik Powszechny*, September 1, 2002.

93. See especially his homily in Ełk and speech in the Polish Parliament in 1999 in John Paul II, *Jan Paweł II: Polska 1999: przemówienia i homilie* (Marki: Michalineum, 1999), esp. 76–77, 108–10. See also John Paul II, *Program dla Kościoła w Polsce: Jan Paweł II do polskich biskupów; wizyta ad limina 1998* (Cracow: Znak, 1998), 36–38.

94. See the classic statement in Milton Friedman, *Capitalism and Freedom* (Chicago: University of Chicago Press, 1962), 2, 8–9. While Friedman's work merits attention, his naivety or agenda comes across in statements such as: "The kind of economic organization that provides economic freedom directly, namely, competitive capitalism, also promotes political freedom because it separates economic power from political power and in this way enables the one to offset the other." For a cogent critique of this idea, see Michael Walzer, *Spheres of Justice: A Defense of Pluralism and Equality* (New York: Basic Books, 1983).

95. Janusz Lewandowski, "Wolność, nie równość," *Gazeta Wyborcza*, January 15–16, 2000, 22.

96. Krzemiński and Śpiewak, "Awantura w rodzinie: jakiego liberalizmu Polacy potrzebują? Doktryner wolności."

97. Leszek Balcerowicz, "Demokracja nie zastąpi kapitalizmu," in *Spór o Polskę: 1989–1999*, ed. Paweł Śpiewak (Warsaw: PWN, 2000), 640.

98. Krzemiński and Śpiewak, "Awantura w rodzinie: jakiego liberalizmu Polacy potrzebują? Doktryner wolności."

99. Friedrich A. von Hayek, *The Constitution of Liberty* (Chicago: University of Chicago Press, 1960), 12.

100. Walicki, "Ideolog epoki postchlubnej," 18. See also Walicki, *Polskie zmagania z wolnością*, 230–31.

101. This analysis of Hayek's understanding of negative freedom is indebted to Janina Filek, *O wolności i odpowiedzialności podmiotu gospodarującego* (Cracow: Wydaw. AE, 2002), 92–103.

102. Friedrich A. von Hayek, *Law, Legislation, and Liberty: A New Statement of the Liberal Principles of Justice and Political Economy*, 3 vols. (Chicago: University of Chicago Press, 1973), 1:51. See also Hayek, *The Constitution of Liberty*, 205–33.

103. Filek, *O wolności i odpowiedzialności podmiotu gospodarującego*, 102–3.
104. Hayek, *The Constitution of Liberty*, 16–17.
105. Wojciech Orliński claims that Polish liberals accept the designation "neoliberal" and follow Hayek and Friedman, the heralds of economic freedom, as opposed to John Stuart Mill and Isaiah Berlin, the defenders of political freedom. Wojciech Orliński, "Wolność, równość, liberalizm," *Gazeta Wyborcza*, July 24–25, 1999, 16. It is interesting to note that Lewandowski translated Hayek's works in the Polish underground during the 1980s.
106. Leszek Balcerowicz, *Wolność i rozwój: ekonomia wolnego rynku* (Znak, 1995 [cited June 20, 2003]); available from http://www.balcerowicz.pl/ksiazki.html.
107. Szacki refers to Balcerowicz, Lewandowski, and Bielecki in this vein. See Szacki, *Liberalizm po komunizmie*, 194–95.
108. See Walicki, "Ideolog epoki postchlubnej." Walicki discusses Hayek's staunch aversion to "social justice." For examples of this aversion, see Adam Michnik and Alina Białkowska, "Mam zdjąć okulary? Adam Michnik and Alina Białkowska rozmawiają z wicepremierem Leszkiem Balcerowiczem," *Gazeta Wyborcza*, August 12, 1991, 11; and Tadeusz Kowalik, "Czy sprawiedliwość społeczna kosztuje? Artykuł polemiczny na marginesie książki pt. *Efektywność a sprawiedliwość*," *Ekonomista* 3 (1997): 291–92.
109. Jan Krzysztof Bielecki, "Duch indywidualizmu," *Wprost*, December 25, 1994. This article is also in Śpiewak, ed., *Spór o Polskę: 1989–1999*, 643.
110. Kowalski, "Jedynie słuszny liberalizm." See also Winiecki's polemic with Kowalski. He equates capitalism and liberalism with the well-being and freedom of individuals. He also denounces the welfare state for promoting "dignity by stealing from other people's pockets." Jan Winiecki, "Godność z cudzej kieszeni," *Polityka* 4, no. 2229 (2000).
111. See Lewandowski, "Wolność, nie równość." Some neoliberals qualify this claim. Friedman, for example, states that economic freedom is "an extremely important part of total freedom." However, because all freedom ultimately follows from economic freedom for neoliberals, this statement holds. The point is that economic freedom construed in this way is given ultimate priority.
112. Charles Taylor, "Kilka refleksji na temat solidarności," *Znak* 543, no. 8 (2000): 31, 34.
113. Gawin, "'Solidarność'—republikańska rewolucja Polaków," 186. See also Gowin, "Kościół a 'Solidarność,'" 36; and Smolar, "Rocznice, pamięć, przyszłość," 38.
114. Cited in Mariański, "Kryzys moralny czy transformacja wartości? Na przykładzie wartości 'wolność,'" 115. He repeated "nie ma wolności bez solidarności" in his speech to the Polish Parliament in 1999. John Paul II, *Jan Paweł II: Polska 1999: przemówienia i homilie*, 106. It is important to note that John Paul utilized this axiom in a different way. He used the word solidarity (*solidarność*) in reference to the principle, value, or virtue, not the movement (*Solidarność*).

115. Maciej Zięba, *Papieże i kapitalizm: od Rerum Novarum po Centesimus Annus* (Cracow: Znak, 1998), 128.

116. John Paul II, *Centesimus Annus*, in *Catholic Social Thought: The Documentary Heritage*, ed. David J. O'Brien and Thomas A. Shannon (Maryknoll, N.Y.: Orbis Books, 1992), 471, no. 42.

117. John Paul II, *Sollicitudo Rei Socialis*, in *Catholic Social Thought: The Documentary Heritage*, ed. David J. O'Brien and Thomas A. Shannon (Maryknoll, N.Y.: Orbis Books, 1992), 418, no. 33.

118. Zięba, *Papieże i kapitalizm: od Rerum Novarum po Centesimus Annus*, 129. See also Dylus, *Zmienność i ciągłość: polskie transformacje ustrojowe w horyzoncie etycznym*, 105; Anton Rauscher, "Odkrycie społecznej gospodarki rynkowej," in *Centesimus Annus: tekst i komentarze*, ed. Franciszek Kampka and Cezary Ritter (Lublin: Redakcja Wydawnictw KUL, 1998), 252; and Jerzy Michałowski, "Centesimus Annus—jaki kapitalizm?" in *Centesimus Annus: tekst i komentarze*, ed. Franciszek Kampka and Cezary Ritter (Lublin: Redakcja Wydawnictw KUL, 1998), 241. According to Rauscher, the pope did not use the term *Sozialmarktwirtschaft* because he did not want to single out the "German model," but it is clear that he had it in mind.

119. See the Preamble and the discussion of social and cultural rights.

120. See Skąpska, "Czy instytucje publiczne budowane są w oparciu o ideę solidarności?"

121. Mariański, "Kryzys moralny czy transformacja wartości? Na przykładzie wartości 'wolność,'" 117; Tadeusz Pieronek, *Kościół nie boi się wolności* (Cracow: Znak, 1998), 27; the homily of John Paul II in Wrocław, 1997, in John Paul II, *Jan Paweł II w Polsce, 31 maja 1997–10 czerwca 1997: przemówienia i homilie* (Cracow: Znak, 1997), 34. See also Jarosław Gowin, *Kościół w czasach wolności 1989–1999* (Cracow: Znak, 1999), 40–45, 106–32; Dylus, *Gospodarka, moralność, chrześcijaństwo*, 99–104; and Piotr Mazurkiewicz, *Kościół i demokracja* (Warsaw: Pax, 2001), 288–89.

122. Krzysztof Hajdamowicz and Marian Filar, "Najpiękniejsza jest wolność," *Gazeta Wyborcza*, November 25–26, 2003, 21.

123. Mariański, "Kryzys moralny czy transformacja wartości? Na przykładzie wartości 'wolność,'" 120–23.

124. See Koralewicz and Ziółkowski, *Mentalność Polaków: sposoby myślenia o polityce, gospodarce i życiu społecznym 1988–2000*, 200.

125. Dylus, *Gospodarka, moralność, chrześcijaństwo*, 98. Dorota Lepianka maintains that this desire for more and more goods is one of the causes of indifference towards poverty in Poland. Dorota Lepianka, "Polacy a biedacy—społeczny obraz ubóstwa i stosunek społeczeństwa polskiego do osób ubogich," in *Przeciw biedzie: programy, pomysły, inicjatywy*, ed. Elżbieta Tarkowska (Warsaw: Oficyna Naukowa, 2002), 64.

126. Konferencja Episkopatu Polski, *Potrzeba i zadania nowej ewangelizacji na przełomie II i III tysiąclecia chrześcijańskiego* (Konferencja Episkopatu Polski,

2001 [cited January 24, 2003]); available from http://www.episkopat.pl/dokumenty/synoddokumenty.pdf. no. 26, 27. See also Konferencja Episkopatu Polski, *Kościół wobec życia społeczno-gospodarczego*, no. 52. For an interesting analysis of the cult of "success" in Poland using Robert K. Merton's theory of anomie, see Krystyna Szafraniec, "Anomia okresu transformacji a orientacje normatywne młodzieży: perspektywa międzygeneracyjna," in *Kondycja moralna społeczeństwa polskiego*, ed. Janusz Mariański (Cracow: Wydawnictwo WAM, 2002).

127. On abortion, see especially John Paul II, "Homilia w czasie mszy św. odprawionej na lotnisku w Maślowie" (Opoka, 1991 [cited December 7, 2003]); available from http://www.opoka.org; John Paul II, *Program dla Kościoła w Polsce: Jan Paweł II do polskich biskupów; wizyta ad limina 1998*, 31; John Paul II, "Przemówienie do przedstawicieli władz państwowych wygłoszone na zamku królewskim" (Opoka, 1991 [cited December 7, 2003]); available from http://www.opoka.org.

128. John Paul II, *Jan Paweł II w Polsce, 31 maja 1997–10 czerwca 1997: przemówienia i homilie*, 34. For an extended discussion of John Paul II's understanding of the relationship between freedom and truth, see Beyer, "Freedom, Truth, and Law in the Mind and Homeland of John Paul II."

129. Świda-Ziemba, "Permisywizm moralny a postawy polskiej młodzieży," 439. For similar claims based on research, see Miszalska, "Moralność a demokracja—uwagi o stylu moralnym współczesnego społeczeństwa polskiego," 164, 169–72. See also Krzysztof Kiciński, "Orientacje moralne społeczeństwa polskiego," in *Kondycja moralna społeczeństwa polskiego*, ed. Janusz Mariański (Cracow: Wydawnictwo WAM, 2002), 375–77; and Janusz Mariański, "Religia i moralność w społeczeństwie polskim," in *Kondycja moralna społeczeństwa polskiego* (Cracow: Wydawnictwo WAM, 2002), 492–501. Interestingly, Mariański, who shares the view that permissivism is growing in Poland, shows that social acceptance of abortion has fallen in the last decade. Nonetheless, it remains at a relatively high number (roughly one half) given that more than 90 percent of Poles are Roman Catholics. Agnieszka Graff contends, however, that only 26 percent of women are against the right to abortion. Graff, *Świat bez kobiet: płeć w polskim życiu publicznym*, 112. For the Church's stance, see Gowin, *Kościół w czasach wolności 1989–1999*, 150–94. For an alternative point of view, see Graff, *Świat bez kobiet: płeć w polskim życiu publicznym*, 111–51.

130. Kojder, "Korupcja i poczucie moralne Polaków," 242–45. According to Kojder, the upshot is that from 1990 to 2000, some 20 percent of Poles acknowledged having paid a bribe. See also his discussion of what is and is not considered a bribe.

131. Tischner, *Nieszczęsny dar wolności*, 7.

132. Ibid., 9.

133. For a slightly different but compatible interpretation of this phenomenon, see Krzemiński, *Solidarność: projekt polskiej demokracji*, 211 ff. Like Tischner, he points to the negative role that the Church has played.

134. Józef Tischner, *Świat ludzkiej nadziei* (Cracow: Znak, 2000), 26–37; Gowin, *Religia i ludzkie biedy: księdza Tischnera spory o Kościół*, 68–73; Tischner, *Nieszczęsny dar wolności*, 13.

135. Gowin, *Religia i ludzkie biedy: księdza Tischnera spory o Kościół*, 74.

136. Tischner, *Nieszczęsny dar wolności*, 12.

137. Józef Tischner, *Ksiądz na manowcach*, 1st ed. (Cracow: Znak, 1999), 27.

138. Tischner, *W krainie schorowanej wyobraźni*, 74–75, 148. For a more detailed analysis of Tischner's relationship to democracy, see Gowin, *Religia i ludzkie biedy: księdza Tischnera spory o Kościół*, 145–73.

139. Tischner, *Nieszczęsny dar wolności*, 141.

140. Ibid., 13.

141. Tischner, "Solidarność po latach."

142. See Miszalska, "Moralność a demokracja—uwagi o stylu moralnym współczesnego społeczeństwa polskiego," 171 ff.

143. Ibid., 172. Appealing to Tadeusz Szaweł's research, she points out that in the United States only 18 percent do not belong and in Germany only 32 percent do not.

144. Ibid.

145. Miszalska, "Moralność a demokracja—uwagi o stylu moralnym współczesnego społeczeństwa polskiego," 173; Krzemiński, *Solidarność: projekt polskiej demokracji*, 231.

146. Joanna Kurczewska, Katarzyna Staszyńska, and Hanna Bojar, "Blokady społeczeństwa obywatelskiego: czyli słabe społeczeństwo obywatelskie i słabe państwo," in *Społeczeństwo w transformacji, ekspertyzy i studia*, ed. Andrzej Rychard and Michał Federowicz (Warsaw: Instytut Filozofii i Socjologii, Polska Akademia Nauk, 1993), 92.

147. Miszalska, "Moralność a demokracja—uwagi o stylu moralnym współczesnego społeczeństwa polskiego," 180. For statistics on voter turnout, though somewhat dated at this point, see United Nations Development Programme Poland, *National Report on Human Development: The Changing Role of the State, Poland '97*.

148. Andrzej Potocki OP demonstrates the vibrancy of solidarity within the family. However, he also argues that solidarity "on the macro scale" is quite weak. See Potocki, "Czy społeczeństwo polskie jest społeczeństwem solidarnym?" See also Miszalska, "Moralność a demokracja—uwagi o stylu moralnym współczesnego społeczeństwa polskiego," 172.

149. For a modern version of this teaching that strongly emphasizes the duties of the family to the larger society, see John Paul II, *Familiaris Consortio* (Vatican website, 1981 [cited May 20, 2004]); available from http://www.vatican.va/holy_father/john_paul_ii/apost_exhortations/documents/hf_jp-ii_exh_19811122_familiaris-consortio_en.html#top. See also Dylus, *Zmienność i ciągłość: polskie transformacje ustrojowe w horyzoncie etycznym*, 119–22.

150. See Józef Tischner's statement on Catholicism in Poland in Michnik, Tischner, and Żakowski, *Między panem a plebanem*, 286.
151. Tischner, *Etyka solidarności oraz homo sovieticus*, 180.
152. See Miszalska, "Moralność a demokracja—uwagi o stylu moralnym współczesnego społeczeństwa polskiego," 174. See Ost, *The Defeat of Solidarity*, in which he blames the Solidarity union after 1989 for fanning the flames of hatred towards post-Communists, Jews, foreigners, and "phony" Catholics.
153. Zuziak, "Znaczenie myśli Józefa Tischnera w rozwoju idei solidarności," 39.
154. Agata Bielik-Robson, "'Solidarność' uliczna—elementarz tożsamości," in *Lekcja sierpnia: dziedzictwo "Solidarności" po dwudziestu latach*, ed. Dariusz Gawin (Warsaw: Wydawnictwo IFiS PAN, 2002), 131–41.
155. Michalski, "'Desolidaryzacja,' czyli wspólnota jako przedmiot roszczeń."
156. Krzemiński, *Solidarność: projekt polskiej demokracji*, 242.
157. Zbigniew Stawrowski, "O zapomnianej solidarności," *Znak* 543, no. 8 (2000).

CHAPTER THREE Poverty in Poland after 1989

1. Elżbieta Tarkowska, *Zrozumieć biednego: o dawnej i obecnej biedzie w Polsce* (Warsaw: Typografika, 2000), 56.
2. Tischner, *Etyka solidarności oraz homo sovieticus*, 18.
3. Bonowicz, "Słowa, których nie wolno zapomnieć," 71.
4. This statement implicitly rejects Hayek's contention that people are not responsible for the unintended consequences of their choices concerning economic policies. For a discussion of Hayek's position and persuasive rejection of it, see Kazimierz Sosenko, "Etyczne problemy transformacji systemu gospodarczego i możliwości ich rozważania," in *Etyczny wymiar przekształceń gospodarczych w Polsce*, ed. Adam Węgrzecki (Cracow: Oficyna Cracovia, 1996), 32; and Sen, *On Ethics and Economics*, 75.
5. Aniela Dylus criticizes this kind of "moralizing" pertaining to ethics and economics, especially among theologians. See Dylus, *Zmienność i ciągłość: polskie transformacje ustrojowe w horyzoncie etycznym*, 55–62; and Dylus, *Gospodarka, moralność, chrześcijaństwo*, 106, 110. She names, for example, those who simply demand the right to work without recognizing the difficulties of realizing this right in practice. Dylus is a leading author in ethics and economics in Poland and has served as an advisor to the Polish government and to the Roman Catholic bishops' conference.
6. Leszek Balcerowicz, *Państwo w przebudowie*, 1st ed. (Cracow: Znak, 1999), 65.

7. In this vein, the task and nature of this book echo what the Roman Catholic bishops in the United States and England and Wales have said in their documents concerning the move from principle to policy by making prudential judgments. See United States Catholic Conference of Bishops, "Economic Justice for All: A Catholic Framework for Economic Life," in *Catholic Social Thought: The Documentary Heritage*, ed. David J. O'Brien and Thomas A. Shannon (Maryknoll, N.Y.: Orbis Books, 1992), 576, 610, nos. 20, 134, 135; and Catholic Bishops' Conference of England and Wales, *The Common Good and the Catholic Church's Social Teaching* (1996 [cited May 1, 2003]); available from http://www.osjspm.org/cst/britbish.htm.

8. See Catholic Bishops' Conference of England and Wales, *The Common Good and the Catholic Church's Social Teaching*. The bishops consider remaining on the level of generalities in order to avoid controversy or a "failure in moral courage."

9. Drèze, "Ethics, Efficiency, and the Social Doctrine of the Church," 45.

10. S. M. Ravi Kanbur, Nora Lustig, and World Bank, *Attacking Poverty, World Development Report, 2000/2001* (New York: Oxford University Press, 2000), 15.

11. Stanisława Golinowska, "Badania nad ubóstwem: założenia i metodologia," in *Polska bieda II: kryteria, ocena, przeciwdziałanie*, ed. Stanisława Golinowska (Warsaw: IPiSS, 1997), 20. Golinowska reviews the most commonly used standards in the measurement of poverty. She discusses absolute, relative, and subjective poverty lines. On this issue, see also Kazimierz Frieske, "Bieda: miary i interpretacje," in *Polska bieda II: kryteria, ocena, przeciwdziałanie*, ed. Stanisława Golinowska (Warsaw: IPiSS, 1997); and Tarkowska, *Zrozumieć biednego: o dawnej i obecnej biedzie w Polsce*, 19.

12. Golinowska, "Badania nad ubóstwem: założenia i metodologia," 29.

13. Włodzimierz Okrasa, *Who Avoids and Who Escapes from Poverty during the Transition? Evidence from Polish Panel Data, 1993–96, Policy Research Working Papers; WPS/2218* (Washington, D.C.: World Bank, 1999), 3. See Golinowska, "Ubóstwo w Polsce: synteza wyników badań," 308–9.

14. Golinowska states that the income threshold is currently about 20 percent of average earnings. Stanisława Golinowska, "Poverty in Poland: Causes, Measures, and Studies," in *Poverty Dynamics in Poland: Selective Quantitative Analyses* (Warsaw: CASE—Center for Social and Economic Research, 2002), 25.

15. Golinowska and Tarkowska have slightly different opinions concerning the amount of censorship of poverty studies that took place. Golinowska enumerates several studies from the 1970s and 1980s, which in her opinion were important for "identifying the problem and for social policy." Golinowska, "Ubóstwo w Polsce: synteza wyników badań," 307. Tarkowska, however, contends that many important studies were either published in extremely limited numbers or forbidden altogther until 1989. Tarkowska, *Zrozumieć biednego: o dawnej i obecnej biedzie w Polsce*, 10.

16. Golinowska, "Ubóstwo w Polsce: synteza wyników badań," 307; and Golinowska, "Poverty in Poland: Causes, Measures, and Studies," 24.

17. Golinowska, "Poverty in Poland: Causes, Measures, and Studies," 24. The calculation of the social minimum is described in much greater detail in Lucyna Deniszczuk and Barbara Sajkiewicz, "Kategoria minimum socjalnego," in *Polska bieda II*, ed. Stanisława Golinowska (Warsaw: Instytut Pracy i Spraw Społecznych, 1997), 150–97. In 2003 it was equivalent to 789 złoty per month for a single person of working age. See the Institute's website at http://www.ipiss.com.pl/teksty/min_wrzesien_2003.html.

18. Deniszczuk and Sajkiewicz, "Kategoria minimum socjalnego," 150–51; and Golinowska, "Badania nad ubóstwem: założenia i metodologia," 21. Sen argues for a similar understanding of poverty in Amartya Kumar Sen, *Development as Freedom*, 1st ed. (New York: Knopf, 1999), esp. 89.

19. Golinowska, "Ubóstwo w Polsce: synteza wyników badań," 309–10. In addition, see the union's current program: Niezależny Samorządny Związek Zawodowy Solidarność, *Uchwała programowa XV KZD* (NSZZ Solidarność, 2004 [cited February 28, 2004]); available from http://www.solidarnosc.org.pl/dokumenty/xv_kzd/u_prog.htm.

20. Frieske, "Bieda: miary i interpretacje," 218.

21. Sen, *Development as Freedom*, 87.

22. Ibid., 36, 74–75. Although the World Bank has resisted at times, Sen's thinking has influenced it. The 2000 World Bank report advocates an approach that acknowledges poverty's many dimensions, including low levels of income and consumption, low achievements in health and education, vulnerability, risk, voicelessness, and powerlessness. See Kanbur, Lustig, and World Bank, *Attacking Poverty*, esp. 15.

23. On the capabilities approach, see also Martha Craven Nussbaum, *Women and Human Development: The Capabilities Approach* (New York: Cambridge University Press, 2000). In addition, a website has been devoted to the study of the capabilities approach: http://www.capabilityapproach.org.

24. Stanisława Golinowska, "Minimalne dochody a walka z ubóstwem," in *Polska bieda II: kryteria, ocena, przeciwdziałanie*, ed. Stanisława Golinowska (Warsaw: IPiSS, 1997), 383.

25. Teresa Bogucka, "Polska bieda," *Gazeta Wyborcza*, February 26–27, 2000, 9. For an example, see Balcerowicz, *Wolność i rozwój: ekonomia wolnego rynku*; and Leszek Balcerowicz, "Awans biednych olbrzymów" (*Wprost* 47, (2002) [cited March 29, 2003]); available from http://www.balcerowicz.pl.wprost/awans.pdf.

26. See, for example, Jan Winiecki, *Instytucjonalne bariery rozwoju gospodarczego: polska niezakończona transformacja* (Warsaw: Centrum im. Adama Smitha, 1995); Jan Winiecki, "Polacy kontra Polska," *Wprost* (1999); and Michał Zieliński, "Klęska sukcesu," *Wprost* (1999).

27. Golinowska, "Poverty in Poland: Causes, Measures, and Studies," 24.

28. Golinowska, "Minimalne dochody a walka z ubóstwem," 383.

29. Golinowska, "Poverty in Poland: Causes, Measures, and Studies," 24. For a clear distinction between the subsistence and social minimums, see the Institute

of Labor and Social Policy (IPiSS) website at http://www.ipiss.com.pl/badania/ minsoc_i_ minegz.html. For a very detailed description of the contents of the subsistence minimum basket, see Lucyna Deniszczuk and Barbara Sajkiewicz, "Kategoria minimum egzystencji," in *Polska bieda II*, ed. Stanisława Golinowska (Warsaw: Instytut Pracy i Spraw Społecznych, 1997).

30. In addition to Frieske, see Krzysztof Lecki and Kazimierz Wódz, "Droga do ubóstwa? Gwara śląska jako bariera edukacyjna," in *Przeciw biedzie: programy, pomysły, inicjatywy*, ed. Elżbieta Tarkowska (Warsaw: Oficyna Naukowa, 2002), 53. See also Tarkowska, *Zrozumieć biednego: o dawnej i obecnej biedzie w Polsce*, 55, 233.

31. See, for example, Piotr Jarecki, *Od zasłuchania do działania: społeczne echo pielgrzymki* (Warsaw: "Pax," 1999), 51; Leon Dyczewski, "Kościół katolicki wobec ubóstwa i ludzi ubogich," in *Polska bieda II: kryteria, ocena, przeciwdziałanie*, ed. Stanisława Golinowska (Warsaw: IPiSS, 1997), 370–71; and Aniela Dylus, "Wolny rynek—ubóstwo—uczestnictwo," *Tygodnik Powszechny*, October 18, 1998. The Roman Catholic bishops also point to the many dimensions of poverty in Konferencja Episkopatu Polski, *Posługa charytatywna Kościoła* (Konferencja Episkopatu Polski, 2001 [cited January 24, 2003]); available from http://www.episkopat.pl/dokumenty/synoddokumenty.pdf. no. 21.

32. Mieczysław Kabaj, *Program przeciwdziałania ubóstwu i bezrobociu, Raport IPiSS, z. 19* (Warsaw: Instytut Pracy i Spraw Socjalnych, 2000), 21, n. 9. For the year 1998, the social minimum for one person was 566 złoty per month (approx. $144 U.S.), whereas the subsistence minimum was 254 złoty per month (approx. $64 U.S.). The present author has provided the dollar conversions.

33. See Kowalik and Kabaj's polemic with Jeffrey Sachs on this topic. Mieczysław Kabaj and Tadeusz Kowalik, "Who Is Responsible for Postcommunist Successes in Eastern Europe?" *Transition*, vol. 6, nos. 7–8, July/August, 1995, World Bank Group Newsletter (accessed March 2, 2004); available from http://www.worldbank.org/transitionnewsletter/ja95/aug-ar3.htm.

34. Tadeusz Kowalik, "Zmiany w podziale dochodu narodowego w czasie transformacji," in *Dynamika transformacji polskiej gospodarki*, ed. Marek Belka and Władysław Trzeciakowski (Warsaw: PolText, 1997), 117–18.

35. Golinowska, "Badania nad ubóstwem: założenia i metodologia," 19, 24.

36. See Frieske, "Bieda: miary i interpretacje," 213. Frieske also warns against the manipulation of data by those who research problems of poverty.

37. Parts of the following material appear in Gerald J. Beyer, "Towards an Ethical Evaluation of Poland's Transition to a Free-Market Economy and the Roman Catholic Church's Response," *Religion in Eastern Europe* 21, no. 4 (2001).

38. For representative examples of negative and positive evaluations, see, respectively, Krzysztof Mądel's statement in Ryszard Bugaj et al., "Odchodzenie od złudzeń?" *Więź* 2, no. 496 (2000): 47; and Witold Gadomski, "Kapitalizm jest zdrowy," *Gazeta Wyborcza*, December 7, 1999.

39. The World Bank report on poverty uses this terminology. See Kanbur, Lustig, and World Bank, *Attacking Poverty*.

40. In his arguments with Polish economists about the effects of the socioeconomic policies of the 1990s, Jeffrey Sachs has referred to mortality rates and a purported rise in consumption. He discredits the use of income to gauge poverty. See Jeffrey Sachs, "Postcommunist Parties and the Politics of Entitlement," *Beyond Transition* 6, no. 3 (1995); and Jeffrey Sachs, "Old Myths about Poland's Reforms Die Hard," *Beyond Transition* 6, no. 11–12 (1995).

41. Czesław Bywalec, "Transformacja gospodarcza a poziom życia społeczeństwa polskiego," *Ekonomista* 4 (1995): 690. Amartya Sen correctly argues that one must look deeper into a given society's mortality rates to find out about the lives of its various groups, either geographically, racially, or by gender. He shows that African-American males in cities have much shorter average lifespans than Bangladeshi or Chinese men. See Sen, *Development as Freedom*, 21–24.

42. United Nations Development Programme Poland, *Raport: milenijne cele rozwoju Polska* (Warsaw: UNDP Poland, 2001), 47.

43. United Nations Development Programme Poland, *Human Development Report: Poland and the Information Society: Logging On* (Warsaw: UNDP Poland, 2002), 148.

44. United Nations Development Programme Poland, *Raport: milenijne cele rozwoju Polska*, 15. While there has been improvement, the risk for males is still twice as high as it is in Western Europe. UNDP Poland enumerates smoking, alcohol abuse, and diet among the leading causes.

45. Ibid.

46. Bywalec, "Transformacja gospodarcza a poziom życia społeczeństwa polskiego," 690.

47. These statistics are taken from the Polish government's official statistical webpage (*Główny Urząd Statystyczny*), which is at http://www.stat.gov.pl/.

48. Golinowska, "Badania nad ubóstwem: założenia i metodologia," 25.

49. Sen, *Development as Freedom*, 72.

50. Mieczysław Kabaj, *Reduction of Poverty and Social Exclusion* (UNDP Poland, 2000 [cited March 3, 2000]); available from http://www.undp.org.pl/pages/pl_pov.htm.

51. See the statistics on the subsistence minimum at the Institute's website: http://www.ipiss.com.pl/teksty/wykres1.gif.

52. United Nations Development Programme Poland, *Raport: milenijne cele rozwoju Polska*, 9.

53. See Tarkowska, *Zrozumieć biednego: o dawnej i obecnej biedzie w Polsce*; Golinowska, "Poverty in Poland: Causes, Measures, and Studies," 30, 31; and Bogumiła Szopa, "Podstawowe uwarunkowania ubóstwa w Polsce," in *Etyczne aspekty bogacenia się i ubóstwa*, ed. Adam Węgrzecki (Cracow: Wydawnictwo Akademii Ekonomicznej w Krakowie, 2003), 146.

54. Golinowska, "Ubóstwo w Polsce: synteza wyników badań," 314. Golinowska reaches this conclusion, despite acknowledging that income figures from 1988 to 1989 did not accurately reflect households' abilities to convert income into consumption because of the deficit of goods at the time. On poverty's rise in the early years of the transformation, see also Kowalik, "Zmiany w podziale dochodu narodowego w czasie transformacji," 118–19; Jan J. Rutkowski, *Welfare and the Labor Market in Poland: Social Policy during Economic Transition* (Washington, D.C.: World Bank, 1998), 61; and Kabaj and Kowalik, *Who Is Responsible for Postcommunist Successes in Eastern Europe?* Kabaj and Kowalik argue against Sachs's contention that in post-Communist societies, "the living standard . . . did not actually drop if one examines actual household consumption behavior." They claim that a reduction in food consumption from the years 1989 to 1994 took place. Sachs's argument is found in Sachs, "Postcommunist Parties and the Politics of Entitlement." See also Sachs's response to Kabaj and Kowalik in Sachs, "Old Myths about Poland's Reforms Die Hard"; and *Commanding Heights: Interview with Jeffrey Sachs* (PBS, 2000 [cited March 16, 2004]); available from http://www.pbs.org/wgbh/commandingheights/shared/minitextlo/int_jeffreysachs.html#11. For a detailed discussion of consumption patterns in Poland in the 1990s, see Czesław Bywalec, *Transformacja gospodarcza a zróżnicowanie poziomu życia społeczeństwa polskiego* (Cracow: Wydaw. Akademii Ekonomicznej, 1999), 23–42.

55. For statistics confirming this rise, in addition to Golinowska, see http://www.ipiss.com.pl/teksty/wykres1.gif.

56. Okrasa, *Who Avoids and Who Escapes from Poverty during the Transition?* 2, 3. For uses of the term "underclass" regarding the poor in Poland, see Katarzyna Korzeniewska, "Biedni (i) emeryci: o ekonomicznej zależności biednych rodzin od pomocy z zewnątrz i o 'underclass' po polsku," in *Lata tłuste, lata chude: spojrzenia na biedę w społecznościach lokalnych: praca zbiorowa*, ed. Katarzyna Korzeniewska and Elżbieta Tarkowska (Warsaw: Wydaw. IFiS PAN, 2002); and Elżbieta Tarkowska, "Czy dziedziczenie biedy? Bariery i szanse edukacyjne młodzieży wiejskiej z gminy Kościelec," in *Lata tłuste, lata chude: spojrzenia na biedę w społecznościach lokalnych: praca zbiorowa*, ed. Katarzyna Korzeniewska and Elżbieta Tarkowska (Warsaw: Wydaw. IFiS PAN, 2002).

57. Rutkowski, *Welfare and the Labor Market in Poland*, 62.

58. See Tarkowska, *Zrozumieć biednego: o dawnej i obecnej biedzie w Polsce*, 57; and Tarkowska, "Czy dziedziczenie biedy? Bariery i szanse edukacyjne młodzieży wiejskiej z gminy Kościelec."

59. Working with a team of international scholars on the relationship between poverty, gender, and ethnicity, Tarkowska and her colleagues concluded that in Poland, which is a highly homogeneous country, an ethnically based underclass does not exist. She contends that there is the danger of an "underclass without ethnicity" arising, mainly comprised of agricultural laborers in the regions where farming was collectivized by the Communist state (known as PGR-y

Notes to Pages 62–63   245

in Poland). One of her colleagues, Justyna Laskowska-Otwinowska, notes that she was surprised to find in her research that Roma, one of the largest minorities in Poland, do not represent a marginalized group as a whole. The economic status within the group, about 30,000 in Poland, is quite diverse. Thus, this chapter will not create a particular category of impoverished based on ethnicity. See Katarzyna Korzeniewska and Elżbieta Tarkowska, "Spojrzenie na biedę: wprowadzenie," in *Lata tłuste, lata chude: spojrzenia na biedę w społecznościach lokalnych: praca zbiorowa*, ed. Katarzyna Korzeniewska and Elżbieta Tarkowska (Warsaw: Wydaw. IFiS PAN, 2002); Justyna Laskowska-Otwinowska, "Elementy kultury romskiej jako źródło marginalizacji i bogacenia się Romów polskich," in *Lata tłuste, lata chude: spojrzenia na biedę w społecznościach lokalnych: praca zbiorowa*, ed. Katarzyna Korzeniewska and Elżbieta Tarkowska (Warsaw: Wydaw. IFiS PAN, 2002); Justyna Laskowska-Otwinowska, "Stereotyp biednego Roma," in *Lata tłuste, lata chude: spojrzenia na biedę w społecznościach lokalnych: praca zbiorowa*, ed. Katarzyna Korzeniewska and Elżbieta Tarkowska (Warsaw: Wydaw. IFiS PAN, 2002); and Elżbieta Tarkowska, "An Underclass without Ethnicity: The Poverty of Polish Women and Agricultural Laborers," in *Poverty, Ethnicity, and Gender in Eastern Europe during the Market Transition*, ed. Rebecca Jean Emigh and Iván Szelényi (Westport, Conn.: Praeger, 2001).

60. For further elucidation of how the Organization for Economic Cooperation and Development (OECD) equivalency scales are used to compare households of different sizes, see Golinowska, "Poverty in Poland: Causes, Measures, and Studies," 24; and Golinowska, "Badania nad ubóstwem: założenia i metodologia," 27.

61. Okrasa, *Who Avoids and Who Escapes from Poverty during the Transition?* 18–19.

62. Ibid., 18; and Elżbieta Tarkowska, "Zróżnicowanie biedy: wiek i płeć," in *Jak żyją Polacy?* ed. Henryk Domański, Antonina Ostrowska, and Andrzej Rychard (Warsaw: Wydawnictwo IFiS PAN, 2000), 261, 277–78; Tarkowska, *Zrozumieć biednego: o dawnej i obecnej biedzie w Polsce*, 56. Tarkowska states that people above age 65 account for 5 percent of the poor, while children under 14 account for 30 percent.

63. Elżbieta Tarkowska, "'Dzieciństwa żadnego nie miałem': bieda i dzieci," *Więź* 488, no. 6 (1999): 65.

64. Tarkowska, "Zróżnicowanie biedy: wiek i płeć," 262.

65. Ibid., 263.

66. Ibid., 264–65; Tarkowska, "'Dzieciństwa żadnego nie miałem': bieda i dzieci," 67.

67. See Tarkowska, "'Dzieciństwa żadnego nie miałem': bieda i dzieci," 70–71.

68. See Golinowska, "Poverty in Poland: Causes, Measures, and Studies," 35.

69. Ibid., 34; Golinowska, "Ubóstwo w Polsce: synteza wyników badań," 323–24.

70. Tarkowska, "Zróżnicowanie biedy: wiek i płeć," 261.

71. For the Catholic bishops' conference stance on this, see the Synodal document on the vocation of marriage and the family. The bishops write: "Another child is sometimes treated like a heavy burden. The ideal for a large portion of couples is one child. This negative trend is driven by a weakness of faith and a related misunderstanding of the parental vocation that God gave men and women, for the sake of one or both partner's material comfort and by the fear of a difficult financial and housing situation" (no. 30). They also criticize the tax system, which does not grant tax reductions for each dependent, as "antifamily" (no. 20). While the bishops acknowledge the Church's official approval of "natural methods" of birth control, the above statement and their numerous condemnations of "artificial" birth control make it clear that large families are the desired norm. Konferencja Episkopatu Polski, *Powołanie do życia w małżeństwie i rodzinie* (Konferencja Episkopatu Polski, 2001 [cited January 24, 2003]); available from http://www.episkopat.pl/dokumenty/synoddokumenty.pdf. For a critique of profamily politics, see Ewa Nowakowska, "Karuzela z rodzinami," *Polityka*, September 12, 1998.

72. Golinowska, "Ubóstwo w Polsce: synteza wyników badań," 323. See also Bożena Balcerzak-Paradowska, "Zagrożenie ubóstwem rodzin wielodzietnych," in *Polska bieda II: kryteria, ocena, przeciwdziałanie*, ed. Stanisława Golinowska (Warsaw: IPiSS, 1997), 231.

73. Tarkowska, "Zróżnicowanie biedy: wiek i płeć," 269.

74. Golinowska, "Poverty in Poland: Causes, Measures, and Studies," 34.

75. There is a growing amount of research on this subject. Among those conducting it are Elżbieta Tarkowska and Irena Reszke, whose articles will provide much of the following information.

76. See the interviews with poor women in Tarkowska, "Zróżnicowanie biedy: wiek i płeć," 265; and Tarkowska, "Czy dziedziczenie biedy? Bariery i szanse edukacyjne młodzieży wiejskiej z gminy Kościelec," 169–70.

77. See "Education of Women in Poland," in Urszula Nowakowska, *Polish Women in the 90's* (Women's Rights Center, 2000 [cited March 19, 2003]); available from http://free.ngo.pl/temida/rapcont.htm. The report is available in English and Polish. Although this statistic may be revealing, Tarkowska finds some evidence that in farming families, girls are more encouraged to get an education because boys are expected to remain at home to manage the farm. Tarkowska, "Czy dziedziczenie biedy? Bariery i szanse edukacyjne młodzieży wiejskiej z gminy Kościelec," 170–71.

78. See "Women in the Family," in Nowakowska, *Polish Women in the 90's*.

79. Ibid. See also Tarkowska, "Zróżnicowanie biedy: wiek i płeć," 269–71; Irena Reszke, "Uwarunkowania feminizacji biedy w Polsce," *Kultura i społeczeństwo* 2 (2001): 73; and Graff, *Świat bez kobiet: płeć w polskim życiu publicznym*, 64, 82, 97.

80. Tarkowska, "Zróżnicowanie biedy: wiek i płeć," 268.

81. Ibid., 271–72; Joanna Jastrzębska-Szklarska and Bohdan Szklarski, "Od klientelizmu do paternalizmu—biednej społeczności popegierowska droga przez transformację," in *Lata tłuste, lata chude: spojrzenia na biedę w społecznościach lokalnych: praca zbiorowa*, ed. Katarzyna Korzeniewska and Elżbieta Tarkowska (Warsaw: Wydaw. IFiS PAN, 2002), 125. Both authors reach this conclusion on the basis of numerous interviews with men and women in poor households.

82. Tarkowska, "Zróżnicowanie biedy: wiek i płeć," 275–77. See Barbara Perepeczko, "Swoistość biedy w rodzinach rolniczych i jej oswajanie," in *Przeciw biedzie: programy, pomysły, inicjatywy*, ed. Elżbieta Tarkowska (Warsaw: Oficyna Naukowa, 2002), 35.

83. Rutkowski, *Welfare and the Labor Market in Poland*, 63. He importantly points out that causality runs both ways. Alcohol abuse often leads to unemployment; and poverty, unemployment, and despair often lead to alcoholism.

84. Tarkowska, "Zróżnicowanie biedy: wiek i płeć," 275–77. The UNDP Millennium Goals report names alcohol abuse among males as one of the major reasons for their lower life expectancy in Poland than in the rest of Western Europe.

85. Elżbieta Tarkowska, "O ubóstwie i moralności: czego można dowiedzieć się o moralnej kondycji społeczeństwa, badając biedę i biednych," in *Kondycja moralna społeczeństwa polskiego*, ed. Janusz Mariański (Cracow: Wydawnictwo WAM, 2002), 311.

86. See "Violence against Women," in Nowakowska, *Polish Women in the 90's*. The report admits that the term "abusive environment" is subjective and open to interpretation in surveys. Nonetheless, it cannot be denied that violence against women in Poland is a serious problem, which occurs more often than domestic violence against men.

87. Tarkowska, "Zróżnicowanie biedy: wiek i płeć," 267.

88. See Kanbur, Lustig, and World Bank, *Attacking Poverty*, 17–18.

89. Reszke, "Uwarunkowania feminizacji biedy w Polsce," 74–79. See also Golinowska, "Poverty in Poland: Causes, Measures, and Studies," 32; United Nations Development Programme Poland, *Raport: milenijne cele rozwoju Polska*, 13–14.

90. See Matthew Valencia, "Poland: Limping towards Normality," *The Economist*, October 27, 2001, 14.

91. Tarkowska, "Czy dziedziczenie biedy? Bariery i szanse edukacyjne młodzieży wiejskiej z gminy Kościelec."

92. United Nations Development Programme Poland, *Raport o rozwoju społecznym Polska 2000: rozwój obszarów wiejskich* (Warsaw: UNDP Poland, 2000), vii–viii.

93. Ibid., 54.

94. Golinowska, "Poverty in Poland: Causes, Measures, and Studies," 34.

95. Tarkowska, *Zrozumieć biednego: o dawnej i obecnej biedzie w Polsce*, 58.

96. Valencia, "Poland: Limping towards Normality," 14.

97. See Irena Wóycicka and Anna Mateja, "Zagłębie biedy, źródło szans," *Tygodnik Powszechny*, November 19, 2003.

98. Rutkowski, *Welfare and the Labor Market in Poland*, 59. Rutkowski defines households with incomes in the bottom quintile as poor.

99. Golinowska, "Poverty in Poland: Causes, Measures, and Studies," 33. Golinowska generally uses the subsistence minimum to denote poverty.

100. Valencia, "Poland: Limping towards Normality," 14. See Wóycicka and Mateja, "Zagłębie biedy, źródło szans." UNDP Poland challenges the claim that as many as 30 percent of all Poles earn their living from agriculture. They argue that those who have small farms but live mainly from social transfers should not be counted. Nonetheless, they agree that the number is still larger compared to other European countries. See United Nations Development Programme Poland, *Raport o rozwoju społecznym Polska 2000: rozwój obszarów wiejskich*, viii.

101. For example, one quarter of the homes in villages do not have bathrooms. See United Nations Development Programme Poland, *Raport o rozwoju społecznym Polska 2000: rozwój obszarów wiejskich*, 59.

102. Ibid., viii, 63–64.

103. For example, Professor Grażyna Skąpska mentions that in small towns where most workers were employed by a factory that then closed, poverty increased dramatically. Grażyna Skąpska, interview, March 30, 2004.

104. See Tarkowska, *Zrozumieć biednego: o dawnej i obecnej biedzie w Polsce*, 106. She relies on the research of several scholars. Among the unemployed, some do work in the black market, but estimates to what extent vary. On this topic, see Katarzyna Sadłowska, "Milion pozornie bezrobotnych," *Rzeczpospolita*, November 9, 2003.

105. United Nations Development Programme Poland, *Raport o rozwoju społecznym Polska 2000: rozwój obszarów wiejskich*, 54.

106. Jastrzębska-Szklarska and Szklarski, "Od klientelizmu do paternalizmu—biednej społeczności popegierowska droga przez transformację," 124, 134. Despite the differences between the poverty of farmers and post-PGR-y poverty, Tarkowska still classifies the latter as "shallow." She maintains that hunger is not widespread; rather, people in these regions face chronic undernourishment. In my judgment, however, when milk for children must be mixed with water, one can begin to speak of the problem of hunger.

107. Tarkowska, *Zrozumieć biednego: o dawnej i obecnej biedzie w Polsce*, 92. See United Nations Development Programme Poland, *Raport o rozwoju społecznym Polska 2000: rozwój obszarów wiejskich*, 53.

108. Bogucka, "Polska Bieda," 10; United Nations Development Programme Poland, *Raport o rozwoju społecznym Polska 2000: rozwój obszarów wiejskich*, 53. Jastrzębska-Szklarska and Szklarski, "Od klientelizmu do paternalizmu—biednej społeczności popegierowska droga przez transformację," 124.

109. This reconstruction, which cannot be thorough and complete given this chapter's limitations, relies on Tarkowska's "Bieda popegierowska," in Tarkowska, *Zrozumieć biednego: o dawnej i obecnej biedzie w Polsce*, 90–117; United Nations Development Programme Poland, *Raport o rozwoju społecznym Polska 2000: rozwój obszarów wiejskich*; and Jastrzębska-Szklarska and Szklarski, "Od klientelizmu do paternalizmu—biednej społeczności popegierowska droga przez transformację."

110. Two contemporary Polish films, *Arizona* (1997) and *Zmruż oczy* (2003), depicted this desolation.

111. United Nations Development Programme Poland, *Raport o rozwoju społecznym Polska 2000: rozwój obszarów wiejskich*, 53.

112. See Bogucka, "Polska bieda," 10. In this vein, Bogucka claims that "in the PGR-y the socialism of the People's Republic of Poland fully realized itself."

113. It is important here to remember that because of shortages at various points during the Communist era, staples such as meat or milk became "rare goods."

114. See the discussion of this problem in chapter 3; and Bogucka, "Polska bieda," 10.

115. Jastrzębska-Szklarska and Szklarski, "Od klientelizmu do paternalizmu—biednej społeczności popegierowska droga przez transformację," 123–34.

116. Chapter 2 mentioned, for example, that Poland negotiated with the IMF and World Bank for debt relief. Wojciech Roszkowski also mentions the negative effects of the economic sanctions against Iraq and the Gulf War and Poland's decreased exports to the former Soviet Union in addition to Balcerowicz's reforms. Roszkowski, *Najnowsza historia Polski: 1980–2002*, 133.

117. See, for example: Golinowska, "Ubóstwo w Polsce: synteza wyników badań," 321; Tarkowska, *Zrozumieć biednego: o dawnej i obecnej biedzie w Polsce*, 56–57; and Kabaj, *Program przeciwdziałania ubóstwu i bezrobociu*, 22. This may seem obvious, but if one considers that other forms of income (social transfers, gifts, savings, assets, etc.) may lift persons out of poverty, the correlation between unemployment and poverty is not automatic.

118. See Tischner, *W krainie schorowanej wyobraźni*, 89–92.

119. See Golinowska, "Poverty in Poland: Causes, Measures, and Studies," 12, 15. Even the Roman Catholic bishops named the process of privatization and concurrent job losses a "painful but necessary remedy." See Gowin, *Kościół w czasach wolności 1989–1999*, 272.

120. See Dylus, *Zmienność i ciągłość: polskie transformacje ustrojowe w horyzoncie etycznym*, 13.

121. Golinowska, "Poverty in Poland: Causes, Measures, and Studies," 11–15. Golinowska points out that employment in the agricultural sector began to rise again in 1994 after a period of decline when those who could not find work in other sectors returned to farms. However, she refers to these farms as "storerooms"

for those who simply could not find work elsewhere. Thus, the agricultural sector has a relatively high rate of "hidden unemployment."

122. Stanisława Golinowska, "Polska droga do bezrobocia: o przyczynach bezrobocia i polityce jego zwalczania," *Tygodnik Powszechny*, July 29, 2001, 1.

123. Ibid., 5. Golinowska estimates that this demographic factor has increased unemployment by one third. See Stanisława Golinowska, *Warunki tworzenia miejsc pracy* (Warsaw: CASE—Centrum Analiz Społeczno-Ekonomicznych, 1999), 9.

124. Statistics taken from *Główny Urząd Statystyczny*, Polska Statystyka Publiczna, *Mały Rocznik Statystyczny, 2003*, and "Stopa bezrobocia w latach 1990–2004" at http://www.stat.gov.pl/.

125. Kabaj, *Program przeciwdziałania ubóstwu i bezrobociu*, 22–23. Reszke shows that 23.8 percent of all women were without work for more than two years, while only 11.8 percent of unemployed men fell into this category. She also notes that 56 percent of all registered unemployed are women. Reszke, "Uwarunkowania feminizacji biedy w Polsce," 74.

126. Golinowska, "Minimalne dochody a walka z ubóstwem," 389. See also Kabaj, *Program przeciwdziałania ubóstwu i bezrobociu*, 30. Kabaj writes that in 1998 the unemployment benefit was lowered to 29 percent of the average wage. In 2004 the basic unemployment benefit was 504 złoty, which lies in between the social minimum for one person (789 złoty) and the subsistence minimum for one person (354 złoty). Unemployment benefit levels are found on the Ministry of Economics, Labor, and Social Policy website at: http://www.mgpips.gov.pl/_swiadczenia.php?dzial=186&poddzial=208&dokument=750. The social and subsistence minimums are found on the Institute of Labor and Social Policy website at: http://www.ipiss.com.pl/opracowania_min.html.

127. Rutkowski, *Welfare and the Labor Market in Poland*, 22.

128. See "Chłopi wielozawodowi," *Gazeta Wyborcza*, March 2, 2000. According to the article, the new legislation "will eliminate the discriminatory rules against farmers."

129. From 1990 to 1998, the number of attempted suicides in Poland almost doubled, with the most occurring in the age bracket of 31–50, that is, in the prime of one's vocational life. See the statistics on suicide at http://www.stat.gov.pl/. One dramatic story alleges that the unemployed citizens of a town in Poland asked the government to assist them in committing suicide if it could not provide them with work. See the story at http://www.polandonline.com/news/newspolback1.html. On the social and psychological consequences of unemployment, see Sen, *Development as Freedom*, 94–96; and United States Catholic Conference of Bishops, "Economic Justice for All: A Catholic Framework for Economic Life," 141–43.

130. Dylus, *Zmienność i ciągłość: polskie transformacje ustrojowe w horyzoncie etycznym*, 13. For a description of "shock therapy," see Dudek, *Pierwsze lata III Rzeczypospolitej: 1989–2001*, 88–98; and *Commanding Heights: Interview with Jeffrey Sachs*. For a detailed, critical analysis of Polish "shock therapy," see Józef

Kaleta, "Harakiri?" in *Spór o Polskę: 1989–1999*, ed. Paweł Śpiewak (Warsaw: PWN, 2001); and Modzelewski, *Dokąd od komunizmu?* 27–70.

131. Patrycja Maciewicz, "Bezrobocie w Polsce spadnie poniżej 10 proc.?" *Gazeta Wyborcza*, March 7, 2007.

132. "KE: W Polsce nawet praca nie chroni przed biedą," *Gazeta Wyborcza*, February 25, 2008. Three recent European Commission reports signal the problem of poverty and low wages in Poland. See Directorate-General for Employment and Social Affairs, "Child Poverty and Well-Being in the EU: Current Status and Way Forward" (Luxembourg: Office for Official Publications of the European Communities, 2008); Directorate-General for Employment and Social Affairs, "Joint Report on Social Protection and Social Inclusion" (Luxembourg: Office for Official Publications of the European Communities, 2008); and Directorate-General for Employment and Social Affairs, "Joint Report on Social Protection and Social Inclusion" (Luxembourg: Office for Official Publications of the European Communities, 2007). All of these are available at http://ec.europa.eu/index_en.htm#. Poland's most recent governmental statistics list 18 percent below the official poverty line and 12.3 percent below the subsistence minimum at http://www.stat.gov.pl/cps/rde/xchg/gus.

133. "'Solidarność' przeciw niskim płacom," *Gazeta Wyborcza*, July 30, 2008.

134. More detailed information can be found in Urszula Sztanderska, Elżbieta Drogosz-Zabłocka, and Barbara Minkiewicz, *Edukacja dla pracy: raport o rozwoju społecznym Polska 2007* (Warsaw: Program Narodów Zjednoczonych ds. Rozwoju, 2007).

135. From 1990 to 1992, Poland experienced a recession. Then, in the years from 1993 to 1999, Poland's GDP grew steadily. In 2001 a period of stagnation began. Growth in terms of the GDP began again in the second quarter of 2003. See http://www.stat.gov.pl/. The fact is that wages increased much less than the rate of growth. When wages did grow robustly, it was to a large degree the result of very high wages in some sectors. See Szopa, "Podstawowe uwarunkowania ubóstwa w Polsce," 147.

136. The Gini coefficient of disposable income rose from 28 to 33 from the end of the 1980s to 1996, placing Poland on the same level as OECD countries in just a few years. Golinowska, "Poverty in Poland: Causes, Measures, and Studies," 17. See Kowalik, "Zmiany w podziale dochodu narodowego w czasie transformacji"; and Mieczysław Kabaj, *Programme Outline for Actively Counteracting Poverty and Social Exclusion* (UNDP Poland, 2000 [cited March 3, 2000]); available from http://www.undp.org.pl/pages/pl_pov2.htm., 16.

137. See the chapter on inequalities, "Trochę o nierównościach," in Balcerowicz, *Wolność i rozwój: ekonomia wolnego rynku*; and Wacław Wilczyński, "Plaga nierówności," *Polityka* 2, no. 2142 (1998).

138. For example, see Kowalik's position in Wilczyński, "Plaga nierówności."

139. Golinowska, "Poverty in Poland: Causes, Measures, and Studies," 17. See also Rutkowski, *Welfare and the Labor Market in Poland*, 28.

140. Kabaj, *Programme Outline for Actively Counteracting Poverty and Social Exclusion*, 16.

141. Rutkowski, *Welfare and the Labor Market in Poland*, 26.

142. Barbara Kieniewicz and Bogumiła Szopa, *Polityka dochodowa na tle rynku pracy w Polsce w warunkach transformacji systemowej* (Cracow: AE. Wydaw. Uczelniane, 1997), 88.

143. White-collar workers represent about 10–15 percent of all households in Poland; the self-employed, roughly 8–12 percent; blue-collar workers, about 25–30 percent; agricultural workers, approximately 15 percent; and farmers, 7–9 percent. Households of old-age pensioners and the disabled comprise about 30 percent of the total population. However, those who receive "unearned income," such as unemployment benefits, temporary welfare benefits, and alimony, represent only 3–5 percent. Czesław Bywalec, *Społeczne aspekty transformacji gospodarczej w Europie Środkowowschodniej* (Cracow: Wydaw. Akademii Ekonomicznej, 1998), 23.

144. Poland increasingly resembles OECD countries in this regard.

145. United Nations Development Programme Poland, *Raport o rozwoju społecznym Polska 1999: ku godnej aktywnej starości* (Warsaw: UNDP Poland, 1999), 59.

146. Rutkowski, *Welfare and the Labor Market in Poland*, 13–14. By comparison, the ratio is much lower in the Czech Republic, Slovakia, and Hungary: 45 percent, 45 percent, and 47 percent, respectively.

147. Ibid., 28, 29. See Kieniewicz and Szopa, *Polityka dochodowa na tle rynku pracy w Polsce w warunkach transformacji systemowej*, 87. Kieniewicz and Szopa claim that the instance of low wages rose from 2 percent in 1987 to 15.7 percent in 1996.

148. Reszke, "Uwarunkowania feminizacji biedy w Polsce." See "W pracy kobiety nie są solidarne: rozmowa z prof. ekonomii Stanisławą Golinowską," *Gazeta Wyborcza*, December 4, 1999; and Ewa Nowakowska, "Szklany sufit, lepka podłoga," *Polityka*, February 21, 2004.

149. Perepeczko, "Swoistość biedy w rodzinach rolniczych i jej oswajanie," 33.

150. Rutkowski, *Welfare and the Labor Market in Poland*, 54.

151. The average monthly salary in Poland was (after taxes in parenthesis) in: 2002: 2113 PLN; 2000: 1,894 PLN; 1998: 1,232 PLN (1,027); 1997: 1,066 PLN (877); 1995: 691 PLN (561); 1994: 525 PLN; (425); 1993: 390 PLN (320); 1992: 290 PLN (244). Statistics for 1998 and earlier are taken from *Rocznik Statystyczny, GUS: 1999*; and *Rocznik Statystyczny, GUS: 1996*. Statistics for later years are taken from the *Główny Urząd Statystyczny* website http://www.stat.gov.pl/. The Polish złoty has fluctuated around $4 U.S. for the last five years or so. This gives the American reader a sense of the meager average monthly wage in Poland, particularly if he or she is cognizant of the fact that many expenses, such as rent, food, and train travel, are fast approaching the equivalent cost in the American context. For example, the 2002 average monthly salary does not cover the social minimum for a family of four (2,308 PLN).

152. Rutkowski, *Welfare and the Labor Market in Poland*, 53.

153. For Balcerowicz's argument that wages needed to be cut, see Leszek Balcerowicz, *Socjalizm, kapitalizm, transformacja: szkice z przełomu epok*, 1st ed. (Warsaw: Wydawn. Nauk. PWN, 1997), 359.

154. United Nations Development Programme Poland, *National Report on Human Development: The Changing Role of the State, Poland '97*, 124.

155. Kowalik, "Zmiany w podziale dochodu narodowego w czasie transformacji," 99.

156. See, for example, Mieczysław Kabaj, "Searching for a New Results-Oriented Wage Negotiation System in Poland," in *Paying the Price: The Wage Crisis in Central and Eastern Europe*, ed. Daniel Vaughan-Whitehead (New York: St. Martin's Press, 1998); Kaleta, "Harakiri?"; Kowalik, "Zmiany w podziale dochodu narodowego w czasie transformacji"; and Kowalik, "Czy sprawiedliwość społeczna kosztuje? Artykuł polemiczny na marginesie książki pt. *Efektywność a sprawiedliwość*."

157. See Kabaj, "Searching for a New Results-Oriented Wage Negotiation System in Poland," 241; and Skąpska, "Czy instytucje publiczne budowane są w oparciu o ideę solidarności?" 51, 52.

158. United Nations Development Programme Poland, *National Report on Human Development: The Changing Role of the State, Poland '97*, 126. On the minimum wage levels, see also Ministerstwo Gospodarki, Pracy i Polityki Społecznej, *Historia minimalnego wynagrodzenia* (Ministerstwo Gospodarki, Pracy i Polityki Społecznej, 2004 [cited March 30, 2004]); available at http://www.mgpips.gov.pl/wydruk.php?nr=763.

159. Joanna Solska, "Goło, Niewesoło," *Polityka*, April 1, 2000, 56. See the NSZZ Solidarność union's program, which demands legally mandated raises in the minimum wage in relation to the average pay, at http://www.solidarnosc.org.pl/dokumenty/xv_kzd/u_prog.htm.

160. See "Manifest kapitalistyczny," *Gazeta Wyborcza*, April 28, 2000.

161. Kabaj, "Searching for a New Results-Oriented Wage Negotiation System in Poland," 251; Michał Dąbrowski, "Płaca minimalna i jej wpływ na wielkość zatrudnienia" (Master's Thesis, Cracow Academy of Economics, 1998), 92. I am grateful to the author and Professor Andrzej Wojtyna, who provided access to this thesis and to numerous other articles and references. In 2002 the minimum wage (760 złoty) was equivalent to just 35 percent of the average wage. In 2003 the minimum wage (800 złoty) did reach the social minimum level for one person for the first time (789 złoty). See Ministerstwo Gospodarki, *Historia minimalnego wynagrodzenia*.

162. Kabaj, *Programme Outline for Actively Counteracting Poverty and Social Exclusion*.

163. The president of the National Bank of Poland, Hanna Gronkiewicz-Waltz, claimed that limiting her salary to the designated 12,000 PLN per month was outrageous. If it were to go into effect, then the salaries of 135 employees who

earned more than 12,000 PLN per month at the National Bank would also have to be lowered. See *Gazeta Wyborcza*, February 17, 2000.

164. United Nations Development Programme Poland, *National Report on Human Development: The Changing Role of the State, Poland '97*, 126–27.

165. Statistics taken from *Rocznik Statystyczny Rzeczpospolitej Polskiej, GUS: 1999*.

166. United Nations Development Programme Poland, *National Human Development Report Poland 1998: Access to Education* (Warsaw: UNDP Poland, 1998), 12. See also Jarosław Gowin, Andrzej Wiśniewski, and Jerzy Zdrada, "Kryzys po chińsku," *Znak* 2, no. 537 (2000): 29; Sztanderska, Drogosz-Zabłocka, and Minkiewicz, *Edukacja dla pracy: raport o rozwoju społecznym Polska 2007*, 22.

167. See United Nations Development Programme Poland, *Human Development Report: Poland and the Information Society: Logging On* (Warsaw: UNDP Poland, 2002), xxxii, 135.

168. Golinowska, "Poverty in Poland: Causes, Measures, and Studies," 9. See also Tarkowska, "Zróżnicowanie biedy: wiek i płeć," 266.

169. Tarkowska, "Czy dziedziczenie biedy? Bariery i szanse edukacyjne młodzieży wiejskiej z gminy Kościelec," 163.

170. Golinowska, "Ubóstwo w Polsce: synteza wyników badań," 325.

171. United Nations Development Programme Poland, *National Human Development Report Poland 1998: Access to Education*, 29.

172. Golinowska, "Poverty in Poland: Causes, Measures, and Studies," 32.

173. United Nations Development Programme Poland, *National Human Development Report Poland 1998: Access to Education*, 63–64. See also Rutkowski, *Welfare and the Labor Market in Poland*, 36. Rutkowski shows the increasing differentials among those with higher education and those without it.

174. Frieske, "Bieda: miary i interpretacje," 217.

175. Polish sociologist Zygmunt Bauman refers to two categories of poor: those who have the means to potentially revolt against their oppressive surroundings and those who experience such deep deprivation that they cannot possibly revolt. He refers to the latter as "the expendable, unwanted, and thrown-away." Zygmunt Bauman, "Zbędni, niechciani, odtrąceni," *Kultura i społeczeństwo* 2 (1998). For a discussion of these categories, and the implications for the social policy towards these groups, see Katarzyna Górniak, "O współczesnej dobroczynności," in *Przeciw biedzie: programy, pomysły, inicjatywy*, ed. Elżbieta Tarkowska (Warsaw: Oficyna Naukowa, 2002), 82–83.

176. See Sen, *Development as Freedom*, 36–38, 51–52, 191–92. Sen shows that this is particularly true in regard to women's literacy.

177. United Nations Development Programme Poland, *National Human Development Report Poland 1998: Access to Education*, 23, 34, 35.

178. Golinowska, "Ubóstwo w Polsce: synteza wyników badań," 325.

179. Professor Jacek Filek of the Department of Philosophy at Jagiellonian University expressed to me in conversation a common attitude among Poles. In

his view, if one wants a good education in Poland, one can get it thanks to a decent system of public schooling.

180. United Nations Development Programme Poland, *National Human Development Report Poland 1998: Access to Education*, 45.

181. For example, in grammar schools in villages, 11 percent of pupils learn English, in which 80 percent of all information on the Internet appears, while 29 percent of pupils in large cities learn the language. English is also crucial because many businesses in Poland require it of their job candidates. See ibid., 71.

182. Roman Dolata, Krzysztof Konarzewski, and Elżbieta Putkiewicz, *Rekomendacje dla polityki oświatowej po trzech latach reformy szkolnictwa* (Instytut Spraw Publicznych, 2003 [cited March 13, 2004]); available from http://www.isp.org.pl/docs/briefs/analizy5.pdf.

183. Piotr Legutko, "Dwie szkoły, dwie Polski," *Tygodnik Powszechny*, January 5, 2003. For more on educational segregation, see Ewa Winnicka, "Dzieci i dzieci-śmieci," *Polityka*, June 28, 2008.

184. United Nations Development Programme Poland, *National Human Development Report Poland 1998: Access to Education*, 44–45.

185. Ibid., 43–44.

186. Ibid., 46. See Gowin, Wiśniewski, and Zdrada, "Kryzys po chińsku," 32–24. Wiśniewski, then the minister of education, goes as far as to say that free higher education is a way of subsidizing the "well-situated" in Polish society, whose children inevitably fill most of the admissions slots to public universities.

187. United Nations Development Programme Poland, *National Human Development Report Poland 1998: Access to Education*, 46. See also Joanna Kostyła, "Lekcja po lekcjach: system korepetycji zaczyna być postrzegany w kategoriach korupcji," *Wprost*, May 21, 2000. According to a recent survey by the Świętokrzyskie (one of seventeen *voivodships*, or provinces, in Poland) school board, close to one half of all high-school students in that school system attend private tutoring sessions. See Piotr Burda, "Korki pod przymusem," *Gazeta Wyborcza*, March 5, 2004.

188. United Nations Development Programme Poland, *National Human Development Report Poland 1998: Access to Education*, 42.

189. Stiglitz, *Globalization and Its Discontents*, 216.

190. On this claim in Catholic social thought, see United States Catholic Conference of Bishops, "Economic Justice for All: A Catholic Framework for Economic Life," 654, no. 382.

191. Lepianka, "Polacy a biedacy—społeczny obraz ubóstwa i stosunek społeczeństwa polskiego do osób ubogich," 58.

192. Ibid., 59–60. See also Lidia Beskid, "Potoczna percepcja biedy w Polsce w latach 1989–1995," in *Polska bieda II: kryteria, ocena, przeciwdziałanie*, ed. Stanisława Golinowska (Warsaw: IPiSS, 1997), 143; and Tarkowska, "O ubóstwie i moralności: czego można dowiedzieć się o moralnej kondycji społeczeństwa, badając biedę i biednych," 319–20. Tarkowska explains that often the poor refuse to seek

social assistance out of shame and a fear of being shunned by society. Moreover, the paternalistic attitudes of social workers contribute to these anxieties.

193. See Tischner, *W krainie schorowanej wyobraźni*, 7–8. Tischner censures a "new Polish messianism" regarding the suffering that Poles have endured in the last several centuries: partitions, invasion, and, more recently, destruction by the Nazis and forty years of Soviet domination.

194. Lidia Beskid confirms this general trend in her research pertaining to the first half of the 1990s. Moreover, she notes that most Poles believed that more people would fall into poverty in the near future. Beskid, "Potoczna percepcja biedy w Polsce w latach 1989–1995," 139–41.

195. Lepianka, "Polacy a biedacy—społeczny obraz ubóstwa i stosunek społeczeństwa polskiego do osób ubogich," 62.

196. Ibid., 64–65.

197. See ibid., 66.

198. Ibid., 56–57. See also Tarkowska, "O ubóstwie i moralności: czego można dowiedzieć się o moralnej kondycji społeczeństwa, badając biedę i biednych," 306–7.

199. Lepianka, "Polacy a biedacy—społeczny obraz ubóstwa i stosunek społeczeństwa polskiego do osób ubogich," 56–57.

200. See ibid., 57. Lepianka states that social workers who interact with the poor often repeated this adage in describing their perception of society's attitude towards the poor.

201. Beskid, "Potoczna percepcja biedy w Polsce w latach 1989–1995," 139.

202. On this, see Tarkowska, "O ubóstwie i moralności: czego można dowiedzieć się o moralnej kondycji społeczeństwa, badając biedę i biednych," 320.

203. John XXIII referred to this method: "The teachings in regard to social matters for the most part are put into effect in the following three stages: first, the actual situation is examined; then, the situation is evaluated carefully in relation to these teachings; then only is it decided what can and should be done in order that the traditional norms may be adapted to circumstances of time and place. These three steps are at times expressed by the three words: *observe, judge, act*." John XXIII, *Mater et Magistra*, in *Catholic Social Thought: The Documentary Heritage*, ed. David J. O'Brien and Thomas A. Shannon (Maryknoll, N.Y.: Orbis Books, 1992), 122, no. 236.

CHAPTER FOUR Recovering and Applying an Ethic of Solidarity to Polish Poverty

Significant portions of this chapter have been published as "Freedom as a Challenge to an Ethic of Solidarity in a Neoliberal Capitalist World: Lessons from Post-1989 Poland," *Journal of Catholic Social Thought* 6, no. 1 (Winter 2009): 133–67. Reprinted here with permission.

1. Potocki, "Czy społeczeństwo polskie jest społeczeństwem solidarnym?" 82–83.
2. Tischner, *Etyka solidarności*, 10–15.
3. John Paul II, *Sollicitudo Rei Socialis*, 423–25, nos. 40–42.
4. See his homily in Ełk and speech in the Polish Parliament in 1999 in John Paul II, *Jan Paweł II: Polska 1999: przemówienia i homilie*, esp. 76–77, 108–10.
5. All biblical quotations are taken from the Revised Standard Version (RSV). Biblical citations used by Polish authors have been translated by using the equivalent RSV texts.
6. John Paul II, *Jan Paweł II: Polska 1999: przemówienia i homilie*, 75–76.
7. Ibid., 76–77. The Polish text reads, "Kościół współczesny głosi i stara się realizować opcję i miłość preferencyjną na rzecz ubogich." Thus, John Paul does not say option *or* preferential love for the poor (the conjunction *lub* in Polish). Charles Curran notes that in *Sollicitudo Rei Socialis*, no. 42, the pope refers to the "option or love of preference for the poor," which Curran claims signals the pope's ambivalence towards the option for the poor. Curran, *Catholic Social Teaching, 1891–Present*, 183. The pope's affirmation of the option for the poor is unambiguous in this homily in Ełk.
8. Tischner, *Etyka solidarności oraz homo sovieticus*, 17, 23.
9. Mercy, according to Jon Sobrino, moves from compassion beyond the emotive to the praxis of seeking to alleviate the causes of the suffering of others and the suffering itself. See especially the first two essays in Jon Sobrino, *The Principle of Mercy: Taking the Crucified People from the Cross* (Maryknoll, N.Y.: Orbis Books, 1994). The relationship between this understanding of mercy and solidarity would be another question worth examining.
10. See Józef Tischner, *Drogi i bezdroża miłosierdzia* (Cracow: Wydawnictwo AA, 1999), 15.
11. See Gowin, "Kościół a 'Solidarność,'" 28.
12. Kampka, "Solidarność w nauczaniu Jana Pawła II," 8–9.
13. Ibid. Rauscher points out that Pesch spoke of "factual solidarity." This pertains to the recognition that the good of individuals is predicated on the development and good of the whole community. See Anton Rauscher, "Źródła idei solidarności," in *Idea solidarności dzisiaj*, ed. Władysław Zuziak (Cracow: Wydawnictwo Naukowe PAT, 2001), 25. John Paul II also discusses the recognition of interdependence as an aspect of solidarity in John Paul II, *Sollicitudo Rei Socialis*, 421, no. 38.
14. Leonardo Boff's "three moments of liberation theology" correspond to this method. See his essay in Ignacio Ellacuría and Jon Sobrino, *Mysterium Liberationis: Fundamental Concepts of Liberation Theology* (Maryknoll, N.Y.: Orbis Books, 1993). I am grateful to Anna Kasafi Perkins for pointing out the similarities to me.
15. Kampka, "Solidarność w nauczaniu Jana Pawła II," 8–9.

16. This section relies on but goes beyond Tischner's discussion of hearing the cry of the wounded in Tischner, *Etyka solidarności oraz homo sovieticus*, 17. See also Bonowicz, "Słowa, których nie wolno zapomnieć," 70–71.

17. See Kampka, "Solidarność w nauczaniu Jana Pawła II," 8–9.

18. Earlier stress on democratic participation can be found in Catholic social thought. Pius XII initially affirmed it in his writing. However, *Justice in the World* most prominently emphasizes the right to participation as it is being used in this book.

19. David Hollenbach, *Claims in Conflict: Retrieving and Renewing the Catholic Human Rights Tradition* (New York: Paulist Press, 1979), 86–87. The discussion here of the right to participation is indebted to Hollenbach's analysis.

20. World Synod of Bishops, *Justice in the World* (*Justitia in Mundo*), in *Catholic Social Thought: The Documentary Heritage*, ed. David J. O'Brien and Thomas A. Shannon (Maryknoll, N.Y.: Orbis Books, 1992), 289.

21. Ibid., 291.

22. Wojtyła, *Osoba i czyn oraz inne studia antropologiczne*, 310.

23. Ibid., 307.

24. See John XXIII, *Pacem in Terris*, in *Catholic Social Thought: The Documentary Heritage*, ed. David J. O'Brien and Thomas A. Shannon (Maryknoll, N.Y.: Orbis Books, 1992), 140, no. 53.

25. John XXIII, *Mater et Magistra*, 1961, no. 73; John XXIII, *Pacem in Terris*, no. 82.

26. See Konferencja Episkopatu Polski, *Kościół wobec rzeczywistości politycznej* (Konferencja Episkopatu Polski, 2001 [cited January 24, 2003]); available from http://www.episkopat.pl/dokumenty/synoddokumenty.pdf., no. 4 Unlike universal Catholic social teaching, the Polish bishops did not explicitly link participation to the economic conditions that preclude or enable it.

27. Wojtyła, *Osoba i czyn oraz inne studia antropologiczne*, 323.

28. Ibid., 313, 310. Wojtyła stresses that personalistic values must be fulfilled in order to speak of authentic participation. In other words, acting with others must not be transformed into being "acted upon." He contends that human history reveals this tendency.

29. Ibid., 321.

30. Ibid., 313.

31. See John Paul II, *Laborem Exercens*, 373, no. 14; John Paul II, *Sollicitudo Rei Socialis*, 411, no. 27; John Paul II, *Centesimus Annus*, 464–66, nos. 33, 34. See also his World Day of Peace Messages from 1998, 1999, 2000, available at http://www.vatican.va. Especially relevant to the present thesis is his discussion of the right to participation in the 1999 message, no. 6.

32. John Paul II, *Christifideles Laici* (Vatican website, 1988 [cited May 22, 2004]); available from http://www.vatican.va/holy_father/john_paul_ii/apost_exhortations/documents/hf_jp-ii_exh_30121988_christifideles-laici_en.html., no. 42.

33. Potocki, "Czy społeczeństwo polskie jest społeczeństwem solidarnym?" 70.
34. Rauscher, "Źródła idei solidarności," 27.
35. For classic statements of this principle, see Pius XI, *Quadragesimo Anno*, in *Catholic Social Thought: The Documentary Heritage*, ed. David J. O'Brien and Thomas A. Shannon (Maryknoll, N.Y.: Orbis Books, 1992), 60, no. 80; and John XXIII, *Mater et Magistra*, 92, nos. 51–59. See also Jean-Yves Calvez, *The Social Thought of John XXIII: Mater et Magistra* (Chicago: H. Regnery, 1964), 1–14; Curran, *Catholic Social Teaching, 1891–Present*, 138–45; and Hollenbach, *Claims in Conflict*, 158.
36. John XXIII, *Mater et Magistra*, 92, no. 53.
37. John Paul II, *Centesimus Annus*, 475, no. 48.
38. John Paul II, "Przemówienie w Parlamencie Polskiej Rzeczpospolitej," in *Jan Paweł II: Polska 1999: przemówienia i homilie* (Marki: Michalineum, 1999), 110.
39. David Hollenbach, *The Common Good and Christian Ethics* (Cambridge: Cambridge University Press, 2002), 159. In this sense, Hollenbach speaks of "institutionalizing solidarity."
40. See United States Catholic Conference of Bishops, "Economic Justice for All: A Catholic Framework for Economic Life," 600, no. 88.
41. Franciszek Kampka, "Działanie i inspiracja: rzecz o mirażach akcyjności," in *Ziarno czynu: refleksje po V pielgrzymce Jana Pawła II do ojczyzny: praca zbiorowa*, ed. Franciszek Kampka (Cracow: Wydaw. WAM, 1998), 73. See also Sobrino, *The Principle of Mercy*, 159.
42. See, especially, Bonowicz, "Światła etyki solidarności." Poles such as Tischner and Bonowicz do not see heroism as the performance of spectacular acts such as that of Kolbe and so-called supererogatory deeds. It may include these, but it also describes the necessary self-sacrifice of everyday moral life.
43. John Paul II, *Sollicitudo Rei Socialis*, 421, no. 38.
44. John Paul II, *Jan Paweł II: Polska 1999: przemówienia i homilie*, 77.
45. See Lepianka, "Polacy a biedacy—społeczny obraz ubóstwa i stosunek społeczeństwa polskiego do osób ubogich," 70–71.
46. Ibid., 72.
47. Ibid., 68. For a similar conclusion, see Skąpska, "Czy instytucje publiczne budowane są w oparciu o idei solidarności?" esp. 55.
48. Lepianka, "Polacy a biedacy—społeczny obraz ubóstwa i stosunek społeczeństwa polskiego do osób ubogich," 74.
49. Kampka, "Działanie i inspiracja: rzecz o mirażach akcyjności," 68–70.
50. For an interesting analysis of fundraisers as a sociopsychological phenomenon, see Górniak, "O współczesnej dobroczynności." See also Kampka, "Działanie i inspiracja: rzecz o mirażach akcyjności." He discusses the desire to conform as one motivation.
51. Kampka, "Działanie i inspiracja: rzecz o mirażach akcyjności," 73. See also Sobrino, *The Principle of Mercy*, 145.

52. Kampka, "Działanie i inspiracja: rzecz o mirażach akcyjności," 66–67. In regard to this contemplative dimension of solidarity, Kampka points out its peripatetic and Thomistic roots. See also Górniak, "O współczesnej dobroczynności." Górniak describes how the Wielka Orkiestra Świątecznej Pomocy initially concentrated on collecting donations while giving little thought to how the money was spent.

53. See Kampka, "Działanie i inspiracja: rzecz o mirażach akcyjności," 67; and Gowin, *Kościół w czasach wolności 1989–1999*, 459.

54. See Skąpska, "Czy instytucje publiczne budowane są w oparciu o idei solidarności?" 54.

55. Potocki, "Czy społeczeństwo polskie jest społeczeństwem solidarnym?" 83.

56. Ibid., 83, 84.

57. Hollenbach, *The Common Good and Christian Ethics*, 190. Hollenbach raises the issue that solidarity in Catholic social thought is related closely to Christian charity, which is too demanding a norm to be used to create policy in a pluralistic society.

58. John Paul II, *Familiaris Consortio*, nos. 42, 44–48. See also John Paul II, "Królewstwo Boże i chrześcijańska rodzina," in *Jan Paweł II o małżenstwie i rodzinie: 1972–82* (Warsaw: Pax, 1983). In *Familiaris Consortio*, John Paul moves beyond the level of abstract claims to concrete ways in which the family is called to participate in social life. He enumerates the practice of hospitality in imitation of Christ and adoption of a "preferential option for the poor" through special concern for the hungry, the poor, the old, the sick, drug victims, and those without families. Dedication to social services that aid those members of society is a requisite. Moreover, Christian families should also assume responsibility for "transforming society" through political intervention. They are also called to advocate a new international order that spreads fraternity and peace among all human beings. Education of children according to a model of life "based on the values of truth, freedom, justice, and love and active involvement in associations devoted to international issues serves that end."

59. See Józef Tischner, *Jak żyć?* 2nd ed. (Wrocław: Tum, 1995), 80; and Dylus, *Zmienność i ciągłość: polskie transformacje ustrojowe w horyzoncie etycznym*, 119–21. I am indebted to Gene Outka for the term "build-up" strategy or ethic.

60. Along with the evidence already presented in this book, see Potocki, "Czy społeczeństwo polskie jest społeczeństwem solidarnym?"; and Karol Edward Soltan, "Agape, Civil Society, and the Task of Social Reconstruction," *Cardozo Journal of International and Comparative Law* 4, no. 24 (1996).

61. See Potocki, "Czy społeczeństwo polskie jest społeczeństwem solidarnym?" 82.

62. See the research discussed in Katarzyna Korzeniewska, "Biedni (i) emeryci: o ekonomicznej zależności biednych rodzin od pomocy z zewnątrz i o 'underclass' po polsku," 148–58.

63. See John Paul II, *Centesimus Annus*, no. 49.
64. Dylus, *Zmienność i ciągłość: polskie transformacje ustrojowe w horyzoncie etycznym*, 119.
65. Erik Erikson describes this element of parenthood in Erik H. Erikson, *Identity: Youth and Crisis* (New York: Norton & Norton, 1968), 92–107, 232–33.
66. Tischner and Żakowski, *Tischner czyta katechizm*, 94.
67. John Paul II, *Familiaris Consortio*, nos. 44–48.
68. John Paul II, *Novo Millennio Ineunte* (Vatican website, 2001 [cited August 15, 2008]); available from http://www.vatican.va/holy_father/john_paul_ii/apost_letters/documents/hf_jp-ii_apl_20010106_novo-millennio-ineunte_en.html. See also John Paul II, *Sollicitudo Rei Socialis*, 423, no. 40. The pope's argument here resembles Karl Rahner's famous argument for the unity of the love of God and neighbor. For an explanation of Rahner's position and full bibliography, see Gerald J. Beyer, "Karl Rahner on the Radical Unity of the Love of God and Neighbor: Excessive Claim or Exigent Insight?" *Irish Theological Quarterly* 68, no. 3 (2003): 251–80.
69. Tischner, *Etyka solidarności oraz homo sovieticus*, 16–17.
70. Kampka, "Solidarność w nauczaniu Jana Pawła II," 9.
71. Rauscher, "Źródła idei solidarności," 26. See Heinrich Pesch, *Heinrich Pesch on Solidarist Economics: Excerpts from the Lehrbuch der Nationalökonomie* (Lanham, Md.: University Press of America, 1998), esp. 86–89.
72. John XXIII, *Mater et Magistra*, 88, no. 23. See also no. 92. I am indebted here to Franciszek Kampka's analysis of solidarity as a regulatory principle in economic life according to Catholic social thought in Franciszek Kampka, *Antropologiczne i społeczne podstawy ładu gospodarczego w świetle nauczania Kościoła* (Lublin: Redakcja Wydawnictw KUL, 1995), 60–61.
73. John XXIII, *Pacem in Terris*, no. 80.
74. Paul VI, *Populorum Progressio*, in *Catholic Social Thought: The Documentary Heritage*, ed. David J. O'Brien and Thomas A. Shannon (Maryknoll, N.Y.: Orbis Books, 1992), 255, no. 62.
75. John Paul II, *Redemptor Hominis* (Vatican website, 1979 [cited May 21, 2004]); available from http://www.vatican.va/holy_father/john_paul_ii/encyclicals/documents/hf_jp-ii_enc_04031979_redemptor-hominis_pl.html., no. 16. This citation has been translated from the Polish text because the English text seems to carry a slightly different meaning at points. For similar teaching regarding solidarity and globalization, see, for example, John Paul II, "Message of His Holiness Pope John Paul II for the Celebration of the World Day of Peace: 'From the Justice of Each Comes Peace for All' " (Vatican website, 1998 [cited May 21, 2004]); available from http://www.vatican.va/holy_father/john_paul_ii/messages/peace/documents/hf_jp-ii_mes_08121997_xxxi-world-day-for-peace_en.html; and John Paul II, *Sollicitudo Rei Socialis*, 422–23, no. 39.
76. Hollenbach, *The Common Good and Christian Ethics*, 190–91. Hollenbach's argument refers to John Paul II's claim in *Sollicitudo Rei Socialis* (no. 40)

that "there are many points of contact between solidarity and charity, which is the distinguishing mark of Christ's disciples." The pope illustrates what he means by invoking the living examples of Saint Peter Claver, who served slaves at Cartagena de Indias, and Saint Maximilian Kolbe, who sacrificed his own life in Auschwitz to save the life of another prisoner. Hollenbach correctly argues that demanding this kind of sacrificial love in public life as the mark of solidarity is not feasible.

77. Ibid., 193.
78. United States Catholic Conference of Bishops, "Economic Justice for All: A Catholic Framework for Economic Life," 597, no. 79.
79. Hollenbach, *The Common Good and Christian Ethics*, 159.
80. John Paul II, "Przemówienie do przedstawicieli władz państwowych wygłoszone na zamku królewskim," no. 4.
81. David Hollenbach points out that the 1971 Synod of Bishops' document *Justitia in Mundo* portrays the interrelationship of the fundamental right of participation to all other human rights. See Hollenbach, *Claims in Conflict*, 84–89.
82. See Sen, *Development as Freedom*, esp. 16, 75, 188.
83. Ibid., 104–6. Sen discusses here his famous research pertaining to so-called missing women.
84. United States Catholic Conference of Bishops, "Economic Justice for All: A Catholic Framework for Economic Life," 598, no. 80. For the full panoply of rights defended in Catholic social teaching, see John XXIII, *Pacem in Terris*.
85. See the section entitled, "Bread, Freedom, and the Common Good," in chapter 1, which includes references on this topic in Garton Ash, Tischner, and on the NSZZ Solidarność website.
86. I have presented a more sustained argument for the distribution of correlative duties of human rights in accordance with subsidiarity in Gerald J. Beyer, "Beyond 'Nonsense on Stilts': Towards Conceptual Clarity and Resolution of Conflicting Economic Rights," *Human Rights Review* 6, no. 4 (2005).
87. Dylus, *Zmienność i ciągłość: polskie transformacje ustrojowe w horyzoncie etycznym*, 111.
88. Ibid., 120.
89. Górniak, "O współczesnej dobroczynności," 81.
90. United Nations Development Programme, *Human Development Report 2000: Human Rights and Human Development* (New York: Oxford University Press, 2000).
91. Sen, *Development as Freedom*, 231. Sen may be correct in arguing that in some cases a right can "be effectively invoked in contexts even where its *legal* enforcement would appear to be most inappropriate." Sen, *Development as Freedom*, 229.
92. Henry Shue, *Basic Rights: Subsistence, Affluence, and U.S. Foreign Policy*, 2nd ed. (Princeton, N.J.: Princeton University Press, 1996), 52–53. Shue's typology

is helpful for thinking about correlative duties. His emphasis on the inherent relationships between these kinds of duties is extremely insightful and useful. However, it may at times lack the perspective of the principle of subsidiarity. He seems to be skeptical about the ability of individuals to act on behalf of others, which necessitates a greater role for the protection of the state. He is correct, however, to point out that the state or multinational agencies must protect the individual from rights violations brought about by transnational corporations. His afterword in the updated edition of *Basic Rights* is helpful because he emphasizes both personal agency and the institutions needed to sustain it. See ibid., 166 ff.

93. For treatment of this issue and the concept of "socialization," see John XXIII, *Mater et Magistra*, 93–94, nos. 59–60; Second Vatican Council, *Gaudium et Spes: Pastoral Constitution on the Church in the Modern World*, in *Catholic Social Thought: The Documentary Heritage*, ed. David J. O'Brien and Thomas A. Shannon (Maryknoll, N.Y.: Orbis Books, 1992), 180–81, no. 25, and 271, no. 75. See also Shue, *Basic Rights: Subsistence, Affluence, and U.S. Foreign Policy*, 63, 97, 138, 143, afterword. In addition, Nicholas Wolterstorff treats the rights and obligations between rich and poor nations in Nicholas Wolterstorff, *Until Justice and Peace Embrace: The Kuyper Lectures for 1981 Delivered at the Free University of Amsterdam* (Grand Rapids, Mich.: W.B. Eerdmans, 1983).

94. Skąpska, "Czy instytucje publiczne budowane są w oparciu o ideę solidarności?" 48–50. The following section is indebted to Skąpska's analysis. Translations of portions of the Constitution of the Republic of Poland are the present author's and taken directly from the Constitution.

95. Ibid., 49.

96. Ibid., 50.

97. Esteemed Polish philosopher Leszek Kołakowski exhibits this kind of misunderstanding of human rights. See Leszek Kołakowski, "Po co nam prawa człowieka?" *Gazeta Wyborcza*, November 25–26, 2003. Aniela Dylus also appears to interpret economic rights in this way in Dylus, *Zmienność i ciągłość: polskie transformacje ustrojowe w horyzoncie etycznym*, 137–42. See also the response to Kołakowski in defense of human rights in Wiktor Osiatyński, "Czy zmierzch praw człowieka?" *Gazeta Wyborcza*, December 6–7, 2003. Like the present author, Osiatyński finds it disconcerting that many of Poland's most ardent defenders of human rights before 1989 have now abandoned their position. Polish politicians generally show little concern for the respect of human rights, as evidenced by their attitudes towards the UN High Commission for Human Rights' recommendations. On this, see "Przemówił komitet do obrazu," *Gazeta Wyborcza*, December 11–12, 2000; and Ewa Siedlicka and Marek Nowicki, "Wyroki na kołku," *Gazeta Wyborcza*, December 11–12, 2000. For a particular example, see the report of human rights abuses by Wałęsa's government published by Human Rights Watch at http://hrw.org/doc/?t=europe_pub&c=poland.

98. The UN High Commission for Human Rights called attention to this and other denials of women's rights in a memorandum. See United Nations Human Rights Committee, *Concluding Observations of the Human Rights Committee: Poland*. 7/29/99 (1999 [cited May 30, 2004]); available from http://www.unhchr.ch/tbs/doc.nsf/(Symbol)/a61db0e519524575802567c200595e9c? Opendocument.

99. Skąpska, "Czy instytucje publiczne budowane są w oparciu o ideę solidarności?" 53.

100. A most blatant example of this attitude can be found in Janusz Korwin-Mikke, *Naprawić Polskę: no problem* (Lublin: Fabryka Słów, 2004), 61–67, 131–32.

101. Filek, *O wolności i odpowiedzialności podmiotu gospodarującego*, 75. See also Berlin, Hardy, and Harris, *Liberty: Incorporating Four Essays on Liberty*, 168.

102. Filek, *O wolności i odpowiedzialności podmiotu gospodarującego*, 93–94, 221–22.

103. See Walicki, *Polskie zmagania z wolnością*, 30.

104. Filek, *O wolności i odpowiedzialności podmiotu gospodarującego*, 21.

105. Citing Saint Augustine, John Paul II argues that keeping the Commandments is the "first necessary step on the journey towards freedom, its starting point." He states that they are the precondition for the love of one's neighbor. John Paul II, *Veritatis Splendor* (Vatican website, 1993 [cited May 20, 2004]); available from http://www.vatican.va/holy_father/john_paul_ii/encyclicals/documents/hf_jp-ii_enc_06081993_veritatis-splendor_en.html.

106. In the Catholic tradition, Karl Rahner has presented one of the most trenchant accounts of a theology of freedom. While one could appeal to his theology of freedom here, the limits of this book demand confining the scope of these reflections on the nature of freedom. Because this book proposes a retrieval of the ethics of solidarity, it makes sense to appeal most heavily to the thought of Tischner and of John Paul II. I have expounded on Rahner's theology of freedom elsewhere. See Beyer, "Karl Rahner on the Radical Unity of the Love of God and Neighbor."

107. Jarsoław Gowin contends that early in his career, Tischner was convinced that official Catholic social teaching did not adequately address the plight of the poor. See his afterword in Józef Tischner, *Polski kształt dialogu* (Cracow: Znak, 2002), 274–75.

108. Józef Tischner, *Spór o istnienie człowieka* (Cracow: Znak, 1998), 298. The above portion of the analysis of Tischner's notion of freedom is indebted to Gowin, *Religia i ludzkie biedy: księdza Tischnera spory o Kościół*, 66–85, 154–60.

109. Tischner, *Ksiądz na manowcach*, 208.

110. Tischner, *Myśli wyszukane*, 84. See also Tischner, *Nieszczęsny dar wolności*, 11.

111. See, for example, Tischner, *Myślenie według wartości*, 196.

112. Tischner, *W krainie schorowanej wyobraźni*, 75. See also 140–41.

113. In one of his lesser known works, Tischner states explicitly that hope liberates the human person. See Józef Tischner, *Książeczka pielgrzyma* (Warsaw: Libellus, 1996), 9.

114. See Gowin, *Religia i ludzkie biedy: księdza Tischnera spory o Kościół*, 180.

115. See, for example, Tischner, *Myślenie według wartości*, 196.

116. Tischner, *Etyka solidarności*, 90. See Stawrowski, "O zapomnianej solidarności," 62. Stawrowski contends that solidarity arises "in freedom and from freedom."

117. Tischner, *Myślenie według wartości*, 196. Tischner bases his analysis of John Paul II's discussion of freedom and truth on *Redemptor Hominis*.

118. Gowin, *Religia i ludzkie biedy: księdza Tischnera spory o Kościół*, 167. See Tischner, *Etyka solidarności oraz homo sovieticus*, 100–101.

119. Tischner, *Etyka solidarności oraz homo sovieticus*, 101.

120. See Tischner, *Myśli wyszukane*, 81.

121. Tischner, *Spór o istnienie człowieka*, 321. Tischner often returns to the role of heroism (that is, self-sacrifice) in his ethics. I have described this in more detail in Beyer, "Fr. Józef Tischner (1931–2000)."

122. Viktor Emil Frankl, *Man's Search for Meaning; An Introduction to Logotherapy* (Boston: Beacon Press, 1963), 104.

123. Tischner, *Jak żyć?* 102. It is interesting to note that Tischner reflected on the meaning of the Beatitudes for the "liberation" of Poland in 1982 in articles published during the martial law period. See Tischner, *Książeczka pielgrzyma*.

124. Gowin, *Religia i ludzkie biedy: księdza Tischnera spory o Kościół*, 179. Gowin makes this claim based on the following text: Tischner, *Etyka solidarności oraz homo sovieticus*, 181. On Tischner's relationship to neoliberals such as Bielecki and Balcerowicz, see also Gowin's afterword in Tischner, *Polski kształt dialogu*, 274–310; Bonowicz, *Tischner*, 431; and Tischner, *Etyka solidarności oraz homo sovieticus*, 181–84. Bonowicz believes that perhaps Tischner's frustration with the inability of workers and farmers to organize and meet the demands of the new market economy led him to support the neoliberal reforms. Wojciech Bonowicz, interview, December 12, 2003.

125. Tischner himself alluded to this need. He stated that "in post-Communist societies the measure of freedom became economic success, not the ideal of authentic humanity. The liberal revolution, which overthrew Communism, was an incomplete one." Tischner, *W krainie schorowanej wyobraźni*, 86.

126. John Paul II used this term in contrast to an individualistic notion of freedom. Kampka, *Antropologiczne i społeczne podstawy ładu gospodarczego w świetle nauczania Kościoła*, 153.

127. John Paul II, *Redemptor Hominis*, no. 16.

128. In *Redemptor Hominis*, no. 12, he states: "Jesus Christ meets the man of every age, including our own, with the same words: 'You will know the truth, and the truth will make you free.' These words contain both a fundamental requirement and a warning: the requirement of an honest relationship with regard

to truth as a condition for authentic freedom, and the warning to avoid every kind of illusory freedom, every superficial unilateral freedom, every freedom that fails to enter into the whole truth about man and the world. Today also, even after two thousand years, we see Christ as the one who brings man freedom based on truth, frees man from what curtails, diminishes, and, as it were, breaks off this freedom at its root, in man's soul, his heart, and his conscience." See also John Paul II, *Centesimus Annus,* 441, 470, 474, nos. 4, 41, 46; and John Paul II, *Familiaris Consortio,* nos. 1, 4, 13, 30, 31, 32, 34.

129. John Paul II, "Message of His Holiness Pope John Paul II for the Celebration of the World Day of Peace: 'From the Justice of Each Comes Peace for All.'" The words immediately preceding this section should serve as an admonition to those who maintain that John Paul II unequivocally endorsed existing forms of capitalism in *Centesimus Annus.*

130. See Kampka, *Antropologiczne i społeczne podstawy ładu gospodarczego w świetle nauczania Kościoła,* 147–48.

131. This does not equate with an unequivocal endorsement of currently existing capitalism, nor is it tantamount to the neoliberal assertion that a market economy free of government interference is the best way to promote human development. On this, see especially John Paul II, *Centesimus Annus,* 471, no. 42; and John Paul II, "What Church Social Teaching Is and Is Not," *Origins* 23 (1993).

132. John Paul II, *Centesimus Annus,* 471, no. 42.

133. See Hollenbach, *The Common Good and Christian Ethics,* 71–77.

134. See, for example, Second Vatican Council, *Gaudium et Spes: Pastoral Constitution on the Church in the Modern World,* 214, no. 71.

135. John XXIII, *Mater et Magistra,* 101, no. 109.

136. This argument resembles one regarding the nature of human dignity and human rights. Human rights are ontologically rooted. Just as universal human dignity cannot be eradicated, that which flows from it, human rights, cannot be eviscerated despite invidious efforts to do so. Human dignity can, of course, be affronted. This is what happens when men and women cannot fully flourish and exercise their inherent capabilities as a result of human rights violations.

137. John Paul II, *Centesimus Annus,* 470, no. 40.

138. Ibid., 462, no. 32. John Paul II's thought here strongly resembles Tischner's philosophy of work. See, for example, Tischner, *Etyka solidarności oraz homo sovieticus,* 19–34.

139. John Paul II, *Centesimus Annus,* 463, no. 32.

140. Ibid., 449, no. 13. See also John Paul II, *Sollicitudo Rei Socialis,* 403, no. 15.

141. On the relationship between economic freedom, private property, and the right to economic initiative, see Józef Majka, *Etyka życia gospodarczego* (Warsaw: Ośrodek Dokumentacji i Studiów Społecznych, 1980), 33–34.

142. On this topic, see Curran, *Catholic Social Teaching, 1891–Present,* 173–82; Kampka, *Antropologiczne i społeczne podstawy ładu gospodarczego w świetle nauc-*

zania Kościoła, 161–90; Majka, *Etyka życia gospodarczego*, 87–126; and Anton Rauscher, "Odkrycie społecznej gospodarki rynkowej."

143. John Paul II, *Centesimus Annus*, 471, no. 42.

144. Leo XIII, *Rerum Novarum*, in *Catholic Social Thought: The Documentary Heritage*, ed. David J. O'Brien and Thomas A. Shannon (Maryknoll, N.Y.: Orbis Books, 1992), 31, no. 34.

145. See John Paul II, *Laborem Exercens*, 378, no. 19.

146. For a classic Roman Catholic definition of the living wage, see John A. Ryan, *A Living Wage* (New York, London: Macmillan, 1906), 126. See also Christine Firer Hinze, "Bridging Discourse on Wage Justice: Roman Catholic and Feminist Perspectives on the Family Living Wage," in *Feminist Ethics and the Catholic Moral Tradition*, ed. Charles E. Curran, Margaret A. Farley, and Richard A. McCormick (New York: Paulist Press, 1996). For business perspectives and discussion of the campaigns for the living wage, see Karen Kraut, Scott Klinger, and Chuck Collins, *Choosing the High Road: Businesses That Pay a Living Wage and Prosper* (United for a Fair Economy, 2000 [cited December 3, 2001]); available from http://www.responsiblewealth.org/living_wage/choosing.html.

147. For a description of the similarities and differences between a just and living wage, see Patricia Ann Lamoureaux, "Is a Living Wage a Just Wage?" *America*, February 19, 2001.

148. See Hinze, "Bridging Discourse on Wage Justice."

149. I am indebted to Professor Piotr Mazurkiewicz of the Cardinal Wyszyński University for bringing this to my attention.

150. Pius XI, *Quadragesimo Anno*, 58–59, nos. 70–74. See also Second Vatican Council, *Gaudium et Spes: Pastoral Constitution on the Church in the Modern World*, 211, no. 67, which explicitly names "each man's assignment and productivity" as a factor in determining wages.

151. See Dąbrowski, "Płaca minimalna i jej wpływ na wielkość zatrudnienia," 123. Dąbrowski also reviews the recent theoretical and empirical literature on the issue.

152. Kowalik, "Czy sprawiedliwość społeczna kosztuje? Artykuł polemiczny na marginesie książki pt. *Efektywność a sprawiedliwość*," 85. See also Kraut, Klinger, and Collins, *Choosing the High Road*.

153. On the economic impact of the minimum wage, see David E. Card and Alan B. Krueger, *Myth and Measurement: The New Economics of the Minimum Wage* (Princeton, N.J.: Princeton University Press, 1995); and Liana Fox, *Minimum Wage Trends: Understanding Past and Contemporary Research* (Washington, D.C.: Economic Policy Institute, 2006). On the economic impact of the living wage, see Jeff Thompson and Jeff Chapman, *The Economic Impact of Local Living Wages* (Washington, D.C.: Economic Policy Institute, 2006). See also Kraut, Klinger, and Collins, *Choosing the High Road*.

154. Stiglitz, *Globalization and Its Discontents*, 84–85.

268   Notes to Pages 114–117

155. Cited in Joseph A. Ritter and Lowell J. Taylor, "Economic Models of Employee Motivation," *Review* 1 (1997): 17.

156. As Kabaj points out, Henry Ford made this claim long ago. Kabaj, "Searching for a New Results-Oriented Wage Negotiation System in Poland," 259. One recent example is the case of casino workers in Las Vegas. After a long history of union-busting in the industry, casino owners realized that picket lines and slowed production led to far greater costs than would paying a living wage. Thus, more than 45,000 low-skilled workers have been able to purchase houses and receive excellent health care, while the casinos have turned greater profits. See Steven Greenhouse, "Local 226 'The Culinary' Makes Las Vegas the Land of the Living Wage," *New York Times*, June 3, 2004.

157. See Kraut, Klinger, and Collins, *Choosing the High Road*.

158. Krishna Fells, founder of Small Business Owners of Washington State, makes this case in ibid.

159. See John Paul II, *Laborem Exercens*, 19.

160. For example, Cardinal Roger Mahoney, the chairman of the U.S. Catholic Bishops' Domestic Policy Committee, urged members of the House and Senate to pass the minimum-wage increase bill. Citing a pastoral letter written by the bishops' conference, he contended that the minimum wage must become a living wage in order to protect the "well-being and stability of families." Cardinal Roger Mahoney, *Raise the Minimum Wage: September 2000* (United States Catholic Conference of Bishops, 2000 [cited January 6, 2001]); available from http://usccb.org/sdwp/national/minimumalert.htm.

161. Dąbrowski, "Płaca minimalna i jej wpływ na wielkość zatrudnienia," 92.

162. John Paul II, *Laborem Exercens*, 362–63, no. 8.

163. See Dąbrowski, "Płaca minimalna i jej wpływ na wielkość zatrudnienia," 123.

164. Pius XI, *Quadragesimo Anno*, 59, no. 74.

165. John Paul II, *Laborem Exercens*, 380, no. 20.

166. Wojtyła, *Osoba i czyn oraz inne studia antropologiczne*, 325.

167. John XXIII, *Mater et Magistra*, 97, no. 79.

168. Ibid., 95, no. 70.

169. Kowalik, "Czy sprawiedliwość społeczna kosztuje? Artykuł polemiczny na marginesie książki pt. *Efektywność a sprawiedliwość*," 302. See Kabaj, "Searching for a New Results-Oriented Wage Negotiation System in Poland," 249.

170. Michael Novak, "The Executive Joneses," *Forbes* (May 29, 1989). Cited in Michael Naughton and Robert G. Kennedy, "Executive Compensation: An Evaluation from the Catholic Social Tradition," *Social Justice Review* 84, no. 11 (1993).

171. In 1998 the average monthly wage in Poland was 1,232.69 PLN. In the same year, the average salary in education was 1,116.16 PLN in the public sector, and 1,229.61 in the private sector. In health-care and social services it was 1,003.35 PLN in the public sector, and 986.26 PLN in the private sector. These figures represent gross wages and are taken from *Główny Urząd Statystyczny, Rocznik Staty-*

styczny Rzeczpospolitej Polskiej, 1999. Mieczysław Kabaj cites exorbitant salaries of managers and CEOs. For example, the chairman of Public Television earned 35,000 PLN per month, which is 25.8 times greater than the average monthly salary. The heads of coal companies earn up to 25,000 PLN, which is 18.4 times greater than the average. See the wage chart in Kabaj, *Reduction of Poverty and Social Exclusion.*

172. See "Uniwersytet przed reanimacją," *Znak* 2, no. 537 (2000).
173. Dariusz Rosati, "Powrót socjalizmu," *Gazeta Wyborcza,* March 7, 2000.
174. See Kabaj, "Searching for a New Results-Oriented Wage Negotiation System in Poland," 251.
175. John XXIII, *Pacem in Terris,* 147, no. 98.
176. John Paul II, *Sollicitudo Rei Socialis,* 422, no. 39.
177. There are a number of organizations in the United States and the United Kingdom, for example, that do this kind of work. See, for example, Global Exchange at http://www.globalexchange.org; United for a Fair Economy at http://www.ufenet.org; Co-Op America at http://www.sweatshops.org; and Corporate Watch at http://www.corporatewatch.org.uk/.

CHAPTER FIVE Freedom and Participation as Social Products

1. See Franklin Delano Roosevelt, "The Economic Bill of Rights," in *The Public Papers and Addresses of Franklin Delano Roosevelt,* ed. Samuel Rosenman (New York: Harper, 1950).

2. Józef Kaleta, "Plusy i minusy," in *Spór o Polskę: 1989–1999,* ed. Paweł Śpiewak (Warsaw: PWN, 2001), 655.

3. Compare to Andrzej Walicki, "Ideolog epoki postchlubnej." Walicki discusses Hayek's staunch aversion to "social justice." For more examples of disdain for the concept of social justice, see Michnik and Białkowska, "Mam zdjąć okulary? Adam Michnik and Alina Białkowska rozmawiają z wicepremierem Leszkiem Balcerowiczem," 11; and Kowalik, "Czy sprawiedliwość społeczna kosztuje? Artykuł polemiczny na marginesie książki pt. *Efektywność a sprawiedliwość,*" 291–92. Balcerowicz declared that "we should not involve the term 'justice' in analysis of precisely measurable economic issues. The term should be used sparingly." He implies that the idea of social justice is so prone to manipulation that it is unsalvageable. Therefore, it should not be used in discussing public policy.

4. See Jerzy Wratny, "Partycypacja pracownicza w zarządzaniu i jej etyczne uzasadnienie," in *Etyka biznesu,* ed. Jerzy Dietl and Wojciech Gasparski (Warsaw: Wydaw. Naukowe PWN, 1999), 236, 244.

5. Catholic social teaching first advocated economic and social rights; only later did it come to accept democracy, citizen participation in governing a society, and civil and political rights. (Leo XIII in 1891 already had advocated the natural law right to a just wage.) Although Pius XII had tilted towards democratic

participation, *Pacem in Terris* represents the first explicit listing of both sets of rights in Catholic social teaching. *Pacem in Terris*, like the United Nations Declaration of Human Rights, embraces both groups of rights: civil and political, and economic and social. See David Hollenbach, *Claims in Conflict*, 41–106.

6. The phrase is borrowed from Norman Davies, *Heart of Europe: A Short History of Poland* (Oxford: Clarendon Press, 1984).

7. Taken from the online version of Balcerowicz, *Wolność i rozwój: ekonomia wolnego rynku*, chapter 1.

8. See ibid.

9. See Leszek Balcerowicz, "Toward a Limited State" (The World Bank Group, Distinguished Lecture, 2003 [cited June 20, 2004]); available from http://www.balcerowicz.pl/ksiazki/tls_en.pdf. Balcerowicz states: "If the state justice system is busy enforcing numerous state-imposed restrictions on economic freedom, would it find enough time and motivation to protect adequately what remained of this freedom against intrusions from third parties? It is hard to imagine that a highly regulatory state could—in the long run—have a justice system providing good protection of the remaining economic liberty. In other words, a limited state not only gives individuals the broadest possible economic freedom but also may be able to protect this freedom better than could be the case with much reduced liberty in a highly regulated state."

10. See Sen, *Development as Freedom*, 25–30, 111–45.

11. Polish ethicist Wojciech Gasparski refers to Sen's work in this way ("prace ... z pozycji lewicowych"). See Wojciech Gasparski, "Kwestia bogactwa i ubóstwa w literaturze przedmiotu," in *Etyczne aspekty bogacenia się i ubóstwa*, ed. Adam Węgrzecki (Cracow: Wydawnictwo Akademii Ekonomicznej w Krakowie, 2003), 17.

12. See Sen, *Development as Freedom*, 284–85; see 31–32. In a public lecture given at the Boston Research Institute in 2000, Sen acknowledged that environmentally friendly legislation should not be adopted if it is against the will of the people in the United States, even though he personally recognizes the irresponsible way in which Americans use natural resources such as oil. On Sen's reluctance to impose legislative measures on societies in order to protect human rights, see also Nussbaum, *Women and Human Development*, 12–13; and Sen, *Development as Freedom*, 269.

13. Sen, *Development as Freedom*, 19.

14. Ibid., 151–52.

15. Professor Janina Filek of the Academy of Economics in Cracow mentioned that Sen's work is known in Poland but for the most part has not been seriously considered. She has appealed to Sen's thought in her article on poverty, freedom, and responsibility. See Janina Filek, "Problem ubóstwa w perspektywie wolności i odpowiedzialności," in *Etyczne aspekty bogacenia się i ubóstwa*, ed. Adam Węgrzecki (Cracow: Wydawnictwo Akademii Ekonomicznej w Krakowie, 2003).

16. Sen, *Development as Freedom*, 36; see 16–17. For an alternate, more complete list, see Nussbaum, *Women and Human Development*, 78–80. Sen plays a central role in this book because he explicitly advances an understanding of freedom, whereas Nussbaum only refers to capabilities. While there are great similarities in their thought, Sen's work applies better to this book's argument for this reason.

17. Sen, *Development as Freedom*, 5.
18. Ibid., 41.
19. Ibid., 38–40.
20. Ibid., 40.
21. Ibid., 39.
22. Aristotle, *Nicomachean Ethics*, trans. D. Ross, rev. ed. (Oxford: Oxford University Press, 1980), 7, book I, section 6. Cited in Sen, *Development as Freedom*, 289.
23. See Sen, *Development as Freedom*, 73.
24. Ibid., 74–75.
25. John Rawls, *A Theory of Justice*, rev. ed. (Cambridge, Mass.: Belknap Press of Harvard University Press, 1999), 199.
26. Norman Daniels, "Equal Liberty and Unequal Worth of Liberty," in *Reading Rawls: Critical Studies on Rawls' A Theory of Justice*, ed. Norman Daniels (Stanford, Calif.: Stanford University Press, 1989), 256–57.
27. Sen, *Development as Freedom*, 8.
28. See ibid., 31; and Rawls, *A Theory of Justice*, 198–200.
29. See Michael Novak, "The Rights and Wrongs of 'Economic Rights': A Debate Continued," *This World* 17 (Spring 1987): 43, 45. In addition to the many Polish neoliberal perspectives cited above, see also Wacław Wilczyński's piece on the "enemy welfare state." Wacław Wilczyński, "Wrogie państwo opiekuńcze," in *Wrogie państwo opiekuńcze czyli trudna droga Polski do gospodarki rynkowej: felietony z tygodnika "Wprost" z lat 1995–1999* (Warsaw: Wydaw. Naukowe PWN, 1999).
30. Sen, *Development as Freedom*, 283–88.
31. Ibid., 284.
32. Hollenbach makes a similar argument against "freedom to be left alone," appealing to Taylor rather than Sen in Hollenbach, *The Common Good and Christian Ethics*, 67–78.
33. See chapter 3 above for evidence and explanations.
34. Sen, *Development as Freedom*, 119.
35. It is somewhat unclear as to what Sen believes constitutes "overall freedom." In one sense, he sees "overall freedom" as the sum of "individual freedoms." See ibid., 18. His reluctance to make overarching truth claims about the nature of freedom is palpable in the following statement: "freedom is an inherently diverse concept, which involves—as was discussed extensively—considerations of processes as well as substantive opportunities." Ibid., 298. See also Sen, *On Ethics and Economics*, 58–61.

36. Sen, *Development as Freedom*, 94.

37. For more on the educational deprivations of those in these regions, see Elżbieta Tarkowska, "Czy dziedziczenie biedy? Bariery i szanse edukacyjne młodzieży wiejskiej z gminy Kościelec."

38. See United Nations Development Programme Poland, *National Human Development Report Poland 1998: Access to Education*, 12–13. See also United Nations Development Programme Poland, *Human Development Report: Poland and the Information Society: Logging On*.

39. The entire party and financing system appears to favor those with personal wealth and/or the support of corporations. See, for example, Janina Paradowska, "Lewa kasa, prawa kasa," *Polityka* 4, no. 2220 (2000). The article also mentions that women have a more difficult time raising money for campaigns.

40. Ewa Nowakowska, "Szklany sufit, lepka podłoga," 82. On these issues, see also Urszula Nowakowska, *Polish Women in the 90's*; Anna Titkow, ed., *Szklany sufit—bariery i ograniczenia karier kobiet* (Warsaw: Instytut Spraw Publicznych, 2003); and Graff, *Świat bez kobiet: płeć w polskim życiu publicznym*, esp. 51–58.

41. See Janina Paradowska, "Sztuka naciskania: słowem, krzykiem, układem," *Polityka*, March 25, 2000.

42. Rafał Kalukin, "Rewolucja w zasiłkach," *Gazeta Wyborcza*, November 27, 2003.

43. See "Kobiety za przywróceniem funduszu alimentacyjnego," *Gazeta Wyborcza*, June 7, 2004.

44. Dariusz Facon and Monika Adamowska, "Zamieszanie wokół wypłat zasiłków rodzinnych," *Gazeta Wyborcza*, June 17, 2004.

45. See Sen, *Development as Freedom*, 198–99.

46. See Tarkowska, "Zróżnicowanie biedy: wiek i płeć." In Tarkowska's interviews, poor women in large families admitted, "No way. None of them were planned. The reason [for getting pregnant] was alcohol. He came home drunk many times," or "Somehow year after year children popped out."

47. Paul VI, *Humanae Vitae* (Vatican website, 1968 [cited June 13, 2004]); available from http://www.vatican.va/holy_father/paul_vi/encyclicals/documents/hf_p-vi_enc_25071968_humanae-vitae_en.html, no. 10. Pius XII had spelled out these reasons more clearly. He stated in a 1951 address that there may be "medical, eugenic, economic or social" reasons to avoid the duty of procreation. See John Thomas Noonan, *Contraception: A History of Its Treatment by the Catholic Theologians and Canonists*, enlarged ed. (Cambridge, Mass.: Belknap Press, 1986), 446.

48. Sen demonstrates that optional family planning in places such as India, as opposed to mandatory family planning such as China's one-child policy, is more effective. This is an important insight. However, I wish to state that any family planning that relies on abortion as birth control should be seen as morally illicit.

49. John Paul II, *Familiaris Consortio*, nos. 22–23.

50. John Paul II, *Laborem Exercens*, 378–79, no. 19.

51. The new benefit was 400 złoty per month for those whose income does not exceed 504 złoty per person in a given family. See Kalukin, "Rewolucja w zasiłkach."
52. United Nations Development Programme, *Human Development Report 1999* (New York: Oxford University Press, 1999), 82.
53. "Working Mothers, Unite!" *The Economist*, July 10, 2008.
54. "Family and Work: The Juggling Act Continues," *Zenit Catholic News Service*, www.zenit.org, December 1, 2001.
55. United Nations Development Programme, *Human Development Report 1999*, 82.
56. See Reszke on how stereotypes of women and pro-family policies that encourage having children affect their wages. Reszke, "Uwarunkowania feminizacji biedy w Polsce," 80–81.
57. United States Catholic Conference of Bishops, "Economic Justice for All," 595, no. 71.
58. These claims are made on the basis of personal experience as a Catholic married in Poland and as a young father in a country that relegates fathers to the sidelines, thus negatively impacting both parents.
59. Some notable economists now contend that the wars against inflation led by Alan Greenspan, the International Monetary Fund, and many central banks were grounded in irrational fears. They also say that the cost of these wars—high interest rates leading to high unemployment—outweighed the benefits. See, for example, Thurow, *The Future of Capitalism*, 185–93; and Stiglitz, *Globalization and Its Discontents*, 81–82.
60. See Sen, *Development as Freedom*, 3–6, 46–48, 144–45. For similarly cogent critiques, see Stiglitz, *Globalization and Its Discontents*, 80–83; United Nations Development Programme, *Human Development Report 1999*; and Herman E. Daly, John B. Cobb, and Clifford W. Cobb, *For the Common Good: Redirecting the Economy toward Community, the Environment, and a Sustainable Future*, 2nd ed. (Boston: Beacon Press, 1994), 62–84.
61. See Greider, *One World, Ready or Not*, 427–28.
62. Sen, *Development as Freedom*, 110.
63. Ibid., 145.
64. For example, the U.S. government loaned $3.8 billion to Poland for the purchase of forty-eight F-16 jet fighters, built by Lockheed Martin in Texas. Critics have called the deal a prime example of U.S. corporate welfare, as the government paid for an expensive flight in one of the fighters for Prime Minister Leszek Miller, among other perks. Moreover, fighter planes manufactured by France and Sweden were said to have been more technologically advanced and offered at a lower price. See Charles M. Sennott, "Arms Deal Criticized as Corporate U.S. Welfare," *Boston Globe*, January 14, 2003, A1.
65. The percentages of the state's budget are as follows: national defense: 5.1 (2002), 5.1 (2001), 6.6 (2000), 6.8 (1999), 6.0 (1998), 5.8 (1995); primary and

secondary education: 1.1 (2002), 1.0 (2001), 1.3 (2000), 2.1 (1999), 5.0 (1998), 11.3 (1995); higher education: 3.7 (2002), 3.7 (2001), 3.5 (2000), 3.7 (1999), 3.1 (1998), 2.4 (1995); health care: 2.0 (2002), 2.7 (2001), 2.8 (2000), 4.6 (1999), 15.0 (1998), 14.4 (1995).

66. For examples, see Marcin Murmyło, "Od 1 stycznia nie leczymy," *Gazeta Wyborcza*, December 29, 2003; and Małgorzata Lampa, "Ścieżka zdrowia," *Gazeta Wyborcza*, January 3–4, 2004.

67. See, for example, John Paul II, *Redemptor Hominis*; John XXIII, *Pacem in Terris*, 148–49, nos. 9–19; and Second Vatican Council, *Gaudium et Spes: Pastoral Constitution on the Church in the Modern World*, 222–23, nos. 81–82. During the height of the Cold War, the U.S. bishops wrote: "We are aware that the precise relationship between disarmament and development is neither easily demonstrated nor easily reoriented. But the fact of a massive distortion of resources in the face of crying human need creates a moral question... When we consider how and what we pay for defense today, we need a broader view than the equation of arms with security." United States Catholic Conference of Bishops, "The Challenge of Peace: God's Promise and Our Response," in *Catholic Social Thought: The Documentary Heritage*, ed. David J. O'Brien and Thomas A. Shannon (Maryknoll, N.Y.: Orbis Books, 1992), 550, no. 270; see also nos. 59–73.

68. Cited in Tischner, *W krainie schorowanej wyobraźni*, 92.

69. Wacław Wilczyński, *Wrogie państwo opiekuńcze czyli trudna droga Polski do gospodarki rynkowej: felietony z tygodnika "Wprost" z lat 1995–1999* (Warsaw: Wydaw. Naukowe PWN, 1999), 67–68.

70. Frieske, "Bieda: miary i interpretacje," 207–8. See also Golinowska, "Badania nad ubóstwem: założenia i metodologia," 19–20.

71. Golinowska, "Badania nad ubóstwem: założenia i metodologia," 20.

72. Sen, *Development as Freedom*, 71.

73. See United Nations Development Programme Poland, *Human Development Report: Poland and the Information Society: Logging On*, xxxi–xxxii.

74. A recent study in the *American Journal of Clinical Nutrition* said that giving all children an adequate diet could save over 2.5 million lives per year. It estimated that 52.5 percent of all deaths in young children were caused by undernourishment. See "Better Diet Would Save Millions" (Health) (BBC News, 2004 [cited June 17, 2004]); available from http://news.bbc.co.uk/go/pr/fr/-/2/hi/health/3814925.stm.

75. See Curran, *Catholic Social Teaching, 1891–Present*, 217. Curran trenchantly states that human rights in the Catholic tradition are not primarily immunities protecting freedom; rather, they are empowerments that give freedom for a particular end or purpose.

76. For unequivocal endorsements of economic rights as demands of justice, see especially John Paul II, *Centesimus Annus*, 475–76, no. 48; John Paul II, "Message of His Holiness Pope John Paul II for the Celebration of the World

Day of Peace: 'Respect for Human Rights: The Secret of True Peace'" (Vatican website, 1999 [cited May 21, 2004]); United States Catholic Conference of Bishops, "Economic Justice for All." Aniela Dylus seems to disagree with this claim in regard to economic rights. See Dylus, *Zmienność i ciągłość: polskie transformacje ustrojowe w horyzoncie etycznym*, 137–42.

77. Hollenbach, *Claims in Conflict*, 91.
78. Leo XIII, *Rerum Novarum*, 15, no. 2.
79. Ibid., 31, no. 34.
80. John XXIII, *Pacem in Terris*, 135, no. 26.
81. Paul VI, *Populorum Progressio*, 243, nos. 14, 15.
82. International Theological Commission, "Human Development and Christian Salvation," cited in Arthur F. McGovern, *Liberation Theology and Its Critics: Toward an Assessment* (Maryknoll, N.Y.: Orbis Books, 1989), 51. See also Second Vatican Council, *Gaudium et Spes: Pastoral Constitution on the Church in the Modern World*, 185, 188, nos. 34, 39.
83. Paul VI, *Populorum Progressio*, 241, no. 6, and 42, no. 14. See also United States Catholic Conference of Bishops, "Economic Justice for All," 598, no. 80.
84. David Hollenbach, "The Growing End of an Argument," *America* 153, no. 15 (1985): 363.
85. World Synod of Bishops, *Justice in the World (Justitia in Mundo)*, 290. See also David Hollenbach's detailed discussion of the interrelatedness of human rights in Hollenbach, *Claims in Conflict*, 94–99.
86. Majka, *Etyka życia gospodarczego*, 34.
87. Steiner and Alston point out that the language used here indicates this and thus deviates from the less flexible language of the International Covenant on Civil and Political Rights. This caused and continues to cause discontent among some critics. Henry J. Steiner and Philip Alston, *International Human Rights in Context: Law, Politics, Morals: Text and Materials*, 2nd ed. (Oxford: Oxford University Press, 2000), 246.
88. Shue, *Basic Rights: Subsistence, Affluence, and U.S. Foreign Policy*, 19.
89. John Paul II, "Message of His Holiness Pope John Paul II for the Celebration of the World Day of Peace: 'Dialogue for Peace, a Challenge for Our Time'" (1983 [cited May 21, 2004]); available from http://www.jesus.2000.years.de/holy_father/john_paul_ii/messages/peace/documents/hf_jp-ii_mes_19821208_xvi-world-day-for-peace_en.html; United States Catholic Conference of Bishops, "Economic Justice for All," 598, no. 80.
90. Shue, *Basic Rights: Subsistence, Affluence, and U.S. Foreign Policy*, 25.
91. John Paul II, "Message of His Holiness Pope John Paul II for the Celebration of the World Day of Peace: 'Peace, a Gift of God Entrusted to Us'" (1982 [cited May 21, 2004]); available from http://www.jesus.2000.years.de/holy_father/john_paul_ii/messages/peace/documents/hf_jp-ii_mes_19811208_xv-world-day-for-peace_en.html.

92. John Paul II, "Message of His Holiness Pope John Paul II for the Celebration of the World Day of Peace: 'Dialogue for Peace, a Challenge for Our Time.'"

93. Golinowska, "Minimalne dochody a walka z ubóstwem," 383.

94. See Bonowicz, "Światła etyki solidarności"; and Tischner, "Solidarność po latach," 706. One may note in this regard the resistance to Vice Premier Hausner's reforms on retirement and disability, which would entail stricter controls regarding disability benefits, but little resistance among politicians to the elimination of alimony.

95. To use Shue's language, a mere preference can never trump a basic right. See Shue, *Basic Rights: Subsistence, Affluence, and U.S. Foreign Policy*, 104, 112, 118, 120, 122, 127, 130.

96. Dylus, "Wolny rynek—ubóstwo—uczestnictwo."

97. Jastrzębska-Szklarska and Szklarski, "Od klientelizmu do paternalizmu—biednej społeczności popegierowska droga przez transformację"; Joanna Podgórska, "Nie robim, bo się narobim," *Polityka*, May 8, 2004.

98. John Paul II, "Message of His Holiness Pope John Paul II for the Celebration of the World Day of Peace: 'Respect for Human Rights: The Secret of True Peace,'" no. 6.

99. Dylus, "Wolny rynek—ubóstwo—uczestnictwo." It is not clear if Dylus sees participation as a right, or simply a desired good. See also Dylus, *Gospodarka, moralność, chrześcijaństwo*, 110–12.

100. William Greider quotes Jeffrey Sachs's opinion. See his chapter on worker ownership, which treats Poland in detail, in Greider, *One World, Ready or Not*, esp. 426.

101. Wratny, "Partycypacja pracownicza w zarządzaniu i jej etyczne uzasadnienie," 244. Wratny makes a much fuller argument for the ethical merits of worker participation than can be provided here.

102. Elmer W. Johnson, "Whither Capitalism?" (paper presented at the Executive in Residence Program, University of Notre Dame, Notre Dame, Indiana, October 5, 1999), 4.

103. Wratny, "Partycypacja pracownicza w zarządzaniu i jej etyczne uzasadnienie," 237.

104. Dylus, *Zmienność i ciągłość: polskie transformacje ustrojowe w horyzoncie etycznym*, 17, 32.

105. See ibid., 32; and Wratny, "Partycypacja pracownicza w zarządzaniu i jej etyczne uzasadnienie," 238–44.

106. John Paul II, *Laborem Exercens*, 372–73, no. 14.

107. Dylus, *Zmienność i ciągłość: polskie transformacje ustrojowe w horyzoncie etycznym*, 16–17, 23–44; Józef Majka, "Przemiany społeczno-gospodarcze w świetle etyki społecznej" (paper presented at the I ogólnopolska konferencja naukowa nt. "Transformacja gospodarki polskiej—doświadczenia i perspektywy," Warsaw, 1993).

108. Dylus, *Zmienność i ciągłość: polskie transformacje ustrojowe w horyzoncie etycznym*, 31.
109. Ibid., 32.
110. Greider, *One World, Ready or Not*, 425–27.
111. See World Synod of Bishops, *Justice in the World*, 291; see also United States Catholic Conference of Bishops, "Economic Justice for All," nos. 71, 72.
112. Skąpska, "Czy instytucje publiczne budowane są w oparciu o ideę solidarności?" 51. In 2003 the national leader of the NSZZ Solidarity union, Janusz Śniadek, announced that Solidarity would no longer partake in the Trilateral Commission's discussion. He believed that the Polish government was not fairly attending to the workers' interests in the negotiations.
113. Józef Majka, *Jaka Polska? Węzłowe problemy katolickiej nauki społecznej* (Wrocław: Wydaw. Wrocławskiej Księgarni Archidiecezjalnej, 1991), 211.
114. See Joanna Solska, "Ogłupianie chłopa," *Polityka*, September 25, 1999. Solska discusses the fact that while a few positive examples exist, for the most part Polish farmers do not raise or grow new products that are in demand not only in Western markets but also by Polish consumers.
115. Majka, *Jaka Polska? Węzłowe problemy katolickiej nauki społecznej*, 224–25.
116. These programs are described in United Nations Development Programme Poland, *Raport o rozwoju społecznym Polska 2000: rozwój obszarów wiejskich*, 101–10. The UNDP report concludes that while much has been accomplished, the scale of the problem requires a "national undertaking." Thus far, there has been a lack of will and agreement among the multiple sectors of Polish society, both governmental and nongovernmental, needed to tackle the problems of rural Poland. In other words, there has been a lack of solidarity.
117. Balcerowicz tried to popularize the Grameen model.
118. Marcin Makowiecki, "Inwestycje wspierane przez państwo," *Nowe Życie Gospodarcze* 33 (2000).
119. See, for example, John XXIII, *Mater et Magistra*, 106–7, nos. 37–40.
120. See Adam Leszczyński, "My, wyzyskiwacze," *Gazeta Wyborcza*, December 13–14, 2003.
121. The theme appears time and again in his World Day of Peace messages; and in John Paul II, *Sollicitudo Rei Socialis*, 422–23, no. 39. See also Kampka, "Solidarność w nauczaniu Jana Pawła II."
122. See Makowiecki, "Inwestycje wspierane przez państwo."
123. See chapter 3, pp. 70–71.
124. See Valencia, "Poland: Limping towards Normality."
125. United Nations Development Programme Poland, *Raport o rozwoju społecznym Polska 2000: rozwój obszarów wiejskich*, 103.
126. The new legislation is described in "Chłopi wielozawodowi." According to the author, the "new legislation will eliminate the discriminatory rules against farmers."

127. United States Catholic Conference of Bishops, "Economic Justice for All," 595, no. 71.

128. Of course, this also applies to those who work in antiquated and unprofitable industries, which were created by the Polish government during Communism.

129. See Wóycicka and Mateja, "Zagłębie biedy, źródło szans."

130. See ibid.

131. In one case an unemployment-office worker was outraged that a client would not accept a job in a sex shop.

132. This is discussed in detail in United Nations Development Programme Poland, *Raport o rozwoju społecznym Polska 2000: rozwój obszarów wiejskich*. See also Valencia, "Poland: Limping towards Normality."

133. See Majka, *Jaka Polska? Węzłowe problemy katolickiej nauki społecznej*, 220.

134. Podgórska, "Nie robim, bo sie narobim."

135. See Kabaj, *Program przeciwdziałania ubóstwu i bezrobociu, Raport IPiSS*, z. 19.

136. Wóycicka and Mateja, "Zagłębie biedy, źródło szans."

137. Tischner, *Etyka solidarności oraz homo sovieticus*, 43.

138. See, for example, Thurow, *The Future of Capitalism*, 180–81. Thurow states that skills, education, and knowledge constitute human capital, which has become "the dominant factor of production—not just an important adjunct to physical capital."

139. See Kanbur, Lustig, and World Bank, *Attacking Poverty*, 34, 77–83.

140. John Paul II, *Centesimus Annus*, 462–63, nos. 32–33.

141. Thurow, *The Future of Capitalism*, 180–81.

142. See Rutkowski, *Welfare and the Labor Market in Poland*, 13–16. He shows that the "soaring costs" of retirement and disability pensions have led to a large overall increase in social expenditures, despite decreases in education and health care.

143. John XXIII, *Pacem in Terris*, 133, no. 13. According to John XXIII, this is a requirement of the natural law.

144. For a more complete argument for the right to higher education in Catholic social thought, see Gerald J. Beyer, "Catholic Universities, Solidarity, and the Right to Higher Education in the American Context," *Journal of Catholic Social Thought* (forthcoming). See also Anthony B. Atkinson, "Economic Transformation and Economic Justice," in *Social and Ethical Aspects of Economics: A Colloquium in the Vatican*, ed. Catholic Church, Pontificium Consilium de Iustitia et Pace (Vatican City: Pontifical Council for Justice and Peace, 1992).

145. For an account of the virtues of a cosmopolitan education, see her essay in Martha C. Nussbaum, ed., *Debating the Limits of Patriotism* (Boston: Beacon Press, 1996). On the farming subsidies of the European Union and how they

eliminate goods from Africa entering the EU's market, see Leszczyński, "My, wyzyskiwacze."
146. Kampka, "Solidarność w nauczaniu Jana Pawła II," 10. See John Paul II, *Sollicitudo Rei Socialis*, 422, no. 39.
147. This phrase is borrowed from the title of Jarosław Gowin's analysis of the Roman Catholic Church in Polish society after 1989. See Gowin, *Kościół w czasach wolności 1989–1999*. The following chapter relies on this book and on several fruitful conversations with its author. The conclusions, however, are the sole responsibility of the author of this book.

CHAPTER SIX Promoting an Ethic of Solidarity as Evangelization

1. Roman Graczyk, *Polski kościół—polska demokracja* (Cracow: Towarzystwo Autorów i Wydawców Prac Naukowych "Universitas," 1999), 41.
2. See World Synod of Bishops, *Justice in the World* (*Justitia in Mundo*), 289.
3. One exception is in the Synod document on socioeconomic life, where the Catechism's mention of economic rights is repeated. See Konferencja Episkopatu Polski, *Kościół wobec życia społeczno-gospodarczego*.
4. Aniela Dylus provides helpful documentation of Catholic movements and organizations and their role in the Polish transformations in Dylus, *Zmienność i ciągłość: polskie transformacje ustrojowe w horyzoncie etycznym*, 187–217.
5. On this dimension of Catholic social teaching, see Marvin L. Krier Mich, *Catholic Social Teaching and Movements* (Mystic, Conn.: Twenty-Third Publications, 1998).
6. Garton Ash, *The Polish Revolution: Solidarity*, 280–81. Garton Ash maintains that many of the Solidarity leaders felt abandoned by Cardinal Glemp at the dawn of martial law in Poland in 1981.
7. See, for example, Anna Anusz and Andrzej Anusz, *Samotnie wśród wiernych: kościół wobec przemian politycznych w Polsce (1944–1994)* (Warsaw: Alfa, 1994); Andrzej Micewski, *Cardinal Wyszynski: A Biography* (San Diego: Harcourt, Brace, Jovanovich, 1984); and Weigel, *The Final Revolution*. Garton Ash also gives many accounts of the Church's involvement in Garton Ash, *The Polish Revolution: Solidarity*.
8. Leszek Kołakowski, "Myślenie—albo przymus samookreślenie: rozmowa Siegfreda Lenza z Leszkiem Kołakowskim," *Aletheia* no. 1 (1987). Cited in Anusz and Anusz, *Samotnie wśród wiernych: kościół wobec przemian politycznych w Polsce (1944–1994)*, 16.
9. Gowin, *Kościół po komunizmie*, 7. Piotr Mazurkiewicz points out that the Church's authority did not decrease in the initial stages after 1989. Rather, it declined sometime later, as the Church began to see its role in society differently. Mazurkiewicz, *Kościół i demokracja*, 13–14.

10. Gowin, *Kościół po komunizmie*, 29–30.
11. Mazurkiewicz, *Kościół i demokracja*, 286–91.
12. See Czesław Miłosz, "Państwo wyznaniowe?" in *Spór o Polskę: 1989–99*, ed. Paweł Śpiewak (Warsaw: PWN, 2000); and Leszek Kołakowski, "Krótka rozprawa o teokracji," in *Spór o Polskę: 1989–99*, ed. Paweł Śpiewak (Warsaw: PWN, 2000). For an analysis of their arguments, see Tischner, *Nieszczęsny dar wolności*; and Gowin, *Kościół w czasach wolności 1989–1999*, 106–13. Both contend that these fears were not well founded. I have examined this issue more closely in Beyer, "Freedom, Truth, and Law in the Mind and Homeland of John Paul II."
13. Michnik, *Kościół, lewica, dialog*, 322. For further discussion of the Church's "besieged fortress" syndrome in Poland, see Gowin, *Kościół w czasach wolności 1989–1999*, 46–47. See also Graczyk, *Polski kościół—polska demokracja*, 23–27. For an alternate view that suggests this "syndrome" was created by anti-Catholic propaganda and not based in reality, see Adam Lepa, "Pięć lat 'zdrowej krtytyki' oblężonej twierdzy," in *Spór o Polskę: 1989–99*, ed. Paweł Śpiewak (Warsaw: PWN, 2000). Bishop Lepa's article illustrates the claim that the Church often reacted to criticism defensively, rather than by seeing it as an opportunity for self-examination.
14. David Hume, *Dialogues Concerning Natural Religion* (New York: MacMillan, 1947), 221.
15. Jan Woleński, "Iluzja mesjanizmu," in *Spór o Polskę: 1989–1999*, ed. Paweł Śpiewak (Warsaw: PWN, 2000).
16. See Samuel Huntingdon, "The Clash of Civilizations," *Foreign Affairs* 72, no. 3 (Summer 1993). David Hollenbach discusses much of this research in Hollenbach, *The Common Good and Christian Ethics*.
17. Peter L. Berger, *The Sacred Canopy: Elements of a Sociological Theory of Religion*, 1st ed. (Garden City, N.Y.: Doubleday, 1967), 3.
18. R. Scott Appleby, *The Ambivalence of the Sacred: Religion, Violence, and Reconciliation* (Lanham, Md.: Rowman & Littlefield, 1999), 76.
19. Ibid., 248.
20. Mazurkiewicz, *Kościół i demokracja*, 295.
21. Roman Andrzejewski et al., *Katolicyzm polski dziś i jutro* (Cracow: Wydawnictwo M, 2001), 9–20.
22. Michnik, *Kościół, lewica, dialog*, 306. See also Graczyk, *Polski kościół—polska demokracja*, esp. 37–45.
23. Marcin Król, "Gorzkie żale," *Res Publica Nova* 2 (2004): 39.
24. See, for example, Jan Woleński, "Niech kościół walczy duchem, a nie prawem," *Gazeta Wyborcza*, August 26, 1994.
25. For a similar proposal pertaining to domestic work, see, for example, John Paul II, *Laborem Exercens*, no. 19.
26. Ewa Nowakowska, "Cnota w komórce," *Polityka* 25 (1998). The remainder of the agenda includes: counting mothers' parental duties at home towards retirement pensions, helping to create small "domestic" businesses, and issuing a

yearly report on the status of the family in Poland. According to Minister Kapera, the program is a "battle to save the Polish family from distintegration, as a result of the influence of Western liberalism."

27. Gowin, *Kościół po komunizmie*, 30.

28. Gowin, *Kościół w czasach wolności 1989–1999*, 60. For more statements by bishops and theologians of a similar nature, see Graczyk, *Polski kościół—polska demokracja*, 23–27.

29. See Gowin, *Kościół w czasach wolności 1989–1999*, 265–67.

30. Tischner, *Nieszczęsny dar wolności*, 23.

31. Marek Zając, "Patron trudnej jedności," *Tygodnik Powszechny*, May 18, 2003.

32. It should be noted that this defense of "liberals" seems to have led to an uncritical stance towards economic liberalism in some cases. This explains Tischner's support of some of the reforms described in previous chapters.

33. She has published perhaps the only constructive work in feminist theology in Polish. See Elżbieta Adamiak, *Milcząca obecność* (Warsaw: Biblioteka Więzi, 1999). Another important contribution to the growing awareness of feminist theology is Jarosław Makowski, ed., *Kobiety uczą kościół* (Warsaw: Wydawnictwo W.A.B., 2007).

34. This section of this chapter has been published as Gerald J. Beyer, "Evangelization and Social Justice in Poland after 1989," in *Spirit, Church, World: College Theology Society Annual*, vol. 49, ed. Bradford Hinze (Maryknoll, N.Y.: Orbis Books, 2004). I am grateful to Orbis Books for permission to republish the original article.

35. Richard P. McBrien, "The Future Role of the Church in American Society," in *Religion and Politics in the American Milieu*, ed. Leslie Griffin (Notre Dame, Ind.: University of Notre Dame Press, 1986), 92.

36. See, for example, Second Vatican Council, *Gaudium et Spes: Pastoral Constitution on the Church in the Modern World*, 185–89, nos. 34, 39, 40.

37. World Synod of Bishops, *Justice in the World* (*Justitia in Mundo*), 289.

38. Charles M. Murphy, "Action for Justice as Constitutive of the Preaching of the Gospel: What Did the 1971 Synod Mean?" *Theological Studies* 44 (1983): 305. I rely here on Murphy's illuminating discussion of the drafting of *Justitia in Mundo* and its subsequent interpretation. Paul VI states: "evangelization would not be complete if it did not take account of the unceasing interplay between the Gospel and of man's concrete life, both personal and social. This is why evangelization involves an explicit message, adapted to the different situations constantly being realized, about the rights and duties of every human being, about family life without which personal growth and development is hardly possible, about life in society, about international life, peace, justice, and development." Paul VI, *Evangelii Nuntiandi*, in *Catholic Social Thought: The Documentary Heritage*, ed. David J. O'Brien and Thomas A. Shannon (Maryknoll, N.Y.: Orbis Books, 1992), 313, no. 29, see also 313–14, nos. 30, 31.

39. Paul VI, *Evangelii Nuntiandi*, 313, no. 27.
40. Ibid., 317, no. 41.
41. Paul VI, *Octogesima Adveniens*, in *Catholic Social Thought: The Documentary Heritage*, ed. David J. O'Brien and Thomas A. Shannon (Maryknoll, N.Y.: Orbis Books, 1992), 266, no. 4.
42. World Synod of Bishops, *Justice in the World* (*Justitia in Mundo*), 294.
43. See John Paul II, *Laborem Exercens*, no. 1, 352.
44. John XXIII, *Mater et Magistra*, 106, no. 37.
45. John Paul II, *Laborem Exercens*, 370, no. 14, and 78, no. 19. In regard to wages, John Paul II states that proper remuneration for a worker responsible for a family can and should be achieved by one of two means: a family wage, or grants to mothers who devote themselves "exclusively to their families." Generally speaking, J. Bryan Hehir refers to the "moral and political specificity" of John Paul II's social teaching. See J. Bryan Hehir, "The Right and Competence of the Church in the American Case," in *One Hundred Years of Catholic Social Thought: Celebration and Challenge*, ed. John Aloysius Coleman (Maryknoll, N.Y.: Orbis Books, 1991), 62.
46. United States Catholic Conference of Bishops, "Economic Justice for All," 582, no. 20, and 610, nos. 134–35.
47. Catholic Bishops' Conference of England and Wales, *The Common Good and the Catholic Church's Social Teaching*.
48. Ibid. A lengthier analysis would examine the work of other bishops' conferences as well.
49. See McBrien, "The Future Role of the Church in American Society," 92.
50. See Curran, *Catholic Social Teaching, 1891–Present*, 113.
51. Paul VI, *Evangelii Nuntiandi*, 331, no. 68.
52. It should be acknowledged that many observers disagree with this argument. J. Bryan Hehir discusses the criticisms of the "legislative-policy" function of the Church in Hehir, "The Right and Competence of the Church in the American Case."
53. See Gowin, *Kościół w czasach wolności 1989–1999*, 273–78; and Dylus, *Zmienność i ciągłość: polskie transformacje ustrojowe w horyzoncie etycznym*, 27. Gowin provides a detailed analysis of the bishops' general stance towards the socioeconomic reforms of the 1990s. Bishop Pieronek has acknowledged this with remorse on several occasions. See Pieronek, *Kościół nie boi się wolności*, 46–47, 103.
54. This explains the difference of opinions between those, such as Ochocki, who state that the Church relentlessly calls attention to the problems of poverty and unemployment, and Gowin, who admits this but claims that these are largely "sound bites." In other words, Gowin and others maintain that it is not enough to simply "draw attention to" the problem of poverty. It should be obvious that this book fully endorses Gowin's point of view. The present author thanks Jarosław Gowin for his willingness to discuss his view in conversation.

55. John Paul II, *Jan Paweł II w Polsce, 31 maja 1997–10 czerwca 1997: przemówienia i homilie*, 176. See also John Paul II, *Jan Paweł II: Polska 1999: przemówienia i homilie*, 76–77; and John Paul II, *Program dla Kościoła w Polsce: Jan Paweł II do polskich biskupów; wizyta ad limina 1998*, 27, 37, 48.

56. The most noteworthy attempts, which shall be discussed below, are the following: Konferencja Episkopatu Polski, *Kościół wobec życia społeczno-gospodarczego*; Jan Chrapek, *Tylko miłość się liczy* (Opoka, 2000 [cited March 16, 2001]); available from www.jubileusz2000.opoka.org.pl; and Damian Zimoń, "Kościół katolicki na Śląsku wobec bezrobocia" (Konferencja Episkopatu Polski, 2001 [cited January 24, 2003]); available from www.episkopat.pl/dokumenty/bezrobocie1.html.

57. See the interview with the bishop in Tomasz Gołąb, "Kościół ubogich" (*Gość Niedzielny*, January 21, 2001 [cited February 1, 2001]); available from http://www.opoka.org.pl/biblioteka/T/TA/TAC/kosciol_ubogich.html.

58. Ibid.

59. This does not imply that the bishops said and did nothing at all to address the problem of poverty. The claim that they exhibited "inertia" pertains to: 1) their relatively scant attention to poverty, compared to other social problems such as abortion; and 2) their reluctance to be specific about the kinds of policies that should be enacted to combat poverty.

60. Konferencja Episkopatu Polski, "Szukając światła na nowe tysiąclecie: słowo biskupów polskich na temat niektórych problemów społecznych" (Opoka, 2000 [cited January 12, 2001]); available from http://www.opoka.org.pl/biblioteka/W/WE/kep/problemy_spoleczne_17122000.html. See also Konferencja Episkopatu Polski, "Komunikat z 322. Zebrania Plenarnego" (Konferencja Episkopatu Polski, 2003 [cited May 23, 2003]); available from http://www.episkopat.pl/dokumenty/komunikat322.html. In the latter document, the bishops deem care for the unemployed a part of the "mission of the Church."

61. John Paul II, *Centesimus Annus*, 442, no. 5.

62. Konferencja Episkopatu Polski, *Potrzeba i zadania nowej ewangelizacji na przełomie II i III tysiąclecia chrześcijańskiego*.

63. Konferencja Episkopatu Polski, *Sól ziemi. Powołanie i posłannictwo świeckich* (Konferencja Episkopatu Polski, 2001 [cited January 24, 2003]); available from http://www.episkopat.pl/dokumenty/synoddokumenty.pdf.

64. Konferencja Episkopatu Polski, *Misyjny Adwent Nowego Tysiąclecia* (Konferencja Episkopatu Polski, 2001 [cited January 24, 2003]); available from http://www.episkopat.pl/dokumenty/synoddokumenty.pdf.

65. The citation of John Paul II is taken from the English translation of *Redemptoris Missio*, no. 11.

66. John Paul II, *Redemptoris Missio* (Vatican website, 1990 [cited May 15, 2003]); available from http://www.vatican.va/holy_father/john_paul_ii/encyclicals/documents/hf_jp-ii_enc_07121990_redemptoris-missio_en.html. Cited in Konferencja Episkopatu Polski, *Misyjny Adwent Nowego Tysiąclecia*, no. 70. See also

nos. 59, 63, 73 of the bishops' document, which stress charitable activities as a part of evangelization.

67. John Paul II reminded the Roman Catholic bishops of Brazil that "it is not an act of charity to feed the poor or visit the suffering by taking human resources to them but not communicating to them the Word that saves." See "Church's Social Work Is Not Political, John Paul II Says: Gospel Message Must Accompany Aid, He Tells Brazilian Bishops" (Zenit News Agency, October 21, 2002 [cited November 7, 2002]); available from http://www.zenit.org.

68. See Karl Rahner, "Anonymous Christianity and the Missionary Task of the Church," in *Theological Investigations XII* (New York: Seabury Press, 1974), 177. For Rahner, missionary activity constitutes a form of love for God and one's neighbor.

69. One could adduce myriad biblical texts to support this claim. Amos 5:21 and Jeremiah 22:13–16 are among the well-known examples. New Testament scholar John R. Donahue contends that knowing Yahweh is to take the cause of the needy and poor. In his view, doing justice is the "substance, not the application of religious faith." See John R. Donahue, "Biblical Perspectives on Justice," in *The Faith That Does Justice: Examining the Christian Sources for Social Change*, ed. John C. Haughey (New York: Paulist Press, 1977), 76.

70. Murphy describes the effort to change "constitutive" by Bishop Torrella and later by John Paul II. See Murphy, "Action for Justice as Constitutive of the Preaching of the Gospel," 301–3.

71. John Paul II, *Program dla Kościoła w Polsce: Jan Paweł II do polskich biskupów; wizyta ad limina 1998*, 36–37.

72. Marian Gołębiewski, "Co Sobór zmienił w Polsce?" *Znak* 1, no. 524 (1999): 24–25.

73. Ibid., 26–27.

74. See Stanisław Janecki, "Kościół niezgody," *Wprost*, May 31, 1995, 26. Jarosław Gowin stated that this is the case in regard to the emphasis on socioeconomic problems. Jarosław Gowin, interview, July 20, 2004. This will become clearer throughout this chapter.

75. Some of the following material has been discussed in Gerald J. Beyer, "Towards an Ethical Evaluation of Poland's Transition to a Free-Market Economy and the Roman Catholic Church's Response." I am grateful to the editor for permission to reprint the material.

76. Dylus, *Zmienność i ciągłość: polskie transformacje ustrojowe w horyzoncie etycznym*, 27–28.

77. Gowin, *Kościół w czasach wolności 1989–1999*, 274.

78. This phenomenon is fairly widely recognized and criticized in Poland. Stanisława Grabska describes it in Stanisława Grabska, "Obywatele Kościoła," in *Dzieci Soboru zadają pytania: rozmowy o Soborze Watykańskim II*, ed. Zbigniew Nosowski (Warsaw: Biblioteka Więzi, 1996), 308. The bishops themselves criticize the lack of cooperation between the laity and the clergy in the parishes. See

also Konferencja Episkopatu Polski, "Sól ziemi. Powołanie i posłannictwo świeckich." However, the bishops place the onus on laypersons who are ignorant of their responsibilities in the Church.

79. Gowin, *Kościół w czasach wolności 1989–1999*, 107.

80. Ibid., 273.

81. The controversy over Radio Maryja, a "Catholic" radio station that tells its listeners whom to vote for and which parties to support, also contributed to the problem. Its anti–European Union and antiliberalism campaigns, along with the anti-Semitic comments of its listeners, caused considerable consternation. See Jarosław Gowin, "Katolicy i polityka," *Rzeczpospolita*, October 4–5, 2003.

82. Gowin, *Kościół w czasach wolności 1989–1999*, 278.

83. Tadeusz Pieronek, "Zatroskanie o człowieka," *Więź* 488, no. 2 (1999): 47.

84. Pieronek, *Kościół nie boi się wolności*, 105.

85. Zimoń, "Kościół katolicki na Śląsku wobec bezrobocia."

86. See Mirosława Marody, "Polak-katolik w Europie," *Odra* 2, no. 387 (1994): 6. Only 46 percent said that the Church should pronounce on unemployment. Marody points out that in Ireland, 76 percent said that the Church should pronounce on unemployment. For more recent statistics, see Andrzejewski, *Katolicyzm polski dziś i jutro*, 75; and Andrzej Ochocki, "Kościół katolicki a sprawy publiczne w Polsce," in *Kościół katolicki na początku tysiąclecia w opinii Polaków*, ed. Witold Zdaniewicz and Sławomir Zaręby (Warsaw: Instytut Statystyki Kościoła Katolickiego SAC, 2004), 209.

87. Kampka, *Antropologiczne i społeczne podstawy ładu gospodarczego w świetle nauczania Kościoła*, 26.

88. Reprivatization refers to property appropriated by the Communists and its subsequent return to its original owner.

89. See, for example: Konferencja Episkopatu Polski, "Społeczny wymiar Jubileuszu Odkupienia: list na luty" (Konferencja Episkopatu Polski, 2000 [cited January 12, 2001]); available from http://www.episkopat.pl/dokumenty/d-17c.htm; and Konferencja Episkopatu Polski, "Komunikat z 303. Zebrania Plenarnego" (2000 [cited January 12, 2001]); available from http://www.episkopat.pl/dokumenty/komunikat303.htm. The latter document contains a slightly higher degree of specificity than the other cited documents. It cites *Centesimus Annus* in regard to the primary duty of the state (see John Paul II, *Centesimus Annus*, no. 48). Yet, concrete directives as to how to fulfill that duty are absent.

90. See Konferencja Episkopatu Polski, "Szukając światła na nowe tysiąclecie: słowo biskupów polskich na temat niektórych problemów społecznych."

91. Konferencja Episkopatu Polski, *Kościół wobec życia społeczno-gospodarczego*, no. 3, see also no. 9

92. See Konferencja Episkopatu Polski, *Kościół wobec rzeczywistości politycznej*, nos. 3, 10.

93. Konferencja Episkopatu Polski, *Sól ziemi. Powołanie i posłannictwo świeckich*, no. 19.

94. Konferencja Episkopatu Polski, *Kościół wobec rzeczywistości politycznej*, no. 15.

95. Second Vatican Council, *Gaudium et Spes: Pastoral Constitution on the Church in the Modern World*, 471, no. 43.

96. Gowin, *Kościół w czasach wolności 1989–1999*, 456.

97. See Bishop Pieronek's statement in "Co Sobór zmienił w Polsce?" *Znak* 524, no. 1 (1999): 15. Cited in Gowin, *Kościoł w czasach wolności 1989–1999*.

98. Gowin, *Kościoł w czasach wolności 1989–1999*, 459. Given the limitations here, I cannot examine all of the Synodal documents in detail. Rather, I provide a sampling in order to portray their overall character and the differences among them.

99. By contrast, for example, the document on charitable work states the following: "The years of transformations following 1989 are marked not only by indicators of growth, but also by myriad difficulties causing the impoverishment of many social groups, while others become rich. The state and local governments are not handling the social questions in this area. As a result, a mechanism of social degradation has appeared, which envelops the unemployed, large families, the homeless, the disabled, children, and inhabitants of villages and small towns." Konferencja Episkopatu Polski, *Posługa charytatywna Kościoła* (Konferencja Episkopatu Polski, 2001 [cited January 24, 2003]); available from http://www.episkopat.pl/dokumenty/synoddokumenty.pdf., no 16.

100. See Konferencja Episkopatu Polski, *Szkoła i uniwersytet w życiu Kościoła i narodu* (Konferencja Episkopatu Polski, 2001 [cited January 24, 2003]); available from http://www.episkopat.pl/dokumenty/synoddokumenty.pdf. Discrimination in access to education is described in United Nations Development Programme Poland, *National Human Development Report Poland 1998: Access to Education*, 45. See also Legutko, "Dwie szkoły, dwie Polski."

101. See his homily in Cracow on August 18, 2002. John Paul II, "Misterium nieprawości i wyobraźnia miłosierdzia."

102. On this topic, see "Enough," *The Economist*, April 17, 2003.

103. See Konferencja Episkopatu Polski, *Powołanie do życia w małżeństwie i rodzinie*, no. 15.

104. Daly, Cobb, and Cobb, *For the Common Good*, 315–31. In addition, Susan Pace Hamill, a professor of tax law and former IRS attorney, has made the case for progressive taxation from a Christian perspective in Susan Pace Hamill, *The Least of These: Fair Taxes and the Moral Duty of Christians* (Birmingham, Ala.: Crane Hill Publishers, 2003). Her arguments led Governor Bob Riley of the state of Alabama to attempt to raise taxes on the wealthy in 2003 by instituting a heavily progessive taxation scheme.

105. Rawls, *A Theory of Justice*, 246, 263.

106. Konferencja Episkopatu Polski, *Posługa charytatywna Kościoła*, no. 57.

107. Franciszek Kampka articulated to me in conversation that the bishops have not undertaken an analysis of the magnitude of *Economic Justice for All*

partly because it is difficult enough to convince priests in Poland of the importance of Catholic social teaching. On the neglect of Catholic social teaching, see Stanisław Pyszka, "Zaangażowanie chrześcijan w politykę dzisiaj," in *Katolicka nauka społeczna wobec wybranych problemów współczesnego świata*, ed. Tomasz Homa (Cracow: WAM, 1995), 92–93; and Gowin, "Katolicy i polityka," A5.

108. See Konferencja Episkopatu Polski, *W trosce o nową kulturę życia i pracy* (Konferencja Episkopatu Polski, 2001 [cited January 24, 2003]); available from http://www.opoka.org.pl/biblioteka/W/WE/kep/list_spoleczny_30102001.html.

109. Ibid., no. 2.

110. Ibid.

111. See pages 66–68 in Konferencja Episkopatu Polski, *Kościół wobec życia społeczno-gospodarczego*.

112. Zimoń, "Kościół katolicki na Śląsku wobec bezrobocia," 6.

113. Ibid.

114. Ibid.

115. Ibid.

116. Ibid.

117. Gowin, "Katolicy i polityka"; Mazurkiewicz, *Kościół i demokracja*, 290.

118. See Terence McGoldrick, "Episcopal Conferences Worldwide on Catholic Social Teaching," *Theological Studies* 59, no. 1 (1998).

119. United States Catholic Conference of Bishops, "Economic Justice for All: Ten Years Later," *America* 176 (1997). Cited in McGoldrick, "Episcopal Conferences Worldwide on Catholic Social Teaching," 23.

120. See above, note 55.

121. On this topic, see Mazurkiewicz, *Kościół i demokracja*, 323–24; and Gowin, *Kościół w czasach wolności 1989–1999*, 261–63.

122. Zimoń, "Kościół katolicki na Śląsku wobec bezrobocia."

123. Dyczewski, "Kościół katolicki wobec ubóstwa i ludzi ubogich," 375.

124. Ochocki, "Kościół katolicki a sprawy publiczne w Polsce," 209, 211. In this vein, Ochocki discusses the fact that 66.6 percent of those polled believe that the Church gets "mixed up" in politics (*miesza się do polityki*). Ochocki considers one part of a massive study recently undertaken at the request of the Polish bishops' conference as the most comprehensive report on the self-understanding of the Roman Catholic Church in Poland.

125. This is the conclusion, drawn by Ochocki, based on the most recent data concerning the Church's social activity. See ibid., 213. I am also grateful to Jarosław Gowin for discussing this issue in an interview.

126. Konferencja Episkopatu Polski, *Sól ziemi. Powołanie i posłannictwo świeckich*, no. 23.

127. The bishops draw attention to this fact in the same paragraph.

128. Franciszek Kampka expressed this view in conversation. See also Pyszka, "Zaangażowanie chrześcijan w politykę dzisiaj," 90–91.

129. Interview with Jarosław Gowin, July 20, 2004.

130. One notable example pertains to the right to work in Konferencja Episkopatu Polski, *W trosce o nową kulturę życia i pracy*, 5. Both Gowin and Bonowicz agreed that the bishops seldom spoke of economic rights, though they gave different rationales for this omission. Gowin, interview, July 20, 2004; and Wojciech Bonowicz, interview, July 8, 2004.

131. See Jan Winiecki, "Ideały Solidarności, czyli o antykomunistycznych bolszewikach," in *Spór o Polskę: 1989–1999*, ed. Paweł Śpiewak (Warsaw: PWN, 2000).

132. Dylus, *Zmienność i ciągłość: polskie transformacje ustrojowe w horyzoncie etycznym*, 140–41.

133. See the U.S. bishops website at http://www.usccb.org/sdwp/national/minwage0406.shtml; and Catholic Bishops' Conference of England and Wales, *The Common Good and the Catholic Church's Social Teaching*, nos. 97–98.

134. Zimoń, "Kościół katolicki na Śląsku wobec bezrobocia," 14.

135. See, for example, Konferencja Episkopatu Polski, *Sól ziemi. Powołanie i posłannictwo świeckich*, no. 49.

136. For a much more nuanced discussion of this issue, see Beyer, "Freedom, Truth, and Law in the Mind and Homeland of John Paul II."

137. The following discussion is heavily indebted to Charles Curran's detailed exposition of public order and the relationship between law and morality in Curran, *Catholic Social Teaching, 1891–Present*, 227–43. Curran discusses *Dignitatis Humanae* and, to a lesser degree, the 1974 Declaration on Procured Abortion of the Congregation of the Doctrine of the Faith.

138. The Declaration on Religious Freedom, "Dignitatis Humanae," in Walter M. Abbott, *The Documents of Vatican II* (New York: Guild Press, 1966), no. 7.

139. Curran, *Catholic Social Teaching, 1891–Present*, 237.

140. Ibid.

141. See ibid., 238–42. Curran mentions that Cardinal Bernadin appealed to the concept of public order to condemn abortion.

142. See Tischner, *Spór o istnienie człowieka*, 132.

143. Tischner's understanding of the relationship between grace, hope, human freedom, and solidarity is explored in detail in Beyer, "Fr. Józef Tischner (1931–2000)."

144. See Metz, "Bread of Survival," in Johannes Baptist Metz, *The Emergent Church: The Future of Christianity in a Postbourgeois World* (New York: Crossroad, 1981), 37–38.

145. I borrow these categories from Hehir. See Hehir, "The Right and Competence of the Church in the American Case," 66–68.

146. Much has been written on this topic. See, for example, Gowin, *Kościół po komunizmie*, 21; and Stefan Świeżawski, "Określanie tożsamości Kościoła," in *Dzieci Soboru zadają pytania: rozmowy o Soborze Watykańskim II*, ed. Zbigniew Nosowski (Warsaw: Więź, 1996). In a previous research project on the reception of Vatican II's teaching in Poland, the present author discussed this issue with,

Notes to Pages 190–198   289

among others, Jarosław Gowin, Jacek Woźniakowski, Fr. Józef Tischner, Fr. Andrzej Bardecki, and Fr. Maciej Zięba, O.P.

147. Dylus, *Zmienność i ciągłość: polskie transformacje ustrojowe w horyzoncie etycznym*, 201.

148. Ibid., 202–7.

149. Dyczewski, "Kościół katolicki wobec ubóstwa i ludzi ubogich," 377. The information in this section is gathered from the following sources, unless otherwise noted: Dyczewski, "Kościół katolicki wobec ubóstwa i ludzi ubogich"; Agnieszka Homan, interview, July 15, 2004; and the Caritas Polska website at http://www.caritas.pl/.

150. Dyczewski, "Kościół katolicki wobec ubóstwa i ludzi ubogich," 378. The following statistics from the years 1990 to 1997 are taken from Dyczewski.

151. The most recent statistics (from 1997 to 2004) are taken from the Caritas Polska website.

152. Dyczewski, "Kościół katolicki wobec ubóstwa i ludzi ubogich," 379.

153. See Caritas Polska, *800,000 PLN i 47,000 USD dla ofiar trzęsienia ziemi*. (Data pub. 31.12.2004) (Caritas Polska, 2004 [cited January 6, 2005]); available from http://caritaspolska.caritas.pl/index.php?strona=akt&id=20041231172723.

154. Dyczewski, "Kościół katolicki wobec ubóstwa i ludzi ubogich," 377.

155. Ibid.

156. Rawls, *A Theory of Justice*, 3.

157. Barbara Czarnocka, *Umiłować Chrystusa: wigilijne dzieło pomocy dzieciom* (Warsaw: Pro Caritate, 2002).

158. In the Archdiocese of Cracow alone, about 4,264 meals are served daily. The author thanks Agnieszka Homan for providing access to her detailed report on Caritas's activity in 2003 in the archdiocese, which she prepared for the bishops' conference.

159. Thus, Henry Shue deems the right to subsistence "basic" to all other rights. See Shue, *Basic Rights: Subsistence, Affluence, and U.S. Foreign Policy*.

160. Information on the program is taken from Mariusz Konowrocki, *Wakacyjna przygoda: materiały dla wychowawców* (Warsaw: Pro Caritate, 2002); and the Caritas Polska website.

161. Interview with Agnieszka Homan, July 15, 2004.

162. Taken from the Caritas Polska website at http://caritaspolska.caritas.pl/index.php?strona=jak_pom.

163. This assessment is based on the description of the programs on the Caritas Polska website and the detailed description of Cracow's Klub Aktywizacji i Treningu provided by Agnieszka Homan.

164. Interview with Agnieszka Homan, July 15, 2004.

165. R. Scott Appleby describes the changes at Catholic Relief Services in Appleby, *The Ambivalence of the Sacred*.

166. See the website of "Dzieło nowego tysiąclecia" at http://www.dzielo.pl/program_stypendialny.html.

167. See the Fundacja nadzieja website at http://www.fundacja-nadzieja .org.pl/.
168. Hehir, "The Right and Competence of the Church in the American Case," 68.
169. John Paul II, "Misterium nieprawości i wyobraźnia miłosierdzia."
170. See Bishop Pieronek's statement in Gołębiewski, "Co Sobór zmienił w Polsce?" 21.
171. Graczyk, *Polski kościół—polska demokracja*, 40.
172. See Bishop Gołębiewski's statement in Gołębiewski, "Co Sobór zmienił w Polsce?" 26.
173. See Archbishop Damian Zimoń, "Górnicy to nie balast," *Gazeta Wyborcza*, September 12, 2003, 21.
174. Stanisław Musiał, *Dwanaście koszy ułomków* (Cracow: Wydawnictwo Literackie, 2002), 89–95.
175. Johannes Baptist Metz, "Messianic or Bourgeois Religion?" in *Faith and the Future: Essays on Theology, Solidarity, and Modernity*, ed. Johannes Baptist Metz and Jurgen Moltmann (Maryknoll, N.Y.: Orbis Books, 1995), 23.
176. Jarosław Gowin in Andrzejewski, *Katolicyzm polski dziś i jutro*, 114.
177. Ibid., 118.
178. See Gołębiewski, "Co Sobór zmienił w Polsce?" 21.

Conclusion: Is Solidarity Possible in a Neoliberal Capitalist World?

1. Jesuit Provincials of Latin America, "A Letter on Neoliberalism in Latin America."
2. Greider, *One World, Ready or Not*, 263–84.
3. Baum, "Are We in a New Historical Situation?" 32.
4. Peters, *In Search of the Good Life*; Ramadan, *Western Muslims and the Future of Islam*, 199. I am grateful to Dr. Gregory Baum for the latter reference. He mentioned the increasing Islamic criticism of neoliberalism in his paper "Alternative Models of Economic Development: The Social Economy," which he delivered at Villanova University on September 26, 2006. See also Tripp, *Islam and the Moral Economy*.
5. See "Admire the Best, Forget the Rest: The Swedish Model," *The Economist*, September 7, 2006; and "Reinfeldt Explained," *The Economist*, September 21, 2006.
6. On Germany, see Greider, *One World, Ready or Not*, 360–87.
7. "On Their Own Track: Germany's Trade Unions," *The Economist*, August 23, 2007.
8. I have described American resistance to the right to education in Beyer, "Catholic Universities, Solidarity, and the Right to Higher Education in the Ameri-

can Context." For a discussion of the American aversion to economic rights in general, see Beyer, "Beyond 'Nonsense on Stilts.'"

9. See, for example, David K. Shipler, *The Working Poor: Invisible in America*, 1st ed. (New York: Knopf, 2004).

10. For examples of those calling for just taxation in the United States, see Edward M. Welch, "Taxing Work," *America*, November 14, 2005; Susan Pace Hamill, *As Certain as Death: A Fifty-State Survey of State and Local Tax Laws: K–12 Funding, Poverty Trends, and Other Characteristics* (Durham, N.C.: Carolina Academic Press, 2008); and the United for a Fair Economy Tax Fairness Organizing Collaborative at http://www.faireconomy.org/TFOC/index.html. On the level of global finance, see Greider, *One World, Ready or Not*, 316–30.

11. On the increasing numbers of working poor and their children globally, see, for example, Jody Heymann, *Forgotten Families: Ending the Growing Crisis Confronting Children and Working Parents in the Global Economy* (Oxford: Oxford University Press, 2006).

12. Mary Ann Glendon, "Knowing the Universal Declaration of Human Rights," *Notre Dame Law Review* 73, no. 5 (1998): 1174.

13. Garton Ash, *The Polish Revolution: Solidarity*, 376.

14. Hollenbach, *The Common Good and Christian Ethics*, 26. Hollenbach draws on the empirical research of Alan Wolfe in Alan Wolfe, *Moral Freedom: The Impossible Idea That Defines the Way We Live Now*, 1st ed. (New York: W.W. Norton, 2001).

15. Hollenbach, *The Common Good and Christian Ethics*, 32–41.

16. For sociological evidence of the individualistic orientation in the United States, see ibid., 22–31. On American culture, see Joshua Charles Taylor, *America as Art* (Washington, D.C.: Smithsonian Institution Press, 1976), esp. 90. Taylor writes that the image of the frontiersman led to what has become "typically American" and was "wholeheartedly embraced by those who were in search of an operational myth on which to base a distinctively American culture ... anything that did not follow the pattern of the colloquial and the self-made was simply not American." See also Robert Neelly Bellah, *Habits of the Heart: Individualism and Commitment in American Life: Updated Edition with a New Introduction*, 1st pbk. ed. (Berkeley: University of California Press, 1996), 32–35, 144–47. One finds here an interesting commentary on Benjamin Franklin's role in the American myth of self-reliance.

17. See Erich Fromm, *On Disobedience and Other Essays* (New York: Seabury Press, 1981). See also Juliet Schor, *The Overspent American: Upscaling, Downshifting, and the New Consumer*, 1st ed. (New York: Basic Books, 1998).

18. Two recent, important books address this issue. See Tom Beaudoin, *Consuming Faith: Integrating Who We Are with What We Buy* (Lanham, Md.: Sheed & Ward, 2003); and Vincent Jude Miller, *Consuming Religion: Christian Faith and Practice in a Consumer Culture* (New York: Continuum, 2004).

19. United Nations General Assembly, *United Nations Millennium Declaration* (2000 [cited October 7, 2007]); available from http://www.un.org/millennium/declaration/ares552e.htm.
20. Zbigniew Brzeziński, *Out Of Control: Global Turmoil on the Eve of the Twenty-first Century*, 1st ed. (New York: Collier Books, 1994), 17.
21. Giles B. Gunn, *Beyond Solidarity: Pragmatism and Difference in a Globalized World* (Chicago: University of Chicago Press, 2001).
22. On this view, see Stephen J. Pope, *Human Evolution and Christian Ethics* (Cambridge: Cambridge University Press, 2007), 158–87, 214–49; F. B. M. de Waal, *Our Inner Ape: A Leading Primatologist Explains Why We Are Who We Are* (New York: Riverhead Books, 2005), 22–23, 243; and David Sloan Wilson, *Darwin's Cathedral: Evolution, Religion, and the Nature of Society* (Chicago: University of Chicago Press, 2002), 224–25.
23. Ada Maria Isasi-Diaz, "Solidarity: Love of Neighbor in the Eighties," in *Lift Every Voice: Constructing Christian Theologies from the Underside*, ed. Susan Brook Thistlethwaite and Mary Potter Engle (New York: Harper, 1990), 32; Wilson, *Darwin's Cathedral*.
24. Jeffrey Stout, *Democracy and Tradition* (Princeton, N.J.: Princeton University Press, 2004), 1–2.
25. Paul Locatelli, "The Catholic University of the 21st Century: Educating for Solidarity" (2005 [cited October 9, 2007]); available from http://www.loyola.edu/Justice/documents/commitment2005/keynote_locatelli.doc.
26. Christine Firer Hinze, "Straining toward Solidarity in a Suffering World: *Gaudium et Spes* after Forty Years," in *Vatican II Forty Years Later*, ed. William Madges (Maryknoll, N.Y.: Orbis Books, 2006).
27. See Thomas Winfried Menko Pogge, *World Poverty and Human Rights: Cosmopolitan Responsibilities and Reforms* (Malden, Mass.: Polity, 2002); and Thomas Winfried Menko Pogge, *Freedom from Poverty as a Human Right: Who Owes What to the Very Poor?* (Paris: UNESCO, 2007).
28. See especially Thomas Massaro, *United States Welfare Policy: A Catholic Response* (Washington, D.C.: Georgetown University Press, 2007). Mary Hobgood has also done interesting work in this area. See Mary E. Hobgood, "Poor Women, Work, and the U.S. Catholic Bishops," *Journal of Religious Ethics* 25 (1997).
29. On reactions to *Deus Caritas Est*, see Thomas Massaro, "Don't Forget Justice," *America* 194, no. 9 (2006).

Epilogue

1. Ost, *The Defeat of Solidarity*, 197.
2. Joanna Derkaczew, Monika Strzępka, and Paweł Demirski, "Dwie Polski i przepaść," *Gazeta Wyborcza*, August 1, 2008. They speak of the Church using the

language of the National Democracy movement (*język endecki*) of the early twentieth century.

3. Marcin Markowski, "Państwo niesolidarne," *Gazeta Wyborcza*, August 28, 2007.

4. E. J. Dionne, "The Death of Reaganomics," in *Truthdig*, available at http://www.truthdig.com/report/item/20080710_the_death_of_reaganomics/ (July 10, 2008 [accessed October 11, 2008]).

5. David Brooks, "Democratic Party Has Collapsed Not Just Politically but Morally," in *The Olympian*, available from http://www.theolympian.com/opinion/v-print.story/70528.html (March 15, 2007 [accessed September 29, 2008]).

6. Philip Blond, "The Failure of Neo-Liberalism," *International Herald Tribune*, January 22, 2008.

7. Carol Glatz, "Vatican Newspaper Says Crisis Shows Failure of 'New Economy,'" *Catholic News Service*, September 24, 2008.

8. See Greider, *One World, Ready or Not*, 263–64.

BIBLIOGRAPHY

Abbott, Walter M. *The Documents of Vatican II*. New York: Guild Press, 1966.
Adamiak, Elżbieta. *Milcząca obecność*. Warsaw: Biblioteka Więzi, 1999.
"Admire the Best, Forget the Rest: The Swedish Model." *The Economist*, September 7, 2006.
Albert, Michel. *Capitalism vs. Capitalism: How America's Obsession with Individual Achievement and Short-term Profit Has Led It to the Brink of Collapse*. New York: Four Walls Eight Windows, 1993.
Andrzejewski, Roman, et al. *Katolicyzm polski dziś i jutro*. Cracow: Wydawnictwo M, 2001.
Anusz, Anna, and Andrzej Anusz. *Samotnie wśród wiernych: kościół wobec przemian politycznych w Polsce (1944–1994)*. Warsaw: Alfa, 1994.
Appleby, R. Scott. *The Ambivalence of the Sacred: Religion, Violence and Reconciliation*. Lanham, Md.: Rowman & Littlefield, 1999.
Aristotle. *Nicomachean Ethics*. Translated by D. Ross. Rev. ed. Oxford: Oxford University Press, 1980.
Atkinson, Anthony B. "Economic Transformation and Economic Justice." In *Social and Ethical Aspects of Economics: A Colloquium in the Vatican*, edited by Catholic Church. Pontificium Consilium de Iustitia et Pace, 23–30. Vatican City: Pontifical Council for Justice and Peace, 1992.
Balcerowicz, Leszek. "Awans biednych olbrzymów." *Wprost* 47 (2002). http://www.balcerowicz.pl/wprost/awans.pdf. (accessed March 29, 2003).
———. "Demokracja nie zastąpi kapitalizmu." In *Spór o Polskę: 1989–1999*, edited by Paweł Śpiewak, 639–42. Warsaw: PWN, 2000.
———. *Państwo w przebudowie*. 1st ed. Cracow: Znak, 1999.
———. *Socjalizm, kapitalizm, transformacja: szkice z przełomu epok*. 1st ed. Warsaw: Wydawn. Nauk. PWN, 1997.
———. 2003. "Toward a Limited State." The World Bank Group, Distinguished Lecture, 2003. http://www.balcerowicz.pl/ksiazki/tls_en.pdf. (accessed June 20, 2004).

———. *Wolność i rozwój: ekonomia wolnego rynku*. Cracow: Znak, 1995. http://www.balcerowicz.pl/ksiazki.html. (accessed June 20, 2003).
Balcerzak-Paradowska, Bożena. "Zagrożenie ubóstwem rodzin wielodzietnych." In *Polska bieda II: kryteria, ocena, przeciwdziałanie*, edited by Stanisława Golinowska, 225–64. Warsaw: IPiSS, 1997.
Baum, Gregory. "Are We in a New Historical Situation? Must We Rethink What Justice and Solidarity Mean Today?" In *Stone Soup: Reflections on Economic Injustice*, 17–40. Montreal: Paulines, 1998.
Bauman, Zygmunt. "Zbędni, niechciani, odtrąceni." *Kultura i społeczeństwo* 2 (1998).
Beaudoin, Tom. *Consuming Faith: Integrating Who We Are with What We Buy*. Lanham, Md.: Sheed & Ward, 2003.
Bellah, Robert Neelly. *Habits of the Heart: Individualism and Commitment in American Life: Updated Edition with a New Introduction*. 1st pbk. ed. Berkeley: University of California Press, 1996.
Berger, Peter L. *The Sacred Canopy: Elements of a Sociological Theory of Religion*. 1st ed. Garden City, N.Y.: Doubleday, 1967.
Berlin, Isaiah, Henry Hardy, and Ian Harris. *Liberty: Incorporating Four Essays on Liberty*. Oxford: Oxford University Press, 2002.
Beskid, Lidia. "Potoczna percepcja biedy w Polsce w latach 1989–1995." In *Polska bieda II: kryteria, ocena, przeciwdziałanie*, edited by Stanisława Golinowska, 137–49. Warsaw: IPiSS, 1997.
"Better Diet Would Save Millions." 2004. Health, BBC News, http://news.bbc.co.uk/go/pr/fr/-/2/hi/health/3814925.stm. (accessed June 17, 2004).
Beyer, Gerald J. "Beyond 'Nonsense on Stilts': Towards Conceptual Clarity and Resolution of Conflicting Economic Rights." *Human Rights Review* 6, no. 4 (2005): 5–32.
———. "Catholic Universities, Solidarity, and the Right to Education in the American Context." *Journal of Catholic Social Thought* (forthcoming).
———. "Evangelization and Social Justice in Poland after 1989." In *Spirit, Church, World: College Theology Society Annual*, vol. 49, edited by Bradford Hinze, 189–218. Maryknoll, N.Y.: Orbis Books, 2004.
———. "Fr. Józef Tischner (1931–2000): Chaplain of *Solidarność* and Philosopher of Hope." *Religion in Eastern Europe* 21, no. 1 (2001): 17–42.
———. "Freedom, Truth, and Law in the Mind and Homeland of John Paul II." *Notre Dame Journal of Law, Ethics, and Public Policy* 21, no. 1 (2007): 17–49.
———. "Karl Rahner on the Radical Unity of the Love of God and Neighbor: Excessive Claim or Exigent Insight?" *Irish Theological Quarterly* 68, no. 3 (2003): 251–80.
———. "Towards an Ethical Evaluation of Poland's Transition to a Free-Market Economy and the Roman Catholic Church's Response." *Religion in Eastern Europe* 21, no. 4 (2001): 12–42.
Bielecki, Jan Krzysztof. "Duch indywidualizmu." *Wprost*, December 25, 1994.

Bielik-Robson, Agata. "'Solidarność' uliczna—elementarz tożsamości." In *Lekcja sierpnia: dziedzictwo "Solidarności" po dwudziestu latach*, edited by Dariusz Gawin, 123–42. Warsaw: Wydawnictwo IFiS PAN, 2002.

Blond, Philip. "The Failure of Neo-Liberalism." *International Herald Tribune*, January 22, 2008.

Bogucka, Teresa. "Polska bieda." *Gazeta Wyborcza*, February 26–27, 2000, 9–11.

Bonowicz, Wojciech. Interview, December 12, 2003.

———. Interview, July 8, 2004.

———. "Słowa, których nie wolno zapomnieć." In *Lekcja sierpnia: Dziedzictwo 'Solidarności' po dwudziestu latach*, edited by Dariusz Gawin, 63–76. Warsaw: Wydawnictwo IFiS PAN, 2002.

———. "Światła etyki solidarności." *Tygodnik Powszechny*, January 7, 2001.

———. *Tischner*. Cracow: Znak, 2001.

Brzeziński, Zbigniew. *Out of Control: Global Turmoil on the Eve of the Twenty-first Century*. 1st ed. New York: Collier Books, 1994.

Bugaj, Ryszard, Waldemar Kuczyński, Krzysztof Mądel, Andrzej Rychard, Agnieszka Magdziak-Miszewska, and Tomasz Wiścicki. "Odchodzenie od złudzeń?" *Więź* 2, no. 496 (2000): 39–53.

Burda, Piotr. "Korki pod przymusem." *Gazeta Wyborcza*, March 5, 2004, 5.

Bywalec, Czesław. *Społeczne aspekty transformacji gospodarczej w Europie Środkowowschodniej*. Cracow: Wydaw. Akademii Ekonomicznej, 1998.

———. "Transformacja gospodarcza a poziom życia społeczeństwa polskiego." *Ekonomista* 4 (1995).

———. *Transformacja gospodarcza a zróżnicowanie poziomu życia społeczeństwa polskiego*. Cracow: Wydaw. Akademii Ekonomicznej, 1999.

Calvez, Jean-Yves. *The Social Thought of John XXIII: Mater et Magistra*. Chicago: H. Regnery, 1964.

Card, David E., and Alan B. Krueger. *Myth and Measurement: The New Economics of the Minimum Wage*. Princeton, N.J.: Princeton University Press, 1995.

Caritas Polska. 2004. *800,000 PLN i 47,000 USD dla ofiar trzęsienia ziemi*. Caritas Polska, http://caritaspolska.caritas.pl/index.php?strona=akt&id=2004 1231172723. (accessed January 6, 2005).

Catholic Bishops' Conference of England and Wales. 1996. *The Common Good and the Catholic Church's Social Teaching*. http://www.osjspm.org/cst/britbish.htm. (accessed May 1, 2003).

"Chłopi wielozawodowi." *Gazeta Wyborcza*, March 2, 2000.

Chrapek, Jan. 2000. *Tylko miłość się liczy*. Opoka, www.jubileusz2000.opoka.org.pl. (accessed March 16, 2001).

"Church's Social Work Is Not Political, John Paul II Says: Gospel Message Must Accompany Aid, He Tells Brazilian Bishops." October 21, 2002. Zenit News Agency, http://www.zenit.org. (accessed November 7, 2002).

Cichocki, Marek. "Doświadczenie pierwszej 'Solidarności'—między moralnym absolutyzmem a polityczną samowiedzą Polaków." In *Lekcja sierpnia: Dziedzictwo 'Solidarności' po dwudziestu latach,* edited by Dariusz Gawin, 77–102. Warsaw: Wydawnictwo IFiS PAN, 2002.

Commanding Heights: Interview with Jeffrey Sachs. 2000. PBS, http://www.pbs.org/wgbh/commandingheights/shared/minitextlo/int_jeffreysachs.html#11. (accessed March 16, 2004).

"Corruption in Poland: Enough!" *The Economist,* April 17, 2003.

Curran, Charles E. *Catholic Social Teaching, 1891–Present: A Historical, Theological, and Ethical Analysis,* Moral Traditions Series. Washington, D.C.: Georgetown University Press, 2002.

Czarnocka, Barbara. *Umiłować Chrystusa: wigilijne dzieło pomocy dzieciom.* Warsaw: Pro Caritate, 2002.

Dąbrowski, Michał. "Płaca minimalna i jej wpływ na wielkość zatrudnienia." Master's Thesis, Cracow Academy of Economics, 1998.

Daly, Herman E., John B. Cobb, and Clifford W. Cobb. *For the Common Good: Redirecting the Economy toward Community, the Environment, and a Sustainable Future.* 2nd ed. Boston: Beacon Press, 1994.

Daniels, Norman. "Equal Liberty and Unequal Worth of Liberty." In *Reading Rawls: Critical Studies on Rawls' A Theory of Justice,* edited by Norman Daniels, 253–82. Stanford, Calif.: Stanford University Press, 1989.

Davies, Norman. *Heart of Europe: A Short History of Poland.* Oxford: Clarendon Press, 1984.

Deniszczuk, Lucyna, and Barbara Sajkiewicz. "Kategoria minimum egzystencji." In *Polska bieda II,* edited by Stanisława Golinowska, 31–64. Warsaw: Instytut Pracy i Spraw Społecznych, 1997.

———. "Kategoria minimum socjalnego." In *Polska bieda II,* edited by Stanisława Golinowska, 150–98. Warsaw: Instytut Pracy i Spraw Społecznych, 1997.

Derkaczew, Joanna, Monika Strzępka, and Pawel Demirski. "Dwie Polski i przepaść." *Gazeta Wyborcza,* August 1, 2008.

Dionne, E. J. "The Death of Reaganomics." *Truthdig,* http://www.truthdig.com/report/item20080710_the_death_of_reaganomics/ July 10, 2008 (accessed October 11, 2008).

Dolata, Roman, Krzysztof Konarzewski, and Elżbieta Putkiewicz. 2003. *Rekomendacje dla polityki oświatowej po trzech latach reformy szkolnictwa.* Instytut Spraw Publicznych, http://www.isp.org.pl/docs/briefs/analizy5.pdf. (accessed March 13, 2004).

Donahue, John R. "Biblical Perspectives on Justice." In *The Faith That Does Justice: Examining the Christian Sources for Social Change,* edited by John C. Haughey, 68–112. New York: Paulist Press, 1977.

Drèze, Jacques H. "Ethics, Efficiency, and the Social Doctrine of the Church." In *Social and Ethical Aspects of Economics: A Colloquium in the Vatican,* edited by Pontificium Consilium de Iustitia et Pace, 39–50. Vatican City: Pontifical Council for Justice and Peace, 1992.

Dudek, Antoni. *Pierwsze lata III Rzeczypospolitej: 1989–2001*. 2nd ed. Arkana Historii. Cracow: Arcana, 2002.

———. "Rewolucja robotnicza i ruch narodowowyzwoleńczy." In *Lekcja sierpnia: Dziedzictwo 'Solidarności' po dwudziestu latach*, edited by Dariusz Gawin, 143–60. Warsaw: Wydawnictwo IFiS PAN, 2002.

Dyczewski, Leon. "Kościół katolicki wobec ubóstwa i ludzi ubogich." In *Polska bieda II: kryteria, ocena, przeciwdziałanie*, edited by Stanisława Golinowska, 370–80. Warsaw: IPiSS, 1997.

Dylus, Aniela. *Gospodarka, moralność, chrześcijaństwo*. Warsaw: Wydawnictwo Fundacji ATK, 1994.

———. "Wolny rynek—ubóstwo—uczestnictwo." *Tygodnik Powszechny*, October 18, 1998.

———. *Zmienność i ciągłość: polskie transformacje ustrojowe w horyzoncie etycznym*. Warsaw: Centrum im. Adama Smitha: Wydaw. Akademii Teologii Katolickiej, 1997.

Ellacuría, Ignacio, and Jon Sobrino. *Mysterium Liberationis: Fundamental Concepts of Liberation Theology*. Maryknoll, N.Y.: Orbis Books, 1993.

"Enough." *The Economist*, April 17, 2003.

Erikson, Erik H. *Identity: Youth and Crisis*. New York: Norton & Norton, 1968.

European Commission, Directorate-General for Employment and Social Affairs. "Child Poverty and Well-Being in the EU: Current Status and Way Forward." Luxembourg: Office for Official Publications of the European Communities, 2008.

———. "Joint Report on Social Protection and Social Inclusion." Luxembourg: Office for Official Publications of the European Communities, 2007.

———. "Joint Report on Social Protection and Social Inclusion." Luxembourg: Office for Official Publications of the European Communities, 2008.

Facon, Dariusz, and Monika Adamowska. "Zamieszanie wokół wypłat zasiłków rodzinnych." *Gazeta Wyborcza*, June 17, 2004.

Filek, Janina. *O wolności i odpowiedzialności podmiotu gospodarującego*. Cracow: Wydaw. AE, 2002.

———. "Problem ubóstwa w perspektywie wolności i odpowiedzialności." In *Etyczne aspekty bogacenia się i ubóstwa*, edited by Adam Węgrzecki, 57–66. Cracow: Wydawnictwo Akademii Ekonomicznej w Krakowie, 2003.

Fox, Liana. *Minimum Wage Trends: Understanding Past and Contemporary Research*, Washington, D.C.: Economic Policy Institute, 2006.

Frankl, Viktor Emil. *Man's Search for Meaning: An Introduction to Logotherapy*. Boston: Beacon Press, 1963.

Friedman, Milton. *Capitalism and Freedom*. Chicago: University of Chicago Press, 1962.

Frieske, Kazimierz. "Bieda: miary i interpretacje." In *Polska bieda II: kryteria, ocena, przeciwdziałanie*, edited by Stanisława Golinowska, 207–21. Warsaw: IPiSS, 1997.

Fromm, Erich. *Escape from Freedom*. 1st ed. New York: Henry Holt, 1994.

———. *On Disobedience and Other Essays*. New York: Seabury Press, 1981.

Gadomski, Witold. "Kapitalizm jest zdrowy." *Gazeta Wyborcza*, December 7, 1999, 23.

Garton Ash, Timothy. *The Polish Revolution: Solidarity*. 3d ed. New Haven, Conn.: Yale University Press, 2002.

Gasparski, Wojciech. "Kwestia bogactwa i ubóstwa w literaturze przedmiotu." In *Etyczne aspekty bogacenia się i ubóstwa*, edited by Adam Węgrzecki, 7–24. Cracow: Wydawnictwo Akademii Ekonomicznej w Krakowie, 2003.

Gawin, Dariusz. "'Solidarność'—republikańska rewolucja Polaków." In *Lekcja sierpnia: dziedzictwo 'Solidarności' po dwudziestu latach*, edited by Dariusz Gawin, 161–88. Warsaw: Wydawnictwo IFiS PAN, 2002.

Glatz, Carol. "Vatican Newspaper Says Crisis Shows Failure of 'New Economy.'" *Catholic News Service*, September 24, 2008.

Glendon, Mary Ann. "Knowing the Universal Declaration of Human Rights." *Notre Dame Law Review* 73, no. 5 (1998): 1153–76.

Glyn, Andrew. *Social Democracy in Neoliberal Times: The Left and Economic Policy since 1980*. Oxford: Oxford University Press, 2001.

Gołąb, Tomasz. 2001. "Kościół ubogich." *Gość Niedzielny*, http://www.opoka.org.pl/biblioteka/T/TA/TAC/kosciol_ubogich.html. (accessed February 1, 2001).

Gołębiewski, Marian. "Co Sobór zmienił w Polsce?" *Znak* 1, no. 524 (1999): 7–29.

Golinowska, Stanisława. "Badania nad ubóstwem: założenia i metodologia." In *Polska bieda II: kryteria, ocena, przeciwdziałanie*, edited by Stanisława Golinowska, 19–30. Warsaw: IPiSS, 1997.

———. "Minimalne dochody a walka z ubóstwem." In *Polska bieda II: kryteria, ocena, przeciwdziałanie*, edited by Stanisława Golinowska. Warsaw: IPiSS, 1997.

———. "Polska droga do bezrobocia: o przyczynach bezrobocia i polityce jego zwalczania." *Tygodnik Powszechny*, July 29, 2001, 1, 5.

———. "Poverty in Poland: Causes, Measures, and Studies." In *Poverty Dynamics in Poland: Selective Quantitative Analyses*, 11–36. Warsaw: CASE—Center for Social and Economic Research, 2002.

———. "Ubóstwo w Polsce: synteza wyników badań." In *Polska bieda II: kryteria, ocena, przeciwdziałanie*, edited by Stanisława Golinowska, 307–30. Warsaw: IPiSS, 1997.

———. *Warunki tworzenia miejsc pracy*. Warsaw: CASE—Centrum Analiz Społeczno-Ekonomicznych, 1999.

Górniak, Katarzyna. "O współczesnej dobroczynności." In *Przeciw biedzie: programy, pomysły, inicjatywy*, edited by Elżbieta Tarkowska, 77–90. Warsaw: Oficyna Naukowa, 2002.

Gowin, Jarosław. Interview, July 20, 2004.
———. "Katolicy i polityka." *Rzeczpospolita*, October 4–5, 2003, A5–A7.
———. "Kościół a 'Solidarność.'" In *Lekcja sierpnia: dziedzictwo 'Solidarności' po dwudziestu latach*, edited by Dariusz Gawin, 13–38. Warsaw: Wydawnictwo IFiS PAN, 2002.
———. *Kościół po komunizmie*. Cracow: Znak, 1995.
———. *Kościół w czasach wolności 1989–1999*. Cracow: Znak, 1999.
———. *Religia i ludzkie biedy: księdza Tischnera spory o Kościół*. Cracow: Znak, 2003.
———. "Zmącona pieśń Pana." *Znak* 3, no. 550 (2001): 89–101.
Gowin, Jarosław, Andrzej Wiśniewski, and Jerzy Zdrada. "Kryzys po chińsku." *Znak* 2, no. 537 (2000): 28–45.
Grabska, Stanisława. "Obywatele Kościoła." In *Dzieci Soboru zadają pytania: rozmowy o Soborze Watykańskim II*, edited by Zbigniew Nosowski. Warsaw: Biblioteka Więzi, 1996.
Graczyk, Roman. *Polski kościół—polska demokracja*. Cracow: Towarzystwo Autorów i Wydawców Prac Naukowych "Universitas," 1999.
Graff, Agnieszka. *Świat bez kobiet: płeć w polskim życiu publicznym*. 1st ed. Warsaw: Wydawn. W. A. B., 2001.
Gray, John. "The Case for Decency." *New York Review of Books* 53, no. 12 (2006).
Greenhouse, Steven. "Local 226 'The Culinary' Makes Las Vegas the Land of the Living Wage." *New York Times*, June 3, 2004.
Greider, William. *One World, Ready or Not: The Manic Logic of Global Capitalism*. New York: Simon & Schuster, 1997.
Gunn, Giles B. *Beyond Solidarity: Pragmatism and Difference in a Globalized World*. Chicago: University of Chicago Press, 2001.
Hajdamowicz, Krzysztof, and Marian Filar. "Najpiękniejsza jest wolność." *Gazeta Wyborcza*, November 25–26, 2003, 20–22.
Hamill, Susan Pace. *As Certain as Death: A Fifty-State Survey of State and Local Tax Laws: K–12 Funding, Poverty Trends, and Other Characteristics*. Durham, N.C.: Carolina Academic Press, 2008.
———. *The Least of These: Fair Taxes and the Moral Duty of Christians*. Birmingham, Ala.: Crane Hill Publishers, 2003.
Hayek, Friedrich A. von. *The Constitution of Liberty*. Chicago: University of Chicago Press, 1960.
———. *Law, Legislation, and Liberty: A New Statement of the Liberal Principles of Justice and Political Economy*. 3 vols. Chicago: University of Chicago Press, 1973.
Hehir, J. Bryan. "The Right and Competence of the Church in the American Case." In *One Hundred Years of Catholic Social Thought: Celebration and Challenge*, edited by John Aloysius Coleman. Maryknoll, N.Y.: Orbis Books, 1991.
Herbert, Zbigniew. "Przesłanie Pana Cogito/The Envoy of Mr. Cogito." In *Poezje Wybrane/Selected Poems*. Cracow: Wydawnictwo Literackie, 2000.

Heymann, Jody. *Forgotten Families: Ending the Growing Crisis Confronting Children and Working Parents in the Global Economy.* Oxford: Oxford University Press, 2006.

Hinze, Christine Firer. "Bridging Discourse on Wage Justice: Roman Catholic and Feminist Perspectives on the Family Living Wage." In *Feminist Ethics and the Catholic Moral Tradition,* edited by Charles E. Curran, Margaret A. Farley, and Richard A. McCormick, 511–40. New York: Paulist Press, 1996.

———. "Straining toward Solidarity in a Suffering World: *Gaudium et Spes* after Forty Years." In *Vatican II Forty Years Later,* edited by William Madges, 165–95. Maryknoll, N.Y.: Orbis Books, 2006.

Hobgood, Mary E. "Poor Women, Work, and the U.S. Catholic Bishops." *Journal of Religious Ethics* 25 (1997): 307–29.

Hollenbach, David. *Claims in Conflict: Retrieving and Renewing the Catholic Human Rights Tradition.* New York: Paulist Press, 1979.

———. *The Common Good and Christian Ethics.* Cambridge: Cambridge University Press, 2002.

———. "The Growing End of an Argument." *America* 153, no. 15 (1985).

Homan, Agnieszka. Interview, July 15 2004.

Hugo-Bader, Jacek. "Chłopcy z motykami." *Gazeta Wyborcza,* September 29, 2003, 4–13.

Hume, David. *Dialogues Concerning Natural Religion.* New York: MacMillan, 1947.

Huntingdon, Samuel. "The Clash of Civilizations." *Foreign Affairs* 72, no. 3 (Summer 1993).

Isasi-Diaz, Ada Maria. "Solidarity: Love of Neighbor in the Eighties." In *Lift Every Voice: Constructing Christian Theologies from the Underside,* edited by Susan Brook Thistlethwaite and Mary Potter Engle, 31–40. New York: Harper, 1990.

Jacher, Władysław, and Urszula Swadzba. "Etos pracy w Polsce." In *Kondycja moralna społeczeństwa polskiego,* edited by Janusz Mariański, 141–62. Cracow: Wydawnictwo WAM, 2002.

Janecki, Stanisław. "Kościół niezgody." *Wprost,* May 31, 1995.

Jarecki, Piotr. *Od zasłuchania do działania: społeczne echo pielgrzymki.* Warsaw: "Pax," 1999.

Jastrzębska-Szklarska, Joanna, and Bohdan Szklarski. "Od klientelizmu do paternalizmu—biednej społeczności popegierowska droga przez transformację." In *Lata tłuste, lata chude: spojrzenia na biedę w społecznościach lokalnych: praca zbiorowa,* edited by Katarzyna Korzeniewska and Elżbieta Tarkowska, 105–40. Warsaw: Wydaw. IFiS PAN, 2002.

Jedlicki, Jerzy. "Czas zwątpienia." *Znak* 558, no. 11 (2001): 44–55.

Jesuit Provincials of Latin America. "A Letter on Neoliberalism in Latin America." *Promotio Justitiae* 67 (1997): 43–49.

John XXIII. *Mater et Magistra.* In *Catholic Social Thought: The Documentary Heritage,* edited by David J. O'Brien and Thomas A. Shannon, 82–128. Maryknoll, N.Y.: Orbis Books, 1992.

———. *Pacem in Terris*. In *Catholic Social Thought: The Documentary Heritage*, edited by David J. O'Brien and Thomas A. Shannon, 129–62. Maryknoll, N.Y.: Orbis Books, 1992.

John Paul II. *Centesimus Annus*. In *Catholic Social Thought: The Documentary Heritage*, edited by David J. O'Brien and Thomas A. Shannon, 437–88. Maryknoll, N.Y.: Orbis Books, 1992.

———. 1988. *Christifideles Laici*. Vatican website, http://www.vatican.va/holy_father/john_paul_ii/apost_exhortations/documents/hf_jp-ii_exh_30121988_christifideles-laici_en.html. (accessed May 22, 2004).

———. 1981. *Familiaris Consortio*. Vatican website, http://www.vatican.va/holy_father/john_paul_ii/apost_exhortations/documents/hf_jp-ii_exh_19811122_familiaris-consortio_en.html#top. (accessed May 20, 2004).

———. 1991. "Homilia w czasie mszy św. odprawionej na lotnisku w Maślowie." Opoka, http://www.opoka.org. (accessed December 7, 2003).

———. *Jan Paweł II: Polska 1999: przemówienia i homilie*. Marki: Michalineum, 1999.

———. *Jan Paweł II w Polsce, 31 maja 1997–10 czerwca 1997: przemówienia i homilie*. Cracow: Znak, 1997.

———. "Królewstwo Boże i chrześcijańska rodzina." In *Jan Paweł II o małżeństwie i rodzinie: 1972–82*, 155. Warsaw: Pax, 1983.

———. *Laborem Exercens*. In *Catholic Social Thought: The Documentary Heritage*, edited by David J. O'Brien and Thomas A. Shannon, 350–92. Maryknoll, N.Y.: Orbis Books, 1992.

———. 1983. "Message of His Holiness Pope John Paul II for the Celebration of the World Day of Peace: 'Dialogue for Peace, a Challenge for Our Time.'" http://www.jesus.2000.years.de/holy_father/john_paul_ii/messages/peace/documents/hf_jp-ii_mes_19821208_xvi-world-day-for-peace_en.html. (accessed May 21, 2004).

———. 1998. "Message of His Holiness Pope John Paul II for the Celebration of the World Day of Peace: 'From the Justice of Each Comes Peace for All.'" Vatican website, http://www.vatican.va/holy_father/john_paul_ii/messages/peace/documents/hf_jp-ii_mes_08121997_xxxi-world-day-for-peace_en.html. (accessed May 21, 2004).

———. 1982. "Message of His Holiness Pope John Paul II for the Celebration of the World Day of Peace: 'Peace, a Gift of God Entrusted to Us.'" http://www.jesus.2000.years.de/holy_father/john_paul_ii/messages/peace/documents/hf_jp-ii_mes_19811208_xv-world-day-for-peace_en.html. (accessed May 21, 2004).

———. 1999. "Message of His Holiness Pope John Paul II for the Celebration of the World Day of Peace: 'Respect for Human Rights: The Secret of True Peace.'" Vatican website (accessed May 21, 2004).

———. "Misterium nieprawości i wyobraźnia miłosierdzia." *Tygodnik Powszechny*, August 25, 2002.

———. "Niech Solidarność wróci do korzeni." *Gazeta Wyborcza*, November 13, 2003.

———. 2001. *Novo Millennio Ineunte*. Vatican website, http://www.vatican.va/holy_father/john_paul_ii/apost_letters/documents/hf_jp-ii_apl_20010106_novo-millennio-ineunte_en.html. (accessed August 15, 2008).

———. *Program dla Kościoła w Polsce: Jan Paweł II do polskich biskupów; wizyta ad limina 1998*. Cracow: Znak, 1998.

———. 1991. "Przemówienie do przedstawicieli władz państwowych wygłoszone na zamku królewskim." Opoka, http://www.opoka.org. (accessed December 7, 2003).

———. "Przemówienie w Parlamencie Polskiej Rzeczpospolitej." In *Jan Paweł II: Polska 1999; przemówienia i homilie*, 103–12. Marki: Michalineum, 1999.

———. 1979. *Redemptor Hominis*. Vatican website, http://www.vatican.va/holy_father/john_paul_ii/encyclicals/documents/hf_jp-ii_enc_04031979_redemptor-hominis_pl.html. (accessed May 21, 2004).

———. 1990. *Redemptoris Missio*. Vatican website, http://www.vatican.va/holy_father/john_paul_ii/encyclicals/documents/hf_jp-ii_enc_07121990_redemptoris-missio_en.html. (accessed May 15, 2003).

———. *Sollicitudo Rei Socialis*. In *Catholic Social Thought: The Documentary Heritage*, edited by David J. O'Brien and Thomas A. Shannon, 393–436. Maryknoll, N.Y.: Orbis Books, 1992.

———. 1993. *Veritatis Splendor*. Vatican website, http://www.vatican.va/holy_father/john_paul_ii/encyclicals/documents/hf_jp-ii_enc_06081993_veritatis-splendor_en.html. (accessed May 20, 2004).

———. "What Church Social Teaching Is and Is Not." *Origins* 23 (1993): 257–58.

Johnson, Elmer W. "Whither Capitalism?" Paper presented at the Executive in Residence Program, University of Notre Dame, Notre Dame, Indiana, October 5, 1999.

Kabaj, Mieczysław. *Program przeciwdziałania ubóstwu i bezrobociu, Raport IPiSS, z. 19*. Warsaw: Instytut Pracy i Spraw Socjalnych, 2000.

———. 2000. *Programme Outline for Actively Counteracting Poverty and Social Exclusion*. UNDP Poland, http://www.undp.org.pl/pages/pl_pov2.htm. (accessed March 3, 2000).

———. 2000. *Reduction of Poverty and Social Exclusion*. UNDP Poland, http://www.undp.org.pl/pages/pl_pov.htm. (accessed March 3, 2000).

———. "Searching for a New Results-Oriented Wage Negotiation System in Poland." In *Paying the Price: The Wage Crisis in Central and Eastern Europe*, edited by Daniel Vaughan-Whitehead, 234–71. New York: St. Martin's Press, 1998.

Kabaj, Mieczysław, and Tadeusz Kowalik. "Who Is Responsible for Postcommunist Successes in Eastern Europe?" *Transition*, vol. 6, nos. 7–8, July/August 1995. World Bank Group Newsletter, http://www.worldbank.org/transitionnewsletter/ja95/aug-ar3.htm. (accessed March 2, 2004).

Kaleta, Józef. "Harakiri?" In *Spór o Polskę: 1989–1999*, edited by Paweł Śpiewak, 635–36. Warsaw: PWN, 2001.

———. "Plusy i minusy." In *Spór o Polskę: 1989–1999*, edited by Paweł Śpiewak, 655–66. Warsaw: PWN, 2001.

Kalukin, Rafał. "Rewolucja w zasiłkach." *Gazeta Wyborcza*, November 27, 2003, 15.

Kampka, Franciszek. *Antropologiczne i społeczne podstawy ładu gospodarczego w świetle nauczania Kościoła*. Lublin: Redakcja Wydawnictw KUL, 1995.

———. "Działanie i inspiracja: rzecz o mirażach akcyjności." In *Ziarno czynu: refleksje po V pielgrzymce Jana Pawła II do ojczyzny: praca zbiorowa*, edited by Franciszek Kampka, 55–80. Cracow: Wydaw. WAM, 1998.

———. "Solidarność w nauczaniu Jana Pawła II." In *Idea solidarności dzisiaj*, edited by Władysław Zuziak, 7–16. Cracow: Wydawnictwo Naukowe PAT, 2001.

Kanbur, S. M. Ravi, Nora Lustig, and World Bank. *Attacking Poverty, World Development Report, 2000/2001*. New York: Oxford University Press, 2000.

"KE: W Polsce nawet praca nie chroni przed biedą." *Gazeta Wyborcza*, February 25, 2008.

Kiciński, Krzysztof. "Orientacje moralne społeczeństwa polskiego." In *Kondycja moralna społeczeństwa polskiego*, edited by Janusz Mariański, 369–405. Cracow: Wydawnictwo WAM, 2002.

Kieniewicz, Barbara, and Bogumiła Szopa. *Polityka dochodowa na tle rynku pracy w Polsce w warunkach transformacji systemowej*. Cracow: AE. Wydaw. Uczelniane, 1997.

"Kobiety za przywróceniem funduszu alimentacyjnego." *Gazeta Wyborcza*, June 7, 2004.

Kojder, Andrzej. "Korupcja i poczucie moralne Polaków." In *Kondycja moralna społeczeństwa polskiego*, edited by Janusz Mariański, 233–52. Cracow: Wydawnictwo WAM, 2002.

Kołakowski, Leszek. "Krótka rozprawa o teokracji." In *Spór o Polskę: 1989–99*, edited by Paweł Śpiewak. Warsaw: PWN, 2000.

———. "Laik nad katechizmem się wymądrza." *Puls* 62 (1992).

———. "Po co nam prawa człowieka?" *Gazeta Wyborcza*, November 25–26, 2003, 11–13.

Konferencja Episkopatu Polski. 2000. "Komunikat z 303. Zebrania Plenarnego." Konferencja Episkopatu Polski, http://www.episkopat.pl/dokumenty/komunikat303.htm. (accessed January 12, 2001).

———. 2003. "Komunikat z 322. Zebrania Plenarnego." Konferencja Episkopatu Polski, http://www.episkopat.pl/dokumenty/komunikat322.html. (accessed May 23, 2003).

———. 2001. *Kościół wobec rzeczywistości politycznej*. Konferencja Episkopatu Polski, http://www.episkopat.pl/dokumenty/synoddokumenty.pdf. (accessed January 24, 2003).

———. 2001. *Kościół wobec życia społeczno-gospodarczego*. Konferencja Episkopatu Polski, http://www.episkopat.pl/dokumenty/synoddokumenty.pdf. (accessed January 24, 2003).
———. 2001. *Misyjny Adwent Nowego Tysiąclecia*. Konferencja Episkopatu Polski, http://www.episkopat.pl/dokumenty/synoddokumenty.pdf. (accessed January 24, 2003).
———. 2001. *Posługa charytatywna Kościoła*. Konferencja Episkopatu Polski, http://www.episkopat.pl/dokumenty/synoddokumenty.pdf. (accessed January 24, 2003).
———. 2001. *Potrzeba i zadania nowej ewangelizacji na przełomie II i III tysiąclecia chrześcijańskiego*. Konferencja Episkopatu Polski, http://www.episkopat.pl/dokumenty/synoddokumenty.pdf. (accessed January 24, 2003).
———. 2001. *Powołanie do życia w małżeństwie i rodzinie*. Konferencja Episkopatu Polski, http://www.episkopat.pl/dokumenty/synoddokumenty.pdf. (accessed January 24, 2003).
———. 2001. *Sól ziemi. Powołanie i posłannictwo świeckich*. Konferencja Episkopatu Polski, http://www.episkopat.pl/dokumenty/synoddokumenty.pdf. (accessed January 24, 2003).
———. 2000. "Społeczny wymiar Jubileuszu Odkupienia: list na luty." Konferencja Episkopatu Polski, http://www.episkopat.pl/dokumenty/d-17c.htm. (accessed January 12, 2001).
———. 2001. *Szkoła i uniwersytet w życiu Kościoła i narodu*. Konferencja Episkopatu Polski, http://www.episkopat.pl/dokumenty/synoddokumenty.pdf. (accessed January 24, 2003).
———. 2000. "Szukając światła na nowe tysiąclecie: słowo biskupów polskich na temat niektórych problemów społecznych." Opoka, http://www.opoka.org.pl/biblioteka/W/WE/kep/problemy_spoleczne_17122000.html. (accessed January 12, 2001).
———. 2001. *W trosce o nową kulturę życia i pracy*. Konferencja Episkopatu Polski, http://www.opoka.org.pl/biblioteka/W/WE/kep/list_spoleczny_30102001.html. (accessed January 24, 2003).
Konowrocki, Mariusz. *Wakacyjna przygoda: materiały dla wychowawców*. Warsaw: Pro Caritate, 2002.
Koralewicz, Jadwiga, and Marek Ziółkowski. *Mentalność Polaków: Sposoby myślenia o polityce, gospodarce i życiu społecznym 1988–2000*. Warsaw: Wydawnictwo Naukowe SCHOLAR, 2003.
Korwin-Mikke, Janusz. *Naprawić Polskę: no problem*. Lublin: Fabryka Słów, 2004.
Korzeniewska, Katarzyna. "Biedni (i) emeryci: o ekonomicznej zależności biednych rodzin od pomocy z zewnątrz i o 'underclass' po polsku." In *Lata tłuste, lata chude: spojrzenia na biedę w społecznościach lokalnych: praca zbiorowa*, edited by Katarzyna Korzeniewska and Elżbieta Tarkowska, 141–60. Warsaw: Wydaw. IFiS PAN, 2002.

Korzeniewska, Katarzyna, and Elżbieta Tarkowska. "Spojrzenie na biedę: Wprowadzenie." In *Lata tłuste, lata chude: spojrzenia na biedę w społecznościach lokalnych: praca zbiorowa*, edited by Katarzyna Korzeniewska and Elżbieta Tarkowska, 7–22. Warsaw: Wydaw. IFiS PAN, 2002.

Kostyła, Joanna. "Lekcja po lekcjach: system korepetycji zaczyna być postrzegany w kategoriach korupcji." *Wprost*, May 21, 2000, 66–68.

Kowalik, Tadeusz. "Czy sprawiedliwość społeczna kosztuje? Artykuł polemiczny na marginesie książki pt. *Efektywność a sprawiedliwość*." *Ekonomista* 3 (1997): 291–319.

———. "Joseph Stiglitz a polska transformacja." *Myśl socjaldemokratyczna* 1 (2002): 93–99.

———. "Społeczna gospodarka rynkowa—konstytucyjnym wyzwaniem dla Polski." In *Człowiek—rynek—sprawiedliwość*, edited by Krystyna Goldbergowa, 111–54. Warsaw: Towarzystwo Wydawnicze i Literackie, 2001.

———. "Zmiany w podziale dochodu narodowego w czasie transformacji." In *Dynamika transformacji polskiej gospodarki*, edited by Marek Belka and Władysław Trzeciakowski, 83–100. Warsaw: PolText, 1997.

Kowalski, Sergiusz. "Jedynie słuszny liberalizm." *Polityka*, February 12, 2000, 65.

Krasnodębski, Zdzisław. *Demokracja peryferii*. 2nd ed. Gdańsk: Wydawnictwo Słowo/Obraz Terytoria, 2005.

Kraut, Karen, Scott Klinger, and Chuck Collins. 2000. *Choosing the High Road: Businesses That Pay a Living Wage and Prosper*. United for a Fair Economy, http://www.responsiblewealth.org/living_wage/choosing.html. (accessed December 3, 2001).

Krier Mich, Marvin L. *Catholic Social Teaching and Movements*. Mystic, Conn.: Twenty-Third Publications, 1998.

Król, Marcin. "Gorzkie żale." *Res Publica Nova* 2 (2004): 39–48.

———. "Liberalizm—co to wlaściwie znaczy?" *Tygodnik Powszechny*, September 1, 2002.

Krzemiński, Ireneusz. *Solidarność: projekt polskiej demokracji*. Warsaw: Oficyna Naukowa, 1997.

Krzemiński, Ireneusz, and Pawel Śpiewak. "Awantura w rodzinie: jakiego liberalizmu Polacy potrzebują? doktryner wolności." *Gazeta Wyborcza*, February 16, 2000, 14.

Kurczewska, Joanna, Katarzyna Staszyńska, and Hanna Bojar. "Blokady społeczeństwa obywatelskiego: czyli słabe społeczeństwo obywatelskie i słabe państwo." In *Społeczeństwo w transformacji, ekspertyzy i studia*, edited by Andrzej Rychard and Michał Federowicz. Warsaw: Instytut Filozofii i Socjologii, Polska Akademia Nauk, 1993.

Kurczewski, Jacek. *The Resurrection of Rights in Poland*. Oxford: Clarendon Press, 1993.

Kurczewski, Jacek, and Beata Łaciak. *Korupcja w życiu społecznym*. Warsaw: Instytut Spraw Publicznych, 2000.

Kuroń, Jacek, and Jacek Żakowski. *Siedmiolatka, czyli, kto ukradł Polskę*. 1st ed. Wrocław: Wydawn. Dolnośląskie, 1997.
Lamoureaux, Patricia Ann. "Is a Living Wage a Just Wage?" *America*, February 19, 2001, 12–15.
Lampa, Małgorzata. "Ścieżka zdrowia." *Gazeta Wyborcza*, January 3–4, 2004, 1.
Laskowska-Otwinowska, Justyna. "Elementy kultury romskiej jako źródło marginalizacji i bogacenia się Romów polskich." In *Lata tłuste, lata chude: spojrzenia na biedę w społecznościach lokalnych: praca zbiorowa*, edited by Katarzyna Korzeniewska and Elżbieta Tarkowska, 211–38. Warsaw: Wydaw. IFiS PAN, 2002.
———. "Stereotyp biednego Roma." In *Lata tłuste, lata chude: spojrzenia na biedę w społecznościach lokalnych: praca zbiorowa*, edited by Katarzyna Korzeniewska and Elżbieta Tarkowska, 239–58. Warsaw: Wydaw. IFiS PAN, 2002.
Lecki, Krzysztof, and Kazimierz Wódz. "Droga do ubóstwa? Gwara śląska jako bariera edukacyjna." In *Przeciw biedzie: programy, pomysły, inicjatywy*, edited by Elżbieta Tarkowska, 42–53. Warsaw: Oficyna Naukowa, 2002.
Legutko, Piotr. "Dwie szkoły, dwie Polski." *Tygodnik Powszechny*, January 5, 2003.
Leo XIII. *Rerum Novarum*. In *Catholic Social Thought: The Documentary Heritage*, edited by David J. O'Brien and Thomas A. Shannon, 12–39. Maryknoll, N.Y.: Orbis Books, 1992.
Lepa, Adam. "Pięć lat 'zdrowej krtytyki' oblężonej twierdzy." In *Spór o Polskę: 1989–99*, edited by Paweł Śpiewak. Warsaw: PWN, 2000.
Lepianka, Dorota. "Polacy a biedacy—społeczny obraz ubóstwa i stosunek społeczeństwa polskiego do osób ubogich." In *Przeciw biedzie: programy, pomysły, inicjatywy*, edited by Elżbieta Tarkowska, 54–77. Warsaw: Oficyna Naukowa, 2002.
Leszczyński, Adam. "My, wyzyskiwacze." *Gazeta Wyborcza*, December 13–14, 2003, 16–17.
Lewandowski, Janusz. "Wolność, nie równość." *Gazeta Wyborcza*, January 15–16, 2000, 21–22.
Locatelli, Paul. 2005. "The Catholic University of the 21st Century: Educating for Solidarity." http://www.loyola.edu/Justice/documents/commitment2005/keynote_locatelli.doc. (accessed October 9, 2007).
MacCallum, Gerald C. "Negative and Positive Freedom." *Philosophical Review* 76, no. 3 (1967).
Maciewicz, Patrycja. "Bezrobocie w Polsce spadnie poniżej 10 proc.?" *Gazeta Wyborcza*, March 7, 2007.
Mahoney, Roger. *Raise the Minimum Wage: September 2000*. United States Conference of Catholic Bishops, http://usccb.org/sdwp/national/minimumalert.htm. (accessed January 6, 2001).
Majka, Józef. *Etyka życia gospodarczego*. Warsaw: Ośrodek Dokumentacji i Studiów Społecznych, 1980.
———. *Jaka Polska? Węzłowe problemy katolickiej nauki społecznej*. Wrocław: Wydaw. Wrocławskiej Księgarni Archidiecezjalnej, 1991.

———. "Przemiany społeczno-gospodarcze w świetle etyki społecznej." Paper presented at the I ogólnopolska konferencja naukowa nt. "Transformacja gospodarki polskiej—doświadczenia i perspektywy," Warsaw, 1993.

Makowiecki, Marcin. "Inwestycje wspierane przez państwo." *Nowe Życie Gospodarcze* 33 (2000): 30–32.

Makowski, Jarosław, ed. *Kobiety uczą kościół.* Warsaw: Wydawnictwo W.A.B., 2007.

"Manifest kapitalistyczny." *Gazeta Wyborcza,* April 28, 2000.

Mariański, Janusz. "Kryzys moralny czy transformacja wartości? Na przykładzie wartości 'wolność.'" In *Ziarno czynu: refleksje po V pielgrzymce Jana Pawła II do ojczyzny: praca zbiorowa,* edited by Franciszek Kampka, 103–28. Cracow: Wydaw. WAM, 1998.

———. "Religia i moralność w społeczeństwie polskim." In *Kondycja moralna społeczeństwa polskiego,* edited by Janusz Mariański, 481–504. Cracow: Wydawnictwo WAM, 2002.

Maritain, Jacques, and John J. Fitzgerald. *The Person and the Common Good.* New York: C. Scribner's Sons, 1947.

Markowski, Marcin. "Państwo niesolidarne." *Gazeta Wyborcza,* August 28, 2007.

Marody, Mirosława. "Polak-katolik w Europie." *Odra* 2, no. 387 (1994): 2–10.

Massaro, Thomas. "Don't Forget Justice." *America* 194, no. 9 (2006): 18–20.

———. *United States Welfare Policy: A Catholic Response.* Washington, D.C.: Georgetown University Press, 2007.

Mazurkiewicz, Piotr. *Kościół i demokracja.* Warsaw: Pax, 2001.

McBrien, Richard. "The Future Role of the Church in American Society." In *Religion and Politics in the American Milieu,* edited by Leslie Griffin. Notre Dame, Ind.: University of Notre Dame Press, 1986.

McGoldrick, Terence. "Episcopal Conferences Worldwide on Catholic Social Teaching." *Theological Studies* 59, no. 1 (1998).

McGovern, Arthur F. *Liberation Theology and Its Critics: Toward an Assessment.* Maryknoll, N.Y.: Orbis Books, 1989.

Metz, Johannes Baptist. *The Emergent Church: The Future of Christianity in a Postbourgeois World.* New York: Crossroad, 1981.

———. "Messianic or Bourgeois Religion?" In *Faith and the Future: Essays on Theology, Solidarity, and Modernity,* edited by Johannes Baptist Metz and Jurgen Moltmann. Maryknoll, N.Y.: Orbis Books, 1995.

Micewski, Andrzej. *Cardinal Wyszynski: A Biography.* San Diego: Harcourt, Brace, Jovanovich, 1984.

Michałowski, Jerzy. "Centesimus Annus—jaki kapitalizm?" In *Centesimus annus: tekst i komentarze,* edited by Franciszek Kampka and Cezary Ritter, 227–45. Lublin: Redakcja Wydawnictw KUL, 1998.

Michalski, Cezary. "'Desolidaryzacja,' czyli wspólnota jako przedmiot roszczeń." In *Lekcja sierpnia: dziedzictwo 'Solidarności' po dwudziestu latach,* edited by Dariusz Gawin, 189–206. Warsaw: Wydawnictwo IFiS PAN, 2002.

Michnik, Adam. *The Church and the Left*. Translated by David Ost. Chicago: University of Chicago Press, 1993.
———. *Kościół, lewica, dialog*. 2nd ed. Warsaw: Świat Książki, 1998.
———. *Letters from Freedom: Post–Cold War Realities and Perspectives*. Translated by Irena Grudzińska-Gross. Berkeley: University of California Press, 1998.
———. *Letters from Prison and Other Essays*. Berkeley: University of California Press, 1985.
———. "The Moral and Spiritual Origins of Solidarity." In *Without Force or Lies: Voices from the Revolution of Central Europe in 1989–90: Essays, Speeches, and Eyewitness Accounts*, edited by William M. Brinton and Alan Rinzler, 239–50. San Francisco: Mercury House, 1990.
Michnik, Adam, and Alina Białkowska. "Mam zdjąć okulary? Adam Michnik and Alina Białkowska rozmawiają z wicepremierem Leszkiem Balcerowiczem." *Gazeta Wyborcza*, August 12, 1991, 8–11.
Michnik, Adam, Józef Tischner, and Jacek Żakowski. *Między panem a plebanem*. 1st ed. Cracow: Znak, 1995.
Miller, Vincent Jude. *Consuming Religion: Christian Faith and Practice in a Consumer Culture*. New York: Continuum, 2004.
Miłosz, Czesław. "Państwo wyznaniowe?" In *Spór o Polskę: 1989–99*, edited by Paweł Śpiewak. Warsaw: PWN, 2000.
Ministerstwo Gospodarki, Pracy i Polityki Społecznej. 2004. *Historia minimalnego wynagrodzenia*. Ministerstwo Gospodarki, Pracy i Polityki Społecznej, http://www.mgpips.gov.pl/wydruk.php?nr=763. (accessed March 30, 2004).
Miszalska, Anita. "Moralność a demokracja—uwagi o stylu moralnym współczesnego społeczeństwa polskiego." In *Kondycja moralna społeczeństwa polskiego*, edited by Janusz Mariański, 163–88. Cracow: Wydawnictwo WAM, 2002.
Modzelewski, Karol. *Dokąd od komunizmu?* Warsaw: "BGW," 1993.
———. *Życiodajny impuls chuligaństwa*. Cracow: Universitas, 2003.
Morawski, Witold. "Realizacja zasad sprawiedliwości społecznej w Polsce jako miara 'powrótu do normalności.'" In *Kondycja moralna społeczeństwa polskiego*, edited by Janusz Mariański, 117–40. Cracow: Wydawnictwo WAM, 2002.
Murmyło, Marcin. "Od 1 stycznia nie leczymy." *Gazeta Wyborcza*, December 29, 2003, 1, 3.
Murphy, Charles M. "Action for Justice as Constitutive of the Preaching of the Gospel: What Did the 1971 Synod Mean?" *Theological Studies* 44 (1983): 298–311.
Musiał, Stanisław. *Dwanaście koszy ułomków*. Cracow: Wydawnictwo Literackie, 2002.
Naughton, Michael, and Robert G. Kennedy. "Executive Compensation: An Evaluation from the Catholic Social Tradition." *Social Justice Review* 84, no. 11 (1993).
Niebuhr, Reinhold. *Moral Man and Immoral Society: A Study in Ethics and Politics*. New York, London: C. Scribner's, 1932.

Niezależny Samorządny Związek Zawodowy Solidarność. 1980. *21 Postulatów z 17 sierpnia 1980 roku*. NSZZ Solidarność, http://www.solidarnosc.org.pl/archiwum/historia/21_post.htm. (accessed February 28, 2004).

———. 2004. *Uchwała programowa XV KZD*. NSZZ Solidarność, http://www.solidarnosc.org.pl/dokumenty/xv_kzd/u_prog.htm. (accessed February 28, 2004).

Noonan, John Thomas. *Contraception: A History of Its Treatment by the Catholic Theologians and Canonists*. Enlarged ed. Cambridge, Mass.: Belknap Press, 1986.

Novak, Michael. "The Executive Joneses." *Forbes* (May 29, 1989): 95.

———. "The Rights and Wrongs of 'Economic Rights': A Debate Continued." *This World* 17 (Spring 1987).

Nowakowska, Ewa. "Cnota w komórce." *Polityka* 25 (1998).

———. "Karuzela z rodzinami." *Polityka*, September 12, 1998, 78–81.

———. "Szklany sufit, lepka podłoga." *Polityka*, February 21, 2004, 82–86.

Nowakowska, Urszula. 2000. *Polish Women in the 90's*. Women's Rights Center, http://free.ngo.pl/temida/rapcont.htm. (accessed March 19, 2003).

Nussbaum, Martha Craven. *Women and Human Development: The Capabilities Approach*. New York: Cambridge University Press, 2000.

———, ed. *Debating the Limits of Patriotism*. Boston: Beacon Press, 1996.

Ochocki, Andrzej. "Kościół katolicki a sprawy publiczne w Polsce." In *Kościół katolicki na początku tysiąclecia w opinii Polaków*, edited by Witold Zdaniewicz and Sławomir Zaręby. Warsaw: Instytut Statystyki Kościoła Katolickiego SAC, 2004.

Okrasa, Włodzimierz. *Who Avoids and Who Escapes from Poverty during the Transition? Evidence from Polish Panel Data, 1993–96, Policy Research Working Papers; WPS/2218*. Washington, D.C.: World Bank, 1999.

"On Their Own Track: Germany's Trade Unions." *The Economist*, August 23, 2007.

Orliński, Wojciech. "Wolność, równość, liberalizm." *Gazeta Wyborcza*, July 24–25, 1999, 16–17.

Osiatyński, Wiktor. "Czy zmierzch praw człowieka?" *Gazeta Wyborcza*, December 6–7, 2003, 12–13.

Ost, David. *The Defeat of Solidarity: Anger and Politics in Postcommunist Europe*. Ithaca, N.Y.: Cornell University Press, 2005.

Paczkowski, Andrzej. *Pół wieku dziejów Polski: 1939–1989*. 4th ed. Warsaw: Wydaw. Naukowe PWN, 2000.

Paradowska, Janina. "Król Lew. Bilans Lecha Wałęsy: 1990–95." In *Spór o Polskę: 1989–1999*, edited by Paweł Śpiewak, 693–94. Warsaw: PWN, 2000.

———. "Lewa kasa, prawa kasa." *Polityka* 4, no. 2220 (2000): 3–9.

———. "Sztuka naciskania: słowem, krzykiem, układem." *Polityka*, March 25, 2000, 3–8.

Paul VI. *Evangelii Nuntiandi*. In *Catholic Social Thought: The Documentary Heritage*, edited by David J. O'Brien and Thomas A. Shannon, 303–46. Maryknoll, N.Y.: Orbis Books, 1992.

———. 1968. *Humanae Vitae*. Vatican website, http://www.vatican.va/holy_father/paul_vi/encyclicals/documents/hf_p-vi_enc_25071968_humanaevitae_en.html. (accessed June 13, 2004).

———. *Octogesima Adveniens*. In *Catholic Social Thought: The Documentary Heritage*, edited by David J. O'Brien and Thomas A. Shannon, 263–87. Maryknoll, N.Y.: Orbis Books, 1992.

———. *Populorum Progressio*. In *Catholic Social Thought: The Documentary Heritage*, edited by David J. O'Brien and Thomas A. Shannon, 238–62. Maryknoll, N.Y.: Orbis Books, 1992.

Penn, Shana. *Podziemie kobiet*. Warsaw: Wydawnictwo Rosner i Wspólnicy, 2003.

Perepeczko, Barbara. "Swoistość biedy w rodzinach rolniczych i jej oswajanie." In *Przeciw biedzie: programy, pomysły, inicjatywy*, edited by Elżbieta Tarkowska, 32–41. Warsaw: Oficyna Naukowa, 2002.

Pesch, Heinrich. *Heinrich Pesch on Solidarist Economics: Excerpts from the Lehrbuch der Nationalökonomie*. Lanham, Md.: University Press of America, 1998.

Peters, Rebecca Todd. *In Search of the Good Life: The Ethics of Globalization*. New York: Continuum, 2004.

Pieronek, Tadeusz. *Kościół nie boi się wolności*. Cracow: Znak, 1998.

———. "Zatroskanie o człowieka." *Więź* 488, no. 2 (1999): 45–49.

Pius XI. *Quadragesimo Anno*. In *Catholic Social Thought: The Documentary Heritage*, edited by David J. O'Brien and Thomas A. Shannon, 40–80. Maryknoll, N.Y.: Orbis Books, 1992.

Podgórska, Joanna. "Nie robim, bo się narobim." *Polityka*, May 8, 2004, 1–10.

Pogge, Thomas Winfried Menko. *Freedom from Poverty as a Human Right: Who Owes What to the Very Poor?* Paris: UNESCO, 2007.

———. *World Poverty and Human Rights: Cosmopolitan Responsibilities and Reforms*. Malden, Mass.: Polity, 2002.

Pope, Stephen J. *Human Evolution and Christian Ethics*. Cambridge: Cambridge University Press, 2007.

Popiełuszko, Jerzy. *Myśli wyszukane*. Cracow: Znak, 2002.

Potocki, Andrzej. "Czy społeczeństwo polskie jest społeczeństwem solidarnym?" In *Idea solidarności dzisiaj*, edited by Władysław Zuziak, 69–83. Cracow: Wydawnictwo Naukowe PAT, 2001.

"Przemówił komitet do obrazu." *Gazeta Wyborcza*, December 11–12, 2000.

Pyszka, Stanisław. "Zaangażowanie chrześcijan w politykę dzisiaj." In *Katolicka nauka społeczna wobec wybranych problemów współczesnego świata*, edited by Tomasz Homa. Cracow: WAM, 1995.

Rahner, Karl. "Anonymous Christianity and the Missionary Task of the Church." In *Theological Investigations XII*. New York: Seabury Press, 1974.

Ramadan, Tariq. *Western Muslims and the Future of Islam*. Oxford: Oxford University Press, 2004.

Rauscher, Anton. "Odkrycie społecznej gospodarki rynkowej." In *Centesimus annus: tekst i komentarze*, edited by Franciszek Kampka and Cezary Ritter, 247–62. Lublin: Redakcja Wydawnictw KUL, 1998.

———. "Źródła idei solidarności." In *Idea solidarności dzisiaj*, edited by Władysław Zuziak, 17–30. Cracow: Wydawnictwo Naukowe PAT, 2001.

Rawls, John. *A Theory of Justice*. Rev. ed. Cambridge, Mass.: Belknap Press of Harvard University Press, 1999.

"Reinfeldt Explained." *The Economist*, September 21, 2006.

Reszke, Irena. "Uwarunkowania feminizacji biedy w Polsce." *Kultura i społeczeństwo* 2 (2001): 73–83.

"A Revolution Faces the Voters." *The Economist*, June 29, 2006.

Ritter, Joseph A., and Lowell J. Taylor. "Economic Models of Employee Motivation." *Review* 1 (1997). (Journal of the Federal Reserve Bank of St. Louis.)

Roosevelt, Franklin Delano. "The Economic Bill of Rights." In *The Public Papers and Addresses of Franklin Delano Roosevelt*, edited by Samuel Rosenman, 40–42. New York: Harper, 1950.

Rosati, Dariusz. "Powrót socjalizmu." *Gazeta Wyborcza*, March 7, 2000.

Roszkowski, Wojciech. *Najnowsza historia Polski: 1980–2002*. Vol. 3. Warsaw: Świat Książki, 2003.

Rutkowski, Jan J. *Welfare and the Labor Market in Poland: Social Policy during Economic Transition*. Washington, D.C.: World Bank, 1998.

Ryan, John A. *A Living Wage*. New York, London: Macmillan, 1906.

Sachs, Jeffrey. *The End of Poverty: Economic Possibilities for Our Time*. New York: Penguin Press, 2005.

———. "Old Myths about Poland's Reforms Die Hard." *Beyond Transition* 6, nos. 11–12 (1995): 1–32.

———. "Postcommunist Parties and the Politics of Entitlement." *Beyond Transition* 6, no. 3 (1995): 1–32.

Sadłowska, Katarzyna. "Milion pozornie bezrobotnych." *Rzeczpospolita*, November 9, 2003, 1.

Salij, Jacek. "Solidarność trochę teologiczniej." *Znak* 543, no. 8 (2000): 35–50.

Schor, Juliet. *The Overspent American: Upscaling, Downshifting, and the New Consumer*. 1st ed. New York: Basic Books, 1998.

Second Vatican Council. *Gaudium et Spes: Pastoral Constitution on the Church in the Modern World*. In *Catholic Social Thought: The Documentary Heritage*, edited by David J. O'Brien and Thomas A. Shannon, 164–237. Maryknoll, N.Y.: Orbis Books, 1992.

Sen, Amartya Kumar. *Development as Freedom*. 1st ed. New York: Knopf, 1999.

———. *On Ethics and Economics*. Oxford: Blackwell, 1987.

Sennett, Charles M. "Arms Deal Criticized as Corporate U.S. Welfare." *Boston Globe*, January 14, 2003, A1.

Shipler, David K. *The Working Poor: Invisible in America*. 1st ed. New York: Knopf, 2004.

Shue, Henry. *Basic Rights: Subsistence, Affluence, and U.S. Foreign Policy*. 2nd ed. Princeton, N.J.: Princeton University Press, 1996.

Siedlicka, Ewa, and Marek Nowicki. "Wyroki na kołku." *Gazeta Wyborcza*, December 11–12, 2000.

Skąpska, Grażyna. "Czy instytucje publiczne budowane są w oparciu o ideę solidarności?" In *Idea solidarności dzisiaj*, edited by Władysław Zuziak, 47–56. Cracow: Wydawnictwo Naukowe PAT, 2001.

———. Interview, March 30, 2004.

Smolar, Aleksander. "Rocznice, pamięć, przyszłość." *Znak* 558, no. 11 (2001): 12–38.

Sobrino, Jon. *The Principle of Mercy: Taking the Crucified People from the Cross*. Maryknoll, N.Y.: Orbis Books, 1994.

"'Solidarność' przeciw niskim płacom." *Gazeta Wyborcza*, July 30, 2008.

Solska, Joanna. "Goło, Niewesoło." *Polityka*, April 1, 2000.

———. "Ogłupianie chłopa." *Polityka*, September 25, 1999, 20–21.

Soltan, Karol Edward. "Agape, Civil Society, and the Task of Social Reconstruction." *Cardozo Journal of International and Comparative Law* 4, no. 24 (1996): 241–60.

Sosenko, Kazimierz. "Etyczne problemy transformacji systemu gospodarczego i możliwości ich rozważania." In *Etyczny wymiar przekształceń gospodarczych w Polsce*, edited by Adam Węgrzecki. Cracow: Oficyna Cracovia, 1996.

Śpiewak, Paweł, ed. *Spór o Polskę: 1989–1999*. Warsaw: PWN, 2000.

Stankiewicz, Andrzej. "Młodzi doceniają 'Solidarność,'" *Rzeczpospolita*, August 16, 2005.

Stawrowski, Zbigniew. "Doświadczenie 'Solidarności' jako wspólnoty etycznej." In *Lekcja sierpnia: dziedzictwo 'Solidarności' po dwudziestu latach*, edited by Dariusz Gawin, 103–22. Warsaw: IFiS PAN, 2002.

———. "O zapomnianej solidarności." *Znak* 543, no. 8 (2000): 60–67.

Steiner, Henry J., and Philip Alston. *International Human Rights in Context: Law, Politics, Morals: Text and Materials*. 2nd ed. Oxford: Oxford University Press, 2000.

Stiglitz, Joseph E. *Globalization and Its Discontents*. 1st ed. New York: W.W. Norton, 2002.

———. "The Private Uses of Public Interests: Incentives and Institutions." *Journal of Economic Perspectives* (Spring 1998).

Stout, Jeffrey. *Democracy and Tradition*. Princeton, N.J.: Princeton University Press, 2004.

Świda-Ziemba, Hanna. "Permisywizm moralny a postawy polskiej młodzieży." In *Kondycja moralna społeczeństwa polskiego*, edited by Janusz Mariański, 435–52. Cracow: Wydawnictwo WAM, 2002.

Świeżawski, Stefan. "Określanie tożsamości Kościoła." In *Dzieci Soboru zadają pytania: rozmowy o Soborze Watykańskim II*, edited by Zbigniew Nosowski, 15–30. Warsaw: Więź, 1996.

Szacki, Jerzy. *Liberalism after Communism*. Translated by Chester Adam Kisiel. Budapest: Central European University Press, 1995.
———. *Liberalizm po komunizmie*. Cracow: Znak, 1994.
Szafraniec, Krystyna. "Anomia okresu transformacji a orientacje normatywne młodzieży: perspektywa międzygeneracyjna." In *Kondycja moralna społeczeństwa polskiego*, edited by Janusz Mariański, 453–81. Cracow: Wydawnictwo WAM, 2002.
Szopa, Bogumiła. "Podstawowe uwarunkowania ubóstwa w Polsce." In *Etyczne aspekty bogacenia się i ubóstwa*, edited by Adam Węgrzecki, 139–49. Cracow: Wydawnictwo Akademii Ekonomicznej w Krakowie, 2003.
Szostek, Andrzej. "Sztuka jedności—posługa jednania." In *Ziarno czynu: refleksje po V pielgrzymce Jana Pawła II do ojczyzny*, edited by Franciszek Kampka, 15–34. Cracow: Wydaw. WAM, 1998.
Sztanderska, Urszula, Elżbieta Drogosz-Zabłocka, and Barbara Minkiewicz. *Edukacja dla pracy: raport o rozwoju społecznym Polska 2007*. Warsaw: Program Narodów Zjednoczonych ds. Rozwoju, 2007.
Tarkowska, Elżbieta. "Czy dziedziczenie biedy? Bariery i szanse edukacyjne młodzieży wiejskiej z gminy Kościelec." In *Lata tłuste, lata chude: spojrzenia na biedę w społecznościach lokalnych: praca zbiorowa*, edited by Katarzyna Korzeniewska and Elżbieta Tarkowska, 161–86. Warsaw: Wydaw. IFiS PAN, 2002.
———. "'Dzieciństwa żadnego nie miałem': bieda i dzieci." *Więź* 488, no. 6 (1999): 65–72.
———. "O ubóstwie i moralności: czego można dowiedzieć się o moralnej kondycji społeczeństwa, badając biedę i biednych." In *Kondycja moralna społeczeństwa polskiego*, edited by Janusz Mariański, 305–26. Cracow: Wydawnictwo WAM, 2002.
———. "An Underclass without Ethnicity: The Poverty of Polish Women and Agricultural Laborers." In *Poverty, Ethnicity, and Gender in Eastern Europe during the Market Transition*, edited by Rebecca Jean Emigh and Iván Szelényi. Westport, Conn.: Praeger, 2001.
———. "Zróżnicowanie biedy: wiek i płeć." In *Jak żyją Polacy?* edited by Henryk Domański, Antonina Ostrowska, and Andrzej Rychard, 259–80. Warsaw: Wydawnictwo IFiS PAN, 2000.
———. *Zrozumieć biednego: o dawnej i obecnej biedzie w Polsce*. Warsaw: Typografika, 2000.
Taylor, Charles. "Kilka refleksji na temat solidarności." *Znak* 543, no. 8 (2000): 22–34.
Taylor, Joshua Charles. *America as Art*. Washington, D.C.: Smithsonian Institution Press, 1976.
Thompson, Jeff, and Jeff Chapman. *The Economic Impact of Local Living Wages*. Washington, D.C.: Economic Policy Institute, 2006.

Thurow, Lester C. *The Future of Capitalism: How Today's Economic Forces Shape Tomorrow's World*. 1st ed. New York: W. Morrow, 1996.
Tischner, Józef. *Drogi i bezdroża miłosierdzia*. Cracow: Wydawnictwo AA, 1999.
———. *Etyka solidarności*. Cracow: Znak, 1981.
———. *Etyka solidarności oraz homo sovieticus*. 1st ed. Cracow: Znak, 1992.
———. "Fragment o solidarności." *Znak* 543, no. 8 (2000): 21.
———. *Jak żyć?* 2nd ed. Wrocław: Tum, 1995.
———. *Ksiądz na manowcach*. 1st ed. Cracow: Znak, 1999.
———. *Książeczka pielgrzyma*. Warsaw: Libellus, 1996.
———. *Myślenie według wartości*. 3d ed. Cracow: Znak, 2000.
———. *Myśli wyszukane*. Edited by Wojciech Bonowicz. Cracow: Znak, 2000.
———. *Nieszczęsny dar wolności*. Cracow: Znak, 1996.
———. *Polski kształt dialogu*. Cracow: Znak, 2002.
———. "Solidarność po latach." In *Spór o Polskę: 1989–99*, edited by Paweł Śpiewak. Warsaw: PWN, 2000.
———. *The Spirit of Solidarity*. Translated by Marek B. Zaleski and Benjamin Fiore. San Francisco: Harper & Row, 1984.
———. *Spór o istnienie człowieka*. Cracow: Znak, 1998.
———. *Świat ludzkiej nadziei*. Cracow: Znak, 2000.
———. *W krainie schorowanej wyobraźni*. 1st ed. Cracow: Znak, 1997.
Tischner, Józef, and Jacek Żakowski. *Tischner czyta katechizm*. Cracow: Znak, 1996.
Titkow, Anna, ed. *Szklany sufit—bariery i ograniczenia karier kobiet*. Warsaw: Instytut Spraw Publicznych, 2003.
Tripp, Charles. *Islam and the Moral Economy: The Challenge of Capitalism*. Cambridge: Cambridge University Press, 2006.
Turowicz, Jerzy. "Dekomunizacja, ale jaka?" In *Spór o Polskę: 1989–1999*, edited by Paweł Śpiewak, 181–84. Warsaw: PWN, 2000.
United for a Fair Economy Tax Fairness Organizing Collaborative. http://www.faireconomy.org/TFOC/index.html.
United Nations Development Programme. *Human Development Report 1999*. New York: Oxford University Press, 1999.
———. *Human Development Report 2000: Human Rights and Human Development*. New York: Oxford University Press, 2000.
United Nations Development Programme Poland. *Human Development Report: Poland and the Information Society: Logging On*. Warsaw: UNDP Poland, 2002.
———. *National Human Development Report Poland 1998: Access to Education*. Warsaw: UNDP Poland, 1998.
———. *National Report on Human Development: The Changing Role of the State, Poland '97*. Warsaw: UNDP Poland, 1997.
———. *Raport: milenijne cele rozwoju Polska*. Warsaw: UNDP Poland, 2001.

———. *Raport o rozwoju społecznym Polska 1999: ku godnej aktywnej starości.* Warsaw: UNDP Poland, 1999.

———. *Raport o rozwoju społecznym Polska 2000: rozwój obszarów wiejskich.* Warsaw: UNDP Poland, 2000.

United Nations Human Rights Committee. 1999. *Concluding Observations of the Human Rights Committee: Poland.* 7/29/99. http://www.unhchr.ch/tbs/doc.nsf/ (Symbol)/a61db0e519524575802567c200595e9c?Opendocument. (accessed May 30, 2004).

United Nations General Assembly. 2000. *United Nations Millennium Declaration.* http://www.un.org/millennium/declaration/ares552e.htm. (accessed October 7, 2007).

United States Catholic Conference of Bishops. "The Challenge of Peace: God's Promise and Our Response." In *Catholic Social Thought: The Documentary Heritage,* edited by David J. O'Brien and Thomas A. Shannon, 492–571. Maryknoll, N.Y.: Orbis Books, 1992.

———. "Economic Justice for All: A Catholic Framework for Economic Life." In *Catholic Social Thought: The Documentary Heritage,* edited by David J. O'Brien and Thomas A. Shannon, 572–680. Maryknoll, N.Y.: Orbis Books, 1992.

"Uniwersytet przed reanimacją." *Znak* 2, no. 537 (2000).

Valencia, Matthew. "Poland: Limping towards Normality." *The Economist,* October 27, 2001, Survey 1–16.

"W pracy kobiety nie są solidarne: rozmowa z prof. ekonomii Stanisławą Golinowską." *Gazeta Wyborcza,* December 4, 1999.

Waal, F. B. M. de. *Our Inner Ape: A Leading Primatologist Explains Why We Are Who We Are.* New York: Riverhead Books, 2005.

Wałęsa, Lech. *A Way of Hope.* New York: Henry Holt, 1987.

Walicki, Andrzej. "Ideolog epoki postchlubnej." *Gazeta Wyborcza,* November 8–9, 2003, 17–18.

———. *Polskie zmagania z wolnością.* Cracow: Universitas, 2000.

Walzer, Michael. *Spheres of Justice: A Defense of Pluralism and Equality.* New York: Basic Books, 1983.

Wedel, Janine R. *The Private Poland.* New York: Facts on File, 1986.

Weigel, George. *The Final Revolution: The Resistance Church and the Collapse of Communism.* New York: Oxford University Press, 1992.

Welch, Edward M. "Taxing Work." *America,* November 14, 2005, 7–9.

Wilczyński, Wacław. "Plaga nierówności." *Polityka* 2, no. 2142 (1998): 74–75.

———. "Wrogie państwo opiekuńcze." In *Wrogie państwo opiekuńcze czyli trudna droga Polski do gospodarki rynkowej: felietony z tygodnika "Wprost" z lat 1995–1999,* 145–46. Warsaw: Wydaw. Naukowe PWN, 1999.

Wilson, David Sloan. *Darwin's Cathedral: Evolution, Religion, and the Nature of Society.* Chicago: University of Chicago Press, 2002.

Winiecki, Jan. "Godność z cudzej kieszeni." *Polityka* 4, no. 2229 (2000): 70.

———. "Ideały Solidarności, czyli o antykomunistycznych bolszewikach." In *Spór o Polskę: 1989–1999*, edited by Paweł Śpiewak, 702–3. Warsaw: PWN, 2000.

———. *Instytucjonalne bariery rozwoju gospodarczego: polska niezakończona transformacja, Zeszyty Centrum im. Adama Smitha nr specjalny*. Warsaw: Centrum im. Adama Smitha, 1995.

———. "Polacy kontra Polska." *Wprost* (1999): 46.

Winnicka, Ewa. "Dzieci i dzieci-śmieci." *Polityka*, June 28, 2008.

Władka, Wiesław. "Mocne i słabe strony Polaka: Onizm." *Polityka* 45, no. 2426 (2003): 85–86.

Wnuk-Lipiński, Edmund. "Wyuczona bezradność." In *Spór o Polskę: 1989–1999*, edited by Paweł Śpiewak, 675. Warsaw: PWN, 2000.

Wojtyła, Karol. *Osoba i czyn oraz inne studia antropologiczne*. 3d ed. Lublin: Towarzystwo Naukowe KUL, 2000. English translation: *The Acting Person*. Translated by Andrzej Potocki. Boston: D. Reidel, 1979.

Woleński, Jan. "Iluzja mesjanizmu." In *Spór o Polskę: 1989–1999*, edited by Paweł Śpiewak, 58. Warsaw: PWN, 2000.

———. "Niech kościół walczy duchem, a nie prawem." *Gazeta Wyborcza*, August 26, 1994.

Wolfe, Alan. *Moral Freedom: The Impossible Idea That Defines the Way We Live Now*. 1st ed. New York: W.W. Norton, 2001.

Wolterstorff, Nicholas. *Until Justice and Peace Embrace: The Kuyper Lectures for 1981 Delivered at the Free University of Amsterdam*. Grand Rapids, Mich.: W.B. Eerdmans, 1983.

"Working Mothers, Unite!" *The Economist*, July 10, 2008.

World Synod of Bishops. *Justice in the World (Justitia in Mundo)*. In *Catholic Social Thought: The Documentary Heritage*, edited by David J. O'Brien and Thomas A. Shannon, 288–300. Maryknoll, N.Y.: Orbis Books, 1992.

Wóycicka, Irena, and Anna Mateja. "Zagłębie biedy, źródło szans." *Tygodnik Powszechny*, November 19, 2003, 4.

Wratny, Jerzy. "Partycypacja pracownicza w zarządzaniu i jej etyczne uzasadnienie." In *Etyka biznesu*, edited by Jerzy Dietl and Wojciech Gasparski. Warsaw: Wydaw. Naukowe PWN, 1999.

Zając, Marek. "Patron trudnej jedności." *Tygodnik Powszechny*, May 18, 2003.

Zięba, Maciej. *Papieże i kapitalizm: od Rerum Novarum po Centesimus Annus*. Cracow: Znak, 1998.

Zieliński, Mateusz. "Atak górników." *Gazeta Wyborcza*, September 12, 2003, 6–7.

Zieliński, Michał. "Klęska sukcesu." *Wprost* (1999): 44–45.

Zimoń, Damian. "Górnicy to nie balast." *Gazeta Wyborcza*, September 12, 2003, 21.

———. 2001. "Kościół katolicki na Śląsku wobec bezrobocia." Konferencja Episkopatu Polski, www.episkopat.pl/dokumenty/bezrobocie1.html. (accessed January 24, 2003).

Ziółkowski, Marek. "Społeczno-kulturowy kontekst kondycji moralnej społeczeństwa polskiego." In *Kondycja moralna społeczeństwa polskiego*, edited by Janusz Mariański, 17–43. Cracow: Wydawnictwo WAM, 2002.

Zuziak, Władysław. "Znaczenie myśli Józefa Tischnera w rozwoju idei solidarności." In *Idea solidarności dzisiaj*, edited by Władysław Zuziak, 31–46. Cracow: Wydawnictwo Naukowe PAT, 2001.

———, ed. *Idea solidarności dzisiaj*. Cracow: Wydawnictwo Naukowe PAT, 2001.

INDEX

agriculture. *See also* PGR-y
  agricultural subsidies, 33, 69, 149, 166, 191, 278n.145
  in Poland, 71, 148–50, 178, 197
Akcja Wyborcza Solidarność (Solidarity Electoral Action), 29
Auschwitz, 14, 50, 261n.76

Balcerowicz, Leszek, 149, 153, 228n.26, 235n.107, 241n.25, 253n.153, 269n.3, 270n.9
  role in economic reforms, 35
  tax policies and wages, 76, 127
  understandings of development and freedom, 44–45, 123–25
Berlin, Isaiah, 4, 7, 40
Bielecki, Jan Krzystof, 45, 235n.107
Bonowicz, Wojciech, 54, 259n.42

Capitalist Manifesto (*Manifest kapitalistyczny*), 114, 186
Caritas Polska, 88, 159, 164, 191–201
Catholic Bishops Conference of England and Wales, 166
Catholic Church. *See* Roman Catholic Church
Centesimus Annus (John Paul II), 46, 50, 93, 111, 174, 179, 236n.118, 285n.89

common good, 13–17, 19, 36–37, 42, 88, 142, 161, 182, 194, 207, 209
  Catholic social teaching on, 51, 91, 104, 115, 116, 144, 178, 184, 188
  Hayek's argument against, 45
  Hobbesian anthropology as a negation of, 155–56
  and human rights, 19–21, 41
  participation in, 51, 91–94, 96–97, 105–6, 112, 139, 140–41, 144, 151, 197
  and wages, 115–17, 147, 169, 171
Conference of Catholic Bishops of Poland (Konferencja Episkopatu Polski). *See also* Roman Catholic Church
  criticisms of, 47, 52, 164
  dissention within, 171
  role after 1989, 8, 34, 48, 57, 136, 158–59, 167, 172–74, 180, 182, 186, 189, 246n.71
  during Solidarity era, 20, 159–60
  understanding of relationship between evangelization and social justice, 167–73

319

decommunization, 31. *See also* lustration
development, 81, 117, 140, 169, 220n.11
　economic and human development in Poland, 57, 66, 122–23, 134–37, 180
　neoliberal understanding of, 3, 44, 207
　See also John Paul II; Sen, Amartya Kumar
Dylus, Aniela, 41, 101, 144, 147, 155, 171, 173, 185, 239n.5, 263n.97, 274n.76, 276n.99

economic rights, 7, 19, 104, 122, 128, 138–41, 158, 185–86, 263n.97.
　See also human rights
　relationship to social justice 158, 165–67, 168–70, 175, 181–82, 199, 201–2, 281n.38
Etyka solidarności (Tischner), 13, 21, 87, 153, 176
European Union, 149, 150
　Poland's entry into, 52, 71, 285n.81
Evangelii Nuntiandi (Paul VI), 165, 281n.38
evangelization 158, 171, 175, 179, 183, 189

Familiaris Consortio (John Paul II), 238n.149, 260n.58
freedom
　integral freedom, 110, 145
　negative freedom, 40–44, 105, 108, 123, 208
　personalist freedom, 106, 109–12, 118, 145–46, 154
　positive freedom, 40–42, 106, 108, 118, 232nn.77, 79
　understood as moral permissivism, 47–49
　understood as sovereignty, 41–42, 108, 118

Garton Ash, Timothy, 1, 12, 41, 208
Gdańsk, 1, 14, 16, 21, 30
Geremek, Bronisław, 30, 215
Golinowska, Stanisława, 55, 57, 60–61, 72, 77, 80, 142
Gowin, Jarosław, 15, 160, 172, 175, 185
Graff, Agnieszka, 237n.129
Greider, William, 9, 33, 145, 206, 218, 276n.100

Hayek, Friedrich von
　conception of freedom, 44–45
　influence in Poland, 34, 235n.105
Herbert, Zbigniew, 26
heroism, 16–17, 96, 143, 259n.42
homo sovieticus, 36–40, 50–51, 68, 82, 93, 98, 104, 122, 153–54, 180, 184–85, 216, 230n.50
hope, 19, 27, 161, 170, 189, 265n.113
　relationship to solidarity, 14, 15, 24, 26, 38, 107, 188, 203
　virtue of, 98, 155
human dignity, 18–19, 25, 26, 103, 107, 129, 139–40, 203, 266n.136
human rights, 18, 20–21, 43, 93–94, 100–104, 107, 113, 129, 134, 139–43, 155, 159–62, 165, 169, 185, 208

International Monetary Fund, 36, 249n.116

John XXIII (pope), 93, 103, 111, 116, 166, 262n.84
　on observe, judge, act methodology, 256n.203
　on solidarity, 99, 117
　on subsidiarity and socialization, 263n.93
John Paul II (pope), 2, 49, 50, 97, 107, 162, 166, 170, 201, 213, 215, 216
　contribution to *Solidarność*, 15, 20, 22, 23, 26

critique of Polish socioeconomic
transformations, 34, 43, 48, 88,
100
critique of *Solidarność*, 1, 5
ethic of solidarity, 46, 86, 89, 98,
99, 103, 115, 117, 142, 144, 149, 156,
172, 182, 199, 210, 212, 257n.13
on human and economic
development, 47, 92, 109–12,
113, 133, 141
on the nature of freedom, 111,
118, 154, 186
views concerning capitalism,
47, 93, 110, 144, 146, 266n.129
Justitia in Mundo (World Synod
of Bishops), 91, 140, 165–66,
170
just wage, 19, 20, 23, 112–16, 118, 139,
145, 150, 186, 203, 208, 269n.5

Kabaj, Mieczysław, 58, 60, 70, 242n.33,
244n.54, 250n.126
Kaczyński, Lech, 29, 215
Kampka, Franciszek, 89, 95, 173
Katyń, 26
Kołalowski, Leszek, 40, 160–61,
232n.79, 263n.97
Kolbe, Maximilian, 108, 259n.42,
261n.76
Kolyma, 14, 50
Komitet Obrony Robotników
(Workers' Defense Committee),
11–12
Kowalik, Tadeusz, 35, 58, 220n.11
disagreements with Jeffrey Sachs,
228n.21, 242n.33, 244n.54
Kuroń, Jacek, 19, 27, 30, 215, 229n.34

Laborem Exercens (John Paul II), 22,
115, 146, 166, 176, 179, 282n.45
Leo XIII (pope), 111, 139, 269n.5
Lewandowski, Janusz, 44, 235n.105
lustration, 215

Majka, Józef, 148
Mater et Magistra (John XXIII), 166
Mazowiecki, Tadeusz, 6, 30–31
Michnik, Adam, 218
  assessment of the Roman Catholic
  Church in Poland, 161–63, 186
  on the demise of Solidarity, 30, 161
  on the ethic of solidarity, 12, 14, 16,
  17, 26, 27
Mickiewicz, Adam, 20, 225n.67
Miłosz, Czesław, 160
Modzelewski, Karol, 19, 35
Musiał, Stanisław, 201

Nell-Breuning, Oswald, 99
neoliberalism
  conception of freedom, 3, 7, 8, 40,
  44–50, 105, 109, 186, 202. *See also*
  negative freedom
  global influence, 33, 206–7, 217–18,
  219n.6
  in Poland, 3, 4, 31–32, 34–36,
  42–44, 109, 176, 209, 216–17
noble democracy (*demokracja
szlachecka*), 20
Nowakowska, Ewa, 163
NSZZ Solidarność trade union. *See*
Solidarity

option for the poor, 15, 21–24, 55, 61,
86–88, 92, 97, 104, 115, 143, 149, 152,
169, 171–73, 184, 190, 200–203,
257n.7
Osoba i czyń (Wojtyła), 13, 19, 92
Ost, David, 36, 216

Pacem in Terris (John XXIII), 20, 99
participation
  right to, 18–19, 90–94, 101, 113, 115,
  118, 129, 143, 144–48, 150, 151, 188,
  258n.18
  education as a precondition of,
  152–56

Index

Paul VI (pope), 166, 182
  on evangelization, 165, 170, 281n.38
  on solidarity, 99
Pesch, Heinrich, 89, 99, 257n.13
PGR-y (state-owned farmlands), 64–69, 129–32, 152, 184, 196, 199, 244n.59, 248n.106
Pieńkowska, Alina, 16, 215
Pieronek, Tadeusz (bishop), 172, 173, 175, 202, 282n.53
Pius XI, 114–15
Popiełuszko, Jerzy, 15, 17, 26–27, 226n.99
poverty
  of children, 62–64, 71, 143, 216
  definition of, 23, 58
  as a denial of freedom, 118, 121–29, 132, 134–35, 138, 142
  as a denial of the right to participation, 93, 94, 103, 142
  difficulties measuring, 54–57, 137
  and educational deprivation, 78–81, 152–56
  empirical data on (in post-1989 Poland), 2, 6, 53, 59–68
  and inequality, 72, 85
  neoliberal view of, 123–24, 137
  participation as a remedy for, 144–45, 150–51
  Polish attitudes towards, 69, 82–83, 88, 104, 109, 112
  prior to 1989 in Poland, 22–23
  relationship to agriculture, 66–68
  the Roman Catholic Church's response to in Poland, 158, 167, 173–74, 177–78, 180–83, 190–202
  solidarity as a remedy for, 86–88, 98, 104, 118, 209, 212
  stemming from low wages, 72–78, 113
  unemployment as a cause of, 69–72, 87
  of women, 64–66, 129–34
Poznań, 14

Quadragesimo Anno (Pius XI), 114

Radom, 167
Rawls, John, 127–28, 178, 192
Redemptor Hominis (John Paul II), 99, 109, 129, 265n.117
Rhine model (of capitalism). See *Sozialmarktwirtschaft*
Roman Catholic Church
  during Communist era, 37, 160
  on neoliberal economic reforms in Poland
  role in Polish politics after 1989, 7, 8, 29, 63, 158–63, 201–2
  situation within after 1989 in Poland, 49, 162–63, 201, 230n.52
  and *Solidarność*, 13, 16, 20
Roman Catholicism in Poland. See Roman Catholic Church
Romanticism, 20
Round Table (1989), 13

Sachs, Jeffrey, 34, 243n.40, 244n.54
samorządy pracownicze (worker management), 18
Sen, Amartya Kumar, 102, 186
  on economic and human development, 125, 130, 135–36, 179, 243n.41, 262n.83
  on freedom, 7, 119, 122, 124–33, 135, 138, 140, 153
  models of capitalism, 33
  understanding of poverty, 56, 57, 60, 100, 122, 124, 126, 137
Smolar, Aleksander, 2
social justice, 110, 200
  attitudes towards in Poland, 44, 103, 122, 235n.108
  as a component of solidarity, 92, 115, 146, 147, 149, 150, 203
  relationship to evangelization, 165–75, 181–82, 189, 199, 201
  relationship to freedom, 40, 45

social market economy, 32, 47, 58, 101–103, 144, 207. *See also Sozialmarktwirtschaft*
social minimum (*minimum socjalne*), 23, 56–58, 63, 66, 79, 113, 115, 117, 121, 137–38, 142–43, 173, 241n.17
Solidarity (NSZZ Solidarność trade union)
 criticisms of, 2, 5, 37, 41
 demise after 1989, 1–2, 29–31, 46, 51–52, 208
 differences within in the 1980s, 12–13, 27, 183
 goals and ideals during the 1980s, 1, 11–27, 37–38, 42, 46, 94, 107
 as a movement of workers and intellectuals, 11–12, 16–17
 return to its original ideals, 216
 role of women in, 16–17, 223n.42
 Roman Catholicism's influence on, 13, 15, 16–17, 20, 22, 26, 157–61
 and the social minimum, 56
 understanding of freedom, 19, 46
 and worker management, 18, 145, 185
solidarity (ethic of)
 application to concrete realities, 54–55, 85, 148
 Christian foundations of, 15–17, 20, 23, 26, 98, 156, 189
 and dialogue, 13, 163–64, 186
 amidst differences, 12–14
 different ways of embodying, 25, 96
 distinguished from sympathy and charity, 88–89, 94–96
 and emphasis on equality of all, 17–18
 and emphasis on truth, 24–27, 187–88
 "factual solidarity," 89
 within the family, 51, 96–99, 135, 155
 homo sovieticus as a challenge to, 36–39, 154

 hope as the foundation of, 14–15, 26, 98, 189, 212
 and human nature, 210–11
 and human rights, 19–21, 94, 99–105, 137, 141, 143, 154–55, 185–86
 "imperfect solidarity," 12
 institutionalization of, 89–90, 99–105, 141,
 John Paul II on, 46, 86, 89, 92, 98, 99, 103, 115, 117, 142, 144, 149, 156, 172, 182, 199, 210, 212, 257n.13
 and just wages, 112–19
 misleading understandings of, 96–97, 102, 211–12
 and mutuality, 94, 195
 neoliberalism's threat to, 4, 8, 31, 34, 39, 43, 176, 205–9, 216–18
 participation as a requirement of, 18–19, 86, 90–94, 96, 98, 125, 144, 149, 189
 perseverance as a requirement of, 94–96, 98, 196
 Pesch, Heinrich, on, 89, 99, 257n.13
 in the Polish Constitution, 47, 103
 promoted by the Roman Catholic Church in Poland, 16, 20, 158–65, 167–73, 176, 179–80, 189–99
 relationship to freedom, 3, 5, 7, 9, 40–47, 49, 86, 105–12, 122, 128–29, 135, 158, 208–9
 relationship to the option for the poor, 21–24, 53, 55, 81, 86–88, 143, 149, 152, 176, 200–203, 212
 as the remedy for poverty, 86–88, 98, 104, 118, 209, 212
 Republican ethos of, 20, 42,
 and self-sacrifice and heroism, 16–17, 94, 96, 143, 259n.42
 sequential development of, 54, 89–90
Tischner, Józef, on, 13–16, 18, 19, 21–23, 26, 27, 38, 85, 87, 98, 202

Sollicitudo Rei Socialis (John Paul II), 47, 86, 87, 94, 104, 109, 257n.7, 261n.76
Sozialmarktwirtschaft, 32, 33
Stawrowski, Zbigniew, 14
subsidiarity, principle of, 93–94, 101–2, 113, 128, 134, 155, 179–80
subsistence minimum (*minimum egzystencji*), 61

Tarkowska, Elżbieta, 61, 62, 63, 240n.15, 244n.59, 246n.77, 248n.106, 255n.192
Taylor, Charles, 46
Tischner, Józef, 175, 184, 216
  critique of Catholicism in Poland, 164, 186
  and the ethic of solidarity, 13–16, 18, 19, 21–23, 26, 27, 38, 85, 87, 98, 202
  evaluation of post-1989 Poland, 29, 265nn.124, 125
  on hope 98, 265n.113
  philosophy of freedom, 37, 40, 49–50, 106–10, 118
  on the right to education, 153
Tokarczuk, Ignacy, 16
Turowicz, Jerzy, 30
Tusk, Donald, 233n.90

unemployment, 23, 32, 33, 87, 103, 130, 140
  methods of combatting, 134, 148–52
  after 1989 in Poland, 60, 66–71, 77–79, 81, 83, 113, 114, 129, 135, 168, 173–74, 179–83, 186, 197, 199–200, 216
United States Catholic Conference of Bishops, 141, 166

Veritatis Splendor (John Paul II), 50

Wajda, Andrzej, 17
Walentynowicz, Anna, 1, 21, 108
Wałęsa, Lech, 1, 2, 11, 16, 30–32, 35, 108, 215
Wojtyła, Karol, 13, 20, 91, 92, 116, 224n.60, 258n.28. *See also* John Paul II
Women's Rights Center (Centrum Praw Kobiet), 64
worker ownership, 145–47, 185, 203, 276n.100. *See also samorządy pracownicze*
World Bank, 36, 58, 60, 62, 72, 81, 114, 124, 149, 174
Wyszyński, Stefan, 20, 279n.7

Zimoń, Damian, 173

GERALD J. BEYER is assistant professor of theology at Saint Joseph's University in Philadelphia, Pennsylvania.

www.ingramcontent.com/pod-product-compliance
Lightning Source LLC
Chambersburg PA
CBHW061427300426
44114CB00014B/1569